"Christopher Ash writes beautifully—this book is a delight to read! But that isn't its greatest strength. Nor is the fact that these pages are filled with nuanced and fresh exegetical insights. Christopher has succeeded in producing the richest, most moving, most deeply cross-centered and God-glorifying treatment of Job I have ever read. This book marries brilliant explanation with powerful gospel-driven application. It is simply a 'must-have' resource for anyone intending to preach through Job."

J. Gary Millar, Principal, Queensland Theological College; author, *Now Choose Life*

"This is one of the finest Biblical commentaries I have had the privilege to read, and certainly the best I know on the wonderful but perplexing book of Job. Christopher Ash takes us into the depths of this book, taking no shortcuts. He guides us through the details, helping us to see the brilliance of the poetry and the profundity of the questions raised. More than this he helps us to see how the sufferings of Jesus shed brilliant light into the darkest corners of Job's experience. In turn the book of Job deepens our understanding of Jesus' blameless suffering, and the suffering and darkness experienced by those who share in the sufferings of Christ. This is a powerfully edifying exposition."

John Woodhouse, Former Principal, Moore Theological College

"If like me, you have shied away from the book of Job, daunted by its structure and length, do not despair, help has arrived! Christopher Ash has performed a noble service by 'bashing his head' against the text and providing us with such a lucid, wonderfully helpful commentary. It is both mind-stretching and heart-warming as it reminds us that, like the rest of the Bible, Job is ultimately a book about Jesus."

Alistair Begg, Senior Pastor, Parkside Church, Cleveland, Ohio

"This is the book for any who, like me, have been both fascinated and frightened by Job. Christopher Ash brilliantly engages with the interpretive challenge of understanding the text and the emotional challenge of being confronted by the awful reality of suffering and evil in the world. His exposition combines sober realism about what we can expect in the life of faith and great encouragement as we are pointed to the sufferings and glory of Christ."

Vaughan Roberts, Rector, St. Ebbe's; Director, The Proclamation Trust; author, *God's Big Picture*

"A magnificent study of one of the least read and understood books of the Bible. Here is meticulous, detailed exploration of the text, its vocabulary and poetic structure, which opens up its richness and complexity with interpretive sensitivity. This in turn produces a narrative reading that illuminates the revelatory argument of the book as a whole, with its conflict between redemptive grace and religious systems. 'Honest grappling' is its characteristic as the imponderable questions of the human condition are played out through the drama of Job's individual agony. But this is also a preacher's book, full of human empathy and applicatory wisdom providing nourishment for the deepest recesses of the soul. Supremely, it is a book not about Job's suffering, but about Job's God, which leads us to the ultimate answers to all our human enigmas in the reality of Jesus Christ and him crucified. This is a book to return to again and again as a valuable tool to unpack the message of Job in a generation to whom it is strikingly relevant."

David J. Jackman, Former President, Proclamation Trust, London, England

"This book has reinforced my general rule, 'If Christopher Ash has written it, I should definitely read it.' It is an outstanding exposition of this dramatic but difficult book, at the same time eminently accessible, yet profoundly stretching and thought-provoking. As the book's chapters are opened up masterfully, characteristic attention to textual detail is enriched by a theological trajectory that, like a reverse prism, draws every obscure but colorfully illuminating ray from this ancient story and traces them forward to the pure brightness and clear light revealed in the cross of Christ. The pastoral warmth and power of its message comes from this recognition, that for *every* believer, ancient or modern, it is the reality of our union with Christ, the Christ who was glorified only through suffering, that offers the deepest explanation of all evil that we may encounter on our road to glory. I commend it most warmly to anyone who wants to dig into the riches of this extraordinary book of the Bible."

William J. U. Philip, Senior Minister, The Tron Church, Glasgow

"This commentary is invaluable for personal or group Bible study, and also for preachers. It includes careful study of the text of Job, and the fruits of deep theological and pastoral reflection. It avoids the sadly common question, 'What is the minimum I need to know to understand the book of Job?' and instead asks the godly and productive question, 'What are the full riches that God has provided for us in the book of Job?' Furthermore, Christopher answers this question in the light of Christ and the gospel. And of course, there is much to learn here about suffering, the pastoral Achilles heel of the Church both in the West and in the two-thirds world. It is a persuasive and powerful tool to help us edify God's people by expounding the Scriptures."

Peter Adam, Vicar Emeritus, St Jude's Church, Carlton, Australia; author,
Speaking God's Words: A Practical Theology of Preaching

"This expository commentary provides everything a preacher is looking for. The 'big picture' is kept clear even as technical detail is explained. The text is set in its Biblical context even as the text is unpacked on its own terms. Application is faithful to the book's Biblical purpose, acutely insightful and contemporary. It is readable, profoundly pastorally helpful, and above all Christ-centered. I could not commend it more highly."

William Taylor, Rector, St Helen's Church, Bishopsgate, London

"Christopher has produced something on a much misunderstood (and abused) book that draws us to the anguished questions of a sufferer, deals carefully with all the data, and brings us to Christ. A great help for anyone wishing to preach on Job, and for anyone wishing to hear this word from God."

Nat Schluter, Principal, Johannesburg Bible College

"A marvelous commentary on an important book."

Josh Moody, Senior Pastor, College Church, Wheaton, Illinois; author,
Journey to Joy: The Psalms of Ascent

JOB

PREACHING THE WORD
Edited by R. Kent Hughes

Genesis ǀ R. Kent Hughes

Exodus ǀ Philip Graham Ryken

Leviticus ǀ Kenneth A. Mathews

Numbers ǀ Iain M. Duguid

Deuteronomy ǀ Ajith Fernando

Joshua ǀ David Jackman

Judges and Ruth ǀ Barry G. Webb

1 Samuel ǀ John Woodhouse

2 Samuel ǀ John Woodhouse

1 Kings ǀ John Woodhouse

Job ǀ Christopher Ash

Psalms, vol. 1 ǀ James Johnston

Proverbs ǀ Raymond C. Ortlund Jr.

Ecclesiastes ǀ Philip Graham Ryken

Song of Solomon ǀ Douglas Sean O'Donnell

Isaiah ǀ Raymond C. Ortlund Jr.

Jeremiah and Lamentations ǀ R. Kent Hughes

Daniel ǀ Rodney D. Stortz

Matthew ǀ Douglas Sean O'Donnell

Mark ǀ R. Kent Hughes

Luke ǀ R. Kent Hughes

John ǀ R. Kent Hughes

Acts ǀ R. Kent Hughes

Romans ǀ R. Kent Hughes

1 Corinthians ǀ Stephen T. Um

2 Corinthians ǀ R. Kent Hughes

Galatians ǀ Todd Wilson

Ephesians ǀ R. Kent Hughes

Philippians, Colossians, and Philemon ǀ R. Kent Hughes

1–2 Thessalonians ǀ James H. Grant Jr.

1–2 Timothy and Titus ǀ R. Kent Hughes and Bryan Chapell

Hebrews ǀ R. Kent Hughes

James ǀ R. Kent Hughes

1–2 Peter and Jude ǀ David R. Helm

1–3 John ǀ David L. Allen

Revelation ǀ James M. Hamilton Jr.

The Sermon on the Mount ǀ R. Kent Hughes

<(((PREACHING *the* WORD)))

JOB

The WISDOM
of the CROSS

CHRISTOPHER ASH

R. Kent Hughes
Series Editor

WHEATON, ILLINOIS

Job

Copyright © 2014 by Christopher Ash

Published by Crossway
      1300 Crescent Street
      Wheaton, Illinois 60187

Cover design: Jon McGrath, Simplicated Studio

Cover image: Adam Greene, illustrator

First printing 2014

Printed in China

Unless otherwise indicated, Scripture quotations are from the ESV® Bible (The Holy Bible, English Standard Version®), copyright © 2001 by Crossway. 2011 Text Edition. Used by permission. All rights reserved.

Scripture quotations marked HCSB have been taken from *The Holman Christian Standard Bible*®. Copyright © 1999, 2000, 2002, 2003 by Holman Bible Publishers. Used by permission.

Scripture references marked JB are from *The Jerusalem Bible*. Copyright © 1966, 1967, 1968 by Darton, Longman & Todd Ltd. and Doubleday & Co., Inc.

Scripture quotations marked KJV are from the *King James Version* of the Bible.

Scripture quotations marked MESSAGE are from *The Message*. Copyright © by Eugene H. Peterson 1993, 1994, 1995, 1996, 2000, 2001, 2002. Used by permission of NavPress Publishing Group.

Scripture quotations marked NASB are from *The New American Standard Bible*®. Copyright © The Lockman Foundation 1960, 1962, 1963, 1968, 1971, 1972, 1973, 1975, 1977. Used by permission.

Scripture references marked NEB are from *The New English Bible* © The Delegates of the Oxford University Press and The Syndics of the Cambridge University Press, 1961, 1970.

Scripture quotations marked NET are from *The NET Bible*® copyright © 2003 by Biblical Studies Press, L.L.C. www.netbible.com. All rights reserved. Quoted by permission.

Scripture references marked NIV are taken from The Holy Bible, New Internation Version®, NIV®. Copyright © 1973, 1978, 1984, 2011 by Biblica, Inc.™ Used by permission. All rights reserved worldwide.

Scripture references marked RSV are from *The Revised Standard Version*. Copyright ©1946, 1952, 1971, 1973 by the Division of Christian Education of the National Council of the Churches of Christ in the U.S.A.

Scripture quotations marked TEV are taken from the Good News Bible in Today's English Version – Second Edition, Copyright ©1992 by American Bible Society. Used by Permission.

All emphases in Scripture quotations have been added by the author.

Hardcover ISBN: 978-1-4335-1312-1
ePub ISBN: 978-1-4335-2418-9
PDF ISBN: 978-1-4335-1313-8
Mobipocket ISBN: 978-1-4335-1314-5

Library of Congress Cataloging-in-Publication Data

Ash, Christopher, 1953–
  Job / Christopher Ash.
    pages cm. – (Preaching the word)
  Includes bibliographical references and index.
  ISBN 978-1-4335-1312-1 (hc)
  1. Bible. Job–Commentaries. I. Title.
BS1415.53.A84   2014
223'.107–dc23
                        2013014987

Crossway is a publishing ministry of Good News Publishers.

RRDS   29 28 27 26 25 24 23 22 21
18 17 16 15 14 13 12 11 10 9 8 7

To
Dick Lucas

Behold, we consider those blessed who remained steadfast. You have heard of the steadfastness of Job, and you have seen the purpose of the Lord, how the Lord is compassionate and merciful.

JAMES 5:11

Contents

A Word to Those Who Preach the Word

There are times when I am preaching that I have especially sensed the pleasure of God. I usually become aware of it through the unnatural silence. The ever-present coughing ceases, and the pews stop creaking, bringing an almost physical quiet to the sanctuary—through which my words sail like arrows. I experience a heightened eloquence, so that the cadence and volume of my voice intensify the truth I am preaching.

There is nothing quite like it—the Holy Spirit filling one's sails, the sense of his pleasure, and the awareness that something is happening among one's hearers. This experience is, of course, not unique, for thousands of preachers have similar experiences, even greater ones.

What has happened when this takes place? How do we account for this sense of his smile? The answer for me has come from the ancient rhetorical categories of *logos*, *ethos*, and *pathos*.

The first reason for his smile is the *logos*—in terms of preaching, God's Word. This means that as we stand before God's people to proclaim his Word, we have done our homework. We have exegeted the passage, mined the significance of its words in their context, and applied sound hermeneutical principles in interpreting the text so that we understand what its words meant to its hearers. And it means that we have labored long until we can express in a sentence what the theme of the text is—so that our outline springs from the text. Then our preparation will be such that as we preach, we will not be preaching our own thoughts about God's Word, but God's actual Word, his *logos*. This is fundamental to pleasing him in preaching.

The second element in knowing God's smile in preaching is *ethos*—what you are as a person. There is a danger endemic to preaching, which is having your hands and heart cauterized by holy things. Phillips Brooks illustrated it by the analogy of a train conductor who comes to believe that he has been to the places he announces because of his long and loud heralding of them. And that is why Brooks insisted that preaching must be "the bringing of truth through personality." Though we can never perfectly embody the truth we preach, we must be subject to it, long for it, and make it as much a part of our ethos as possible. As the Puritan William Ames said, "Next to the Scriptures, nothing makes a sermon more to pierce, than when it comes out of the inward affection of the heart without any affectation." When a preacher's *ethos* backs up his *logos*, there will be the pleasure of God.

Last, there is *pathos*—personal passion and conviction. David Hume, the Scottish philosopher and skeptic, was once challenged as he was seen going to hear George Whitefield preach: "I thought you do not believe in the gospel." Hume replied, "I don't, but he does." Just so! When a preacher believes what he preaches, there will be passion. And this belief and requisite passion will know the smile of God.

The pleasure of God is a matter of *logos* (the Word), *ethos* (what you are), and *pathos* (your passion). As you preach the Word may you experience his smile—the Holy Spirit in your sails!

R. Kent Hughes

Preface

"The grandest book ever written with pen." So wrote the Victorian essayist Thomas Carlyle about the Old Testament book of Job.[1] It is a book I have been grappling with for a decade or so. The more I have walked through it and around it, the more deeply convinced I have become that it makes no sense apart from the cross of Christ. That statement would be strictly true of the entire Old Testament, but somehow in Job it seems more sharply and urgently true, for without Jesus the book of Job will be but "the record of an unanswered agony."[2] It could almost be a commentary on Paul's words in 1 Corinthians 1:18–25. The book of Job hinges around the contrast, conflict, and tension between the wisdom of the world and the wisdom of the cross.

Perhaps this is why commentaries that restrict themselves to interpreting the Old Testament in terms of the Old Testament alone find themselves heading up blind alleys. Scripture is to be interpreted by Scripture, and the book of Job can only be understood as a part of the whole Biblical canon as it is fulfilled in Christ.

Again and again as I have beaten my head against these puzzling and seemingly intractable texts, it has been the cross of Christ that has shone light on the page. This is not to say that the book is not about Job in his ancient context. Of course it is. But Job's experiences, Job's debates, Job's struggles, Job's sufferings, and Job's final blessings all come to fruition in the perfect obedience of Jesus Christ in his life and death and then in his resurrection, ascension, and exaltation at God's right hand. I hope I can persuade you of this as the exposition walks through every verse of the book.

This book is not a treatment of a topic, whether the topic of suffering or anything else. It is a study of the Bible book of Job. I want you to venture into the book of Job, to read, meditate, explore, and pray this profound Bible book into your bloodstream. If you have never done so, my prayer is that this study will help you find a way in. If you have ventured in but got bogged down and confused, I hope this book will help you find your way.

Job is a neglected treasure of the Christian life. It has spawned an enormous outpouring of scholarly work, and yet few Christians know quite where to start in appropriating its message for themselves. I hope this book will be sufficiently accessible, clear, accurate, and faithful to help.

Introduction

WHAT IS JOB ALL ABOUT?

The book of Job raises three big questions: What kind of world do we live in? What kind of church should we want? What kind of Savior do we need?

What Kind of World Do We Live In?

This book began as a sermon series on the book of Job in the church where I was pastor.[1] Twelve days before the first sermon, on January 14, 2003, Detective Constable Stephen Oake was stabbed and killed in Manchester. Why? He was an upright man, a faithful husband, a loving father. What is more, he was a Christian, a committed member of his church where he used sometimes to preach. The newspapers reported a moving statement by his father, Robin Oake, a former chairman of the Christian Police Association. He said through his tears that he was praying for the man who had killed his son. The newspaper articles told of the quiet dignity of Stephen's widow Lesley. They showed happy family snapshots with his teenage son Christopher and daughters Rebecca and Corinne.

So why was *he* killed? Does this not make us angry? After all, if we're going to be honest we will surely admit that there were others who deserved to die more than he. Perhaps there was a corrupt policeman somewhere who had unjustly put innocent people in prison or a crooked policeman who had taken bribes. Or perhaps another policeman was carrying on an affair with his neighbor's wife. If one of those had been killed, we might have said that although we were sad, at least there would have appeared to be some moral logic to that death. But the Oakeses, dare we say it, are good people. Not sinless, of course, but believers living upright lives. So why is this pointless and terrible loss inflicted on *them*?

We need to be honest and face the kind of world in which we live. Why does God allow these things? Why does he do nothing to put these things right? And why, on the other hand, do people who couldn't care less about God and justice thrive? Here in contemporary idiom is the angry voice of an honest man from long ago who struggled with this same unfairness:

> Why do the wicked have it so good,
> live to a ripe old age and get rich?
> They get to see their children succeed,

get to watch and enjoy their grandchildren.
Their homes are peaceful and free from fear;
they never experience God's disciplining rod.
Their bulls breed with great vigor
and their calves calve without fail.
They send out their children to play
and watch them frolic like spring lambs.
They make music with fiddles and flutes,
have good times singing and dancing.
They have a long life on easy street,
and die painlessly in their sleep.[2]

That was the voice of Job, in a paraphrase from chapter 21. "Let's be honest," he says. "Let's have no more of this pious make-believe that it goes well for good people and badly for bad people. It's not true; look around the world—it's simply not true. By and large people who could not care less about God live happier, longer lives with less suffering than do believers. Why? What kind of God runs a world like this?"

Armchair Questions and Wheelchair Questions
It is hard questions like this that face us in the book of Job. But there are two ways of asking them. We may ask them as armchair questions or we may ask them as wheelchair questions. We ask them as armchair questions if we ourselves are remote from suffering. As Shakespeare said, "He jests at scars that never felt a wound."[3] The troubled Jesuit poet Gerard Manley Hopkins wrote eloquently and almost bitterly:

O the mind, mind has mountains; cliffs of fall
Frightful, sheer, no-man fathomed. Hold them cheap
May who ne'er hung there.[4]

We grapple with God with wheelchair questions when we do not take this terror lightly when we ourselves, or those we love, are suffering. Job asks wheelchair questions.

Every pastor knows that behind most front doors there lies pain, often hidden, sometimes long and drawn out, sometimes very deep. A few years ago a pastor was discussing how to preach a passage from Job with four fellow ministers when he looked around at the others. For a moment he lost his concentration on the text as he realized that one of them, some years ago, had lost his wife in a car accident in their first year of marriage. The second was bringing up a seriously handicapped daughter. The third had broken his neck and had come within 2 millimeters of total paralysis or death six years previously. The fourth had undergone repeated radical surgeries that had changed his life. As his concentration returned to the text of Job, he thought, *This book is not merely academic. It is both about people and for people who know suffering.*

Robert Gordis writes, "The ubiquity of evil and its apparent triumph everywhere give particular urgency to the most agonizing riddle of human existence, the problem of evil, which is the crucial issue in biblical faith." He calls the book of Job "the most profound and—if such an epithet may be allowed—the most beautiful discussion of the theme," more relevant than ever, "in this, the most brutal of centuries."[5]

Job is a fireball book. It is a staggeringly honest book. It is a book that knows what people actually say and think—not just what they say publicly in church. It knows what people say behind closed doors and in whispers, and it knows what we say in our tears. It is not merely an academic book. If we listen to it carefully, it will touch us, trouble us, and unsettle us at a deep level.

What Kind of Church Should We Want?

But as well as asking what kind of world we live in, the book of Job will force us to ask what kind of church we belong to. What is the greatest threat to Christian churches today? That question was asked to an Any Questions panel at the Proclamation Trust's Cornhill Training Course in London where I work. It is a good question, although answers are bound to be impressionistic. But here's a suggestion: in most of the world churches are liable to be swamped by the so-called prosperity gospel, and in the richer parts of the world churches struggle to guard the gospel against metamorphosing into what we might call the therapeutic gospel. These two closely-related pseudo-gospels threaten to displace the authentic Christian and Biblical gospel.

The prosperity gospel, in its crudest form, is the message that God wants you to be rich, and if you trust him and ask him, he *will* make you rich. One of the largest Christian occasions in Britain is the annual International Gathering of Champions, run by Pastor Matthew Ashimolowo. Preachers tell the congregation how God wants them to be rich and then richer and richer. The American preacher T. D. Jakes has an estimated personal fortune of one hundred million dollars. Such fortunes are regarded as evidence of God's favor.[6]

The first time I visited Nigeria I was astonished at the myriad of ramshackle signs alongside the roadside advertising little independent churches. Most of them seemed to be teaching the prosperity gospel, with names like The Winners Chapel, Divine Call Bible Church (its slogan was "Excellence and Power"), or The Redeemed Evangelical Mission POWER WORD (how to speak a word that gets you power and influence). Come to Jesus and become a winner in life—that seemed to be the message. In our contrasuggestible English way, my traveling companion wanted to start a Losers Chapel, and I suggested an Apostolic Scum of the Earth Church, neither of which would be a marketing man's dream, but each of which would have been closer to the New Testament.

We visited the Ecumenical Centre, the large cathedral-like building at the heart of Abuja, the capital city. This is the flagship Christian building in the country (mirrored by an equally large central mosque not far away). When we were there, the building was being used by a prosperity gospel denomination, headed by self-styled Archbishop Sam Amaga. The bookstall consisted entirely of books by him. Here is a selection of the titles: *Cultivating a Winning Habit* (with the subtitle "Sure Guarantee for a Top Life"), *Created for the Top, Don't Die at the Bottom*, and *Power Pillars for Uncommon Success*.

A Ghanaian student at Cornhill told me that some weddings in his country replace the traditional wording of the wedding vows with the words, "For better, for best, for richer, for richest" because they cannot countenance the possibility that there may, for a Christian couple, be anything "worse" or "poorer."

So that is the prosperity gospel. If I am poor (financially and materially poor) and I come to Jesus, Jesus will make me rich. If I am sick, and I pray to Jesus, Jesus will make me well. If I want a wife or a husband, and I ask Jesus for one, he will give me a wife or husband. If a couple wants children and call out to Jesus, Jesus will give them children. And so on. This, according to the prosperity gospel, is what he has promised.

But what if, as in some parts of the world, I already am rich? I may not think of myself as particularly rich, but I have running water, I do not worry about having enough food, I have a roof over my head and adequate clothing. I may well have much more than these, but these alone suffice to make me very rich in world terms. Perhaps I am also healthy, happily married, and have children. What happens to the prosperity gospel when I already enjoy prosperity? It metamorphoses into the therapeutic gospel. In its simplest form, this false gospel says that if I feel empty and I come to Jesus, Jesus will fill me. The promise of objective goods (money, wife, husband, children) metamorphoses into the claiming of subjective benefits. I feel depressed, and Jesus promises to lift my spirits. I feel aimless, and Jesus commits himself to giving me purpose in life. I feel empty inside, and Jesus will fill me.[7]

This chimes perfectly with prosperous twenty-first-century society. While writing this, I had a survey from our gas supplier asking for customer feedback after a repair job. The survey began with the words, "We want to know how we left you feeling." That is very contemporary. Not "We want to know whether we made your gas heating *work*, whether we did it promptly and efficiently" and so on (objective criteria), but "We want to know how we left you *feeling*" (the subjective focus). Did we help you feel good?

The therapeutic gospel is the gospel of self-fulfillment. It makes me, already healthy and wealthy, feel good.

The book of Job addresses in a deep and unsettling way both the pseudo-gospel of prosperity and the pseudo-gospel of feeling good.

What Kind of Savior Do We Need?

The most significant question, however, is the third one: what kind of Savior do we need? Or to put it another way, what kind of man does the universe need? The more I have bashed my head against the text of Job year after year, the more deeply convinced I have become that the book ultimately makes no sense without the obedience of Jesus Christ, his obedience to death on a cross. Job is not everyman; he is not even every believer. There is something desperately extreme about Job. He foreshadows one man whose greatness exceeded even Job's, whose sufferings took him deeper than Job, and whose perfect obedience to his Father was only anticipated in faint outline by Job. The universe needed one man who would lovingly and perfectly obey his heavenly Father in the entirety of his life and death, by whose obedience the many would be made righteous (Romans 5:19).

We are probably right to view Job as a prophet. James says to suffering Christians, "As an example of suffering and patience, brothers, take the prophets. . . . You have heard of the steadfastness of Job" (James 5:10, 11). If Job is a prophet, then at the heart of his life was "the Spirit of Christ" indicating within him something about "the sufferings of Christ and the subsequent glories" (1 Peter 1:11). Sometimes for the prophets this meant living out in anticipation something of the sufferings of Christ, as it did for Hosea when he was called to marry the immoral woman Gomer. For Job, perhaps supremely among the prophets, the call of God on his life was to anticipate the perfect obedience of Christ.

Two Preliminary Observations

Two introductory points need to be made before we launch into the book.

Job Is a Very Long Book

Job is forty-two chapters long. We may consider that rather an obvious observation. But the point is this: in his wisdom God has given us a very long book, and he has done so for a reason. It is easy just to read or preach the beginning and the end and to skip rather quickly over the endless arguments in between as if it wouldn't much matter if they weren't there. Too many churches, if or when they tackle Job, do so in a very short series of sermons—perhaps one on the first two chapters, one for the end of the book, and one (sometimes assigned to a junior member of the preaching staff) to cover chapters 3—37. But God has given us forty-two chapters!

Why? Well, maybe because when the suffering question and the "where is God?" question and the "what kind of God . . . ?" question are asked from the wheelchair, they cannot be answered on a postcard. If we ask, "What kind of God allows this kind of world?" God gives us a forty-two-chapter book. Far from saying, "The message of Job can be summarized on a postcard, in a Tweet, or on an SMS, and here it is," he says, "Come with me on a journey, a journey that will take time. There is no instant answer—take a spoonful of Job, just add boiling water, and you'll know the answer." Job cannot be distilled. It is a narrative with a very slow pace (after the frenetic beginning) and long delays. Why? Because there is no instant working through grief, no quick fix to pain, no message of Job in a nutshell. God has given us a forty-two-chapter journey with no satisfactory bypass.

Writing about therapy, one writer says, "Many will wonder why therapy can take so long. Why can't pain, once understood and engaged with, allow for a speedy rewrite of a physical or mental template and thus bring quick relief? It is frustrating." She goes on to say that it takes two to four years for a language to become personal and a part of oneself, and therapy is like absorbing a new language. "In therapy the patient has to unlearn one way of being and develop another, more sustainable one"; so it's not surprising that it takes a long time.[8] For a similar reason the book of Job is long. We need to read it, read it all, and read it slowly.

Most of Job Is Poetry

About 95 percent of the book of Job is poetry. Chapters 1, 2 and part of chapter 42 are prose. Almost all the rest is poetry. But so what? Well, poetry does not speak to us in the same way as prose. Poems "are always a personal 'take' on something, communicating not just from head to head but from heart to heart" (J. I. Packer).[9] A poet can often touch us, move us, and unsettle us in ways that prose cannot. Job is a blend of the affective (touching our feelings) and the cognitive (addressing our minds). And poetry is particularly suited to this balanced address to the whole person. But poetry does not lend itself to summing up in tidy propositions, bullet points, neat systems, and well-swept answers. Poetry grapples with our emotions, our wills, and our sensitivities. We cannot just sum up a poem in a bald statement; we need to let a poem get to work on us—we must immerse ourselves in it.

We need therefore to try to sensitize ourselves to the connotations of words, for "speech, particularly poetry, uses words not only for denotation, to refer to concrete, definable objects, but also for connotation, to suggest the penumbra or aura that surrounds the denotation of words and goes beyond them."[10]

It is just so with Job. We shall be immersed in the poetry of Job. As we enter it we must not expect tidy systematic points to jot down and then think we've "done" Job, as a one-day tourist might "do" Florence. Job is to be lived in and not just studied. So during this study let us read the book of Job itself, read it out loud, mull it over, absorb it, wonder, be unsettled, and meditate. And may we let God work on us through this great Bible book. We shall find our faith deepened and our emotional palettes enriched.

The Structure of the Book of Job

The book of Job is divided into three unequal parts. In each part a character or characters is or are introduced in prose. First, from 1:1—2:10 Job is introduced (1:1–5), and we then learn what happened to him. Then, from 2:11 right through to 31:40, the focus is on Job and his three friends, who are introduced in prose in 2:11–13. This long section ends with "The words of Job are ended" (31:40). Finally, from 32:1—42:6, we have the answers to Job, beginning with the prose introduction of Elihu (32:1–5). At the very end there is a short but significant conclusion.[1]

> Part I: Job and What Happened to Him
> *Introducing Job* **1:1–5**
> What happened to Job **1:6—2:10**
> Part II: Job's friends and their "conversations" with Job
> *Introducing Job's three friends* **2:11–13**
> Speeches by Job and his friends **3:1—28:28**
> Job's 1st lament (3)
> 1st Cycle of speeches
> Eliphaz (4, 5)—Job (6, 7)
> Bildad (8)—Job (9, 10)
> Zophar (11)—Job (12—14)
> 2nd Cycle of speeches
> Eliphaz (15)—Job (16, 17)
> Bildad (18)—Job (19)
> Zophar (20)—Job (21)
> 3rd Cycle of speeches (interrupted)
> Eliphaz (22)—Job (23, 24)
> Bildad (25)—Job (26)
> Job's summary speech, part 1 (27:1–23)
> Job's summary speech, part 2 (28:1–28)[2]
> Job's Final Defense **29:1—31:40**
> Part III: The Answers to Job **32:1—42:6**
> *Introducing Elihu* **32:1–5**
> Elihu's Answers **32:6—37:24**
> The Lord's First Answer and Job's Response **38:1—40:5**
> The Lord's Second Answer and Job's Response **40:6—42:6**
> *Conclusion* **42:7–17**

Because 2:11–13 and 3 focus primarily on Job, I have taken all of chapters 1—3 as the first section of my exposition.

25

Part 1

JOB AND WHAT HAPPENED TO HIM

Job 1—3

1

Welcome to a Well-Run World

JOB 1:1–5

IN WHAT SORT OF A WORLD would you like to live? In any society some people come out on top, and others are nearer the bottom; some are great men and women, and others are not. When we give this some thought, we probably say that we would like to live in a society where the great persons are also good persons. In England we have an idiom; when we want to describe a gathering of important people we say, "the great and the good were there," leaving the connection between greatness and goodness unstated and open.

Much misery is caused when evil people govern and rule. And much joy results when good persons become great and govern with justice and righteousness. That is the sort of world we want, or at least the sort of world we ought to want.

That is the world with which the book of Job begins.

There Was a Man . . .

The story begins with the words, "There was a man . . ." (or, in the Hebrew word order, "A man there was . . . ," v. 1). This is the story of a human being.[1]

It is easy not to concentrate when someone is introduced to us. I find that when others kindly tell me their name and something about themselves, all too often what they have said has gone in one ear and out the other. But in the book of Job we need to pay careful attention to the introductions, and supremely to the first one.

This is the first of the three prose introductions that structure the book of Job (see "Structure of the Book of Job" earlier). Although other people

29

are introduced later, the human focus of the book is on the one man Job. It is Job who is introduced first. The scenes that follow focus on what happens to Job. The long speech cycles with his friends are all addressed to Job or spoken by Job. Elihu addresses much of his four speeches to Job. Even the Lord addresses his speeches to Job, and Job replies. It really is "the book of Job." Job is, as it were, either on the stage or the subject of discussion at every point in the book. So we need to pay careful attention to how Job is introduced to us.

The writer tells us five things about Job.

His Place

First, he lived "in the land of Uz" (v. 1). We do not know exactly where Uz was. Probably it was in the land of Edom, just to the east of the promised land. Lamentations 4:21 says, "Rejoice and be glad, O daughter of Edom, you who dwell in the land of Uz."[2] But "[t]he importance of the name Uz lies not in where such a place is, but in where it is not"; namely, it is not in Israel.[3]

We do not know whether or not Job was a Hebrew (the term *Jew* was not used until much later in Old Testament history). But we do know that he lived outside the promised land, and his story does not tie in to any known events in Israel's history. The story does not begin "in the xth year of so-and-so king of Israel or Judah" or at any identifiable time in Israel's history. In fact, as we shall see in verse 5, Job seems to be a kind of patriarch who offers sacrifices on behalf of his family in a way that would have been strictly forbidden after the institution of the priesthood. He seems to have been a contemporary (speaking very loosely) of Abraham, Isaac, or Jacob. He lived independent of the giving of the promises to Abraham, before the captivity in and exodus from Egypt, before the giving of the Law at Mount Sinai, before the conquest of the promised land, and outside that land. All this makes his story all the more wonderful. Here was a man who knew almost nothing of God, and yet, as we shall see, he knew God and trusted and worshipped him as God.

His Name

". . . whose name was Job" (v. 1).

Although various theories have been propounded about the possible meaning of Job's name, there is no convincing evidence that the name had any particular significance.[4] Most likely he is called Job because Job was his name! We are not given his genealogy. His family connections are not significant. He is just a man called Job.

His Godliness

". . . and that man was blameless and upright, one who feared God and turned away from evil" (v. 1). After the more or less incidental historical facts of his place and his name, the first really significant thing the writer tells us is about Job's character. This is of lasting importance, and we need to burn this into our consciousness as we read the book.

We are told four things about Job: his integrity, his treatment of others, his religion, and his morality. These four things tell us, not what Job was from time to time or occasionally, but his "constant nature."[5]

First, he was "blameless." This is a better translation than "perfect" (e.g., KJV, RSV). It does not mean "sinless," for Job himself admits "the iniquities of my youth" (13:26) and "my sin" (14:16). Fundamentally the word "blameless" speaks of genuineness and authenticity. In Joshua 24:14 Joshua exhorts the people of Israel to serve God "in *sincerity*" (the same Hebrew word)—that is to say, genuinely, not just pretending to serve him while their hearts were somewhere else. In Judges 9:16 Jotham challenges the people of Shechem, "Now therefore, if you acted in good faith and *integrity* [same word] when you made Abimelech king . . ." By which he means, "if you meant what you said and were not trying to deceive or double-cross anyone . . ." God said to Abraham, "Walk before me, and be blameless" (Genesis 17:1). And Psalm 119:1 proclaims a blessing on those "whose way is blameless."

The same idea is conveyed by the old expression used by some of the rabbis: "his 'within' was like his 'without.'"[6] Or as we might put it, "what you see is what you get." When you see Job at work, when you hear his words, when you watch his deeds, you see an accurate reflection of what is actually going on in his heart. The word means "personal integrity, not sinless perfection."[7] It is the opposite of hypocrisy, pretending to be one thing on the outside but being something else on the inside. Centuries later Timothy had to deal in Ephesus with the very opposite, men who had "the appearance of godliness, but [denied] its power" (2 Timothy 3:5). Job had the appearance of godliness because there was real godliness in his heart.

This character trait of blamelessness or integrity is pivotal in the book of Job. In 8:20 Bildad will say, "God will not reject a *blameless* man," and in 9:20–22 Job will repeatedly claim that he is "blameless." He does the same in 12:4.[8] As the drama develops, we shall be sorely tempted to think that Job is hiding something, that he is not as squeaky clean as he appears, that he is not blameless. We need to remember that he *is* blameless. The writer has headlined this wonderful characteristic of him.

Second, "that man was . . . upright" (v. 1). This shifts the focus slightly from Job's own integrity to the way he treats other people. In his human relationships Job is "upright," straightforward, a man you can do business with because he will not double-cross you, a man who deals straight. We shall see this upright behavior beautifully described in 31:13–23.

Third, his character was marked by integrity and his relationships by right dealing, and his religion was shaped by a humble piety. "That man was . . . one who feared God" (v. 1). We do not know how much he knew about the God he feared. But he had a reverence, a piety, a bowing down before the God who made the world, so that he honored God as God and gave thanks to him (cf. Romans 1:21).

Later in Israel's history the fear of the Lord was "that affectionate reverence, by which the child of God bends himself humbly and carefully to his Father's law."[9] For Job, not knowing that law in its fullness, the fear of God consisted of a devout, pious reverence for God and a desire to please him in all he knew of him. Job was, in the very best sense of the word, a genuinely religious man.

As the book develops we shall see that Job believed that God was both sovereign and just, that he had the power to make sure the world ran the way he chose to make it run, and that the way he would choose to make it run would be fair and marked by justice. At least that is what Job thought to begin with. The second of these convictions (God's justice) is about to be sorely tested.

Finally, Job's religion issues in godly morality. ". . . and that man was . . . one who . . . turned away from evil" (v. 1). As he walked life's path, he resolutely stayed on the straight and upright path and turned away from the crooked byways of sin. To turn away from sin is to repent. Job's character was marked by daily repentance, a habitual turning away from evil in his thoughts, words, and deeds.

Job is thus presented to us, not as a perfect man—only one perfect man has ever walked this earth—but as a genuine believer. In Ezekiel, Job is bracketed with Noah and Daniel as a man of conspicuous righteousness. God says, "Even if these three men, Noah, Daniel, and Job, were in [a land], they would deliver but their own lives by their righteousness" (Ezekiel 14:14; see also Ezekiel 14:20). What sort of righteousness did these men have? "By faith Noah, being warned by God concerning events as yet unseen, in reverent fear constructed an ark for the saving of his household. By this he condemned the world and became an heir of *the righteousness that comes by faith*" (Hebrews 11:7). Noah was righteous by faith. So was Job. Indeed, no sinner has ever been righteous with God in any other way.

So Job is a real believer, genuine in his integrity, upright in his relationships, pious in his worship, and penitent in his behavior. His life was marked by what we would call repentance and faith, which are still the marks of the believer today, as they have always been.

So the next question is, what will happen to a man like this? The answer appears to be simple and wonderful: he will be a very very great man.

His Greatness

"[And[10]] there were born to him seven sons and three daughters. He possessed 7,000 sheep, 3,000 camels, 500 yoke of oxen, and 500 female donkeys, and very many servants, so that this man was the greatest of all the people of the east" (vv. 2, 3).

We begin with his family. "Behold, children are a heritage from the LORD," and the man whose "quiver" is full of them is "blessed" (Psalm 127:3–5). Job's quiver is certainly full—seven sons and three daughters. These are good numbers. Seven symbolizes completeness. Sons were special blessings in those pastoral cultures. When praising Ruth to the skies, the friends of her mother-in-law Naomi described her as being "more to you than seven sons" (Ruth 4:15). When Hannah celebrates the gospel reversals of God, she says, "The barren has borne seven" (1 Samuel 2:5). What more could a man want than seven sons! Well, I guess some daughters as well. And three is a good number. And seven plus three equals ten, which is also a good number. They are all good numbers and speak of an ideal family.[11]

Consider also his possessions. Job was a farmer. He was not strictly a nomad, for we see later that he was a local dignitary and was prominent in "the gate of the city" where local business was done (see Job 29:7). He seems to have grown crops as well as having herds and flocks.[12] He and his family lived in houses rather than tents (as we see, for example, in 1:18, 19, where the oldest brother's house is destroyed).[13] Job had 7,000 sheep, 3,000 camels for desert transport, 500 yoke (i.e., pairs) of oxen for plowing the land, and 500 female donkeys, used to carry the produce of the fields and also for milk production and breeding. In addition, he had a large staff, huge numbers on his payroll. To identify with this, we may need to transpose this pastoral description of great wealth into our own contexts, whether urban or rural. It is a picture of great wealth and power. He is described as "the greatest of all the people of the east" (v. 3). "The people of the east" is an expression used of the Arameans (to whom Jacob fled in Genesis 29:1; cf. Genesis 25:20), of Israel's eastern neighbors, as opposed to the Philistines in the west (Isaiah 11:14), or of those associated with the Midianites in the days of the Judges

(Judges 6:3). It is a general term referring to various peoples who lived east of the promised land. Among these peoples in his day Job was the greatest.

Job was, on a regional or local scale, what Adam was meant to be on a global scale—a great, rich, and powerful ruler. It is worth reflecting on this. This is, in a way, the prosperity gospel, and it seems to be what we ought to expect in a well-run world. Surely the world would be a better place if godly people got to the top and ungodly people were squashed down at the bottom, where they could do no harm. How terrible it is when ungodly people rise to the top. How miserable are so many countries because they are ruled by the wicked.

So Job's greatness is the natural and right consequence of his godliness. It is what we ought to expect. Or is it? There is just one more thing to note in Job's introduction.

His Anxiety

His sons used to go and hold a feast in the house of each one on his day, and they would send and invite their three sisters to eat and drink with them. And when the days of the feast had run their course, Job would send and consecrate them, and he would rise early in the morning and offer burnt offerings according to the number of them all. For Job said, "It may be that my children have sinned, and cursed God in their hearts." Thus Job did continually. (1:4, 5)

The expression "on his day" probably means an annual feast day for each son, perhaps his birthday (v. 4). This is not a picture of incessant partying, but of regular natural family get-togethers.[14] Their three sisters are presumably unmarried, for there is no mention of their husbands. So we are to think of Job as a man in the prime of life,[15] perhaps in contemporary terms a man in his early forties, with three unmarried daughters perhaps between eighteen and their early twenties. We do not know if the seven sons are married or not. Whatever the details, it is a picture of family harmony and innocent festivity.

And yet, for all the harmony and happiness on the surface, there is a deep anxiety and care in Job's heart. When each birthday party comes to an end,[16] Job summons all his children (or possibly just all his sons) for a religious ceremony of sacrifice. Each time Job "would rise early in the morning" (v. 5). This suggests an eagerness, a zeal, a sense of urgency. He is conscientious about this because he has a sensitive conscience. Before anything else intervenes to distract them, Job summons them for this ceremony. It is important. He impresses on his children the urgency of being present for this.

They gather, and Job the patriarch, the family head, offers a burnt offering for each of them. Later in the history of Israel a burnt offering would be the most expensive form of sacrifice, in which the whole sacrificial animal is consumed. It pictures the hot anger of God burning up the animal in the place of the worshipper, whose sins would have made them liable to be burned up in the presence of God. We can imagine Job doing this for them one at a time: "This one is for you," and he lights the fire, and the animal is consumed. And the son or daughter watches the holocaust and thinks, "That is what would have happened to me if there had not been a sacrifice." And then the next one: "This one is for you." And so on until all the children were covered by sacrifice.

What was so serious that it necessitated such an expensive and urgent sacrifice? Why did Job insist on doing this party by party? Because he said to himself, "It may be that my children have sinned, and cursed God in their hearts" (v. 5). Although the children presumably showed outward piety (they did not curse God with their mouths; their parties were not wild drunken orgies or anything like that), Job is anxious lest in their hearts they did not honor God, lest deep inside lurked the godless wish that there were no God. Job has integrity (or blamelessness); he is not so sure about his children.

Job knows that what matters is not the appearance of godliness but a godly heart. He knows that to curse God in the heart, to wish God dead (as it were), is a terribly serious offense, an offense that carries the eternal death penalty if it is not atoned for. But Job believes in the atoning power of sacrifice, and so he offers burnt offerings. As Proverbs says, "In the fear of the LORD one has strong confidence, and his children will have a refuge" (Proverbs 14:26). And the narrator concludes, "Thus Job did continually" (v. 5). Year after year the godly Job covers any secret sin in his children's hearts with sacrifice.

Conclusion

The story does not begin with this introduction. No event in the drama of Job has yet happened. Verses 1–3 are descriptions of Job and his character. And verses 4, 5 describe what Job habitually did. The whole introduction sets the scene before our story actually starts.

It sets a happy scene with one shadow. The happiness consists in a good man being a great man, a pious man being a prosperous man. It is a picture of the world being as the world ought to be, a world where the righteous lead. It is a world where the prosperity gospel seems to be true.

The shadow is the sad possibility that people might say that they are pious while in their hearts they are being impious, saying in their hearts that they wish God were dead. At this stage we cannot imagine why recipients of such signal favor from God would ever want to curse God. Why would men and women blessed with such harmony and abundant prosperity do anything other than praise and love God from the bottom of their hearts? And yet the possibility is there. It exercises Job at every family gathering. There is something dark in human hearts, and Job knows it. Job knows that by nature we do not honor God as God or give thanks to him (cf. Romans 1:21). Only sacrifice can cover such sin in the heart.

2

The Testing of Your Faith

JOB 1:6—2:10

THE GLORY OF GOD is more important than your or my comfort. That is a statement with which all Christians will readily agree in theory. A Puritan prayer begins:

Lord of all being,
There is one thing that deserves my greatest care,
that calls forth my ardent desires,
That is, that I may answer the great end for which I am made—
to glorify thee who hast given me being. . . .[1]

That is a fine and noble prayer. But it has awesome consequences from which we naturally shy away. Of course, we say, there can be nothing more important than the glory of God. What Christian could possibly disagree with that expression of correct piety? And yet before long we find ourselves recoiling from the implications of this statement.

The introduction of the book of Job in 1:1–5 portrays a world with which Disney would by and large be happy. It is a world in which the right people come out on top. We are ready, as it were, to go home happy, knowing it is all working out as it should. But then the action begins, with four alternating scenes in Heaven and on earth. The story is told sparingly and brilliantly, as a cartoonist might, as a few well-chosen lines on the page conjure up whole worlds of drama. In this drama we shall see that it is necessary for it publicly to be seen that there is in God's world a great man who is great because he is good, and yet who will continue to be a good man when he ceases to be a great man. Ultimately, in the greatest fulfillment of Job's story, we will need to see a man who does not count equality with God (greatness) as something to be grasped but makes himself nothing for the glory of God (Philippians 2:6–11).

Scene 1: Heaven (Job 1:6–12)

> Now there was a day when the sons of God came to present themselves before the Lord, and the Satan[2] also came among them. The Lord said to the Satan, "From where have you come?" The Satan answered the Lord and said, "From going to and fro on the earth, and from walking up and down on it." And the Lord said to the Satan, "Have you considered my servant Job, that there is none like him on the earth, a blameless and upright man, who fears God and turns away from evil?" Then the Satan answered the Lord and said, "Does Job fear God for no reason? Have you not put a hedge around him and his house and all that he has, on every side? You have blessed the work of his hands, and his possessions have increased in the land. But stretch out your hand and touch all that he has, and he will curse you to your face." And the Lord said to the Satan, "Behold, all that he has is in your hand. Only against him do not stretch out your hand." So the Satan went out from the presence of the Lord. (Job 1:6–12)

After the timeless introduction, which describes who Job was and what he habitually did, we read, "there was a day" (v. 6). And what a day! On this particular day something happened in Heaven that would change Job's life forever.

The day began in what seems to have been a routine way: "the sons of God came to present themselves before the Lord" (v. 6). The expression "the sons of God" speaks here of beings whose existence is derivative from God (hence "sons") but whose rank is superhuman.[3] The expression literally translated "sons of God" by the ESV is often translated "angels" (e.g., NIV). We meet them again in Psalm 29 ("Ascribe to the Lord, O sons of God," Psalm 29:1, ESV footnote) and in Genesis 6:2.[4] They form a "divine council" or heavenly cabinet, and we see reference to this in Psalms 82 and 89.

> God has taken his place in the divine council;
> in the midst of the gods he holds judgment. . . .
> I said, "You are gods,
> sons of the Most High, all of you." (Psalm 82:1, 6)

> For who in the skies can be compared to the Lord?
> Who among the sons of God (ESV footnote) is like the Lord . . .
> a God greatly to be feared in the council of the holy ones,
> and awesome above all who are around him? (Psalm 89:6, 7)

As members of God's heavenly cabinet, they come "to present themselves" before him (v. 6). The expression "to present oneself" or "to stand before" means something like "to attend a meeting to which one is summoned" or "to come before a superior ready to do his will."[5] It is the expression used of the wise man in Proverbs: "Do you see a man skillful in his work? He will stand before kings; he will not stand before obscure men" (Proverbs 22:29). That is to say, he will be a senior civil servant or a government minister rather than just a local council employee. The same expression is used with apocalyptic imagery in Zechariah when the four chariots go out to all the world "after presenting themselves before the Lord of all the earth" (Zechariah 6:5). First they present themselves for duty, and then they go out to do what they have been told to do.

This "day" that turns out to be so devastating for Job begins with a normal heavenly cabinet meeting. God summons his ministers rather as an American President might call his senior staff to an early-morning meeting in the Oval Office before sending them out for action.

Only one member of the heavenly cabinet is mentioned individually: ". . . and the Satan also came among them" (v. 6). The expression "the Satan" suggests that here "Satan" is a title, which tells us something about his role. The word "Satan" means something like "adversary, opponent, enemy." The noun is used to mean an adversary in other contexts as well. When the Lord stops Balaam in his tracks, he does so "as his adversary [satan]" (Numbers 22:22). When the Philistine commanders tell the Philistine king Achish they don't want David fighting with them against Israel, they say, "He shall not go down with us to battle, lest in the battle he become an adversary [satan] to us" (1 Samuel 29:4). Here in Job 1, it is not yet clear whose adversary the Satan is. It will soon become apparent that he is Job's adversary.[6]

We are not told explicitly whether or not the Satan is present as a member of the heavenly council or whether he is in some way a gatecrasher. It is sometimes assumed that because the Satan is evil he cannot be a member of the council and must have barged in uninvited. So the Lord's question, "From where have you come?" (v. 7) is read in a hostile voice ("What do you think *you* are doing here?"). But this is unlikely. The word "among" (v. 6) probably suggests that he is a member of the group.[7] There need be no hostility or implied rebuke in the question, "From where have you come?" Probably it represents something like a President asking a Cabinet secretary for his report: "Secretary of War, it is time for your report. Tell us where you have been and what you have seen."

In 1 Kings 22 the prophet Micaiah vividly describes the same heavenly council: "I saw the Lord sitting on his throne, and all the host of heaven standing beside him." Then as Micaiah describes the conversation in the council, "a lying spirit" speaks up and is sent out by the Lord to do his will (1 Kings 22:19–22). So there is apparently no inconsistency in "a lying spirit" being present in God's council. In the same way, it will become clear that the Satan is present at the council because he belongs there. His presence (and indeed that of other lying spirits and evil spirits) has been described as being analogous to the expression in British governance, "Her Majesty's Loyal Opposition."[8] They oppose the government, but they do so in ultimate and unquestioned subservience to the Crown. Their opposition is a necessary and good part of British governance. They in themselves are devoted to trying to bring the government down; and yet in spite of themselves their opposition serves a purpose in making the government better than it would be in the absence of opposition (as tyrannies attest). In the same way the Satan will oppose Job and yet will do so in a way that strangely and paradoxically will eventually be seen to serve the purposes of the Lord. As Luther put it, the Satan is "God's Satan."

How the World Is Governed

This description of the Lord and "the sons of God" gives us an important insight into the way the world is governed. Presumably this language of God sitting surrounded by a heavenly council is anthropomorphic language. God does not literally sit at the head of a council any more than he literally has hands or feet. This kind of language is used of God because we can understand it, to accommodate to our limitations. But what does it mean?

Broadly speaking there are three models for understanding the spiritual government of the world.

The first is polytheism or animism, in which the universe is governed (if that is not too strong a word) by a multiplicity of gods, goddesses, and spirits, none of whom is perfect and some of which are exceedingly evil. There is no absolutely supreme god or goddess, although some are generally more powerful than others. The end result is a universe filled with anxiety, in which we may never know in advance which spiritual power will come out on top in a particular situation, in which different deities have to be appeased and kept friendly, much as a citizen in a corrupt society may offer bribes to different officials, hoping he or she gets the bribes right in their amounts and their recipients. This is the world of animism and of Hinduism. In a strange way, it is also the world of Buddhism, where the "gods and goddesses" are within ourselves. Each person is his or her own god or goddess. Who knows who will win?

At its simplest this view becomes a dualism in which the world is governed by the outcome of an ongoing contest between God and the devil, who are thought of as pretty much equal and opposite powers battling it out for supremacy, like the Empire and the Federation in *Star Wars*. The devil is perceived as having an autonomy and agency independent of God. Some Christians are practical dualists in this way.

The second is a kind of absolute monism, in which the world is governed absolutely and simply by one God. What this God says goes, end of story. Above the visible and material universe there is one, and only one, supernatural power, the absolute power of the Creator of Heaven and earth. This model underlies the classic objection to the goodness of God: "If God is God He is not good. If God is good He is not God."[9]

As I understand it, this is the model of Islam, and many Christians think it is the Biblical model. It is not.

Christian people can veer toward either of these, a dualism or a monism. Neither does justice to the Bible's picture, which is more nuanced and complex. The Bible portrays for us a world that lies under the absolute supremacy and sovereignty of the Creator, who has no rivals, who is unique, such that there is no god like him. And yet he does not govern the world as the sole supernatural power. He governs the world by the means of and through the agency of a multiplicity of supernatural powers, *some of whom are evil*. That is to say, "the sons of God" represent powers that are greater than human powers and yet are less than God's power. They include among their number the Satan and his lying and evil spirits.

Above the visible and measurable material world of human senses lies a world in which is the one Jesus calls "the ruler of this world" (John 12:31) and whom Paul will later call "the prince of the power of the air, the spirit that is now at work in the sons of disobedience" (Ephesians 2:2). "The air" here speaks of a region higher than earth (hence supernatural) but lower than the dwelling-place of God himself (Heaven). Our battle does not just take place at the human level ("against flesh and blood") but "against the rulers, against the authorities, against the cosmic powers over this present darkness, against the spiritual forces of evil in the heavenly places" (Ephesians 6:12).

This model is not dualist; the sovereignty of God is not compromised one iota in this model. But the nature of the government of the world is significantly different than in the monist model. We need to take account of these supernatural agencies, "the sons of God" in the language of Job and other Old Testament passages. And we need to grasp that the evil agencies, the devil and all his angels, while being supernatural and superhuman, are sub-divine. Satan is, to again quote Luther's famous phrase, "God's Satan."

Some will object that since God cannot look at or have fellowship with evil (Habakkuk 1:13), he cannot allow the Satan to be in his presence. But this is to confuse fellowship with government. God can have no fellowship with evil, because he is pure light, and "in him is no darkness at all" (1 John 1:5, 6). But he can use evil in his government of the world, and he does. His having business dealings, so to speak, with the Satan in the government of the world is not the same as suggesting that the Satan enjoys God's presence in the sense of his blessing.

The Conversation in Heaven

The writer of the book of Job is a prophet. How else could he know what happened in the heavenly council? As Eliphaz taunts Job later, "Have you listened in the council of God?" (15:8). Of course he hasn't. But the writer has. And as he listens, this is what he hears.

To the introductory question, the Satan replies, "From going to and fro on the earth, and from walking up and down on it" (v. 7). This may be evasive, like the teenager who, asked by Mom or Dad what he's been doing all day, grunts, "Oh, just stuff" (subtext: "it's none of your business"). And yet the expression "going to and fro" suggests going about with a specific purpose.[10] What that purpose is will become apparent. The Satan has a job to do, and he has been doing it, even if he is reluctant to divulge his findings.

His task becomes clear with the Lord's next question: "Have you considered [literally, "Have you set your heart upon"] my servant Job, that there is none like him on the earth, a blameless and upright man, who fears God and turns away from evil?" (v. 8). This implies that the Satan's job, as God's submissive opposition, is to search men and women to see if there is anyone who is genuinely godly and pious. God claims that there is one and echoes point for point the storyteller's description of Job in the very first verse of the book. We might paraphrase it like this: "I wonder if, in your travels looking for genuine piety, you have noticed my servant Job." The expression "my servant" conveys Job's honor and dignity; he is God's covenant partner. It is a title used forty times of Moses, as a general title for the prophets (e.g., 1 Kings 14:18), and of the patriarchs (e.g., Genesis 24:14; 26:24; Psalm 105:6; Exodus 32:13). Job is loyal to the Lord, and the Lord will be loyal to him: "He is a real believer, with integrity and consistency. It is impossible to find in the whole world such a conspicuously pious and consistent believer."

These fateful words, singling out Job as conspicuously genuine and godly, are to prove devastating in their consequences for Job. The book of Job is not about suffering in general, and certainly not about the sufferings common to men and women the world over. Rather it is about how God treats his friends.[11] Commenting on the words "he whom you love is ill" (John 11:3), John Chrysostom wrote, "Many men, when they see any of those who are pleasing to God suffering anything terrible . . . are offended, not knowing that to those especially dear to God it belongeth to endure these things."[12] In the same way God singles out his friend Job for the Satan's detailed attention. He asks the Satan if he has noticed Job's astonishing and preeminent godliness.

The Satan has. After all, it is his job to notice people like that. But—and this also is a part of his God-given role in the government of the world—the Satan puts a different interpretation on Job's piety. "Does Job fear God for no reason?" he asks (v. 9); or it may be, "Has Job *feared* God for no reason?" implying that Job was fearing God the last time he saw him.[13] He admits that Job looks like one who fears God; he must admit this. But why does Job fear God? Is it because God is God, because God is worthy of his worship and loving obedience? Or is there another reason? "Does God's finest servant, his boasted showpiece, serve him for conscience or convenience?"[14] The Satan suggests that it is merely convenience: "Have you not put a hedge around him and his house and all that he has, on every side?" (v. 10). Outside Job's human skin there is an outer skin, a protective hedge put there by God, so that not only his body but his family and his possessions are kept safe. "You have blessed the work of his hands, and his possessions have increased in the land" (v. 10). Here is a protective hedge that expands as Job's possessions expand. It is not a hedge that constrains him, but simply one that protects him and all that is his.

The Satan insinuates that Job's prosperity is the only cause of his piety. "Sure, he is pious," the Satan says in essence. "I cannot deny that. I see him in church every Sunday and at the church prayer meeting and active in the service of God. His piety is incontrovertible. But why is he pious?" Answer: Job has discovered the prosperity gospel, and it works. He has discovered that if he honors God, God will make him richer and richer. He and his wife will have great sex. His wife will have children. His children will be healthy and successful. And his bank balance will grow and grow. They will enjoy fabulous holidays and a lifestyle to make a pagan billionaire envious. Who wouldn't be pious, if that's what you get out of it? That is his motive. That is why he is pious. He is pious not because he actually loves God, honors God, or believes God is worthy of his worship; he is pious because piety results in prosperity, and for no other reason. That's the Satan's argument.

So the Satan continues, "But stretch out your hand and touch all that he has, and he will curse you to your face" (v. 11). The "hand" of God is the

Bible's way of speaking of God in action. When God stretches out his hand, he acts in human history. To "touch" here means more or less to "smite"[15] or "hit aggressively." "Do that," says the Satan with impudence using the imperative command to God ("stretch out"), and "I'll be damned if he doesn't curse you to your face."[16]

The Satan's logic is impeccable. How can we tell whether Job is pious because he believes God is worthy of his loving worship or whether he is pious because he believes his piety will result in blessing? Does his genuine piety lead to prosperity, or does his prosperity lead to his superficial piety? We must find out, says the Satan. The honor of God depends upon it. And the only way to find out is to take away Job's prosperity. Only when that outer skin or protective hedge is breached and the hand of God breaks in to take away what Job has will we and can we know whether or not his piety is genuine. "If we take those things away and he still fears you and turns from evil, then," implies the Satan, "I will admit that there is a man on earth who worships you because you are worthy of worship. But he won't. You watch and see. He will curse you to your face, directly, impudently. Just try it and we'll see."

Now although the Satan's motives are 100 percent aggressive and malicious, his argument is correct. There is no other way publicly to establish the nature of Job's piety. David Clines has pointed out perceptively that the converse would also be true. If a poor man were pious, it might even be necessary to enrich him to be absolutely sure that his piety were not the result of his poverty.[17]

The Satan is not bullying God, nor is he offering him a casual wager, as though Job's sufferings were just to see who wins a bet in Heaven. No, the Satan, for all his malice, is doing something necessary to the glory of God. In some deep way it is necessary for it to be publicly seen by the whole universe that God is worthy of the worship of a man and that God's worth is in no way dependent on God's gifts.

Exactly the same logic is present when Peter writes to Christians enduring trials and sufferings. Even though in the present "you have been grieved by various trials" there is a reason. And here is the reason: ". . . so that the tested genuineness of your faith—more precious than gold that perishes though it is tested by fire—may be found to result in praise and glory and honor at the revelation of Jesus Christ" (1 Peter 1:6, 7). When Jesus returns, the fact that a Christian has gone on trusting and believing even though all the blessings have been removed and he has suffered severe trials will prove to the universe that another human being considers God to be worthy of worship simply because he is God. God will be praised, his glory adored, and his honor seen by the universe because Christian men and women have gone on worshipping him when all the blessings have been taken away.

The glory of God is more important than your or my or Job's comfort. In some deep way the sufferings of Job are necessary to redound to the glory of God. Paradoxically the Satan, for all his evil motivation, has a necessary ministry in God's government of the world for his glory. If the Satan did not issue this challenge, it would be necessary for God to delegate this terrible task to another supernatural creature. Satan has a ministry; it is the ministry of opposition, the ministry of insisting that the genuineness of the believer be tested and proved genuine. It is a hostile and malicious ministry, but a necessary ministry for the glory of God.

So God gives his terrible instruction and permission: "And the LORD said to the Satan, 'Behold, all that he has is in your hand. Only against him do not stretch out your hand'" (v. 12). This instruction does not betray callousness in God, nor cold-bloodedness. We cannot say that God's insistence that Job's person not be harmed is a sign of God's love, for what then of the next heavenly scene, when that protection is withdrawn? Something deeper is going on here. Nor can we say, as David Clines perversely suggests, that God gives this permission because God himself does not know whether Job's faith is genuine.[18]

We must not draw too clear a line between instruction and permission. We do not like the idea of God instructing the Satan to attack Job, but that is what he does. In all this the Bible insists on the sovereignty of God. It has been fashionable since the late twentieth century to get around the problem of evil by suggesting that God is doing his best and we cannot blame him if he does not manage to arrange everything the way he wants. In his book *When Bad Things Happen to Good People*, Rabbi Harold Kushner "solves" the problem of suffering in this way. Others suggest that God is like a chess grandmaster taking on a roomful of amateur chess players; usually he wins the game against all comers, but once in a while an amateur wins. In the same way God wins most of the "games" but not all. The Bible allows no such idea. God is sovereign. "He [the Satan] cannot touch a hair upon the back of a single camel that belongs to Job, until he has Divine permission."[19] The Satan does what he is told, no more and no less.[20]

What is at stake here is the glory of God. Ultimately the well-being of the universe depends upon the glory of God. A universe in which God is not glorified will be a universe at odds with itself, a self-contradictory universe. Ultimately—and it is ultimately rather than immediately—the well-being of

Job depends upon the glory of God. And the sufferings of Job are necessary for the final blessing of Job.

It is not self-centered of God to desire his own glory. For us it is an inappropriate megalomania; for God, it is to desire the most deeply right thing in the world. We may perhaps use a trivial illustration to cast light on this. If I suggest that I ought to be given a Nobel Prize for Chemistry, I am suggesting something deeply inappropriate, for my knowledge of chemistry is very poor. If this prize were to be awarded to me, there would be something deeply awry with the Nobel Prize committee. But if a brilliant chemist who has done seminal work suggests he ought to be given the prize, this is quite different. Indeed, if he is *not* given the prize there is something wrong! In a faintly similar way, the universe has gone terribly awry when God is not given ultimate glory.

And so at the end of this scene "the Satan went out from the presence of the LORD" to do his terrible but strangely necessary work (v. 12).

Scene 2: Earth (Job 1:13–22)

Now there was a day when his sons and daughters were eating and drinking wine in their oldest brother's house, and there came a messenger to Job and said, "The oxen were plowing and the donkeys feeding beside them, and the Sabeans fell upon them and took them and struck down the servants with the edge of the sword, and I alone have escaped to tell you." While he was yet speaking, there came another and said, "The fire of God fell from heaven and burned up the sheep and the servants and consumed them, and I alone have escaped to tell you." While he was yet speaking, there came another and said, "The Chaldeans formed three groups and made a raid on the camels and took them and struck down the servants with the edge of the sword, and I alone have escaped to tell you." While he was yet speaking, there came another and said, "Your sons and daughters were eating and drinking wine in their oldest brother's house, and behold, a great wind came across the wilderness and struck the four corners of the house, and it fell upon the young people, and they are dead, and I alone have escaped to tell you."

Then Job arose and tore his robe and shaved his head and fell on the ground and worshiped. And he said, "Naked I came from my mother's womb, and naked shall I return. The LORD gave, and the LORD has taken away; blessed be the name of the LORD."

In all this Job did not sin or charge God with wrong. (Job 1:13–22)

Scene 2 is terrifying. We move now from Heaven to earth and from that first "day" (v. 6) to another "day"(v. 13). Like 9/11, this day begins normally enough. It seems to be the oldest brother's party, another in the lovely annual round of family festivities. Job is in his own home, perhaps quietly rejoicing in the harmonious family God has given him, when a messenger knocks on the door and insists on being heard. Job turns from whatever he is doing and listens quietly as this ashen-faced messenger, ragged and distraught, tells his story. He has run in from the farm. "The oxen were plowing" (v. 14), so it was a normal farming day in early winter, preparing the fields after harvest to sow the seed for the next harvest. Beside them "the donkeys [were] feeding" after the hard work of carrying the harvest into the barns. It was just a normal day in the autumn when, quite suddenly, "the Sabeans"—roving peoples from either southwestern or northern Arabia[21]—"fell upon them and took them and struck down the servants with the edge of the sword" (v. 15). It was an unexpected, violent, sudden, and terrifyingly destructive terrorist attack, as terrible in its violence and bloodshed as a car bomb or a suicide bomber today. The protective "hedge" (v. 10) has been breached. Every victim of a house burglary knows the feeling of being violated at this invasion of what they thought was their safe space. It is like this with Job. The world he thought was safe has been turned into a killing field. All Job's oxen and donkeys were stolen and all the associated farm workers were killed in one terrible attack. And—to add to the completeness of the terror, each returning servant said, "I alone have escaped to tell you" (v. 15; cf. vv. 16, 17, 19).

It is a devastating message. But before Job has time even to begin to take this in, while the first messenger is still speaking, another traumatized messenger appears in the doorway and interrupts: "The fire of God" (v. 16)—a conventional way of speaking of lightning[22]—"fell from heaven and burned up the sheep and the servants and consumed them." Not only the oxen and donkeys, but now the sheep too, with all the shepherds, were killed—not this time by terrorism but by a terrible act of God (as the insurance companies call it), a freak storm. The shock is not unlike the trauma experienced by victims of an earthquake or tsunami. And it comes on top of the trauma experienced by victims of terrorism. And again, to press home the completeness of the devastation, Job hears those awful words, "I alone have escaped to tell you" (v. 16).

But the trauma is not over. While this messenger is still telling his shocking story, a third messenger appears. "The Chaldeans"—nomads from southern Mesopotamia—"formed three groups"—a deliberate premeditated strategy of criminal aggression—"and made a raid on the camels and took them and struck down the servants with the edge of the sword" (v. 17). First the oxen and donkeys with their workers are killed, then the sheep with their shepherds, and now the camels are stolen and their keepers killed. And again, as Job listens in shocked silence, come the words, "I alone have escaped to tell you" (v. 17).

Job has been bankrupted. The greatest man of the region has been emptied of all his wealth in a day—from riches to rags. But poor Job doesn't even have time to think about what he will say to the creditors who are even now making their way to his door, for there is worse to come. As we listen to the story, we cannot avoid wondering why we were told at the start that all the children were together in the oldest brother's house. The tension has been rising. While the third messenger is still blurting out his story of disaster, a fourth and final messenger runs in with a tearstained face: "Your sons and daughters were eating and drinking wine in their oldest brother's house"—*yes, I know that*, we can imagine Job thinking, *get on with the news*—"and behold, a great wind came across the wilderness and struck the four corners of the house"—four corners to stress the completeness of the ensuing disaster—"and it fell upon the young people,"[23] and before Job has time to ask if there were casualties, before he even has time to hope, "and they are dead." All the remaining servants, all the children are dead, "and I alone have escaped to tell you" (vv. 18, 19).

An alternation of two human terrorist attacks and two "natural" disasters have deprived Job of everything. If we dwell for a few moments on this scene, it is hard not to weep with Job. Throughout the rest of this long book we must never forget the trauma of this scene. We are used in our cultures to post-traumatic stress disorders and to the training of trauma counselors to assist in times of natural disaster, terrorism, and war. But rarely if ever in human history can there have been a succession of such extreme disasters as this. Bankrupt and bereft, Job is basically left alone. His protective hedge has been broken, his outer skin so to speak violated, and all he had has been taken away.

The four messengers (who perhaps remind us of the four horsemen of the apocalypse in Revelation) fade away, and Job is on the stage alone. The greatest man of the region has now no possessions and no family (except his wife, who will make a brief and unhappy appearance soon). How will he respond? How he responds will reveal the true state of his heart—or so we have been led to believe by the Satan. Does Job serve God for what God gives him, or does Job serve God because God is worthy of his worship?

Job has been sitting to receive his terrible visitors. Now at last he can begin to respond. He "arose" (v. 20); perhaps he began to rise as each of the messengers neared the end of their tale, only to be nailed back to his seat by the onset of the next report of disaster. But now at last he can begin to respond and to grieve. He rises; he tears his robe, the outer mantle worn by people of distinction, perhaps symbolizing the pain that is tearing at his heart.[24] He shaves his head, another conventional symbol of mourning, perhaps indicating identification with the dead. And then he falls on the ground, not (yet) crushed by sadness, but in worship of the God he knows and loves. Quietly, with dignity and restraint, Job worships.

And then he speaks:

> Naked I came from my mother's womb, and naked shall I return. The LORD gave, and the LORD has taken away; blessed be the name of the LORD. (v. 21)[25]

The preacher says something very similar in Ecclesiastes:

> As he came from his mother's womb he shall go again, naked as he came, and shall take nothing for his toil that he may carry away in his hand. (Ecclesiastes 5:15)

Job knows that eventually he will die and take nothing away. It is almost as if he has died today. He understands that all his possessions and all his children were gifts from the Lord. By the nature of the Godness of God he gives, and it is therefore entirely his prerogative to take away as he sees fit, as and when he chooses. This is part of God being God.

So Job blesses the name of the Lord. He expresses the wish that all who hear his story will bless God for it. The Satan said Job would curse God to his face. On the contrary, his response to terrible loss is wonderfully blessing the God who has given and has now seen fit to take away. In the moment of his loss his first thought is of the God who had first given.

The story seems to conclude, "In all this Job did not sin or charge God with wrong" (v. 22). What this man says about God is the key issue at stake. He has been anxious lest his children may have cursed God in their hearts. The Satan has predicted that Job will curse God to his face. Instead he responds with blessing. It is a wonderful conclusion to a terrible story.

But it is not the conclusion. This is the next shock. We need to learn to be shocked and shocked and shocked again by this story and never to let familiarity dull the sharpness of the pain.

Scene 3: Heaven (Job 2:1–7a)

> Again there was a day when the sons of God came to present themselves before the LORD, and the Satan also came among them to present himself before the LORD. And the LORD said to the Satan, "From where have you come?" The Satan answered the LORD and said, "From going to and fro on the earth, and from walking up and down on it." And the LORD said to the Satan, "Have you considered my servant Job, that there is none like him on the earth, a blameless and upright man, who fears God and turns away from evil? He still holds fast his integrity, although you incited me against

him to destroy him without reason." Then the Satan answered the L ORD and said, "Skin for skin! All that a man has he will give for his life. But stretch out your hand and touch his bone and his flesh, and he will curse you to your face." And the L ORD said to the Satan, "Behold, he is in your hand; only spare his life."

So the Satan went out from the presence of the L ORD. . . . (Job 2:1–7a)

Suddenly we are taken back into Heaven to witness another "day," another heavenly cabinet meeting. Job did not witness the first one, and he does not witness this one. But we, the readers, are allowed to be flies on the wall.

We have no indication of what time elapses between the disasters of scene two and the heavenly scene three, but this new scene begins almost word for word the same as the last scene in Heaven. This time we are explicitly told that the Satan "came among them to present himself before the L ORD" (v. 1). If we were in any doubt that the Satan is a minister or servant of the Lord, this lays that doubt to rest. Like all the other powers and principalities that share in the agency of governing the world, the Satan is subservient to the Sovereign God. He comes "to present himself" and specifically to report back on "progress" since the last meeting, when he was sent to deprive Job of all his possessions and children. It is a macabre task that the Satan has carried out.

The report begins with the same formulas as in the previous meeting—the same question, "From where have you come?" and the same evasive answer, "From going to and fro on the earth, and from walking up and down on it," (v. 2).

Then the Lord asks the same question as before but with something extra added: "Have you considered my servant Job, that there is none like him on the earth, a blameless and upright man, who fears God and turns away from evil?" (v. 3). If we were in any doubt about Job's character, surely this must lay it to rest. Three times now he has been called blameless, upright, God-fearing, and penitent, once by the narrator and twice by God himself. Also twice God has called him "my servant."

But now the Lord goes on, "He still holds fast his integrity"—his inside is the same as his outside—"although you incited me against him to destroy him without reason" (v. 3). We learn two more things here. First, that Job has maintained his integrity as a genuine and consistent believer. This is exactly what we thought from the conclusion of the last scene.

But, second, we learn the Satan's actual motive. The Satan sets up the test with a logic that has its foundation in the glory of God. But what he actually wants is not to see Job tested but to see Job destroyed. He wants God to destroy him, to swallow him alive, to kill him. There is no justification for this (it is "without reason" [v. 3]), but this is what the Satan wants. Job's sufferings are undeserved. And yet the Satan is frustrated by the instructions he has been given—to take away what Job has but not to touch his person.

So the Satan presses the matter further. "Skin for skin!" he says, using an idiom the meaning of which is not absolutely clear.[26] "All that a man has he will give for his life" (v. 4). Which is to say, you can breach the protective hedge, the outer skin, around a man's possessions and family, and you will hurt him; but there is an inner skin that protects the man himself, his body and soul. Until that skin is breached, a man will not really be tested to see if his piety is genuine. "But stretch out your hand and touch"—again to "touch" means to "strike"—"his bone and his flesh [the inside and outside of his own person], and he will curse you to your face" (v. 5).

The point here seems to be that there is a distinction between what a person *has* and what a person *is*. What a person is is closer to the person's heart than what he has. I am attached to what I have, whether it be impersonal possessions or personal relations (family); it hurts me to have those taken away. But it does not ultimately hurt me as deeply as when my inner skin is penetrated and the attack reaches to who I am, to my own body and soul. This is what the Satan demands.

Shockingly (and it is truly shocking) the Lord agrees. Having rebuked the Satan for inciting him against Job without valid reason, the Lord says to the Satan, "Behold, he is in your hand; only spare his life" (v. 6). But the Satan is frustrated in his desire to see Job swallowed up and utterly destroyed—he is not allowed to kill him.

Nevertheless, we must think hard about this second permission or instruction. Had we been writing the story, we would have had the Lord say to the Satan, "Enough is enough. The man has suffered more than any human being in one day. He has been taken from riches to bankruptcy, from greatness to destitution, from a happy family to utter bereavement. That is enough, surely, to establish that his piety is genuine. The man worships me because he knows I am worthy of worship. End of trial." That is what we would have said.

That the Lord disagrees with us must teach us something very deep. The glory of God really is more important than your or my comfort. When all that Job has is taken from him, we may get an approximate or provisional demonstration that God is worthy of worship. But an approximate or provisional demonstration is not sufficient for the ultimate glory of God. In the end it is necessary and right that this man should suffer personal and intimate attack upon himself, so that we see absolutely and without doubt that God is worthy of worship. It is necessary for this man to demonstrate a full and deep obedience to the glory of God.

So for a second time "the Satan went out from the presence of the LORD" (v. 7). Thus the third scene comes to an end.

Scene 4: Earth (Job 2:7b–10)

> . . . and struck Job with loathsome sores from the sole of his foot to the crown of his head. And he took a piece of broken pottery with which to scrape himself while he sat in the ashes.
>
> Then his wife said to him, "Do you still hold fast your integrity? Curse God and die." But he said to her, "You speak as one of the foolish women would speak. Shall we receive good from God, and shall we not receive evil?" In all this Job did not sin with his lips. (vv. 7b–10)

The transition from scene 1 to scene 2 was, if we may say so, leisurely. There was a day for the heavenly scene, and then, at some unspecified date later, there was another day when the disasters happened on earth. Similarly there is no indication of how long elapsed between scene 2 and scene 3. The transition between scene 3 and scene 4 is immediate. One scene fades into the next, as in many cinematography sequences. There is no "there was a day" formula this time (1:13). The moment "the Satan went out from the presence of the LORD" he "struck Job with loathsome sores" (v. 7). It was an immediate disaster. The pace has quickened.

The scene is intensified in another way. In the first four disasters the agents were either human (the Sabeans and the Chaldeans) or impersonal (lightning and hurricane). Here the Satan is the immediate agent of Job's sufferings: "the Satan . . . struck Job" (v. 7). We are not told what medical causes are intermediate between the Satan and the suffering. Satan struck Job's person, not just his family or his possessions, afflicting his skin with "loathsome sores" (v. 7). And he did it "from the sole of his foot to the crown of his head" (v. 7). It was a total and intimate affliction with no reprieve. All of Job's person is invaded; the last vestige of protective hedge has been destroyed.

So he sits "in the ashes" (v. 8) on the council incinerator and rubbish dump, where the rubbish is continually burned in a heap outside the city gate, the place that Jesus was later to use as the best human image to represent Hell (Gehenna, the valley of the sons of Hinnom, outside Jerusalem). Job "took a piece of broken pottery with which to scrape himself" (v. 8). Everything about Job is broken now. And he is all alone.

So this really is the test. Now we shall see for a certainty whether he serves God only for what God gives him. Now God has taken it all away. God could not take any more away from Job without killing him, and then we would never know the result of the trial. So Job must live.

And yet there is one more trial. Job's wife makes her only appearance in the drama. We must resist the temptation to romanticize Job and his wife. All we know of her is that at this moment of lonely suffering she pleads with him, "Do you still hold fast your integrity?"—as God says he does before this last trial (2:3)—"Curse God and die" (v. 9). She knows, as Job knows, that to curse God ultimately brings a human being under sentence of death. This is why Job had offered all those burnt offerings to protect his children from this fate. This is what Job has refused to do after the first trials, blessing God wonderfully in 1:21.

But, not for the last time in human history, a wife has seen her husband suffering so terribly that she has wished him the peace of death. We are not invited to make any moral judgment about Job's wife. But whatever her motive, she is the mouthpiece of a terrible temptation, what Augustine calls "the devil's assistant" and Calvin "Satan's tool,"[27] asking Job to do what the Satan wants him to do. Job hears the pleading of his nearest and dearest to abandon his proud principles about God and just give in, let rip against God, and bring upon himself the inevitable judgment of death.

Job's reply is a model of faith under trial. "But he said to her, 'You speak as one of the foolish women would speak'" (v. 10). In kindness he does not actually call her a foolish woman. But he says that what she has suggested is not worthy of her. Hers is the suggestion that you would expect from a fool. She has spoken under stress, as if she were foolish.

Far from cursing God, Job says, "Shall we receive good from God, and shall we not receive evil?" (v. 10). Job speaks not self-centeredly of himself alone but of them both ("Shall we . . . ?") Again, as after the first trials, Job's heart is full of God the Creator who is the author of all good gifts. All the good he has received, he received from God. Can he not trust this same God to give him evil (i.e., harmful) things and to believe that he knows best? The sense of "receive" is to accept, humbly bowing beneath God's loving providence.

Now comes the conclusion: "In all this Job did not sin with his lips" (v. 10). This does not suggest that Job did sin in his heart;[28] sin with the lips is what the Satan had predicted, and sin with the lips is what Job has not done. We have here a simple affirmation that Job has passed the test. The question is settled, the trial concluded. Job's piety results from Job's heart conviction that God is the author of everything, the Creator who is worthy of all his worship in the bad times as well as the good.

In one sense the trial is settled. But as the book continues, Heaven is silent from now until the Lord speaks from chapter 38 onward.[29] Only in chapter 42 will we know for sure that Job is vindicated. In the meantime the damaged and broken skin of Job speaks of a real believer in the process of a terrible and life-changing breakdown.[30]

Conclusion: Does Satan Attack Christians Today?

The glory of God is more important than your or my comfort. It matters for the glory of God that there should be a man who worships God because he is worthy of worship, and for no other reason.

This is a good moment, before Job's comforters are introduced and we launch into the many chapters of poetry, to pause and orient ourselves in the book of Job. How are we as Christian people to read Job today?

The first thing to say is that Job is an extreme book. Job is extravagantly rich, wonderfully happy, and extremely great. He is not only one among many great men—he is the greatest of all the people of his region. And then his downfall is extreme. He does not go from moderate riches to a measure of poverty; he goes from extravagant riches to absolute destitution. He does not do so gradually; he does so in a day. He does not experience the loss of one child or even two. He loses all ten children, and he does so in a day.

This poses a problem for us as we read the book. However deep our suffering, it is unlikely that our experience can ever do more than very approximately mirror Job's. We have neither been so great as Job, nor so fallen, neither so happy, nor so lonely, neither so rich, nor so poor, neither so pious, nor so cursed. All of which points to a fulfillment greater and deeper than your life or mine. Job in his extremity is actually but a shadow of a reality more extreme still, of a man who was not just blameless but sinless, who was not just the greatest man in a region, but the greatest human being in history, greater even than merely human, who emptied himself of all his glory, became incarnate, and went all the way down to a degrading, naked, shameful death on the cross, whose journey took him from eternal fellowship with the Father to utter aloneness on the cross. The story of Job is a shadow of the greater story of Jesus Christ.

And yet we cannot stop there. For the story of Job is, in a measure, your story and mine as Christian believers, as men and women in Christ. Before the cross Jesus said to Simon Peter, "Simon, Simon, behold, Satan demanded to have you ["you" here is plural, referring to all the apostolic band], that he might sift you like wheat." Just as the Satan demanded to have Job to sift and test him, to see if he was—as it were—wheat or chaff, so he demanded to sift the apostolic band. And just as God the Father sent Satan off to do that to Job, so he does with the apostles. Jesus does not go on to say, "But my Father has forbidden Satan from doing this." Rather, he says, "But I have prayed for you ["you" here is singular, Simon Peter specifically] that your faith may not fail. And when you have turned again, strengthen your brothers" (Luke 22:31, 32). Clearly Satan's demand is to be granted; the apostles are to be sifted by Satan, to see if their faith is genuine. And their faith will prove genuine, not least because God the Son prays to God the Father for Peter, and then Peter becomes the instrument to strengthen the faith of the others.

Later in his life, as we have seen, Peter writes to Christian believers under trial to explain that their trials are necessary "so that the tested genuineness" of their faith "may be found to result in praise and glory and honor at the revelation of Jesus Christ" (1 Peter 1:6, 7). An enemy, "your adversary the devil," "prowls around like a roaring lion, seeking someone to devour," and he can be resisted only by faith ("Resist him, firm in your *faith*") (1 Peter 5:8, 9). Paul exhorts Christian people to put on "the whole armor of God, that you may be able to stand against the schemes of the devil" (Ephesians 6:11). So we are naive and mistaken if we suppose that Satan no longer wants to attack believers or that God the Father has changed his mind about giving Satan permission to launch such attacks. We have a dangerous enemy who continues to attack us, as he attacked Job and as he even assaulted the Lord Jesus Christ himself. The book of Job is a scary book, not like a horror movie (where we can enjoy the scariness, knowing that it is not about to strike us), but because of the real understanding that this terrible story may in some way become our story too. Our horror in reading the story of Job is more than an empathetic horror; it is a personal horror.

But there is one difference. We live after the cross of Christ and therefore after the fulfillment of the story of Job. In the cross of Christ, God has "disarmed the rulers and authorities and put them to open shame, by triumphing over them" in Jesus and his cross (Colossians 2:15). Through his death Jesus will "destroy the one who has the power of death, that is, the devil, and deliver all those who though fear of death were subject to lifelong slavery" (Hebrews 2:14, 15). "The reason the Son of God appeared was to destroy the works of the devil" (1 John 3:8). The cross changes things.

We learn what the cross changes from a vivid apocalyptic passage in Revelation 12.

> Now war arose in heaven, Michael and his angels fighting against the dragon. And the dragon and his angels fought back, but he was defeated, and

there was no longer any place for them in heaven. And the great dragon was thrown down, that ancient serpent, who is called the devil and Satan, the deceiver of the whole world—he was thrown down to the earth, and his angels were thrown down with him. And I heard a loud voice in heaven, saying, "Now the salvation and the power and the kingdom of our God and the authority of his Christ have come, for the accuser of our brothers has been thrown down, who accuses them day and night before our God. And they have conquered him by the blood of the Lamb and by the word of their testimony, for they loved not their lives even unto death. Therefore, rejoice, O heavens and you who dwell in them! But woe to you, O earth and sea, for the devil has come down to you in great wrath, because he knows that his time is short!" (Revelation 12:7–12)

As a result of the victory of the cross, the Satan is no longer present in the council of God, as he was in Job 1, 2, to accuse believers before the Father. He has been thrown down to earth. He no longer has access to the throne room of Heaven. What does this mean, since he is still dangerous, ranges the earth and sea with great anger, and indeed can only be conquered by those who "loved not their lives even unto death" (v. 11)? The key truth is that he who was "the accuser of our brothers" is no longer able to accuse Christian believers before God (v. 10). He accuses us, and we need to learn what to do with his accusation. But when he accuses us, God is not listening. The devil no longer has that access. The issue of our justification has been decisively settled at the cross. This is the gospel truth of the cross: there is no longer any condemnation (Romans 8:1), and our consciences have been cleansed by the blood of Christ (Hebrews 9:14).

So as we read the story of Job we think first and primarily of the greater story of Jesus, who walked the way of Job for us, who plumbed the depths of Job's suffering for us, and who was vindicated for us. Satan is still able to attack us, and he spends what short life is left to him angrily doing that, like a hungry lion on the prowl. We must be realistic about this. Still we have to endure ("Here is a call for the endurance and faith of the saints," Revelation 13:10). But if we are in Christ, the Satan is no longer able to accuse us before God. He no longer has that access.

3

The Loneliness of Job

JOB 2:11–13

Alone on the Rubbish Heap

Job is terribly, frighteningly alone. He sits on the rubbish heap. His wife has come and gone after a disagreement. His only companion, if we can call it such, is a broken shard of pottery with which he scratches himself (2:8). At this stage we can only guess what thoughts filled his mind. Did he think back to days of purpose, when he got out of bed with drive and desire, to work energetically, to manage his farm, and to govern his household? Did he remember the accolades given him for his justice, his care for his employees, and his business success?

Were there memories of his sons and daughters in their childhood? Near where I live in central London there used to be a bronze statue of a local man sitting on a bench overlooking the River Thames. A few meters in front of him is a bronze figure of a little girl, his daughter who had died in childhood. As he sits, in his old age, his imagination plays tricks with him, and it is as if he sees his little daughter alive and playing there. That pair of statues always moves me to tears. Did Job's imagination play those kinds of tricks with him? We cannot know.

A Visit of Friends

But what happens next presses home to us Job's loneliness as never before. This is surprising because it seems to start so well. "Now when Job's three friends heard of all this evil [harm] that had come upon him, they came. . . ." (v. 11). So Job has friends. The word "friend" in the Old Testament, and especially in the Wisdom literature, is stronger than our debased use, in which we may have many so-called "friends" (especially on social networking sites).

"A man of many companions [what we might call Facebook friends] may come to ruin, but there is a friend who sticks closer than a brother" (Proverbs 18:24). A friend is bound to you with bonds of steadfast love (the strong Hebrew word is *chesed*, which means pledged, unbreakable, covenant love and loyalty).

Many years later "Hushai the Archite, David's *friend*" pretends to have gone over from David's side to support and counsel his rebel son Absalom. Although Absalom is pleased to have Hushai's counsel, he is surprised and chides Hushai: "Is this your loyalty [*chesed*, steadfast loyalty] to your *friend*? Why did you not go with your *friend*?" (2 Samuel 16:16, 17). Indeed as Job himself says, "He who withholds kindness [*chesed*, steadfast covenant loyalty] from a *friend* forsakes the fear of the Almighty" (6:14).

It is therefore deeply encouraging to know that Job has three friends, men who are bound to him with ties of steadfast love and loyalty. Surely they will be able to help. It begins well. "Now when Job's three friends heard . . . they came. . . . They made an appointment together to come " (v. 11). It must have taken weeks, if not months, for the news of Job's afflictions to reach them, for them to communicate with one another, to rendezvous, and then to travel to visit Job.[1] And all this time Job is alone on the rubbish heap with his shard of pottery for company. Job himself later refers to "months of emptiness" (7:3), and the lament of chapter 30 indicates a long suffering.

Sympathy and Comfort

But at last they come. They come "together" rather than separately, perhaps because they sense that the task of comforting Job will be more than any individual can bear.[2] They come "to show him sympathy"—that is, to enter into and share in his grief[3]—"and comfort him"—that is, to find a way to ease his pain (v. 11).

We must not read back into their coming the later disappointment and anger that their words bring. So far as we can tell, these are "three good men and true."[4] They were bound to Job as Jonathan was to David. They were not fair-weather friends, Facebook friends who were glad to be able to "name-drop" Job's acquaintance when he was rich and famous or to take vacations in his luxurious holiday villas. They were loyal friends who took the considerable trouble to travel and come to sympathize and comfort him when he was bankrupt and bereft. "Theirs was a noble, gentle spirit. They were sincere."[5]

It is worth pausing to ask how "comfort" works. The Hebrew word is *nacham*. It is not the same as empathy. Empathy may be inarticulate, because it focuses on entering into the feelings and experience of the sufferer as best we can. But comfort must be articulate and active. Empathy may be silent, but comfort must include speech. To comfort involves speaking to the mind and heart of the sufferer in such a way as to change his or her mind and heart. Comfort is an action, sometimes called "speaking to the heart," that hopes and intends to bring about a change in how the sufferer thinks and feels about his or her suffering. When Joseph "comforted" his brothers, he did so in such a way as to reduce their fearfulness (Genesis 50:21); his words lowered the level of their fear. The Levite in Judges 19 spoke "kindly to" ("spoke to the heart of") his wife with a view to changing her mind and bringing her back home (Judges 19:3). Boaz cheers Ruth up when he comforts her with his words (Ruth 2:13). Joab tells David that unless he will "speak kindly to" ("speak to the heart of") his army by speaking words to them, they will abandon him (2 Samuel 19:7). His comfort will change their minds. King Hezekiah "spoke encouragingly to" ("spoke to the heart of") his army to make them strong and courageous (2 Chronicles 32:6, 7). Both the verb *nacham* and the expression "speak to the heart" refer to speaking words that bring comfort and change someone's mind or feelings. This is what we expect Job's friends to do.[6]

The Wisdom of the World

And so "they came each from his own place," and we might wonder what resources of comfort were available in the places from which they came (v. 11). We are told their names and places—"Eliphaz the Temanite, Bildad the Shuhite, and Zophar the Naamathite." Eliphaz is from Teman, Bildad from Shuah, and Zophar from Naamah.

Naamah appears in Genesis 4 as the daughter of one of Lamech's wives (Genesis 4:22), but this is a remote hint and tells us very little about Zophar. Shuah is one of Abraham's sons by his wife Keturah, one of a group who (because they were not to inherit the promise through Isaac) were "sent . . . away from his son Isaac, eastward to the east country" (Genesis 25:1–6).[7] This all fits with Job being "the greatest of all the people of the east" (1:3), somewhere to the east of the promised land.

The clearest clue is about Eliphaz. Teman was one of the most important towns of Edom (Jeremiah 49:20; Amos 1:12; Obadiah 9). Eliphaz himself bears an Edomite name. One of the sons of Esau is called Eliphaz (Genesis 36:4). He is even described as "the firstborn of Esau" (Genesis 36:15). Whether the Eliphaz of Job is the same Eliphaz or not, we cannot know. But he does seem to be an Edomite.

Edom was renowned for its wisdom. In Obadiah the Lord says he will "destroy the wise men out of Edom" (Obadiah 8). And in Jeremiah this wisdom is especially associated with Teman: "Concerning Edom. Thus says the LORD of hosts: 'Is wisdom no more in Teman? Has counsel perished from the prudent? Has their wisdom vanished?'" (Jeremiah 49:7). So it is no surprise that one of the friends who will, we hope, bring wise comfort to Job is an Edomite. It is a reasonable assumption that the other two also represent traditions of wise counsel. Certainly they think of themselves as such, as becomes evident when they begin to speak. We have here not just three kind and loyal friends but three wise friends who between them represent, as it were, the combined resources of the wisdom of the world. Can the world's wisdom with the world's kindness and loyalty help this lonely sufferer?

An Unbridgeable Gulf

As they catch their first glimpse of their old friend they are appalled: "And when they saw him from a distance, they did not recognize him" (v. 12). The smoking rubbish heap was often piled higher than the city itself,[8] so we may imagine them approaching the city and spying this lonely figure crouched on the landfill pile in the distance. They knew it was Job. Probably they had been told in advance that was where he was; we may suppose he was by now a well-known sight in the region. But they could hardly believe it was really him. "Is that Job?" we may imagine one saying to another, "so thin, so pale, so harrowed with pain and grief?" And as they approach him, they shrink back in horror.

> Many have had this experience, of visiting a familiar friend or family member and of being shocked at the altered appearance. It is not just the physical features that have altered, but something deeper. It is as though the calamity or the suffering has claimed the other in an experience alien to us. The other is no longer fully or even primarily in our familiar world, but inhabits a realm whose terrain is strange and foreign to us. We sense a chasm across which we cannot or will not venture and from which we draw back in self-protective fear onto the safe ground of our familiar world. Or we attempt to cross the chasm somehow through sympathetic, perhaps symbolic, identification, hoping to draw the other back with us into the familiar world.[9]

Their not "recognizing" him was a painful thing for them, but no doubt it was also a painful thing for him.[10] No longer could there be the old natural friendly embrace, the hug or handshake, the smiles of friendship rekindled, the delighted warmth of welcome into his home. Instead they did not "recognize" him. They found themselves behaving toward him as to a stranger. There was something painfully strange about his appearance, the emptiness in his eyes, the lines in his face, the brokenness of his demeanor. This is a sad assembly, very different from the happy family gatherings that punctuated the ordered life of the introduction (1:4). This one is marked by alienation rather than fellowship, and loneliness rather than joy.[11]

"And they raised their voices and wept" (v. 12). Weeping here (*bakah*) is not the shedding of silent tears. It is "the *sound* of . . . weeping" (Psalm 6:8), something done with the mouth as well as the eyes.[12] But they weep at him and not with him. This cannot be the "weep[ing] with those who weep" of Romans 12:15. They cannot sit "with" him in any meaningful sense. He is unrecognizable. He has been taken away into a different realm, a realm of suffering so deep they cannot reach him.

Silent with a Corpse

Job has torn his robe in mourning (1:20), and they too tear theirs. And they "sprinkled dust on their heads toward heaven" (v. 12).[13] Dust speaks of mortality and death. God says to cursed Adam, "You are dust, and to dust you shall return" (Genesis 3:19). Joshua and the elders of Israel tear their clothes, fall to the ground, and put dust on their heads after the disaster at Ai (Joshua 7:6). The Israelite who reports the capture of the ark by the Philistines comes to Shiloh with his clothes torn and with dirt on his head (1 Samuel 4:12). After Tamar has been raped by her half-brother Amnon, she tears her clothes and puts ashes on her head, mourning for her lost future (2 Samuel 13:19).

To throw dust in the air (toward Heaven) so that it falls on their heads is vividly to identify themselves in their grief with Job's dead children and probably also with Job himself, who has been grasped by death and is already being dragged down into the realm of the dead. Job is to them like a friend being sucked down by quicksand in the desert; they long to draw him up, but he is beyond their reach. He is as good as dead.

"And they sat with him on the ground" (v. 13). They do not sit on a carpet or on cushions but directly on the ground. The ground is the place of the dust of death; it is the closest men on earth can get to Sheol. After the sack of Jerusalem, "The elders of the daughter of Zion sit on the ground in silence; they have thrown dust on their heads and put on sackcloth" (Lamentations 2:10).

Then comes silence, seven days and seven nights of silence! "They sat with him on the ground seven days and seven nights, and no one spoke a word to him, for they saw that his suffering was very great." Job's suffering was, as we shall see, deeper than merely physical. It was made sharper by mental and spiritual grief. It was an anguish and an agony.[14] This man who had been a very great man (1:3) now suffers a very great suffering.

What are we to make of this silence? It is at best ambiguous. Preachers often say that this long silence was the best thing that they did. And certainly, as we shall see in chapter 4, when they begin to speak they do no good at all. So one writer concludes, "If for the most part Job's friends got things wrong . . . here, at the beginning, they do it right." "Here is genuine friendship. Here is deep ministry." He calls this "the compassion of a silent presence."[15] Another says, "Their silence is a further expression of their genuine empathy."[16] Others say, "They do honour by profound silence to his vast grief," for "when grief is so crushing, what form but silence can sympathy take?" "They were true friends, bringing to Job's lonely ash-heap the compassion of a silent presence."[17]

But while their silence may initially have been appropriate, it seems unlikely that it continued so. To sit quietly with a sufferer, to hold his or her hand, to listen patiently as he or she pours out his or her grief is one thing. But this silence is "hugely extended."[18] To refuse to speak a word to a sufferer for seven days and seven nights is eerie and not comforting. It is interesting that we are told they did not speak a word "to him" (v. 13). For all we know, they may have spoken with one another. So it may not have been silence after all, but just a refusal to speak to Job, which is quite another thing.

Even if it was total silence (which seems more likely), a seven-day silence symbolized mourning for the dead. It is what Joseph did for his father Jacob. It is what the loyal city of Ramoth-Gilead did for King Saul (1 Samuel 31:13).[19] "Job's friends mourn for him as one already dead."[20]

It is as if they call for the hearse and sit by Job with the coffin open and ready for him. There is no point talking to a corpse; one just weeps by it. To them Job is no longer a living person. Their silence may be not so much a silence of sympathy (although it may have begun as such) but a silence of bankruptcy. They say nothing because they have nothing to say that will bring him comfort. It seems to them too late for that.

The Loneliness of Suffering

Whatever the meaning of their silence, the book of Job brings home to us the loneliness of suffering. The friends came with kind intentions. They came together. They brought with them the wisdom of the world, all the resources available within the world to comfort their suffering friend. But they were bankrupt, able to sympathize up to a point but utterly unable to comfort. Before they came, Job was all alone on the rubbish heap. After they came, he was yet more deeply alone as he sat alongside them but was utterly ignored by them with not a word addressed to him as a person. Before, there was no one physically or emotionally close to him; now he has proximity (they sit by him) but is still without intimacy.

Sometimes in Scripture there are corporate laments. Psalm 137 is one such. But this is so personal, and Job is so alone. Suffering does that. Even a non-serious illness cuts us off from others; we have to miss out on a family outing, a party, or a gathering. There is (in the title of an old play) "Laughter in the Room Next Door." And if even a trivial suffering begins to isolate the sufferer, heavy suffering isolates acutely. Even a shared loss is experienced uniquely by each bereft person. When a child dies, the father alone knows what it is to be the father of this dead child; only the mother enters the unique depths of loss as the mother of this son or daughter. However much they share, at the deepest level they suffer alone. In his book *The Anatomy of Loneliness* Thomas Wolfe writes, "The most tragic, sublime and beautiful expression of loneliness which I have ever read is the Book of Job."[21] We need to recognize that those who suffer, suffer alone. And Job is terribly alone.

The Loneliness Job Foreshadows

Job in his awesome aloneness foreshadows another believer, an even greater man who endures an even deeper suffering. This believer too was with his dearest friends, in a garden outside Jerusalem. He told them to sit and wait while he prayed. He took with him his three closest friends "and began to be greatly distressed and troubled." He said to them, "My soul is very sorrowful, even to death. Remain here and watch." He went on a little farther, fell on the ground, and prayed "with loud cries and tears." But when he came back he found them sleeping. "Could you not watch one hour?" he asked sadly (Mark 14:32–42; Hebrews 5:7). He prayed and wept alone. And the next day he suffered alone, stripped of his clothes, robbed of his friends, with even his mother having to keep her distance from the cross. He had said to his friends that although they would leave him alone, he was not alone, "for the Father is with me" (John 16:32). But in the deepest intensity of his suffering he cried out in anguish, "My God, my God, why have you forsaken me?" (Mark 15:34). As the old hymn puts it, "He bore the burden to Calvary, and suffered and died alone."[22]

There is a deep sense in which the lonely sufferings of Jesus Christ mean that no believer today is called to enter Job's loneliness in its full depth. As someone has put it:

Suffering encloses a man in solitude. . . . Between Job and his friends an abyss was cleft. They regarded him with astonishment as a strange be-ing. . . . But they could no longer get to him. Only Jesus could cross this abyss, descend into the abyss of misery, plunge into the deepest hell.[23]

However alone the believer in Christ may feel today, the reality is that he or she is not ultimately alone as Job was.

4

Weep with Those
Who Weep

JOB 3

WE COME NOW TO "a poem of immense power and poignancy."[1]

"In the end it was Job who broke the silence" (v. 1 JB). This is like David in Psalm 39, struggling with the presence of the wicked:

I was mute and silent;
    I held my peace to no avail,
and my distress grew worse.
    My heart became hot within me.
As I mused, the fire burned;
    then I spoke with my tongue. . . . (Psalm 39:2, 3)

In a similar way Job's inner anguish has been boiling up within him, and in the end he cannot hold it in. And out it pours in the darkest chapter of the book. And yet this outpouring of grief is not yet the beginning of a conversation.

We have watched the loneliness of Job. Now we listen to his loneliness. Chapter 3 is a soliloquy. Job is not speaking here to anybody. He is not speaking to his friends; the cycles of speeches begin with Eliphaz in chapter 4. He is not speaking to God. He is just speaking with himself. And although no doubt the friends are within earshot, and surely God is listening, this soliloquy deepens the solitariness of Job. Although his friends hear his words, it will become apparent that they have not really heard his heart. And although God has undoubtedly listened with a Father's heart of love, Job has absolutely no awareness of that patient listening ear at this stage of the tragedy.[2]

A true Christian believer may be taken by God through times of deep and dark despair. This may happen to a man or woman who is affirmed by God as a believer before the darkness, who remains a believer in the darkness, and who will finally be vindicated by God as a believer after the darkness. He or she may be taken through this darkness even though he or she has not fallen into sin or backslidden from faith in Jesus Christ. This is a very important truth.

In Job 3 we must "weep with those who weep" (Romans 12:15). When I first preached this chapter at the church where I was pastor, we did not sing at all in the service. Not a hymn, not a song. Although some of us had come to the service feeling quite cheerful, our own circumstances full of hope, we needed to weep with one who wept.

So we read together Psalm 137, where the people of God are asked to sing one of the songs of Zion but cannot sing, so deep is their distress. That is a terribly painful psalm, with its desperate cry for justice wrung from broken hearts: "We have seen our young children murdered, we have heard their screams—well, just maybe someone will do that to your children, you torturers, and when they do, good for them!" Those are strong words, but that is how they felt. "We cannot sing. And if you force us to be happy, it will add torment to our misery." "Cheer up! Pull yourselves together!" said their tormentors. But they could not.

In that church service we listened to the puzzling story of William Cowper, the great Christian poet and hymn-writer—how his life was blighted first by the death of his mother when he was six, how fifty-three years later when someone sent him a portrait of her, he wrote a moving poem that makes it clear his grief was ever fresh. That poem included the lines:

I heard the bell tolled on thy burial day,
I saw the hearse that bore thee slow away,
And turning from my nursery window, drew
A long, long sigh, and wept a last adieu!

We heard how Cowper's father sent him away to a boarding school where he was cruelly bullied, and he probably never recovered in his mind. And how after a two-year engagement his fiancée's father forbade the marriage. How before his conversion he suffered repeated episodes of deep depressive illness. "I was struck," he wrote, "with such a dejection of spirits, as none but they who have felt the same, can have the least conception of. Day and night I was upon the rack, lying down in horror, and rising up in despair."

We listened to how, aged thirty-one, Cowper suffered a catastrophic psy-

chotic breakdown, tried three times to take his own life, and was committed
to an asylum (today it would be called a psychiatric hospital). This asylum
was run by an evangelical Christian, and it was there, six months later, that
Cowper met the Lord Jesus Christ and became his disciple. Describing his
conversion he wrote, "Unless the Almighty arm had been under me, I think
I should have died with gratitude and joy. My eyes filled with tears, and my
voice choked with transport; I could only look up to heaven in silent fear,
overwhelmed with wonder and love."

It was a wonderful change and a real conversion. And yet on four more
occasions in his life he suffered deep depressive illness. And shortly before
he died of dropsy in 1800 one of the last things he said was, "I feel unutterable despair."[3]

Now this was a Christian, a real Christian who bequeathed to the church
some of its deepest and greatest hymns. In that service we looked together at
his great hymn "O for a Closer Walk with God," in which he laments the loss
of the blessedness he had first known when he met the Lord Jesus and how his
diagnosis for his despair is that there must be an idol in his life. If only he can
be helped to tear that idol from God's throne in his life, then again his walk
will be close with God, and calmness and serenity will return.

> Where is the blessedness I knew,
> When first I saw the Lord?
> Where is the soul refreshing view
> Of Jesus and His word?
>
> The dearest idol I have known,
> Whate'er that idol be,
> Help me to tear it from Thy throne,
> And worship only Thee.
>
> So shall my walk be close with God,
> Calm and serene my frame;
> So purer light shall mark the road
> That leads me to the Lamb.

And we considered the possibility that—great though that hymn is, and
as much as it applies to many believers—it may have been written out of a
false diagnosis of Cowper's own condition. His despair might not have had
anything to do with backsliding or turning away from the worship of the true
God. As we shall see in this study, Job's despair was not the result of backsliding or unforgiven sin.

In that service we also listened to the unrelieved laments of Psalm 88 and Jeremiah 20:14–18, where we read:

> Cursed be the day
>   on which I was born!
> The day when my mother bore me,
>   let it not be blessed!
> Cursed be the man who brought the news to my father,
> "A son is born to you,"
>   making him very glad.
> Let that man be like the cities
>   that the Lord overthrew without pity;
> let him hear a cry in the morning
>   and an alarm at noon,
> because he did not kill me in the womb;
>   so my mother would have been my grave,
>   and her womb forever great.
> Why did I come out from the womb
>   to see toil and sorrow,
>   and spend my days in shame?[4]

We listened to the lament of Job 3. And then, after the sermon, we went home. It was a sobering evening with one aim—that we might grasp that a real believer may go through blank despair and utter desperation. That a blameless believer, who has not fallen into sin, may go through utter dereliction, and yet at the end be seen to be a real believer. That we might grasp that we ourselves, if we walk closely with Christ, may go through very deep darkness, deeper even perhaps than if we had not walked faithfully in his footsteps. And that as we grasp this sobering truth we may learn to weep with those who weep.

Job 3 is a very important chapter for contemporary Christianity. There is a version of Christianity around that is shallow, trite, superficial, "happy clappy" (as some put it). It is a kind of Christianity that, as has been said, "would have had Jesus singing a chorus at the grave of Lazarus."[5] We have all met it—easy triumphalism. We sing of God in one song that "in his presence our problems disappear,"[6] in another that "my love just keeps on growing."[7] Neither was true for Job in chapter 3, and yet he was a real and blameless believer.

Someone has written a book about Christians who suffer depression and anxiety; it is called *I'm Not Supposed to Feel Like This*.[8] That is a provocative title. The authors state, "It is bad enough that I feel low or anxious. But on top of that I feel guilty: for I ought not to feel low, as a Christian. I feel that I ought to be able to cast my cares upon him, for he cares for me (1 Peter 5:7). And yet somehow I can't."

In Job 1:1—2:10 we watched this blameless believer suffer heartrending loss—his possessions ruined, his children killed, his health destroyed. And we listened—as Job could not listen—to the conversations in Heaven that lay behind his loss—between God and the Satan, the enemy, and how the Lord gives his terrible permissions to the Satan to torture Job. Job is not being punished for his sin. Exactly the reverse: Job suffers precisely because he is conspicuously godly. And he suffers deep deprivation—physical, mental, emotional, social, and spiritual loss.

And yet still he shows faith. After the first two trials we hear two very remarkable and often celebrated responses.

> Naked I came from my mother's womb, and naked shall I return. The LORD gave, and the LORD has taken away; blessed be the name of the LORD. (1:21)

> Shall we receive good from God, and shall we not receive evil? (2:10)

Both Jewish and Christian piety have wanted to major on Job's faith. This is not surprising, for Job's faith here is very wonderful. But the danger with our focusing on 1:21 and 2:10 is that we make Job's faith two-dimensional. "He suffered; he trusted," we say, "and so should we. End of story."

But it is far from the end of the story, for in 3:1 he curses the day of his birth. And we are brought up short, for Job then goes on lamenting and protesting chapter after chapter. We must not soften this. We must remember that at the end of the book God affirms that Job has spoken rightly of him (42:7), that Job is God's servant, that Job is a righteous man (who can therefore pray and expect his prayers to be heard). The despair of Job 3 is the authentic experience of a man affirmed by God at the start (1:8; 2:3) and affirmed again by God at the end (42:7). We need to remember that. It is very surprising, for Job 3 is a dark chapter.

The Satan has first attacked the outer skin of Job's possessions, wealth, and household. Then he has gone in closer, to ravage the skin so to speak of his family, killing his ten children. And then he has gone deeper still, to strike the literal skin of Job's body. But the Satan's attack has penetrated deeper still, for he has struck at Job's heart. And now for the first (but not the last) time in the book we hear the cry of Job's heart and soul. So far in the story we have mostly been looking *at* Job, listening to the heavenly conversations, looking from above at the earthly disasters, and hearing from Job only the brief affirmations of pious trust (in 1:21; 2:10). We have watched his loneliness as his comforters sit with him in a terrible seven-day and seven-night silence. Chapter 2 ends with the words, "his suffering was very great." We are about to learn just how great as we listen to his inner experience.[9]

So let us go with Job into his dark lament. As we sing with Job verse by dark verse, I want us to notice three features of his lament. The first is that in his darkness Job can only look back. His mind is full of regrets and is empty of hope for the future. The second is that he cannot rest but is unbearably troubled. In each of these themes we will find a paradoxical glimmer of light. It is not easy to find the gospel in Job 3, but—as in all of Scripture—it is there. It will not do to immerse ourselves in the darkness and then say in a shallow and banal way, "Ah, well, it was pretty bad. But thank God Jesus has come, and now it's all OK." It is not OK, and it is dishonest to pretend that it is. Instead we must see how glimmers of the gospel may be seen in the ashes of Job's rubbish heap. The third feature is that Job's lament extends beyond his individual experience to the common experience of undeserved sufferings by the godly throughout the world. In this too there is gospel.

Job's words fall naturally into three parts: a curse (vv. 3–10), a lament (vv. 11–19), and an agonized question (vv. 20–26).

A Curse (3:3–10)

Job's outburst begins with a carefully crafted curse. Job "cursed the day of his birth" (v. 1). He does not curse God, as the Satan has said he would (1:11; 2:5) and as his wife exhorts him to do (2:9). But he comes right to the brink of doing this.[10] He curses (literally) "his day" (the ESV is probably right to translate this as "the day of his birth").[11]

In verses 3–10 he expands on this to give a comprehensive curse on his very existence.

> Let the day perish on which I was born,
>   and the night that said,
>   "A man is conceived." (v. 3)

The day on which Job was born and the night nine months earlier in which he had been conceived together supply the two foundations of his existence as a human being, indeed as "a man." The word usually indicates a grown male in his strength and dignity, as opposed to a child. This lament is not at the troubles that have come upon some insignificant creature, a weakling or a nobody; these disasters have come upon a man of distinction, greatness, and dignity.[12] This is a comprehensive wish not only that he had not been born but that he had not even begun to exist as a fetus.

Verses 4, 5 expand on the day of his birth and then verses 6–10 on the night of his conception.

> Let that day be darkness!
>> May God above not seek it,
>> nor light shine upon it.
> Let gloom and deep darkness claim it.
>> Let clouds dwell upon it;
>> let the blackness of the day terrify it. (vv. 4, 5)

Every moviemaker knows that darkness is associated with sadness, danger, and gloom. Often the sad parts of a movie are set on rainy days or with a blue filter to indicate nighttime! Now we must take that idea and press it far beyond the worst horror film, right to the gates of Hell.

When time began, darkness was everywhere, and "God said, 'Let there be light,' and there was light. And God saw that the light was good. And God separated the light from the darkness. God called the light Day . . ." (Genesis 1:2–5). Light is about God, goodness, creation, order, and life. For a day to become night is for a part of creation to be undone.

Job piles up words for darkness and pours them onto the day of his birth. "Let that day be darkness!" he says. Let it never have come into existence as a day. "May God above not seek it, nor light shine upon it" (v. 4). For God to "seek" or pay attention to something is for it to be a place or time where God is present in his life-giving power. The New Jerusalem will be "called Sought Out, A City Not Forsaken" (Isaiah 62:12). To be "sought" by God is the opposite of being God-forsaken. Here at the root of Job's existence is to be a God-forsaken "day" that is no day at all, a day that is night, a day with "Darkness at Noon."[13]

"Let gloom and deep darkness claim it" (v. 5). This is not the darkness of a naturally cloudy day, but the "deep darkness" that is the shadow of death itself. This word means a thick, deep darkness, like that found in a mineshaft (28:3) or in the regions of the dead (10:21: "before I go . . . to the land of darkness and deep shadow"); it is the place of the gates of death (cf. 38:17 where "the gates of death" stand parallel to "the gates of deep darkness"). When God brings salvation, he "turns deep darkness into the morning" (Amos 5:8).[14] Job's desire is that these death-powers of gloom and deep darkness would lay "claim" to Job's birth day, that they would win back their demonic rights over this created day (Job 3:5). The word "claim" (ga'al) is also used, positively, of the redemption accomplished by the kinsman-redeemer; here, in an ironic reversal, Job wishes that the powers of darkness would "redeem" his day from light into endless darkness.

"Let clouds"—that is, supernatural clouds that blot out every trace of light—"dwell upon it; let the blackness of the day terrify it" (v. 5). The "blackness of the day" means an eclipse, a source of supernatural dread and terror to ancient peoples. The word "terrify" speaks of "an uncanny feeling that causes every fiber of one's being to shudder, leaving one powerless."[15]

Life is so painful that Job wishes the roots of his existence had been recaptured by death and darkness, that he had never existed in the presence of God. He wishes God would rewind the tape of creation and undo the part that led to his existence.

And then, to press this wish home to its most radical conclusion, he does the same for the night of his conception in verses 6–10:

> That night—let thick darkness seize it!
>   Let it not rejoice among the days of the year;
>   let it not come into the number of the months.
> Behold, let that night be barren;
>   let no joyful cry enter it.
> Let those curse it who curse the day,
>   who are ready to rouse up Leviathan. (vv. 6–8)

The night of Job's conception had not been "night" in any spiritual sense. It had been a time of life and joy, a time of sexual joy for his parents, a time when a new human life sprang into being, a time in which that wonderful and astonishing moment had happened when two DNAs fused and a new human being was procreated. It had been a time that imaged the creative power of God triumphing over darkness and evil. But Job cannot rejoice in this. He wishes that night had been truly night in the darkest and deepest sense imaginable. He wishes it would be like the plague of darkness over Egypt at the time of the exodus or the night when Judas went out to betray Jesus (John comments, "And it was night," John 13:30). He wishes it had been that kind of God-forsaken night.

He wishes that "thick darkness," darker than any natural darkness, which is often illuminated by moonlight, starlight, or even candles, would "seize" that day, abduct it, take it out of the calendar. He wants it removed from the days and months of the year, so that every calendar from then on will have that night missing (v. 6).

Far from being an empty time, that night had been fruitful. But Job wishes it had been "barren," like rocky soil yielding no crops, like a barren woman giving no children. There had been in it a "joyful cry," perhaps the literal joyful sound of his parents' lovemaking,[16] but certainly the poetic joyful cry of the night itself personified, giving a shout of joy that a child was conceived. How many childless couples long for the night when that joyful sound will be heard! But Job wishes it had never been (v. 7).

He wishes that someone somewhere had the power and authority to "curse the day"; he wishes for someone to "rouse up Leviathan" (v. 8). Leviathan, whom we shall meet again in Job 41, was the storybook sea monster of chaos, the great enemy of the Creator whose mission it was to undo the order and beauty God had made. Job pictures Leviathan as having keepers, professional curse-bringers, who can whistle for Leviathan and call him to come and destroy part of the created order. He wants them to stir up from the depths[17] this chaotic, evil, supernatural sea monster whose design is always to bring disorder in place of order, death in place of life, darkness swallowing life. It is rather like in The Lord of the Rings, when those making up the Fellowship of the Ring are passing through the mines of Moria, and one of the hobbits accidentally stirs up the monstrous Balrog, with terrible consequences. But Job wants this to be done deliberately. He wishes for a supernatural demonic intervention to have prevented his conception and birth. He summons the most powerful sorcerers in the universe to do this for him. "I wish they would call him to curse the night of my conception, so that I might never have been born," he says in essence.

Of course it is all fanciful. He cannot effectively curse the past. The past is past, and he cannot change it. "The language is fierce, but the curse has no teeth and the wish is hopeless. Its power is wholly literary, its extravagance the violence of Job's feeling."[18]

> Let the stars of its dawn be dark;
>> let it hope for light, but have none,
>> nor see the eyelids of the morning,
> because it did not shut the doors of my mother's womb,
>> nor hide trouble from my eyes. (vv. 9, 10)

Job wishes this night, as well as being supernaturally dark, would have been a night that never ended in day, a night that never saw the morning "stars" (traditionally Venus and Mercury) assuring another victory of light over darkness (v. 9). Here is a night in which watchmen can watch and wait for the morning (as in Psalm 130:5, 6), but they will watch and wait in vain, for morning will never come. They will never see "the eyelids of the morning," the first light in the eastern sky that announces sunrise is at hand, the dawn personified as a beautiful woman whose eyelids are suggestive of the full splendor to be revealed when dawn comes (Job 3:9). But for Job there is no beauty of dawn, no hope, no confident waiting for a light at the end of his dark tunnel.

Why does Job make these terrible wishes? Because that night "did not shut the doors of my mother's womb" to prevent new life from entering at the time of conception, to keep the sperm from fusing with the ovum, to prevent his first beginning to exist (v. 10).[19] This is a retrospective contraceptive wish applied to his own existence.

This is terrible. In normal life almost nothing can rival conception and birth as signs of hope. A wife tells us she is expecting a baby, and we rejoice. Or we ought to. Her position is quite literally pregnant with hope (even if sometimes mixed with feelings of inconvenience, alarm, or anxiety). Fundamentally there is excitement, and there are eager preparations. And when we hear of a safe birth this is even more so. The whole affair is full of looking forward. We ask expectant parents, "Is there anything you are looking forward to?" and they look at us as if we are mad. "What a silly question! Of course we're looking forward. Our lives, and the mother's body, are literally filled with hope and expectation."

But for Job it has all gone into the negative. All he sees is a *No Entry* sign to the future. "If only I had never been." "What are you looking forward to, Job?" "Nothing." If he tries to look forward, all he can see is a blank wall of hopelessness as his affections and longings are turned back upon themselves in despair. "There is no future for me; would that there had been no past." Here is bitter memory unsweetened by hope.

In St. Nicholas' church in the village of Moreton in Dorset, England, there is a beautiful window engraved by Laurence Whistler. It is a memorial to a local fighter pilot shot down and killed in the Battle of Britain. It shows the broken propeller of his plane, and on it are two pairs of initials, his and his young wife's, with the years of their marriage—1939–1940. What did that premature death do to that young widow? What happened in her mind to all the potential and hope with which their marriage began—the children they might have had, their future together? There is no comment in the window, but in those initials and those dates is such a compression of grief.

The last line of verse 10 is the climax of this section: "... nor hide trouble from my eyes." Job's conception and then Job's birth have opened the way for Job's troubles, for had those doors been closed, "trouble" would have been hidden from Job's eyes. The word "trouble" (*'amal*) speaks often in the book of Job of Job's plight. Eliphaz says accusingly that those who "sow trouble" will reap the same, as Job evidently has (4:8). He says that "man is born to trouble" (5:7). Job himself speaks of "nights of *misery*" (*'amal*, 7:3). Zophar promises that if Job repents, "you will forget your *misery*" (*'amal*, 11:16). Eliphaz says the godless "conceive trouble" (15:35). And Job accuses his friends of being "*miserable* [troublesome] comforters" (16:2).

Job would never have known the unrest, the distress, that he now endures. He would never have known the pain of bankruptcy, the grief of bereavement, the misery of sickness, the evils that seem to him so dark that they render life meaningless and worthless. This theme of trouble and unrest dominates the remainder of the chapter. In 3:13 he longs to lie down and be quiet, to sleep, to be at rest. In verse 17 he yearns for a life unsullied by "troubling," a life of rest. And in verse 26, at the very end, he laments that he has no ease, no quiet, no rest, but only trouble. It is not simple pain that hurts Job; it is trouble and unrest.[20] Job is restless, but he is not resigned to his fate. He knows there is something terribly wrong. We will see that this unrest is itself a paradoxical sign of hope. Job has not given up; he will not give up. He is on a journey, we might almost say, through crucifixion to resurrection. But before the resurrection there must be this terrible loneliness as he is increasingly isolated not only from other human beings but from his own past and future.[21] He hangs suspended between past and future, utterly alone and utterly without the experience of hope in his heart. And yet he will not give up.

A Lament (vv. 11–19)

And so Job's pointless, ineffective curse merges into a desperate lament. This lament is carefully structured in two parts. Each part begins with the question "Why?" and ends with a description of the place of the dead (v. 11). Each of these parts helps us to understand the other.

Part I is found in verses 11–15.

> Why did I not die at birth,
>   come out from the womb and expire?
> Why did the knees receive me?
>   Or why the breasts, that I should nurse?
> For then I would have lain down and been quiet;
>   I would have slept; then I would have been at rest,
> with kings and counselors of the earth
>   who rebuilt ruins for themselves,
> or with princes who had gold,
>   who filled their houses with silver.

Part II is seen in verses 16–19.

> Or why was I not as a hidden stillborn child,
>   as infants who never see the light?
> There the wicked cease from troubling,
>   and there the weary are at rest.
> There the prisoners are at ease together;
>   they hear not the voice of the taskmaster.
> The small and the great are there,
>   and the slave is free from his master.

Part I begins with the question, if I had to be conceived and born, why did I have to be born and stay alive? Why could I not have been just another statistic of perinatal mortality, dying at or immediately after birth? There is a movement in verses 11, 12 from womb to knees to breasts. This is a movement toward sustainable life on earth.

The knees may be the knees of Job's father or of his mother. For a father to take a baby on his knees seems to have indicated acceptance of paternity and responsibility for the child's support and future. In a variation of this custom, the children of Joseph's grandson Machir are described as being, literally, "born on Joseph's knees" (Genesis 50:23; the ESV renders this as "counted as Joseph's own"). More naturally here, however, it would seem to refer to a mother taking a baby on her knees prior to putting the baby to her breast. In Isaiah 66:12 those who love Jerusalem are described as being lovingly "bounced upon her knees" in the context of being nursed and fed. This would seem to be the picture here. Job had traveled from his mother's womb to being dandled fondly on his mother's knees and then lovingly put to his mother's breast. It is a beautiful picture of a young life loved and nurtured. But for Job it was a disaster. All it did was to launch him into a life that would end with unbearable misery.

Job longs for the place of the dead. Verse 13 piles up four consecutive images of rest. First, "I would have lain down." That is, "I am tired; I want to lie down." Then he would have "been quiet," away from the noise and tumult. Third, he would have enjoyed the peace of sleep. Lastly, he "would have been at rest." This is normal human experience at night: we lie down, we are quiet, we sleep, we find rest. It is rest for which Job most deeply longs.

But who would have been his resting companions? Here we come up against a surprise. In verses 14, 15 Job speaks of a familiar threesome of powerful men—"kings . . . counselors . . . princes." The word "counselors" means senior ministers of state, such as Hushai and Ahithophel under King David (2 Samuel 15—17). The word "princes" simply means powerful people. This threesome appears in Ezra 7:28 (". . . the king and his counselors, and . . . all the king's mighty officers") and Ezra 8:25 (". . . the king and his counselors and his lords"). These three are a comprehensive way of saying "powerful and influential people in the world." In our terms, they include presidents, prime ministers, senators, media barons, CEOs, billionaires, and anyone else who exercises power.

Job describes these men as having "rebuilt ruins for themselves" and having had "gold" and having "filled their houses with silver" (vv. 14, 15). The word "ruins" may refer to ruined cities that these powerful people sought to rebuild as a mark of their greatness.[22] God himself speaks of his intention to rebuild the ruins of Jerusalem (Isaiah 44:26; 58:12).[23] This is possible. In the twentieth century we saw Saddam Hussein proclaiming his greatness by his plans to rebuild ancient Babylon.

Alternatively, the text may mean not that they *re*built ruins but that the buildings they built in their lifetime are now fallen into ruin. The NIV reads, "who built for themselves places now lying in ruins" (v. 15). This accords better with Job's argument here. The reference to wealth and filling their houses with silver in verse 15 would seem to be parallel to the description of the ruins in verse 14, and this may help us understand the imagery. One persuasive suggestion is that the "houses" of verse 15 are the burial places they built for themselves, which they filled with wealth to take with them to the afterlife.[24] The now ruined state of these monuments and mausoleums shows that in fact these powerful men are in the place of the dead; they are now on the same level as everybody else. They take with them neither their wealth nor their power.

However we understand the detail of verses 14, 15, the main picture is clear: the place of the dead is where powerful people end up, no matter how rich and strong they were in this life. But why does Job specifically speak of his longing to be with *these* people? He is surely not expecting a privileged status in Sheol![25] The key would seem to be found in the second part of the lament, in verses 17–19.[26]

Verse 16 echoes verses 11, 12, with essentially the same question: "Why, if I had to be born, could I not have been stillborn and never see the light of life? I wish I had gone straight from the womb to Sheol."[27]

But in verses 17–19 we see a different portrait of his prospective Sheol companions. Instead of just kings, counselors, and princes, we now have two groups—on the one hand "the wicked" who cause turmoil and trouble, "the taskmaster," "the great," the "master" and on the other hand "the weary," "the prisoners," "the small," and "the slave." The kings, counselors, and princes are now seen as the oppressors. Here humanity is viewed through the lens of power and divided into the powerful and the powerless. Job clearly identifies himself with the latter group. The former are wicked and cause trouble for the latter. The former run slave labor camps. The former exploit the weak and use their power for their own advantage. The former are the slave owners and slave drivers. Surely these are the same as the kings, counselors, and princes. They may have been rich and powerful, but they are wicked. And it is their selfish wickedness that causes so much of the suffering on earth. Job's distress here broadens beyond his own awful suffering. He knows that he is not the only human being on earth to experience unfair misery.

In Isaiah 14 the King of Babylon comes to Sheol, and when he arrives they say, "Is this the man who made the earth tremble, who shook kingdoms . . . ?" (Isaiah 14:16). When alive, he had made people tremble and shake; he had caused trouble and turmoil. He causes it no more.

The image of "the voice of the taskmaster" is a haunting one (v. 18). It contains echoes of the Pharaoh's cruel taskmasters before the exodus (Exodus 3:7), of "the yoke of his burden, and the staff for his shoulder, the rod of his oppressor" in Isaiah 9:4, and of the oppressor who marches roughshod over people in Zechariah 9:8. It is a penetrating image, heavy with the long shadow of human cruelty over the lives of sufferers. At the very end of his classic and deeply moving two-volume account of Auschwitz and his return home, the Italian Jew Primo Levi recounts "a dream full of horror [which] has not ceased to visit me." "It is a dream within a dream" in which he begins in peace, perhaps sitting at a table with his family or friends or in the green countryside. And yet he feels

> a deep and subtle anguish, the definite sensation of an impending threat." And then "everything collapses and disintegrates around me, the scenery, the walls, the people, while the anguish becomes more intense and more precise. Now everything has changed to chaos; I am alone in the centre of a grey and turbid nothing, and now, I *know* what this thing means, and I also know that I have always known it; I am in the Lager [concentration camp] once more, and nothing is true outside the Lager. All the rest was a brief pause, a deception of the senses, a dream; my family, nature in flower, my home. Now this inner dream, this dream of peace, is over, and in the outer dream, which continues . . . a well-known voice resounds: a single word, not imperious, but brief and subdued. It is the dawn command of Auschwitz, a foreign word, feared and expected: get up, "*Wstawàch.*"[28]

The voice of the slave driver cast a long shadow. The nightmare shadow of that voice never left him. Perhaps it echoed in his mind at the time of his death in the 1960s, very possibly by suicide.

Job can find no rest on earth because he is now identified with the small, the weak, the downtrodden. He experiences with them the turmoil and restless misery of being oppressed by forces stronger than himself. It is probably not fanciful to extend this from the oppression of the Sabeans and Chaldeans, who caused him such trouble in chapters 1, 2 to the evil oppression of his spiritual enemy, the Satan.

So in verses 14, 15 it is not that Job particularly wants to be with the kings, counselors, and princes. After all, among them will no doubt be the Sabean and Chaldean chieftains who ravaged his property. Rather he believes that in Sheol at last they will no longer be able to cause him trouble.

"If I had been stillborn," says Job in effect, "I would have been in Sheol, the place of the dead. And that would be peace." In his clearer moments Job knows that is not true, that Sheol is a terrible place. In 17:14 he knows it is where decay and the worm are our father and mother. But in his desperation he thinks it's the place of rest.

The deep reason for Job's unrest is that he cannot understand his sufferings. He cannot understand why a believer, a man of godliness and piety, suffers with such mind-numbing intensity. This inexplicable trouble shakes the foundations of his moral and ordered universe. It is for this reason he cannot and will not rest until he has found some resolution to this cosmic question.[29]

At heart human rest is rooted in the rest of God when he looks on a completed and good creation (Genesis 2:1–3). Rest is predicated on cosmic order, a creation in which there are proper boundaries, in which virtue is rewarded and vice punished, in which there is justice and in which goodness triumphs. Job longs to share that rest with God. At the moment his experience is the polar opposite. So he ends his speech with a desperate question.

An Agonized Question (3:20–26)

> Why is light given to him who is in misery,
>   and life to the bitter in soul,
> who long for death, but it comes not,
>   and dig for it more than for hidden treasures,
> who rejoice exceedingly
>   and are glad when they find the grave?
> Why is light given[30] to a man whose way is hidden,
>   whom God has hedged in?

In verse 20 "him who is in misery" is singular; we think of Job. But "the bitter in soul" is plural. Job's question does not relate to Job alone. Although God is not mentioned by name, the verb "given" implies that God has given it, as in 1:21 ("The LORD gave . . ."); it is from the Lord that we "receive" good things and bad things (2:10). The expression "bitter in soul" speaks of a deep distress. The childless and desperate Hannah experiences this deep distress (1 Samuel 1:10). It is the bitter misery of the defeated and crushed. Hushai says to Absalom that David and his men are "enraged" (literally, "bitter of soul," ESV footnote) after their expulsion from Jerusalem (2 Samuel 17:8). In Ezekiel's lament for the trading city of Tyre, he speaks of the mariners weeping over her "in bitterness of soul" (Ezekiel 27:31). The expression is used of parents who have lost a child in 1 Samuel 30:6 and of the sick and despairing King Hezekiah in Isaiah 38:15. These are men and women who have lost all hope and who cannot see the point of continuing to live. Why does God give them life in the first place? asks Job.

Verses 21, 22 speak with biting irony. These miserable people, of whom Job is one, long for death with the passionate desire of the treasure hunter, rushing out to the wild west in the gold rush, dreaming of death as the gold-hunter dreams of the yellow stuff. And when they die, their exuberance can only be understood when you think of the treasure hunter striking a rich vein of gold. The Roman writer Ovid speaks of a terrible curse so that someone has a reason for dying but not the means.[31] Job feels like a man on a life-support machine who longs for it to be switched off.

Job is obsessed with death as the only way out of trouble because life is so futile. Wilfred Owen gets this so poignantly in his poem "Futility."[32]

> Move him into the sun—
> Gently its touch awoke him once,
> At home, whispering of fields unsown.
> Always it woke him, even in France,
> Until this morning and this snow.
> If anything might rouse him now
> The kind old sun will know.
>
> Think how it wakes the seeds,—
> Woke, once, the clays of a cold star.
> Are limbs, so dear-achieved, are sides,
> Full-nerved—still warm—too hard to stir?
> Was it for this the clay grew tall?
> —O what made fatuous sunbeams toil
> To break earth's sleep at all?

Owen writes of the untimely death of a young British farmer on the fields of the Western Front in World War I. In this poignant poem Owen moves from one particular futile tragedy to a world that seems to have no point. The sun used to wake this young man; it won't wake him now. That same sun gave life to the cold earth (at creation); why? And in his anger he shouts, "O what made fatuous sunbeams toil to break earth's sleep at all?" Why did God bother to make the world at all? This is what Job feels.

In verse 23 he describes himself and others like him as walking on a way or path that is "hidden" from God's blessing and grace, a God-forsaken walk, and a path that is "hedged in" by God. To be "hidden" suggests it has no purpose or meaning. To be "hedged in" is an ironic twist to what the Satan had said. In 1:10 the Satan said that Job's happy prosperous life was hedged in by God's gracious protection.[33] Now he experiences a different kind of hedge, a hedge of razor wire, not to keep the marauder out, but to keep Job imprisoned in a miserable life he longs to leave but cannot, a life that is locked in to trouble, with the key thrown away. He speaks of it again in a later chapter: "[God] has walled up my way, so that I cannot pass, and he has set darkness upon my paths" (19:8).[34]

It is a life of cramped narrowness, just as the world of an elderly person today gradually contracts from the world to the nation (no longer going abroad), from the nation to the neighborhood, from the neighborhood to the occasional walk in the garden, from the garden to being housebound, from the house to the bedroom, and from the bedroom to the coffin or casket. Job feels this is happening to him. He is hedged in, trapped, and he cannot escape. And he wonders why God is doing it. What is the point? Is there a point?

In verses 24–26 there is a great emphasis on what "comes" upon Job. His sighing "comes" to him (v. 24a); his groanings "are poured out" over him like water (v. 24b); what he fears "comes" upon him, and what he dreads "befalls" him (v. 25). He has no rest, but trouble "comes" (v. 26). He is the target. Things happen to him. What is "given" by God "comes" to Job. These things are the reality of his experience. But he does not, and cannot, know why. This is the source of his deep unease. He knows that God is the author, and he knows that these things have come to him. But why?

> For my sighing comes instead of my bread,
>   and my groanings are poured out like water.
> For the thing that I fear comes upon me,
>   and what I dread befalls me.
> I am not at ease, nor am I quiet;
>   I have no rest, but trouble comes. (vv. 24–26)

The word "sighing" or groaning is a strong word (v. 24). It means something like "my shrieks,"[35] the loud moans and wails that come from people devastated by tragedy. It is the kind of thing we see after an earthquake or terrorist bombing, when the injured and bereaved cry out aloud in their misery. Under the Pharaoh, the Hebrew slaves "groaned" (the same word) because of their slavery (Exodus 2:23). At the exile Jerusalem's people wail aloud (Lamentations 1:4, 8). It is an exhausting grief. Jeremiah's companion Baruch says, "I am weary with my groaning, and I find no rest" (Jeremiah 45:3). This is Job's daily diet. It comes to him in place of bread; he can only feed on his own misery. This is the lament of David in Psalm 22:1: "My God, my God, why have you forsaken me? Why are you so far from saving me, from the words of my groaning?" This grief is fulfilled many years later when a man cries out from a cross, "My God, my God, why have you forsaken me?" (Matthew 27:46).

Verse 25 speaks of the things Job had most dreaded, which are now coming upon him. Right at the start, in 1:4, 5, we see Job anxious about possible troubles. But whatever troubles he may have dreaded in his worst nightmares are now fulfilled.

Verse 26 is the climax of the speech, with its four images of rest/unrest. Job is "not at ease," he has no "quiet," he has "no rest," but instead just "trouble." Three negatives (no "ease," no "quiet," "no rest") and one terrible positive ("trouble"). This is torment not just of body, terrible though that is, but of the soul. The word "trouble" is the keynote and the closing word of the speech. What a contrast to the idyllic picture of 1:1–3, a portrayal of a restful prosperity untroubled by pain, a reassuring regularity unbroken by disorder.

The question "Why?" will echo throughout the book (v. 20). We are drawn by the tragedy of Job into bigger and more alarming questions than the individual tragedy of Job himself. Job wants not only to undo his own life but to question the creation of the world. Genesis 1 moves from darkness to light, from night to day, from inanimacy to life. Job wants to put it all into reverse.

Where Is the Gospel in Job 3?

We know if we are Christians that for every believer the best is yet to be. Always there are better things ahead; always there is hope, because the future is God's future, and our destiny is glory. But we need to recognize that there may be times in the life of a believer when that future appears utterly blank and all we can do is look back with regret, consumed with "if only." That is where Job is in Job 3. It is a bleak time.

So where is the gospel in Job 3? It is not very obvious, but it is there in three ways.

Even in the Darkness Job Cannot Avoid God

It seems unlikely that Job is conscious of the presence of God. Perhaps he would have echoed the words of C. S. Lewis in his moving personal reflection after the death of his wife (*A Grief Observed*). Lewis asks the question, in bereavement, "Where is God?" and he answers:

> This is one of the most disquieting symptoms. When you are happy, so happy that you have no sense of needing Him . . . if you remember yourself and turn to Him with gratitude and praise, you will be—or so it feels—welcomed with open arms.
>
> But go to him when your need is desperate, when all other help is vain, and what do you find? A door slammed in your face, and a sound of bolting and double bolting on the inside. After that, silence. You may as well turn away. The longer you wait, the more emphatic the silence will become. There are no lights in the windows. It might be an empty house. Was it ever inhabited? It seemed so once.[36]

And yet Job knows that he cannot turn away from that door. Right here in the depth of his misery he knows he has to deal with God. We shall see as the book unfolds that this is a great theme in his journey. Even in God's felt absence he is somehow there. We see this in the word "given" in verse 20. Light and life have been given, given by God, and therefore it is with God we must deal. Even in his absence God is present as the focus of Job's loss.

There is a glimmer of hope here. But it will take some time for that glimmer to become a ray.

Job's Restlessness Is a Paradoxical Sign of Hope

We have seen that the dominant tone of chapter 3 is restlessness. Job cannot rest with things as they are. And therefore he will not rest. In his weakness, misery, and distress there is yet an energy within Job that surges and drives him to discover the God who has treated him like this. Although he says he has no hope, his restlessness betrays him. A restless man is not a defeated man; a troubled man is not a hopeless man resigned to his fate. If there really is no hope, there is no point asking "Why?" (v. 20). And yet Job does ask "Why?" and he asks it repeatedly and energetically. He says he wants to die, but his restless words betray him, for they point inexorably to life and resurrection.

Job's Darkness Anticipates a Deeper Darkness

At the end of Job 3 we leave Job terribly alone, sitting with friends who want to comfort him but have nothing to say. We leave him able only to look back with bitter regrets that he ever lived, mired in deep darkness. Is there anything that can be said to him?

I believe there is; even at this stage there is something to be said, beyond the silence of bankruptcy, beyond even the silence of sympathy. We saw when considering 2:11–13 that Job's loneliness foreshadowed a greater loneliness. His darkness likewise anticipates a deeper darkness. Two thousand years ago another blameless believer was in deep darkness, hanging on a cross at midday. Deeper than the darkness of night. Deeper even than Job's darkness. And from his lips came the cry of dereliction, "My God, My God, why have you forsaken me?" (Mark 15:33, 34). In some strange way, because Job's darkness of soul foreshadows the darkness of the cross there is within it hope of rescue.

Part 2

JOB AND HIS FRIENDS

Job 4—31

5

Introducing Job's Comforters: What Not to Say to the Suffering Believer

THE PROLOGUE TO the book of Job in the 1560 Geneva Bible begins:

> In this history is set before our eyes the example of a singular patience. For this holy man Job was not only extremely afflicted in outward things and in his body, but also in his mind and conscience, by the sharp temptations of his wife, and chief friends; which, by their vehement words and subtle disputations, brought him almost to despair. . . . These friends came unto him under pretence of consolation, and yet they tormented him more than did all his affliction. Notwithstanding he did constantly resist them, and at length had good success.

We considered earlier the Christian hymn-writer William Cowper. In his hymn "God Moves in a Mysterious Way," Cowper assures us, "Behind a frowning providence [God] hides a smiling face." But is it true? When providence frowns and the believer's circumstances are filled with pain, is there a face smiling with sovereign love? Or is this a fancy, sugary make-believe worthy only of the world of Walt Disney? Cowper himself sometimes doubted the truth of his own hymn in his times of deep depression.

In Job 3 we heard Job utter a black heartrending lament of utter desolation. At the end we left him deeply alone and desperately devoid of hope, wanting the forward progress of the created order to be set in reverse—light to turn back to darkness and his life to dissolve in death. It was a bleak chapter. The chapter ended with a terrible question ringing in our ears. This blameless believer whose possessions are all lost, his children killed, and his health destroyed cries out, "Why?" (3:20). Why indeed? We must ask this question, for it is not suffering that destroys a person, but suffering without a purpose. Why? What do we say to ourselves when we sit where Job sat or to others when we sit with them as Job's three friends did?

There is a time for saying nothing. A time when trauma so numbs feeling that words lose their usefulness, when loss cauterizes the senses and all someone can do is stare blankly into space, and all we can do is sit alongside and maybe hold a hand. But after that the question comes: Why?

So what do we say? And not just afterward but before suffering comes. At my ordination I was charged "to prepare the dying for their death." Although the intention here may have been the narrower one of ministry to those near the point of death, the charge has wider implications. All Christians ought to be engaged in preparing one another for their deaths and for suffering, so that when suffering comes we may be so shaped by God's Word that we may be able, as it were, to put our hands into the hand of God even in the darkness.

The Lutheran pastor Helmut Thielicke, preaching in Stuttgart near the end of the war, during the period of heavy Allied bombing, was walking discouraged through the city, absorbed in gloomy thoughts, when he found himself looking down into the concrete pit of a cellar that had been shattered by a bomb and in which more than fifty young people had been killed. "A woman came up to me and asked whether I was [Pastor Thielicke], since she was not sure who I was in the clothes I wore. Then she said, 'My husband died down there. His place was right under the hole. The clean-up squad was unable to find a trace of him; all that was left was his cap. We were there the last time you preached in the cathedral church. And here before this pit I want to thank you for preparing him for eternity.'"[1]

The privilege of speaking with sufferers is one that is easily abused. In this chapter we are going to learn from the mistakes of three men who said a great deal to a sufferer, and it wasn't very helpful. The men are Eliphaz, Bildad, and Zophar, Job's "comforters," as they are ironically called. They say nothing for a week (2:11–14). But after Job's lament (Job 3) they say much. They speak for nine Bible chapters in nearly three rounds of heated argument. In this chapter we will get our bearings to help us as we come to read their speeches, interspersed with Job's replies.

The three friends are not clones of each other in what they say, and we shall see that there is a measure of development in their speeches as we move through the three cycles. But by and large they say the same things in similar ways, and for the purposes of this overview we will consider them together so that we are introduced to the common salient features of their woeful pastoral theology.

Getting a Feel for the Exchanges

Here are three preliminary points about the tone of the exchanges, to orient us and get a feel for what is going on.

The Comforters Are Not Impressed with Job

For example, in 8:2 Bildad is clearly riled by Job: "How long will you say these things, and the words of your mouth be a great wind?" Eliphaz says much the same in 15:2, 3. While Job's appearance had made his friends sad (2:12), his words make them angry. Why? Because as the exchanges go on, Job repeatedly insists he is not being punished for some particular sin, for he has nothing on his conscience that could justify this treatment from God. So it seems that God is being unfair. This makes his friends livid. We can understand why.

So in 11:2–6 Zophar wishes that God would intervene and speak, because that really would shut Job up and show him what empty babble he is pouring out. (It never crosses Zophar's mind that God might actually do this, let alone what God's verdict might be on him and his friends, as we see in 42:7.) As the exchanges continue, Job's friends become thoroughly fed up with having to listen to him (e.g., 18:2a). They wish he would shut up and listen properly to them.

Job Is Not Impressed with His Comforters

The friends are unimpressed with Job, but Job is not exactly filled with gratitude toward them either. The antipathy and frustration are mutual. There is, in diplomatic language, a full and frank exchange of views. Job had hoped for refreshment from them, but they were like a riverbed to which a parched traveler turns aside, only to find it dry as dust (6:14–30). "Miserable comforters are you all" (16:2), and again in 16:3 he calls them windbags and wishes they would shut up. Or hear the biting sarcasm of Job in 12:2: "No doubt you are the people, and wisdom will die with you." "Oh, yes, you are so wise! You are where wisdom is at. When you die, I am really worried that there won't be any wise people left in the world." This is sharp and cutting sarcasm (cf. 26:2ff.). It is prompted by the error and cruelty of his friends, for they "torment" Job and "break [him] in pieces with words" (19:2).

God Is Not Impressed with Job's Comforters

For twenty-four chapters (4—27) Job and his friends have a blazing row. So who is right to be angry? Are the friends right to be angry because Job accuses God of being unfair? Or is Job right to be angry with his friends for not offering him any substantial comfort? It would be helpful to know. We are told at the end of the book when the Lord says to Eliphaz, "My anger burns against you and against your two friends, for you have not spoken of me what is right" (42:7)

So we learn that God is not impressed with Job's comforters. The anger of Job at his friends is an echo of the anger of God that burns against them.

So when we read the nine Bible chapters of comforters' speeches, we are reading words that are, by and large, a load of rubbish. Except that they are not entirely so! We find ourselves agreeing with many parts of their speeches. If it were total rubbish that would be much easier. It is always like that with false teaching; it is dangerous because it is nearly true. So we will need to look carefully at where Job's comforters go wrong. Let us do that now.

We will consider in turn their system of theology, their pastoral tone, and their gaps or omissions (the vital things they don't believe).

Their System of Theology
The theology that underlies all three friends is very simple and clear.

1. God is absolutely in control. (We have seen that this is indeed one of the foundational markers laid down by our narrator in Job 1, 2.)
2. God is absolutely just and fair.
3. *Therefore* he always punishes wickedness and blesses righteousness— always (and soon and certainly in this life). If he were ever to do otherwise, he would necessarily be unjust, which is inconceivable.
4. *Therefore*, if I suffer I *must* have sinned and am being punished justly for my sin.

(And, presumably, if I am blessed I must have been good—although this isn't relevant here, so they don't develop this side of it.)

This logic undergirds almost all they say. For example, "Remember: Who that was innocent ever perished?" (4:7) "You see," implies Eliphaz, "if the innocent did perish, the world would be unfair, and that cannot be." Again in 5:17–26 Eliphaz says in essence, "Job, your suffering is God's discipline. You sinned, and because God loves you he disciplines you. So learn from his discipline." Now the Bible does teach the truth that God disciplines his spiritual children (Proverbs 3:11, 12, quoted in Hebrews 12:4–13). Eliphaz is sure Job has sinned because he sees Job suffering. It is an entirely valid argument, *assuming* that Job has sinned.

The emotional stakes are raised in 8:4–7, where Bildad draws another conclusion from their system. In effect he said, "So your children died, did they, Job? Well, that means they must have sinned." This is of questionable comfort to Job, even though Bildad interprets the friends' way of thinking sensitively and tells Job (8:5–7) that it may not be too late for Job himself. "If you repent, God may yet restore you." Again, within the terms of their mind-set this is all correct.

The friends' frustration with Job becomes evident when Zophar pushes things even further. "Know then that God exacts of you less than your guilt deserves" (11:6b). In essence he is saying, "God has even forgotten or over-looked some of your sin, Job. Presumably if he hadn't, you'd already be dead like your children." Zophar is fed up with Job's protestations of innocence. "Count yourself lucky because God hasn't really punished you for all your sins!" And then again, as with Bildad in 8:4–7, in 11:13–19 there is another appeal for Job to repent as they deduce that he ought.

The reason the friends feel so strongly about it all is that they have grasped that unless God is just and fair, the moral fabric of the universe will disintegrate. We see this in the imagery of 18:3–5, where Bildad complains (18:3) that Job is treating them as if they are "stupid." Job is getting very angry (18:4a), but it is outrageous of him to imagine (18:4b) that "the earth" may be "forsaken for you, or the rock be removed out of its place"—that is, that the moral order and structure of the cosmos can be rearranged just to suit one individual's whims. "You cannot expect a cosmic exception to be made for you, Job. It is an absolute rule that 'the light of the wicked is put out' [18:5]. So, Job, if you are suffering, you must be wicked." And so it goes on. But Job won't accept it. He stubbornly refuses to repent of sins he hasn't committed. His conscience is clear.

So in 22:5–9 Eliphaz runs out of patience and tells Job precisely what he has done wrong. "Is not your evil abundant? There is no end to your iniquities" (22:5). "And I'll be specific, Job, since you force me to it. You're a rich man, aren't you? Well, don't expect us to believe you got rich quite as honestly and justly and kindly as you would have us think! Come clean, you hypocrite!" And again (22:21–30) there is an appeal for Job to repent. It is a winsome appeal and a beautiful expression of the offer of the gospel. Bible studies have been led on this passage. But they have usually wrenched it out of its context, which is one of utterly inappropriate words directed to the wrong man.

So that is the comforters' outlook. Both sides of this system lie deep in the human psyche. We see one side of the formula in the musical *The Sound of Music*. The handsome Captain Von Trapp declares his love for the young heroine. And in her delight she sings:

> Perhaps I had a wicked childhood
> Perhaps I had a miserable youth
> But somewhere in my wicked, miserable past
> There must have been a moment of truth.
> For here you are standing there loving me
> Whether or not you should
> So somewhere in my youth or childhood
> I must have done something good.
> Nothing comes from nothing
> Nothing ever could
> So somewhere in my youth or childhood
> I must have done something good.

Something good has happened to me, and therefore I deduce that "Somewhere in my youth or childhood I must have done something good." The comforters would agree.

The other side of the comforters' worldview surfaces again and again even today. It appeared when an elderly Christian lady said to me, as she suffered much pain in old age, "Have I done something terribly wrong? What have I done to deserve this?" It came into the open when a dear Christian friend of mine, suffering deep depression, cried out, "I must have done something terrible in the past." It was evident when a man said to a missionary friend of mine in China, "I fear I must have done something wrong because God has punished me." Yes, say the comforters to all these sufferers, you must have.

What are we to make of this theological system? It will not do to dismiss it out of hand as stupid, for it is not stupid. The first two parts of their formula (see Figure 5-1 earlier in this chapter) are absolutely right. God is absolutely in control, and God is absolutely just and fair. Further, we need to recognize that there are many ways in which we may and do suffer as a direct result of our own sin. In Psalm 32 the psalmist says that when he kept his sin secret, the pressure of unresolved guilt was destroying him physically. Only when he confessed it and turned from it did his health return. If I get drunk and drive and crash and injure myself, it is my fault. If I commit adultery and it leads, as it typically does, to misery and often violence (Proverbs 6:32–35), that misery is the result of my sin. If someone hurts me and I refuse to forgive him, and I nurse resentment and become a hard and bitter person, the resulting damage to my character is my fault because I ought to forgive.

So the comforters might be right when they appeal to Job to repent. And yet we must remember that three times in Job 1, 2 (once from the narrator, 1:1, and twice from the Lord, 1:8; 2:3) we have been told that Job is "blameless." So the comforters make a big mistake. Job does not need to repent for any sin that has led to his suffering. He is not being punished for sin. To say that he is adds a cruel burden to his grief. Yet the comforters say exactly that for nine chapters.

So let us jettison their way of thinking.

Their Tone

They are very sure they are right. For example, at the end of Eliphaz's first speech he says, "This we have searched out; it is true" (5:27). "So you'd better listen, Job." The reason they are sure is that their authority is that of tradition (8:8–10). "This was the tradition handed down to us," they say, "so it must be true." (They did not understand the wisdom of Cyprian—a tradition may simply be an error in its old age.)

Again in 15:7–10 Eliphaz pulls rank on Job. "What do you know that we do not know?" (15:9). "We are senior to you and more experienced" (15:10, paraphrase). For the friends there is no puzzle or enigma in the world as they observe it. There is no chink in their dogmatic armor. It is all so tidy, so well-swept. Whatever we do, we must not let evidence get in the way of a good theory.

Why are they so confident?

They Have No Honesty

They have inherited these dogmas, and they are not prepared to look at the world as it is. But they ought to because God's truth fits with God's world. When we look at the world through the spectacles of God's word, the world comes into focus and makes sense. We must not take our theory and squeeze the world into its mold. There is an air of unreality about their theology; it just doesn't fit the real world. It may work in the ghetto when everyone agrees to believe it and doesn't look too closely outside, but it has no power and no persuasiveness for those outside.

They Have No Sympathy

They do not seem to have been where Job is. So in 4:2–5 Eliphaz says in effect, "I can't quite see why you should be so miserable, Job. You used to be the one offering comfort to others, and I must admit you were very good at it. Well, that wasn't so difficult when you weren't suffering; but now it's your turn, and you don't like it, do you?" They are sorry for him at the start, but they don't understand his pain. They are more attached to their theories than to Job their friend. It is a little like the quip by the author James Dobson, who said about parenting, "I used to have four theories on child-rearing and no kids. Now I have four kids and no theories." These comforters have plenty of theories about suffering, but we wonder if they have ever been there.

They Have No Love

It does not look as if the friends really love Job. They do not listen to his cries. The cycles of speeches are like dialogues in which one side (the friends) are deaf to the cries and protestations of the other. They do not respond to what he says and do not engage with him as a fellow human being in need. The German writer Goethe once said that we can only understand what we love. This is true in all human relationships. Because they do not love Job, they cannot understand him.

So we should avoid their tone even as we jettison their system.

What They Don't Believe

The trouble with the comforters is that so much of what they say looks right. It would be a useful exercise to read their speeches with a pencil in hand and to put a check mark in the margin beside every statement they make with which we agree. There would be many marks and generally high marks for their doctrinal orthodoxy. So much so that it is easy to think the friends are doctrinally sound teachers whose fault is simply that they are pastorally insensitive. But more careful consideration suggests that their fault lies deeper than pastoral insensitivity. It is the content, and not only the tone, of their teaching that is false. Their problem is not so much what they do say as what they don't. (This is so often the case with false teaching; we need to be on the lookout not only for the wrong teaching Bible teachers give but also for vital Biblical ingredients they habitually omit.)

There are three vital truths they don't believe.

No Satan

They have no place in their thinking for the Satan. We know from Job 1, 2 that the Satan is a real and influential spiritual person. We know that the whole tragedy of Job has its origin in heavenly arguments between the Lord and the Satan. But the comforters have no place in their thinking for the Satan or for the spiritual battle. There are hints that Job does, in 3:8 where he speaks of Leviathan and in 26:12ff. where he refers to the serpent monster Rahab (another expression in Old Testament symbolism of the great spiritual enemy of the Creator God). We shall return to Leviathan when we reach Job 41. But the point here is that Job's friends have no place for spiritual forces of evil. In their world evil is purely a human phenomenon. It has no spiritual dimension; there is no spiritual battle. How wrong they are.

No Waiting

For them judgment is now. The wicked are punished now; the righteous are blessed now. But the promises of judgment are not for now. They are for the end. So, for example, Psalm 1 makes a clear distinction between the righteous and the wicked. According to Psalm 1:5, "the wicked will not stand in the judgment." And the judgment is (usually) in the future. The comforters' "now theology" seems so neat but is actually disastrous. It is like a slot machine: put in some goodness, and out pops a can of blessing; put in some badness, and out pops a can of poison. Just like that. In terms of the popular *Matrix* films, they would think of God like a deterministic computer program, just part of how the matrix is operating, fixed rules that determine how it all runs.

In a Peanuts cartoon Lucy says to Charlie Brown, "There is one thing you're going to have to learn: you reap what you sow; you get out of life what you put into it, no more and no less." Snoopy mutters from the corner, "I'd kind of like to see a little margin for error." The Bible does indeed teach that we will reap what we sow (Galatians 6:7ff.); in the end there will be no margin for error. But not immediately because what we sow has to grow until the harvest. In Jesus' parable (Matthew 13:24–30) the wheat and the weeds grow together. And they will not be separated until the harvest—that is, the last judgment. Then the wicked will be punished and the righteous saved, but not until then. The comforters are right to believe in retributive justice; they are wrong to assume that it will necessarily be immediate retributive justice. One day the world will be orderly as it was in creation, but our current world isn't.

What are we to make of Bible passages that seem to speak straightforwardly of blessings following obedience and curses following apostasy? For example, Proverbs 3:1ff. promises, "Let your heart keep my commandments, for length of days and years of life and peace they will add to you"—and yet they didn't bring peace to Job! (Many other examples could be cited, especially from Proverbs and Deuteronomy.) There is a distinction between the general truth of such sayings and absolute "every case" truth.

There is perhaps an analogy with a city after an earthquake. Suppose an earthquake struck a well-planned city, such as the Georgian New Town area of Edinburgh with its clear planning and gracious order. If I wanted to go from A to B afterward, I would in general still be best advised to go by the main roads. But whereas before the earthquake that would always be the best route, now I might find that the main road is blocked or that a building had collapsed to open up an unplanned route. It is a little like this with the created order after the disruption of the fall of humankind. Generally, to keep God's commandments, to live in line with his created order, will bring peace and prosperity. For example, if I am honest and work hard I will do better. But not always. And the final proof that righteousness pays will not come until the final judgment, when all disruption will be put right and the creation reordered as it ought to be.

The comforters turn religion into an impersonal slot machine formula. In their view there is no hoping for a promised future but only living in the present. There is no prayer to an unseen God but only moralizing. There is no love for a hidden God or love for people in pain but only well-reasoned answers. There is no personal yearning and longing and faith but only sight. So faith, hope, and love are dissolved into moralism and lectures. There is a kind of Christianity that belongs to this family, that revels in the immediate. *I expect the blessing of God now; I expect to see the triumph of God now; I expect to know the answers now.* There is to be no waiting. We shall see in the next chapter how very different it is with Job himself.

No Cross

In the context of the whole Bible, perhaps the deepest error and omission of the friends is this: they have no place for innocent suffering. They think that if the righteous were ever to suffer or perish, it would be a blot on the moral landscape. As Eliphaz asks, "Who that was innocent ever perished?" (4:7).

The Bible places against that question a large eternal cross.

On the cross the innocent one perished in the place of the guilty, that we might not finally perish. In a profound sense the sufferings of Job are the cost of grace. Or to be more accurate, the sufferings that Job foreshadows will be the cost of grace. With their tidy impersonal theological code, the comforters miss the heart of the universe.

And yet their speeches are in the Scriptures, all of which are able to "make [us] wise for salvation through faith in Christ Jesus" (2 Timothy 3:15). So we cannot just skip these speeches. For each one we must ask ourselves in what way it is intended by God to profit us and to lead us to faith in Christ.

The First Cycle of Speeches

Job 4—14

6

Eliphaz's First Speech:
A Useless Sermon
from a Kind Friend

JOB 4, 5

HAVE YOU HAD THE EXPERIENCE of a well-meaning friend giving kind advice that doesn't help at all? It may be straightforward advice, exactly the kind you would have given to him. But it brings no comfort to you. Or perhaps you have been, as I have, on the other side, as the one giving what you think is wise and discerning counsel, only to find it spurned as unhelpful. Whichever side of the exchange you and I have been on, the experience is deeply unsatisfactory. It always points to a deeper problem, undiagnosed by the counselor or unrecognized by the one in need.

Job's three friends have traveled to show Job sympathy and to "comfort him" (2:11). We have seen that these friends share with Job the privilege of being men associated with wisdom and wise counsel. They are not just any old friends; they are counselors whose advice would naturally be sought. So when they sit for those terrible seven days and seven nights of silence, we know that something is wrong, for there is no advice forthcoming.

In chapter 3 Job breaks that silence with the most moving and passionately unsettled lament, spoken, it would seem, to himself more than to anyone else. But his friends are there listening. Or are they really listening? We will have reason to doubt that before long.

Eliphaz speaks first in all three cycles of speeches. Here is the man from Teman in Edom, renowned for its wisdom. Eliphaz is the senior friend, named first in 2:11 and summoned by the Lord as the representative of all three in 42:7.

He speaks kindly, courteously, deferentially, and sensitively, as best he knows how.[1] He begins, "If one ventures a word with you . . ." (4:2). He is not pushy or aggressive but respectful. He compliments Job on his past: "Behold, you have instructed many" (4:3). He seeks to get alongside Job, saying things like "if I were you" (which is the sense of 5:8), appealing with empathy. Sure, he counsels Job, but in the normal tone of the Wisdom Literature, the tone of voice we find all through Proverbs, for example.[2] And yet he does no good.

We are going to listen as positively as we can to what Eliphaz has to say before asking ourselves what we can learn both from what he gets right and from what he gets wrong. If Eliphaz's speech were a sermon, we might reasonably divide it into four points. "My dear friend Job," he says, "I must speak to you. And I want to say four things. I want to encourage you to be consistent with what you and I both know to be true.[3] I want to exhort you to be realistic about being mortal and human. I need to warn you to be humble and not try to be too clever. And I want to plead with you to be submissive to God's discipline."

Be Consistent (4:1–11)

Then Eliphaz the Temanite answered and said:

> "If one ventures a word with you, will you be impatient?
>   Yet who can keep from speaking?
> Behold, you have instructed many,
>   and you have strengthened the weak hands.
> Your words have upheld him who was stumbling,
>   and you have made firm the feeble knees.
> But now it has come to you, and you are impatient;
>   it touches you, and you are dismayed.
> Is not your fear of God your confidence,
>   and the integrity of your ways your hope?" (4:1–6)

Eliphaz starts somewhat tentatively as Job sputters to a halt; he is bristling with indignation, sweating, and deeply disturbed. He begins (v. 2) in essence, "Excuse me, but I wonder if I might get in a word edgewise. If someone does speak to you, are you going to be impatient, irritated, offended, fed up even before I get started? I hope not, for there are things that simply have to be said."

He essentially goes on, "Listen a moment. I want to remind you that in the good old days you were a jolly good counselor yourself. Many people have been grateful for your advice." Verses 3, 4 reinforce this point. Job has been a good wordsmith. He has spoken well-chosen words that have instructed many (v. 3a) and have been heard by struggling people with "weak hands" (v. 3b) and "feeble knees" (4b),[4] pictures of fear, depression, enervation, loss of morale, being "tired all the time" (as the doctors sometimes describe it), the inability to do things properly ("weak hands") or to stand up tall and strong ("feeble knees"). "And the effect of your words has been to give strength (v. 3b), to uphold (v. 4a), and to make firm (v. 4b)."[5] "You know the words that need to be spoken to people, the right words, words that give instruction and wisdom. I remember how good you used to be at speaking such words to others, even to us." It is as if Eliphaz gently rebukes him, "You comforted others, but you cannot comfort yourself."[6]

"But now [v. 5] hard times have come to you, and you are 'impatient' [the same word as in v. 2]; you are fed up, you will not listen properly, you get irritated. Suffering strikes you[7] as the wind struck the house [cf. 1:19], and you will not heed all the good advice you have known for years and have given to others. If I may say so, you are being inconsistent."

The point is that Job and Eliphaz start with exactly the same worldview. The advice that Eliphaz gives to Job is precisely the advice that Job would have given to Eliphaz had the boot been on the other foot. Eliphaz is simply appealing to Job to be consistent with the worldview they both know and accept.

So what is this worldview? We have outlined its salient features in the last chapter. Its contours will gradually come into view in this and subsequent speeches of the friends. Verse 6 begins to open it up. "Surely," says Eliphaz, "you are a pious man,[8] and you have integrity or blamelessness [the word translated "integrity" is the same word used in 1:1; 1:8; 2:3 of Job]. The fact that you fear God and do so genuinely, with integrity, ought to give you confidence and hope as you look to the future. You and I know that God rewards really pious people with blessings; that is how the universe works. There is moral order. God gives good things to good people. So many times have you said that to others, to encourage them to have strong hands and firm knees. So what is all this about wishing you had never been conceived and born, about wishing you were dead, about speaking as if you have nothing to look forward to [3:3–26]? You know that must be nonsense, for you are a good person, and good things happen to good people. You must be consistent, dear friend."

Then Eliphaz goes on to expand on why piety and integrity ought to give hope.

> Remember: who that was innocent ever perished?
> Or where were the upright cut off? (v. 7)

Verse 7 is a critical verse. Eliphaz says, "Listen to this key truth—give me one example of an innocent person who has died an untimely death, of a morally upright person who has been cut off from life in his prime. You can't, can you? No, of course you can't; it has never happened, and it never will." This is, of course, an unfalsifiable claim, for it assumes what it seeks to prove. It is the kind of claim of which we may say, "Never let the evidence get in the way of a good theory."

But it is the worldview of most morally serious religious persons. This is what the inhabitants of Malta were thinking when they saw a viper fasten itself to the Apostle Paul. What could they conclude from the fact that this man was about to be killed by a poisonous snake? "No doubt this man is a murderer. Though he has escaped from the sea, Justice has not allowed him to live" (Acts 28:4). There was no doubt about this conclusion for these natives of classical Malta, just as there was no doubt for Eliphaz. If a person dies an untimely death, this proves that he cannot be morally upright.

I think the implication at this stage is that Job is pious and upright and therefore has grounds for hope. Eliphaz does not yet conclude that Job must be guilty. For now at least he is seeking to encourage Job.

He goes on to expand, from his own eyewitness evidence, on the foundational truth of verse 7:

> As I have seen, those who plow iniquity
> and sow trouble reap the same.
> By the breath of God they perish,
> and by the blast of his anger they are consumed. (vv. 8–9)

"I have observed," says Eliphaz, "that when people invest bad things in their lives, they get bad stuff out." Using a familiar agricultural analogy, he speaks of the wicked plowing and sowing the seeds of sin in their lives. Just as a farmer sowing corn will not reap barley, so it is with moral actions: we reap what we sow. Paul says just the same in Galatians 6:7, and the Lord Jesus uses the same harvest language in Matthew 13:24–30, 36–43. The world is not a random place; actions have consequences, and the consequences correspond to the actions. What Eliphaz misses—and it is vital—is that the harvest is at the close of the age (Matthew 13:39) and not until then.

And it is not just an impersonal process, as the ideas of sowing and reaping might suggest. Rather (v. 9), this is the personal judgment of God. God is angry with sinners; it is as if he flares his nostrils (the word translated "anger" has this sense) and breathes out a gale of angry judgment on the wicked,[9] so that they perish and are consumed. Eliphaz says he has observed this, but with what must be a very selective memory. He goes on to use a vivid metaphor of predatory wickedness:

> The roar of the lion, the voice of the fierce lion,
>> the teeth of the young lions are broken.
> The strong lion perishes for lack of prey,
>> and the cubs of the lioness are scattered. (vv.10–11)

Five words for lion are used, either referring to different types of lions or to various stages of a lion's development. The lion here is a picture of the wicked, just as David prays against the wicked, "O God, break the teeth in their mouths; tear out the fangs of the young lions, O Lord!" (Psalm 58:6).[10] Although the wicked may roar like lions and prey on the righteous, their teeth will be broken, they will perish, and all the family of wickedness will be scattered. Eliphaz is saying, "That is called moral order, Job, and you know it. And I have observed it over many years."

Eliphaz appeals, firmly but courteously, to Job to consistently hold to the firm convictions of a settled moral order that he shares (or shared) with Eliphaz and his friends.

Be Realistic (4:12—5:7)

But then the tone changes. What follows is a strange, even spooky account of a night vision. The philosophical religious system is about to be buttressed by a kind of mystical spirituality.

> Now a word was brought to me stealthily;
>> my ear received the whisper of it.
> Amid thoughts from visions of the night,
>> when deep sleep falls on men,
> dread came upon me, and trembling,
>> which made all my bones shake.
> A spirit glided past my face;
>> the hair of my flesh stood up.
> It stood still,
>> but I could not discern its appearance.
> A form was before my eyes;
>> there was silence, then I heard a voice . . . (vv. 12–16)

Verses 12–16 are framed by references to "a word" and "a voice." The focus of this strange account is the message that follows in verse 17. But let us notice how it is introduced. Until now Eliphaz has been appealing to Job to be consistent with the shared wisdom of the ages, the settled convictions of all morally serious and religious people, the great traditions of the wise.

But now a strange thing happens: "I want to tell you what happened to me, Job. I want to tell you about a message given specifically 'to me,' a supernatural message. It came to me 'stealthily,' secretly, in a 'whisper' so that I could scarcely discern it [v. 12]." It happened (v. 13) in what seems very close to a nightmare, "thoughts from visions of the night" (NASB, "disquieting thoughts from the visions of the night").[11] It happened in a "deep sleep" of the kind Abraham experienced in Genesis 15:12–21, a stupor induced by God himself, a time of complete human passivity, or so Eliphaz seems to imply. It was very frightening (v. 14). "Dread came upon me, and trembling, which made all my bones shake" (v. 14). This is like a horror movie. And then (v. 15) a breath, a wind, "a spirit [the words are the same] glided past my face; the hair of my flesh stood up." This is terrifying. We are in the presence of the numinous, of the supernatural world, of a world beyond our comprehension, of a scary dimension of the universe. And then, when our pulses are racing, "it stood still" (v. 16). You can feel the tension. "I could not recognize its appearance; a form loomed before my eyes. I heard a quiet voice" (v. 16 HCSB).

What an extraordinary buildup. And yet it is deeply ambiguous. Unlike the oracles given to some of the prophets in visions of the night, there is no clear indication of the source of this vision or of the one who speaks. Eliphaz may imply that this is supernatural and therefore authoritative, but the author of the book subverts that claim and makes us suspect that something less positive is going on here.[12]

Incidentally, it is fascinating to see how Eliphaz combines the traditions of wisdom with the experience of mysticism, although his mysticism seems frighteningly close to the occult.[13] Be that as it may, after this intense crescendo of anticipation, what does the voice say?

> Can mortal man be in the right before God?
> Can a man be pure before his Maker? (v. 17)

This is a remarkable anticlimax. We might have expected some specific revelation about Job and his secret sins or a heavenly revelation of the reason for his sufferings (perhaps an insight into the heavenly scenes of chapters 1, 2). Instead we get a general statement of a kind that would be the staple diet of the wisdom of Eliphaz's tradition!

There is a translation question here. The NIV translates the Hebrew very literally: "Can a mortal be *more* righteous than God? Can even a strong man be *more* pure than his Maker?" (v. 17). Although the word *min* is usually translated "more," it does seem to make better sense to follow the ESV here and take it in the sense of "before." It would be banal to suggest that anyone would assert that human beings could be more righteous or more pure than God. What is at issue is whether or not it is possible for human beings to be in right relationship with God, to stand before God clean and pure in his presence.[14]

And this is the critical question, which is echoed by Job's questions: ". . . how can a man be in the right before God?" (9:2) or "Who can bring a clean thing out of an unclean [i.e., a mortal]?" (14:4). It is raised again by Eliphaz later—"What is man, that he can be pure? Or he that is born of woman, that he can be righteous?" (15:14)—and by Bildad—"How then can man be in the right before God? How can he who is born of woman be pure?" (25:4). The implied answer from Eliphaz is, he cannot. There is no way that imperfect mortal human beings can stand clean and right in the presence of God. Nowhere on earth is there a man in the right with God. This is the answer of human religion.

But it is also the Satan's answer. The substance of the Satan's challenge in chapters 1, 2 is that no human being on earth is genuinely in the right with God. And so, quite unwittingly no doubt, and meaning well, Eliphaz becomes here the spokesman for the Satan.[15] This strange visionary word emanates not from the God of the Bible but from the enemy and the accuser of the brethren.

But we must let Eliphaz continue:

> Even in his servants he puts no trust,
>   and his angels he charges with error;
> how much more those who dwell in houses of clay,
>   whose foundation is in the dust,
>   who are crushed like the moth.
> Between morning and evening they are beaten to pieces;
>   they perish forever without anyone regarding it.
> Is not their tent-cord plucked up within them,
>   do they not die, and that without wisdom? (vv. 18–21)

Eliphaz backs up his implied answer of verse 17 by arguing that even the supernatural beings in the universe, the angels, are not clean in God's sight! How much more we mortals, whose bodies are "houses of clay," are fragile and transient (v. 19). We have our foundation from the dust; we are created from dissolved, incoherent material, fashioned temporarily into a system that is wonderful but has no inherent stability (Genesis 2:7).[16] It takes so little to crush us back to dust. We may be crushed as easily as you or I squash a moth (v. 19b).[17] We wake one morning full of hope and strength, but by evening we are dead, "beaten to pieces," well on the way to dissolution, going back to the dust from which we came[18] (v. 20). All over the world this happens to us. It is so common an occurrence that it is not newsworthy; no one notices (v. 20b). Our existence is as fragile as a tent;[19] it only takes someone to trip on the cord or pull it up, and the whole human being collapses into inanimate matter and decays back into the dust from which he or she came. Suddenly a whole miniature cosmos of activity, thought, and affections collapses into its constituent molecules.

"So be realistic, Job, about your and my mortality. We are mortal, God is immortal, and never the twain shall meet. You must be realistic about this."

Job 5:1–7 continues on this theme:

Call now; is there anyone who will answer you?
To which of the holy ones will you turn? (v. 1)

Eliphaz raises the question of whether there might be a supernatural, heavenly being who will mediate between unclean, dust-like mortals and the immortal God. He says this cannot be. Heaven is quite simply inaccessible to mortals. And yet in asking this, Eliphaz raises a question pregnant with hope for Job. He will later speak of "an arbiter" between him and God (9:33) and of a "witness . . . in heaven" who "testifies for me" (16:19). Elihu too will speak of "a mediator" (33:23).

Surely vexation kills the fool,
and jealousy slays the simple. (v. 2)

"So," says Eliphaz, "there is no point getting all hot and bothered about it all, and specifically about what has happened to you. That would be foolish, to be a hothead, impulsive." The word "jealousy" in verse 2b has the sense of an angry, vexed kicking against what has happened to one. These are "burning, angry emotions that motivate one to erratic behaviour."[20] "Don't be like that, Job," Eliphaz is saying, "for it would be foolish. And you and I (as wise men) know what happens to fools."

I have seen the fool taking root,
but suddenly I cursed his dwelling.
His children are far from safety;
they are crushed in the gate,
and there is no one to deliver them.

The hungry eat his harvest,
  and he takes it even out of thorns,
  and the thirsty pant after his wealth. (vv. 3–5)

Again Eliphaz appeals to his eyewitness experience. "I have seen what happens when fools, people who get hot and bothered about injustice in the world and that kind of thing, appear to be settled and secure. They don't stay that way for long." Verse 3b is unlikely to mean that Eliphaz wished a curse directly on the home of the fool (as the ESV implies). More likely it means either that he declared it to be cursed[21] (he said, as a wise man, that the fool would not last) or that he observed that the fool's home was cursed.[22]

Either way Eliphaz observes that bad things happen to people who get ideas above their station so far as God is concerned. "Be warned, Job, and don't be like that." Disaster comes to the fool. His children can't ever be safe (v. 4). They are "crushed in the gate" (v. 4), which means "crushed in court" (NIV), guilty, imprisoned, whether justly or not. They end up "crushed." And "the hungry" eat the fool's harvest so eagerly that they take every patch of grain, even in the thorn-infested parts on the edges of his fields (v. 5). His farm will be totally ravaged, as Job's has been. There may be a double meaning here; the expression "the hungry" may be a hint of death as "The Hungry One" consumes all his produce.[23] This is what happens to fools, who are unrealistic about being mortal and get ideas above themselves. It is also alarmingly like what happened to Job in 1:13–19.

For affliction does not come from the dust,
  nor does trouble sprout from the ground,
but man is born to trouble
  as the sparks fly upward. (vv. 6, 7)

Verses 6, 7 are not easy to read. They may mean (as in the ESV and NIV) that troubles don't just appear from nowhere (the ground) but are the result of human sinfulness. Just as sparks defy gravity and fly upward, so human sin leads to terrible sufferings, sufferings that were not what God originally intended for the world.

Alternatively, and I think more likely, the Hebrew word translated "not" in verse 6 may be revocalized to read "surely," so that verse 6 says, "For affliction does come from the dust, and trouble sprouts from the ground." The word "sparks" is literally "sons of Reshef," the god of destruction with his traditional arrows of trouble.[24] So the argument may be that human beings are born to trouble because the earth beneath us and the underworld beneath us send troubles upward to us.[25] Job's troubles are "chthonic,"[26] coming up from below the ground, and we just have to be realistic about that. We live in a world under the curse of God, a world of evil, a world in which the powers of the underworld are causing trouble for us all the time. That is just how it is, and only a fool rails against this and thinks he or she ought to have a "Get out of jail free" card to escape these troubles.

This warning not to get ideas above ourselves leads naturally to the third thing that Eliphaz says to Job.

Be Humble (5:8–16)

In verses 8–16 Eliphaz begins to give Job his clear advice. "If I were you,"[27] he says, "I would turn my face toward God and seek his face. I would trust in him. And I would not try to be too clever."

> As for me, I would seek God,
>   and to God would I commit my cause,
> who does great things and unsearchable,
>   marvelous things without number:
> he gives rain on the earth
>   and sends waters on the fields;
> he sets on high those who are lowly,
>   and those who mourn are lifted to safety. (vv. 8–11)

The God whom Eliphaz exhorts Job to seek is a beautiful and wonderful God in many ways. He is the God who gives water to enable crops to grow (v. 10); he is the God who lifts up humble and lowly people[28] (v. 11). But he is also the God we cannot understand (v. 9): he does many things, and we cannot search them out and understand them. So let's not try to be too clever and arrogantly think we can be wiser than God.

> He frustrates the devices of the crafty,
>   so that their hands achieve no success.
> He catches the wise in their own craftiness,
>   and the schemes of the wily are brought to a quick end.
> They meet with darkness in the daytime
>   and grope at noonday as in the night.
> But he saves the needy from the sword of their mouth
>   and from the hand of the mighty.
> So the poor have hope,
>   and injustice shuts her mouth. (vv. 12–16)

There are in the world all sorts of "crafty" people (v. 12), taking after the serpent of Genesis 3:1, full of schemes (what they plan to do with "their hands"). They think they can outthink God and be wiser than God. But God will always frustrate their schemes. Indeed (v. 13) "he catches the wise in their own craftiness"; this is the only saying from Job that is clearly quoted in the New Testament, by Paul in 1 Corinthians 3:19 (alongside a parallel quote from Psalm 94:11, ESV margin). It is perhaps surprising that Paul should quote as a true and authoritative statement something said by one of Job's comforters! And yet he does. And he does so because the statement is true; it is one of the many true things that Eliphaz and his two friends will say. God does trip up men and women who try to be too clever for their own good. Eliphaz thinks that Job is in danger of doing that, and so he warns him. "Don't do that," he says, "for the end for such people is that just when they think all is clear ["daytime . . . noonday"] they find they cannot understand what is happening at all, and they are walking in darkness [v. 14]. But, by contrast [vv. 15, 16] God reaches down to the humble who depend upon him and rescues them. So be humble, and don't try to be too clever."

Be Submissive (5:17–27)

Following his theme of humility, Eliphaz concludes with a moving and beautiful appeal to Job to submit himself to the loving disciplines of God.

> Behold, blessed is the one whom God reproves;
>   therefore despise not the discipline of the Almighty.
> For he wounds, but he binds up;
>   he shatters, but his hands heal.
> He will deliver you from six troubles;
>   in seven no evil shall touch you. (vv. 17–19)

The blessing pronounced by Eliphaz is the blessing echoed repeatedly in the book of Proverbs and reinforced by the letter to the Hebrews.[29] God disciplines those he loves for their own good. "This," Eliphaz implies, "is what God is doing with you, Job. I want to exhort you to believe that there is a blessing coming and to hold on to that in hope. Don't despair. For the God who disciplines will bind up your wounds and heal your brokenness [v. 18, very much as in Hosea 6:1 or Deuteronomy 32:39]. Even if you have six troubles or seven [the idiom speaks of completeness, the full range and entirety of human troubles], you will not finally be scarred by them but will be fully rescued."

He goes on to spell out some of the dimensions of those possible troubles.

In famine he will redeem you from death,
    and in war from the power of the sword.
You shall be hidden from the lash of the tongue,
    and shall not fear destruction when it comes. (vv. 20, 21)

Famine and siege warfare go together (v. 20), and then (v. 21) there is false accusation and threats ("the lash of the tongue") and "destruction." "God will hide you from these, as he did with Lot in the cave while Sodom and Gomorrah were destroyed, and as he did with Noah in the ark."

At destruction and famine you shall laugh,
    and shall not fear the beasts of the earth.
For you shall be in league with the stones of the field,
    and the beasts of the field shall be at peace with you.
You shall know that your tent is at peace,
    and you shall inspect your fold and miss nothing.
You shall know also that your offspring shall be many,
    and your descendants as the grass of the earth.
You shall come to your grave in ripe old age,
    like a sheaf gathered up in its season. (vv. 22–26)

Verses 22–26 give a lovely picture of the blessing of God, protecting his beloved from what we would call natural and supernatural disasters. "The stones of the field" in verse 23 are a way of speaking of agricultural troubles. In the song of Isaiah 5, the vineyard owner clears the vineyard of stones (Isaiah 5:2). In 2 Kings 3 covering fields with stones is a deliberate act of war (2 Kings 3:19, 25). So to be "in league with" (v. 23a; literally, to "have a covenant with") the stones is to be "at peace" with what we loosely call Nature, as a consequence of being at peace with God. It is what in Israel later would come to be associated with covenant blessings (e.g. Deuteronomy 27, 28).

In addition, there will be peace on the farm, in the family, and in one's own body. There will no farm animals missing (v. 24b); there will be many children and grandchildren (v. 25). All of this is beautiful to describe but must have come as a succession of cruel barbs into Job's heart. He has lost his farm, his animals, his offspring, and his health. None of these blessings are for him, or so it would seem.

There is an irony here, for Eliphaz encourages Job to fear God for exactly the reason the Satan said he had always feared God—for the rewards of piety rather than because God is God.[30]

Behold, this we have searched out; it is true.
    Hear, and know it for your good. (v. 27)

Eliphaz concludes with what he hopes is the steady reassuring voice of the experienced counselor. "These are not just my thoughts as a possibly idiosyncratic individual," he says. He uses the word "we," implying a widespread movement of wisdom stretching through the known world of the morally serious and religious. "We—and, Job, remember that you are (or were) one of us—we have searched out these truths of moral order with great care. They are true. So listen [v. 27b] and take this to heart, and it will do you good." Perhaps Eliphaz senses even at the start of the speeches that Job no longer has confidence in their system of wisdom, and he fears lest Job will prove to be a backslider from the wisdom of the world.[31] How right he will be proved to be!

What's Wrong with Eliphaz's Counsel?

It is a powerful, persuasive and in some ways beautiful sermon, is it not? "My friend Job, whom I love enough to travel with my friends to bring you sympathy and comfort, I want to bring you all the resources of comfort and wisdom known to the world of the morally upright and religious. You know these truths, for you have taught them to others many times. I want gently to encourage you to be consistent with your beliefs, to be realistic about our mortal condition, to be humble and not get ideas above yourself, and gladly to submit to the loving discipline of a good God."

What is wrong with exhorting Job to be consistent, realistic, humble, and submissive to God? What is wrong with preaching to him a sermon that is quoted with approval by the Apostle Paul?

The problem is that Job's experience is extreme. Job was much greater than is normal for human experience, and he was brought down much lower than is normal for human experience. Although we sometimes like to think we are like Job, we are not often like him at all. He was richer than we will ever be, greater, finer, and nobler. And he became poorer, much poorer, than we will ever be and was brought down into depths of destitution, multiple bereavement, and chronic, isolating sickness that we know only in part. Both his greatness and his fall speak of a suffering that will ultimately be fulfilled in one unique event in history. Only one human being in history was greater than Job, and only one human being suffered more intensely than he, and utterly without humanly justified cause. Job's sufferings are not the loving discipline of God. Job is not a morally upright man who has embraced ideas above his station. Job is a believer. Job is in the right before God ultimately by faith in the Christ who was to come, as was Abraham the patriarch.

So Job's experience can only begin to be comprehended in the light of the cross of Christ. When as Christians we suffer in part as Job suffered, we do so only as those who are in some strange way filling up what is lacking in the sufferings of Christ. Christian sufferings are in part a taking up of the cross, a sharing in unjust suffering, a participation in the sufferings of Christ in order that glory and honor may be brought to God on the day of Christ. Without the cross of Christ Job cannot be understood. This is Eliphaz's mistake. He and his friends will give us the best that the wisdom of the world can offer, the cream of the wisdom that comes from morality and human religion. But without the cross it makes no final sense.

Excursus: The Undeserved and Redemptive Sufferings of Christians

It is worth pausing to explore this idea of Christians filling up what is lacking in the sufferings of Christ. Let us begin by asking about the connection between sin and suffering. Suffering, which is an anticipation of death, is God's just penalty for sin—not necessarily individually but corporately (Romans 5:12). For the unbeliever, every suffering is a foretaste of final judgment and a warning of the horrors of Hell, to which they are heading if they do not repent. When some men asked Jesus about an atrocity, he warned without compromise that unless his hearers repented, these deaths were a foretaste of what they too would have to face (Luke 13:1–5).

But what about the believer? All the sins of the believer have been borne by the Savior; he has paid the penalty and has borne the wrath for every one of their sins, conscious and unconscious, past, present, and future. It follows, therefore, that no suffering of believers can possibly be a punishment for their sin. In the light of the cross, it is all undeserved. Of course we deserve it by nature, for by nature we are objects of God's wrath (Ephesians 2:3). However, we are no longer considered "by nature" but as objects of grace. Logically, therefore, we might expect that Christians ought never to suffer, and this is pretty much what the prosperity gospel teaches. Christ has taken upon himself not only our sin, this view says, but our illnesses and diseases (Matthew 8:17).

And yet Christians do suffer, and Paul makes so bold as to describe his own sufferings as "filling up what is lacking in Christ's afflictions for the sake of his body, that is, the church" (Colossians 1:24). We are to suffer with Christ if we hope to be glorified with him (Romans 8:17). There is in Christian discipleship a fellowship or sharing in Christ's sufferings and a becoming like Christ in his death (Philippians 3:10). All this is undeserved, for our sin is paid for and all its entailments covered by the cross. And yet it is necessary. Although our sufferings are not payments for anybody's sin (that was entirely covered by Christ), they are necessary and have the character of redemptive suffering in the sense that they are a part of God's redemptive plan to bring the gospel to a needy world. They are "for the sake of the elect" (2 Timothy 2:10). To understand this enables us both to see Job's sufferings as a foreshadowing of the ultimate sufferings of Christ and also to see them as continuing in the sufferings of Christians.

Ultimately any counsel that is devoid of the cross will be discouraging and hurtful. Eliphaz has kind intentions, but the impact of his counsel is deeply painful for Job. As Job listens to the blessings outlined by Eliphaz, it cannot escape his attention that he himself has been deprived of them all. Since the message of Eliphaz is a message of piety and religion rather than the gospel of grace, Job will be driven to despair if he believes it. Any message other than the gospel of the cross will ultimately lead suffering men and women to despair. Only the gospel of the cross can bring true comfort.

Eliphaz says that God "catches the wise in their own craftiness" (5:13). Paul agrees. But the point that Paul makes is that, paradoxically, those who are wise like Eliphaz are reaching beyond themselves. The wisdom of Eliphaz and his friends is turned into foolishness by God, and the foolish things that Job is going to say will, at the end of the day, be fraught with surprising gospel wisdom.

7

Job's First Reply to Eliphaz: The God-Forsaken Living Death

JOB 6, 7

SOME YEARS AGO an awesomely impressive sports car pulled up and parked right in front of my family. I think it was a Ferrari 355. It was the kind of car that makes you shiver with excitement. We waited with some interest to see what powerful and impressive human being would get out. Surely with such a fine car on the outside, the driver inside must be equally awesome. To our dismay a potbellied, balding, unshaven scruff of a man emerged and waddled away. That curious event was a kind of parable. The exterior may mask a very different reality inside.

We begin now the first of Job's eight speeches in these three cycles of speeches with his friends, fourteen whole chapters in our English Bibles (chapters 6 and 7, 9 and 10, 12—14, 16 and 17, 19, 21, 23 and 24, and 26). As we begin, we will see a deeply unimpressive exterior peeled back to reveal an interior of infinite value. We are going to watch as a true worshipper of God is revealed. We will see some surprising and paradoxical marks of the real believer unveiled. These marks will cut right across all human instincts about religion. These hallmarks of a true worshipper are utterly contradictory to what we might expect.

In chapter 5 of this commentary we did an introductory survey of Job's so-called "comforters," and then in chapter 6 we listened to the first and gentlest of their speeches. Now we feel the force of Job's first reply.

Sometimes in the council chamber of Heaven God looks down at the earth, points, and says, "Look at Carlos there: he's a real believer." Or "Look at Lakshmi there: she really worships me." The Satan is no longer in the heavenly council (as we saw earlier, pp. 55–56), but we can be sure that he calls up angrily from earth with the same riposte that he made when God pointed to Job: "Oh, you think so, do you, Lord? Well, I admit they do look a bit like believers on the outside. But I doubt very much if you'll find a real worshipper inside."

And God says of us, as he said of Job, "It is very important for the universe to know publicly and without doubt whether he or she is a real worshipper. So you can take away from her the externals, what she values, and then we'll see. Take away from her some precious relationship, frustrate some hope, inflict some pain, and then we'll all publicly see if she is a real worshipper. Face him with serious loss, strip away his security, dent his status, and then the real person will step out and we'll see."

That was the conversation of Job 1, 2. What is the only sure test by which the world will know who are real worshippers of the true God and who are just pretending? Answer: loss and suffering. The only sure test is to strip from worshippers something of value, and then we will see if they really worship the living God and bow down to him simply because he is God. Only when worship comes at a cost can we tell if it is true. Suffering is the fire that refines and reveals the heart of worship.

We see this again and again in church life when there is a cost to follow Christ. A Christian wants to marry a non-Christian, knowing it will be a union in which at the deepest level they will pull in opposite directions. It will cost to break the relationship off and worship God wholeheartedly. That is when true worship is revealed. It costs to be a Christian openly at school or college or in the office. Perhaps there will be a loss of face, a loss of prestige or reputation. It is loss that reveals the true worshipper and separates the fair-weather Christian from the true worshipper.

We are going to see in Job's speeches a true worshipper revealed. And we may be surprised by the hallmarks that mark him out as the real thing. To the visible eye Job is alone, scratching at his agonized skin, sitting on the rubbish dump outside the city gate (2:8). He has no status, no job, no family, and no hope. And yet we will see here, despised and rejected, outside the city wall, the pure gold of a real believer. In Shakespeare's words:

> Sweet are the uses of adversity,
> Which, like the toad, ugly and venomous,
> Wears yet a precious jewel in his head.[1]

We are going to see the precious jewel of real worship in the midst of ugliness and venom. And as we see this precious jewel unveiled, we will remember a later believer hanging naked outside the city wall, despised, rejected, and yet precious beyond compare.

So as we listen to the first of Job's side of the cycles of speeches we shift our focus away from the three comforters, so confident, so impressive—and so wrong. And we listen to Job in his laments, so pathetic, so poignant, so confused, so full of doubt—and so deeply right with God. These are rich and poignant speeches with much to teach us.

Structure

Job sometimes speaks to his friends and sometimes to God. It is not always easy to be sure which parts of his speeches are which. Sometimes it doesn't much matter. He speaks aloud for all to hear. But sometimes it is clear, especially when the Hebrew verbs are in the plural (addressing his three friends) or the singular (addressing God). In this speech he addresses his friends to start with, and then he directs his speech to God. So, for example, in 6:22–29 (or 30) he is clearly addressing his friends. And by 7:7 ("Remember" is singular) he is addressing God. Probably our chapter division marks the turn from the one to the other.

Job Pleads with His Friends (6:1–30)

Job's plea to his friends is in two parts. "I want you to understand," he says, "that the wrath of God is an unbearable pain [vv. 1–13] and that religion brings no comfort [vv. 14–30]."

The Wrath of God Is an Unbearable Pain (vv. 1–13)

In the first part of verses 1–13 Job begins with an exclamation (vv. 2, 3) and follows this with an explanation (v. 4) and then an illustration (vv. 5–7). The explanation (with three lines instead of the usual two) would seem to be the central point.

> Then Job answered and said: (v. 1)

Exclamation

> "Oh that my vexation were weighed,
>   and all my calamity laid in the balances!
> For then it would be heavier than the sand of the sea;
>   therefore my words have been rash. (vv. 2, 3)

Explanation

> For the arrows of the Almighty are in me;
>   my spirit drinks their poison;
>   the terrors of God are arrayed against me. (v. 4)

Illustration

> Does the wild donkey bray when he has grass,
>   or the ox low over his fodder?
> Can that which is tasteless be eaten without salt,
>   or is there any taste in the juice of the mallow?
> My appetite refuses to touch them;
>   they are as food that is loathsome to me." (vv. 5–7)

Exclamation (vv. 2, 3)

Eliphaz has said that "vexation" is the kind of angry speech that marks a man out as a fool and therefore condemns him to death (5:2). This is not the way wise people speak. Wise people have a clear and logical system by which to understand the cosmos. They don't get all hot and bothered by what they think is innocent suffering, because they know there is no such thing.

Job replies that his troubled, hot outburst (chapter 3), far from showing him to be a fool, is a natural and understandable response to the depth and weight of his misery. His speech reveals his misery, not his folly. The word translated "vexation" (6:1) is used of Hannah when cruelly provoked by Penninah in 1 Samuel 1:6; it is the anger that fuels her urgent prayer in 1 Samuel 1:16 (where she prays "out of my great anxiety and *vexation*"). It is a tiring anger that drains us of energy for living and can make us depressed, as in 17:7 where Job says, "My eye has grown dim from *vexation*." "I want you to grasp," says Job if we were to put it in modern terms, "that if you took the miserable unfairness that has caused my anger, if you could bottle up all the calamity that has befallen me, and if you were to put them on some machine that weighed human pain, you would find it 'heavier than the sand of the sea'" (6:3a). Sand is both literally and proverbially heavy. "A stone is heavy, and sand is weighty" (Proverbs 27:3). "If only you grasped the burden of my pain," says Job, "then you would know why I have cried out with such an extreme lament." The word translated "rash" (v. 3b) means something like "impetuous" or "wild." "The extremity of my words, far from revealing me to be a fool, opens up to the world the depth of my pain."

Explanation (v. 4)

This prepares us for verse 4, which gives the root reason why Job is hurting so deeply. "If you want to know the cause of my pain," he says, "it is not because I have lost my wealth; nor is it because my greatness and power have come to an end. It is not even because I have been terribly bereaved of my children. It is because the Almighty God, who controls everything that happens in the universe, has been firing poisoned arrows at me." In Psalm 91:5, 6 the image of an arrow is used in parallel with "the terror of the night," "the pestilence that stalks in darkness," and "the destruction [LXX, "demon"] that wastes at noonday." Just as in Greek mythology the arrows of Apollo sting and cause plagues, so it is with the Almighty God.

If there was an allusion to the Canaanite god Reshef in 5:7, the god of pestilence sometimes called "the Archer," then Job may be making a contrasting point here. "The arrows that have pierced through the 'skins' of my possessions, my family, and now my own body and health are not ultimately to be understood as arrows fired up from the underworld [the "sons of Reshef" of 5:7, flying upward]; they are the arrows fired down from Heaven by the Almighty God. The pain I experience is the burning sensation of poison from these arrows getting into the bloodstream of my heart and spirit. That is why it hurts so deeply."

Another way of describing these is to call them "the terrors of God," God's supernatural, demonic messengers, the harbingers of death and Sheol. The word translated "terrors" is only used here and in Psalm 88:16: "Your *wrath* has swept over me; your *dreadful assaults* destroy me," where the phrase "dreadful assaults" translates the same word translated "terrors" in Job 6:4.[2] Notice that in Psalm 88 these terrors are expressions of "your wrath." Job sees himself as experiencing the wrath of God, God's hot, settled anger against sinners. And that makes his life unbearable.

Illustration (vv. 5–7)

The illustration is easy enough to understand, but what does it illustrate? In verse 5 Job makes the commonplace point that an animal that is properly fed does not bellow and bray; it brays and bellows because it is not fed or is not fed an edible diet. In the same way Job's wild outburst, a kind of wild human bellowing, is because the diet he has been given is inedible. Verse 6 continues the picture of inedibility. If something is "tasteless," so bland as to be disgusting, it has to be made palatable with salt or spices. The expression translated "the juice of the mallow" in verse 6b is uncertain (as the ESV footnote observes).

Pope translates it "slimy cream cheese." Whatever it is, it is disgusting to think of eating it. This is why (v. 7) Job refuses to eat the diet that is set before him.

But to what is he referring? There are two possibilities. He may simply be using the metaphor of diet to refer to the terrible circumstances of his life, the diet God has set before him. But since he is speaking to his friends and will soon be explicitly rebuking them for their unhelpful speech, it seems more likely that the diet Job is referring to is the unpalatable words of his friends, exemplified so far by Eliphaz's first speech. All they have said, and will say, to him is no more than "insipid pious pap."[3]

We see the same imagery of words of comfort (or not) being compared to a diet in Psalm 69:20, 21:

> I looked for pity, but there was none,
>   and for comforters, but I found none.
> They gave me poison for food,
>   and for my thirst they gave me sour wine to drink.

This is a deeply suggestive parallel, for here we have another innocent sufferer being given, both literally (Matthew 27:34) and figuratively, a diet that was inedible.

The words used in Psalm 69 for "pity" and "comforters" are from the same roots as the words translated "sympathy" and "comfort" in 2:11. It is pity/sympathy and comfort that Job hopes for from his friends. Instead they give him an insipid explanation of what has happened. The point of Job's illustration, therefore, is that if his friends had given him a diet of true (edible) words of comfort, he would not be screaming in anguish. What is unbearable is to suffer the wrath of God and to be given neat religious explanations.

Job goes on to make a request (vv. 8, 9), give a reason (v. 10), and stress the urgency (vv. 11–13).

Request

> Oh that I might have my request,
>   and that God would fulfill my hope,
> that it would please God to crush me,
>   that he would let loose his hand and cut me off! (vv. 8, 9)

Reason

> This would be my comfort;
>   I would even exult in pain unsparing,
>   for I have not denied the words of the Holy One. (v. 10)

Urgency

> What is my strength, that I should wait?
>> And what is my end, that I should be patient?
> Is my strength the strength of stones, or is my flesh bronze?
> Have I any help in me,
>> when resource is driven from me? (vv. 11–13)

The Request (vv. 8, 9)

Job wanted to die in chapter 3. He counted himself among those "who rejoice exceedingly and are glad when they find the grave" (3:22). He still wants to die. This is his "request"; indeed, paradoxically, it is his "hope" (6:8). Eliphaz shallowly says that Job's integrity and piety ought to be his hope (4:6). But Job's cosmology is turned upside down. It is "a sufferer's cosmology"[4] in which bad things come from above and good things are to be hoped for in the place of the dead below. It does not occur to Job to take his own life, for he knows that life is God's to give and God's to take. He understands that the only reason he is still alive is that God has stayed his hand. So he longs that it would please God to "crush" him (v. 9), a violent word resonant with cruel beatings and trampling to death.[5] It speaks of a life turned back to dust. And yet Job will not be crushed to death. The sufferings of Job, terrible as they are, are but a foreshadowing of the sufferings of one who will be "*crushed* for our iniquities" (Isaiah 53:5). Job can think of nothing that will ease his pain except being crushed to death or, using a familiar Old Testament image, having the slender thread of his life snipped off from the loom of human existence ("cut me off," v. 9b).[6]

The Reason (v. 10)

The reason Job longs to die is surprising and revealing. Even in the midst of "pain unsparing" (v. 10b), if God takes his life soon, then he will have "comfort" (v. 10a). How so? He would die not having cursed God; he would have stayed faithful to God right to the point of death itself. "He would die knowing he had maintained his spiritual integrity."[7] Like a prisoner undergoing torture, he fears the moment he will break; he longs to die without betraying his faith in the goodness of God.[8]

In this motivation something of the heart of Job the believer is revealed. He longs for God to be honored by his life and by his death.

The Urgency (vv. 11–13)

As with a prisoner under torture, there is an urgency to Job's prayer. He is very weak. He knows he has so little physical strength, and with his physical weakness there is a psychological fragility. To hold on and not curse God he feels he will need to be as strong as a stone or as bronze, and he isn't. Here is the sense of verse 13: "Do I have the inner resources to help myself, now that all success has been denied me?"[9] That is, "There was a time when I could do things and succeed at them; I had those inner resources. But no longer. Now it is just a case of trying desperately to hang on to being faithful to God in desperate weakness. If only my suffering could come to an end."

The wrath of God brings an unbearable pain to the believer who hoped and trusted that God is good and gracious and whose experience seems to belie this conviction. It is because Job is a believer that he feels this pain so keenly.

Religion Brings No Comfort (vv. 14–30)

But Job has not finished speaking to his friends. In the rest of chapter 6 he berates them sadly for being deeply disappointing friends. Job states a responsibility, illustrates it, and makes a simple request.

A Responsibility

> He who withholds kindness from a friend
>   forsakes the fear of the Almighty.[10] (v. 14)

An Illustration: A Dry Wadi

> My brothers are treacherous as a torrent-bed,
>   as torrential streams that pass away,
> which are dark with ice,
>   and where the snow hides itself.
> When they melt, they disappear;
>   when it is hot, they vanish from their place.
> The caravans turn aside from their course;
>   they go up into the waste and perish.
> The caravans of Tema look,
>   the travelers of Sheba hope.
> They are ashamed because they were confident;
>   they come there and are disappointed.
> For you have now become nothing;
>   you see my calamity and are afraid. (vv. 15–21)

A Request: All I Ask Is Words and Love

Have I said, "Make me a gift"?
  Or, "From your wealth offer a bribe for me"?
Or, "Deliver me from the adversary's hand"?
  Or, "Redeem me from the hand of the ruthless"?
Teach me, and I will be silent;
  make me understand how I have gone astray.
How forceful are upright words!
  But what does reproof from you reprove?
Do you think that you can reprove words,
  when the speech of a despairing man is wind?
You would even cast lots over the fatherless,
  and bargain over your friend.
"But now, be pleased to look at me,
  for I will not lie to your face.
Please turn; let no injustice be done.
  Turn now; my vindication is at stake.
Is there any injustice on my tongue?
  Cannot my palate discern the cause of calamity? (vv. 22–30)

A Responsibility (v. 14)

"Kindness" here is *chesed*, covenant loyalty, sympathy, and love (v. 14). Friendship in the Old Testament carries with it a strong obligation, even a covenant, to show loyalty, especially when the friend is suffering (see our earlier discussion of Absalom and Hushai). Not to show such loyalty is a mark of impiety, of forsaking "the fear of the Almighty" (v. 14). Job implicitly accuses his three friends of failing to show him loyal sympathy and love.

An Illustration: A Dry Wadi (vv. 15–21)

He then illustrates what they have been to him with a vivid and sad picture. A desert wadi in the hills may (in certain climates) be filled with icy water from the melting snows from above in winter. But in the summer the wadi is bone-dry. Imagine a caravan of traders, perhaps from Tema, on the northwest Arabian trade route, or Sheba, in southwest Arabia (v. 19). As they journey, they find they are running out of water. Someone remembers that several miles off the trading route, up in the foothills, there was a flowing stream. Wearily they make the detour, using up their last supplies of water on the way. But when they get to the stream they find it parched and arid. So they "are ashamed" (v. 20), which does not mean they blush but that they are shown to be mistaken in their hopes. They were so "confident," but when they arrive they are "disappointed" and perish (v. 20).

"That's what you are like to me," says Job. "I had such high hopes when you arrived, three wise men who care for me. But 'you have now become nothing' (v. 21). Your words are empty and vacuous. Instead you look at the depth of my distress and 'are afraid' (v. 21), frightened by the terrible suffering you see before you."

A Request: All I Ask Is Words and Love (vv. 22–30)

In verses 22, 23 Job says that his hopes are not demanding or selfish; he has not asked them for money or actually to do anything. All he has hoped for is words that will unlock his perplexity and settle his anxiety (vv. 24–26). "Teach me," he pleads; "make me understand how I have gone astray" (v. 24). In other words, "Tell me where I have gone wrong because I cannot see that I have. Your words might hurt [v. 25a], but they will do me good in the end if they are true and 'upright' (v. 25). But the words you are speaking don't prove anything [v. 25b]." Verse 26 is not easy to understand. The sense is, "'Do you want to put right what I say and treat my despairing words as empty wind? You are not taking me seriously when you try to impose your simple system of religion on my pain."

He goes on, "You do not love me. I am just a pawn in your religious discussions [v. 27]; you are playing a game with me, rolling dice, tossing 'the problem of Job' to and fro as you sip your coffee in comfort. Please just look me in the face [v. 28] and listen to me; take me seriously. I am speaking the truth."

Why Are Job's Friends Such a Disappointment?

Job's friends are wise men in the eyes of the world. They appear to be well-motivated, coming to bring "sympathy and comfort" to Job (2:11). But they prove deeply disappointing, intensifying Job's pain rather than bringing life. They are like a dry wadi to a thirsty traveler.

The reason is that only the gospel of the cross ultimately makes sense of suffering. A world in which there is no such thing as redemptive suffering, suffering that brings glory to God, is a world in which there will be no comfort for the suffering believer. It is a world without grace, and in the end it is a world without love. Human philosophy and all human religions impose upon the human condition a framework of simple cause and effect in which there can be no such thing as suffering that simply and necessarily brings glory to God because it expresses the obedience of the believing heart that bows down to God simply because he is God. And yet it is precisely this obedience, the obedience of the one man (Romans 5:19), that will bring the redemption of the world. The sufferings of Job foreshadow the redemptive sufferings of Christ.

Job Protests to God (7:1–21)

In a hugely significant move Job now turns and addresses the God with whom he grapples. Always he has loved and feared God. He is a true believer. He has never doubted the sovereignty of God. He knows that the imprisoning "hedge" (3:23) has been put in place by God. But up until now he has not explicitly spoken *to* God. Now he does.

We may perhaps sum up Job's protest with a question and a plea. The question (vv. 1–10) is in essence, "Why do I matter?" The plea (vv. 11–21) is in essence, "Leave me alone!"

Why Do I Matter? (vv. 1–10)

> Has not man a hard service on earth,
>   and are not his days like the days of a hired hand?
> Like a slave who longs for the shadow,
>   and like a hired hand who looks for his wages,
> so I am allotted months of emptiness,
>   and nights of misery are apportioned to me.
> When I lie down I say, "When shall I arise?"
>   But the night is long,
>   and I am full of tossing till the dawn.
> My flesh is clothed with worms and dirt;
>   my skin hardens, then breaks out afresh.
> My days are swifter than a weaver's shuttle
>   and come to their end without hope.
>
> Remember that my life is a breath;
>   my eye will never again see good.
> The eye of him who sees me will behold me no more;
>   while your eyes are on me, I shall be gone.
> As the cloud fades and vanishes,
>   so he who goes down to Sheol does not come up;
> he returns no more to his house,
>   nor does his place know him anymore.

Job piles up vivid imagery to draw a portrait of his life under the sun—except there isn't much sun. This is Ecclesiastes on a rainy day.

In verses 1–3 Job compares himself to conscripted labor. The word translated "hard service" (v. 1) refers to military or conscripted slave labor such as Solomon used (1 Kings 5:13, 14). "A hired hand" was a poor domestic or agricultural worker, badly paid, in desperate need of each day's pay at the end of the day. We meet such persons in Jesus' parable of the laborers in the vineyard (Matthew 20:1–16). Such slaves long for "the shadow" (v. 2)—that is, the shadows of evening—because then there will be rest and payment of wages. In the same way Job longs for the shadow of death. In the meantime his life has no dignity, no rest, no joy, and no hope. And it goes on and on; he speaks of "months of emptiness" (v. 3). This is no short-lived crisis but enduring pain.

The reference to "nights of misery" at the end of verse 3 leads to the miserable picture of sleepless nights in verse 4. The night just seems so long, so desperately slow to pass; he tosses and turns, exhausted and longing for rest but unable to find it. The promise we now have in Psalm 127:2 that the Lord "gives to his beloved sleep" seems a cruel taunt to Job. He is disgusting even to himself (v. 5), his skin dirty, ulcers infested with maggots, alternating between dry hardness and filthy suppuration with no healing anywhere. The maggots or worms that infest Job's skin anticipate the worms that will eat his decaying flesh after his death; indeed, his life is a living death.

While the dark nights seem so slow, the days pass "swifter than a weaver's shuttle" (v. 6), which moves to and fro, to and fro too quickly to watch. The prime of Job's life is passing him by with no achievements, no delight, no relationships, no hope. Another birthday, another year of misery gone. This is one of the paradoxes of suffering, that it can be at the same time a slow pain and a fast running away of life itself. It is a life that is disordered in every way. Job feels that his existence is "nasty, poor, brutish and short" (Thomas Hobbes's famous phrase from *Leviathan*).

So in verses 7–10 he laments that he is an insignificant thing, a nonperson with a one-way ticket to nowhere. "Remember," he says implicitly to God (v. 7), that he is "a breath." When people thought in days past that Job was a man of substance, doing things that would endure, they were so wrong. He is like a "cloud" (v. 9), which may temporarily take a shape and appear to be something, as we sometimes see a cloud formation that looks like a city in the sky. But like the cloud, a breath of wind is all it takes to disperse him, and he fades away and vanishes.[11] He will go down "to Sheol," the place of the dead, and those who go there never return (v. 9). "Abandon hope, all ye who enter here."[12] He leaves "his house," his family, "his place" (v. 10) where he belongs and counts for something, his workplace, his neighborhood. He will leave one morning, and then he will die, and he will never ever return. The one we thought was significant and substantial turns out to be evanescent and transient, a breathy irrelevance and no more.

In verse 8a Job talks about "the eye of him who sees me"; in verse 8b it is clear that Job is not thinking generally but specifically of "your [i.e., God's] eyes" (v. 8). God is the one watching him. He will pick up this thought in the next passage. But the central idea in verses 1–10 seems to be that Job feels instinctively that he ought to matter, but everything about his sufferings suggests that he doesn't. His assumption, indeed his past conviction, is that he lived life in covenant relationship with the Almighty, whom he feared with loving reverence. And he believed that the Almighty looked on him with love. If this is so, Job deduces that he ought, as a human being in the image of God and a believer in relationship with God, to have a derivative significance. And he is right. When arguing with the Sadducees, who did not believe in resurrection, the Lord Jesus said that because God is "the God of Abraham, and the God of Isaac, and the God of Jacob" (Matthew 22:32), we ought to know that Abraham, Isaac, and Jacob are bound to have an enduring existence. No one who is in relationship with the eternal God can be transient.

And yet everything about Job's experience points to insignificance and transience. This is why he says in effect, "You will look for me, but I will not be here anymore" (v. 8b). Job is engaged in holy argumentation with God. "You, the eternal God, are watching over me, and yet I shall go to Sheol and never come back. Is this consistent with your power and your eternity? Surely this cannot be." This is the language of a believer.

Leave Me Alone! (vv. 11–21)

Because there seems to be no answer from Heaven, Job goes on to a desperate and paradoxical plea to be God-forsaken. He says to God in essence, "Leave me alone!"

> Therefore I will not restrain my mouth;
>   I will speak in the anguish of my spirit;
>   I will complain in the bitterness of my soul.
> Am I the sea, or a sea monster,
>   that you set a guard over me?
> When I say, "My bed will comfort me,
>   my couch will ease my complaint,"
> then you scare me with dreams
>   and terrify me with visions,
> so that I would choose strangling
>   and death rather than my bones.
> I loathe my life; I would not live forever.
>   Leave me alone, for my days are a breath.
> What is man, that you make so much of him,
>   and that you set your heart on him,
> visit him every morning

and test him every moment?
How long will you not look away from me,
    nor leave me alone till I swallow my spit?
If I sin, what do I do to you, you watcher of mankind?
    Why have you made me your mark?
    Why have I become a burden to you?
Why do you not pardon my transgression
    and take away my iniquity?
For now I shall lie in the earth;
    you will seek me, but I shall not be. (vv. 11–21)

Precisely because of this terrible tension between his convictions and his experience, Job must speak (v. 11): "Therefore I will not restrain my mouth"—as Eliphaz and the others wish he would—"I will speak in the anguish of my spirit; I will complain in the bitterness of my soul." He has spoken in 3:20 of "the bitter in soul." One of the strange signs of hope in Job is that he *must* speak. And it is precisely by speaking that Job is going to argue, cajole, and almost preach his way toward the truth.

He protests to God (v. 12) that he is not "the sea, or a sea monster." This seems a strange protest until we remember that in the stories the Canaanites and others told about the gods, Sea (Yam) was a hostile god, closely allied to The Sea Monster (Tannin, whom we have met as Leviathan in 3:8, and will meet again in chapter 41). Job is not referring to "the sea" in general or any old sea creature. He speaks of "*the* Sea" and "*the* Sea Monster" (NIV, "Am I the sea, or the monster of the deep?"). Job is protesting that the Almighty is attacking him as if he were the personification of supernatural evil, that the Almighty has "set a guard over" him as if he were a danger to the order of the cosmos (v. 12).

This sets the scene for the terrible picture of God that follows, as the hostile Watcher from whom Job cannot escape. God is to Job what Big Brother is to citizens in Orwell's *1984*; his cameras are everywhere, and his secret police are close behind. Even when Job does manage to get to sleep, he cannot escape (vv. 13–15). He goes to bed thinking he can get a moment's rest (v. 13), but God sends him nightmares (v. 14). The pressure is unbearable. Job would prefer to be strangled to death (v. 15); he loathes his life (v. 16a) and pleads with God, "Leave me alone, for my days are a breath" (v. 16b). He is but a breath, and he is choking for breath, and it hurts so much he would rather be strangled. "If I am as insignificant to you as I appear to be, why will you not leave me alone?"

Verses 17, 18 parody and turn upside down the wonderful positive theology we later find expressed in Psalm 8. "What is man?" asks David, and he answers that to be human, to be entrusted by God with dignity and responsibility over the world, is a wonderful thing. For Job it is the opposite: "What is man, that you make so much of him, and that you set your heart on him . . ." ("set your heart" has the sense of "pay him so much unwelcome attention," [v. 17]). "Why do you keep paying inspection visits to test me, always watching to find fault [v. 18]? Why won't you give me a moment's peace [v. 19], just looking away for long enough for me to swallow my spit?"

The burden of Job's protest is this: "If I am as insignificant as I appear to be, why do you pay me so much hostile attention?" So he says (v. 20), "If I sin, what do I do to you, you watcher of mankind?" "Sure, I sin. I am not perfect. But does my sin really justify this constant unrelenting 'hostile attention'?" Usually in the Bible God's watchful eye is a source of hope for those who trust in him. For example, in Psalm 33:18, 19 the psalmist rejoices:

> Behold, the eye of the LORD is on those who fear him [as Job does],
> on those who hope in his steadfast love,
> that he may deliver their soul from death
> and keep them alive in famine.

But for Job God's "eye" is a terrible thing. "Why are you to me like Big Brother, picking on me, making me 'your mark' (v. 20)? I feel like God's punching bag; it is as if he goes to the gym to practice hitting me." Or to put it another way, "I seem to be a terrible 'burden' (v. 20) to him, so that all God's time is taken up with watching me, guarding me, finding fault with me, striking me." It is all deeply sarcastic. "And anyway, why don't you forgive me (v. 21a)?" We must remember that Job is a penitent sinner who understands sacrifice, who believes in a God who forgives those who repent and believe. Job knows—and he is right—that he should not be punished for his sin since the sacrifices have taken away his sin. Or so he had been led to believe. Job is beginning to drive toward the truth that will be revealed in Jesus, that one day a man will fulfill the sufferings of Job; and when he does, he will suffer not for his own sins but for the sins of all who trust in him.

Job concludes (v. 21b) by echoing verse 8: "For now I shall lie in the earth; you will seek me, but I shall not be."

What Can We Learn from Job 6, 7?

We learn first that the wrath of God is an unbearable pain. Job is a believer; the deepest pain he endures is that it seems to him he has fallen under the judgment of God. And he discovers, as do we, that the kindest and most well-meant religious or philosophical counsel can ultimately provide no comfort. Only the truth of the cross can do that, for only the cross reveals redemptive suffering, and only the cross prepares believers to walk in the way of the cross, knowing that as they and we fill up in our bodies what is lacking in the sufferings of Christ, we are partners with God in ushering in the new heavens and new earth. That realization transforms suffering.

We learn also that honest grappling with the perplexities of the believer places him or her on the path to ultimate enlightenment. Eliphaz has a simple and logical system. He will never let the evidence get in the way of this system. In a cold way it provides him with a kind of reassurance. Job began with the same system, but he is learning that it is not true. And by honest belief grappling with this, he is on the path to truth.

The speech presses home to us also the power of words to heal or to harm. It is words of truth and grace that Job longs for from his friends. It is words of a religious system that they give him. The former would bring gospel comfort; the latter would deepen and sharpen his pain.

We learn also that Job's speeches give us a language of lament, as do the Psalms of lament. We need to know how to lament, how to put into words the pain of walking in the way of the cross. So long as we remember that Job's words become Christ's words before they are our words, and that they are only our words as men and women in Christ, we may appropriate them to put our pain into words.

8

Bildad's First Speech:
The System at Its Simplest

JOB 8

HUMAN BEINGS ARE HARDWIRED to think things ought to be fair. From the schoolchild indignant when the teacher punishes the wrong child to the soccer crowd furious at a referee's error in giving a red card, we know with passionate intensity that unfairness is rotten. We know things are not always fair, but we feel deeply that they ought to be. This instinct is testimony to the justice of God and undergirds the strong traditional conviction that God is just.

But what happens when this belief, along with divine sovereignty, is all there is to say about God? This is the worldview of Job's friends, the theological framework of Islam, and the understanding of most religions in which there is believed to be one, and only one, supreme God. It is certainly where Bildad stands.

Where Eliphaz was gentle and sensitive (chapters 4, 5), Bildad is already angry. After an angry expostulation, he gives Job a short, punchy speech built upon a simple axiom, following that with a negative and positive outworking of that axiom, supported by the evidence of tradition and illustrated vividly from the world of plant life, before concluding with a summary.

Then Bildad the Shuhite answered and said: (v. 1)

Expostulation

"How long will you say these things,
and the words of your mouth be a great wind?" (v. 2)

"How long?" asks Bildad. Chapters 6, 7 have been much too long for poor Bildad to listen to! Not because he has no stamina for discussions; indeed, he loves "wise" discussions, the seminars of the intellectual elite. It is too long because, as far as Bildad is concerned, Job's speech is stuff and nonsense, a lot of hot air. Job is a windbag. In 6:26 Job has accused his friends of treating his words as hot air; now Bildad confirms that is exactly what they think.

The reason Job is talking hot air, in their view, is because he begins from an utterly false starting point. So Bildad comes straight to the point.

Axiom: God Is Fair

> Does God pervert justice?
>   Or does the Almighty pervert the right? (v. 3)

Bildad's convictions are, in this regard, the same as those expressed famously in the song of Moses at the end of Deuteronomy:

> The Rock, his work is perfect,
>   for all his ways are justice.
> A God of faithfulness, and without iniquity,
>   just and upright is he. (Deuteronomy 32:4)

To "pervert justice" (v. 3) is to twist it, bend it, make it crooked, like a merchant using false weights (Amos 8:5: ". . . *deal deceitfully* with false balances"); it is to make crooked what ought to be straight. But, says Bildad, it ought to be an unquestioned axiom of religion and philosophy that God never does that. Not ever. So for Job to suggest that God has treated him unfairly is out of order.

So, says Bildad, let's see how this great truth works out in practice:

Outworking A—The Negative

> If your children have sinned against him,
>   he has delivered them into the hand of their transgression. (v. 4)

He begins with a terrible negative—"If your children have sinned . . ." (v. 4). Clearly the "if" here expresses no uncertainty.[1] It is clear that they must have sinned against God; that's why they died sudden and untimely deaths. Had the rest of the Bible already been written, Bildad might have also cited the deaths of Korah and his companions (Numbers 16) or Ananias and Sapphira (Acts 5:1–11). Bad things happen to bad people; and if a really bad thing happens to someone, it proves he or she is a bad person.

There is here not only a brutality of manner, speaking to a man whose children have perished in a day, there is also a riding roughshod over the history of Job's anxiety lest his children might have sinned and over his conscientious care in making sure their sin was covered by sacrifice (1:5). Bildad has no place in his system for sacrifice, because he has no place for redemptive suffering, and ultimately no place for the cross of Christ. For him it is a pretty simple system of double retribution—good things happen to good people, bad things to bad people.

Now Bildad turns to the positive:

Outworking B—The Positive

> If you will seek God
> > and plead with the Almighty for mercy,
> if you are pure and upright,
> > surely then he will rouse himself for you
> > and restore your rightful habitation.
> And though your beginning was small,
> > your latter days will be very great. (vv. 5–7)

Job is not yet dead, and that must mean that he has not done as bad things as his children—or so Bildad thinks. He must have done some bad things, but there is still a chance: "If you will seek God . . ." (v. 5). The word "seek" means literally "go early" (derived from the word for dawn) and carries a sense of urgency. This is an echo of 1:5, where Job did exactly this for his children. "Now you must go urgently to God," says Bildad, "'and plead with the Almighty for mercy' (v. 5). If you really can prove yourself 'pure and upright' [we know that Job is already "upright" from 1:1, 8; 2:3], then your 'habitation' (v. 6)—not only the skin of your body but the wider skins around your family and your property—will be restored." The expression "rightful habitation" may have a double meaning, both the habitation that will be rightfully Job's and also the habitation that is characterized by Job's righteousness.

Verse 7 is surprising: Job's beginnings were hardly "small," for he was "the greatest of all the people of the east" (1:3)! Perhaps by "your beginning" Bildad means the state Job is in now. In any case, if he turns back to God, Bildad says, there is a chance that he will be wonderfully restored. That's how Bildad's system works, with no grace and no redemptive suffering.

To buttress his case Bildad appeals to long tradition.

The Evidence of Tradition

> For inquire, please, of bygone ages,
> > and consider what the fathers have searched out.

> For we are but of yesterday and know nothing,
>> for our days on earth are a shadow.
> Will they not teach you and tell you
>> and utter words out of their understanding? (vv. 8–10)

Earlier Eliphaz claimed to have searched out The System, and he is sure it works (5:27), not least because his strange nightmare confirmed it (4:12–16). Bildad appeals to "bygone ages . . . the fathers" (that is, previous generations and ancestors [v. 8]). This is a sure and tested truth, for they "have searched [it] out" (v. 8). Besides, he says, how can we who live such a short time expect to reinvent truth (v. 9)? It is much safer (v. 10) to consult the unanimous tradition of moral and religious people down the ages. That's where we'll find "understanding" (v. 10).

The justice of God may indeed be discerned through our innate grasp of the created order. What cannot be found, except by revelation, are the truths of redemptive suffering and consequent grace.

In verses 11–19 Bildad develops his axiom by either one or two illustrations. Scholars differ about this. Some read verses 11–19 as one negative illustration. The problem with this is that verse 16 gives a thoroughly positive contrast to verse 15, as do verses 17, 18, and verse 19 seems to conclude on an ultimately positive note. So it seems better to take these verses as giving two complementary illustrations, shining light on both sides of the concluding truths of verses 20–22.[2]

Illustration A—The Negative

> Can papyrus grow where there is no marsh?
>> Can reeds flourish where there is no water?
> While yet in flower and not cut down,
>> they wither before any other plant.
> Such are the paths of all who forget God;
>> the hope of the godless shall perish.
> His confidence is severed,
>> and his trust is a spider's web.
> He leans against his house, but it does not stand;
>> he lays hold of it, but it does not endure. (vv. 11–15)

Here is the first plant (v. 11). The "reeds" from which "papyrus" is taken are common in Egypt. In a damp, swampy area with a warm climate, like the Nile, they grow quickly to between eight and ten feet.[3] They "flourish" just as the wicked may grow metaphorically tall and proud (v. 11). But take away their water supply and they die quickly (v. 12), an untimely death while still in full flower (just as happened with Job's children). Like the fool envisaged by Eliphaz in 5:3, their dwelling is suddenly cursed.

What do we learn from this lesson from nature? "Such are the paths of all who forget God" (v. 13). They have a short-lived "hope" but will perish suddenly (v. 13). Their grounds for "confidence" and "trust" are like leaning on "a spider's web" (v. 14); when the pressure is applied, the support collapses. They trust in their "house" (v. 15), perhaps their family, their career, or their possessions; but when they really have to look to these things to help in time of pressure, they cannot support them. We once had an old garden shed that had a rotten roof; put your weight on it, and it would crumble. This is similar to the one who puts his trust in human beings in Jeremiah's prophecy (Jeremiah 17:5, 6) or the wicked in Psalm 1.

Illustration B—The Positive

> He is a lush plant before the sun,
>> and his shoots spread over his garden.
> His roots entwine the stone heap;
>> he looks upon a house of stones.
> If he is destroyed from his place,
>> then it will deny him, saying, "I have never seen you."
> Behold, this is the joy of his way,
>> and out of the soil others will spring. (vv. 16–19)

But what of the second plant? "He"—that is, a second and very different plant—"is a lush plant" (v. 16a) even in the hot sunshine ("before the sun") because it has a source of water, like the godly in Psalm 1 or Jeremiah 17:7, 8. It has a vigorous life (v. 16b): "his shoots spread over his garden." He has "roots" that spread through piles of "stones" (v. 17). He may suffer setbacks (v. 18), so that "his place" doesn't know him anymore (v. 18); but ultimately his way is full of "joy" (v. 19), and fresh shoots will come forth in his place. This probably is a picture of the righteous. Job has experienced a setback (as in v. 18), but Bildad still hopes he can prove himself righteous and flourish in the end (as in v. 19).

Conclusion

> Behold, God will not reject a blameless man,
>> nor take the hand of evildoers.
> He will yet fill your mouth with laughter,
>> and your lips with shouting.
> Those who hate you will be clothed with shame,
>> and the tent of the wicked will be no more. (vv. 20–22)

Thus Bildad pulls it all together. You can be sure, he says to Job, both that "God will not reject a blameless man" (we remember that word being used repeatedly of Job in 1:1, 8; 2:3) and that he will not "take the hand of evildoers [i.e., bless them]" (v. 20). If Job takes Bildad's advice, his misery will soon be replaced by "laughter" and joyful "shouting," and his enemies "will be no more" (which is exactly what Job fears will happen to him, 7:8, 21).

It is a simple system, supported by many centuries of morally serious religious tradition. But is it true? That is the only question that matters. If it is true, there will be no undeserved suffering in the universe. And if there is no undeserved suffering, there can be no redemptive suffering, no sacrificial substitutionary suffering. And if there is no substitutionary suffering, there can be no grace. Ultimately the religious system to which Bildad subscribes is a system devoid of grace and therefore devoid of comfort. It is certainly no comfort to Job, who is, as we know, suffering because his patient faith will bring glory to God and not because he is being punished for his sins.

9

Job's First Reply to Bildad:
The Trouble-Maker Maker

JOB 9, 10

IT IS POSSIBLE to be wrong and to be right at the same time. God will say that Job has spoken rightly about him (42:7). And yet Job says a great many things about God that are not right. How are we to reconcile this apparent contradiction? When we listen to Job's speeches, we need to bear in mind the distinction between Job's perception and Job's heart. His heart is the heart of a believer, which is why the Lord commends and affirms him at the end. But his perceptions are partial and flawed. We hear in these speeches the honest grapplings of a real believer with a heart for God as he sees what he thought was a secure worldview crumble around him. This is why we will hear Job say some things that are plain wrong, and yet we hear him say them from a heart that is deeply right.

One of the big questions that begins to surface in Job's speeches is, can Job discern the character of God from the actions of God? Job sees and experiences the actions of God. He believes in the sovereignty of God. He therefore believes that when something happens, it happens because God makes it happen. The natural but, as we shall see, flawed conclusion is that because Job sees unfair things happen, God in his character is unjust.

So the question is, when bad things happen, who does them? This question of causation and agency takes us right back to the heavenly council chamber of chapters 1, 2. We gained there an insight into the true model for understanding the government of the world. This is neither polytheism nor a kind of divine tyrannical monism but rather a Sovereign God who governs the world through the intermediate agency of a number of supernatural forces ("the sons of God"), some of whom are evil. He uses evil to work out his purpose ultimately to defeat evil.

We see the tension inherent in this understanding in two revealing parallel accounts of the same Old Testament event. At some stage in his reign King David sinfully takes a census of the fighting men of Israel, a census that appears to be motivated by a desire for autonomy, to feel secure in his army rather than entrusting his safety to the Lord. So David does something evil. The question is, what supernatural power was at work to cause him to do it?

The answer is stated in two apparently contradictory ways. In the account of the books of Samuel we are told, "the anger of the LORD was kindled against Israel, and he [that is, the LORD] incited David against them, saying, 'Go, number Israel and Judah'" (2 Samuel 24:1). But when the same event is recorded later by the Chronicler, he puts it in a strikingly different way: "Then Satan stood against Israel and incited David to number Israel" (1 Chronicles 21:1). So, did the Lord incite David to do this or did Satan incite him to do this? The answer is, both but in different ways. The characteristic perspective of the writer of Samuel and Kings is that if something happens, it happens because God does it. This is Job's perspective. When the Chronicler says that Satan did it, he is not denying that the Lord did it. The Chronicler is not a dualist. He does not believe that Satan has an existence independent from the Lord or that he can exercise autonomy in his actions. But the Chronicler draws attention to the fact that this action is God's action by the agency of Satan. It is therefore God's action in a different way from some of God's other actions. If we may put it this way, some of God's actions express his character, while others are the outworking of his longer plan to deal with evil. When God acts in steadfast love and faithfulness, these actions express his character directly. But when evil things happen, God is acting through the agencies of evil powers, and the actions do not reveal his character. They are part of his grand plan to turn evil to good, to defeat evil, but they do not immediately reveal his character.

It is this distinction that Job does not yet grasp. We can hardly blame him. His grapplings with it all will help us as we too struggle to discern the character of God in a confused and disordered world.

Responding to Bildad and Eliphaz

Bildad has asserted in the strongest possible terms that God is absolutely and unfailingly fair. He never ever perverts justice (8:3); he will never reject a blameless person or bless wrongdoers (8:20). Although Eliphaz has (so far) not been as forthright as Bildad, he agrees. Innocent people never perish (4:7).

Until that terrible day when his troubles began (1:13, 14) Job would have agreed with them both. This was the traditional, unquestioned worldview of them all. God is God, and God is fair.

To Job this axiom no longer seems at all self-evident. Indeed all the evidence suggests to Job that it is false. In this speech Job begins by identifying what matters to him most; he goes on to outline problem after problem with achieving his longing; then he considers possible alternative strategies before closing with a series of anguished questions for God.

What Matters Most to Job Is Right Relationship with God (9:1–4)
Then Job answered and said:

> "Truly I know that it is so:
>   But how can a man be in the right before God?
> If one wished to contend with him,
>   one could not answer him once in a thousand times.
> He is wise in heart and mighty in strength
>   —who has hardened himself against him, and succeeded?"
>   (vv. 1–4)

Job surprises us by agreeing with Bildad: "Truly I know that it is so" (v. 2a). In view of what follows, we cannot conclude that Job really agrees with Bildad. It seems that he is saying something like "Ah, yes, I know The System. I know—or I always thought I knew—that it was true. But . . ." and it is the "but" where the rub lies.

"But how can a man [that is, a mere human being] be in the right before God?" (v. 2b). To "be in the right" is not sinless perfection, but being able to stand before God. It is what we call justification, to "get right with God" (MESSAGE), to have the legal status before God of a justified or acquitted person. Eliphaz, as the punch line of his eerie dream, hears a voice assuring him this cannot be: "Can mortal man be in the right before God?" (4:17). Of course not!

And yet—and we shall see this again and again in Job—it is this above all else for which Job longs. Job longs to stand justified before God more than he longs for his health, his wealth, or his family. Our deepest desires reveal the worship of our hearts. Job's deepest desire is to stand before God. Idolaters long most deeply for what their idols promise, whether it be success, comfort, fame, sexual satisfaction, whatever. But in his ragged desperation the deepest desire of Job's heart is revealed—he longs for God.

The problem is that he can see no way in which this could ever be possible. "If one wished to contend [the word "contend" speaks the language of the courtroom] with him, one could not answer him once in a thousand times" (v. 3).[1] This sheer impossibility of standing before God in court is the main burden of this speech.

It is impossible because God "is wise in heart" (that is, he has a deep wisdom) and "mighty in strength" (v. 4). The only other Old Testament use of the phrase "mighty in strength" is in Isaiah 40:26 (translated "strong in power" in the ESV). God is too strong and too inscrutable for us to stand any chance against him in court. So, as Job asks, "who has hardened himself against him [that is, stood up against him], and succeeded [that is, survived]?" It cannot be done.

So in this speech Job is going to face up to the impossibility of ever achieving the deepest longing of his heart.

Job's Big Problem Is the Arbitrary and Unjust Sovereignty of God (9:5–24)

While Bildad begins his argument with the axiom of God's justice and the assumed axiom of his sovereignty, Job builds his argument on divine sovereignty alone. If God is God, he asks, what can we learn?

He Causes Cosmic Disorder (9:5–10)

he who removes mountains, and they know it not,
    when he overturns them in his anger,
who shakes the earth out of its place,
    and its pillars tremble;
who commands the sun, and it does not rise;
    who seals up the stars;
who alone stretched out the heavens
    and trampled the waves of the sea;
who made the Bear and Orion,
    the Pleiades and the chambers of the south;
who does great things beyond searching out,
    and marvelous things beyond number. (vv. 5–10)

In verses 5–10 Job pours out a cascade of powerful imagery, in which creation language is turned upside down. Verses 5, 6 speak about the "mountains" and "pillars" of the earth. Traditionally these speak of a solidity in creation that extends not only to the physical order of the cosmos but to its moral order.[2] When unjust judges govern, "all the foundations of the earth are shaken" (Psalm 82:1–5). When Hannah is rejoicing in God's justice she sings, "The pillars of the earth are the Lord's, and on them he has set the world" (1 Samuel 2:8). God says, "When the earth totters, and all its inhabitants, it is I who keep steady its pillars" (Psalm 75:3). God "set the earth on its foundations," celebrates Psalm 104, "so that it should never be moved" (Psalm 104:5).

But as far as Job can see, God is the one who, far from keeping the moral order of the universe in place, actually initiates the moral earthquake that replaces order with disorder. This is exactly what has happened in Job's own life; a life of stability has been overturned. Cosmic disorder happens; so God must be the one who does it, if he is God. God is the Maker; but it seems to Job that he is a Maker of trouble, the Trouble-Maker.

In Job's experience, light has been replaced by darkness. So he says (v. 7) that God has told the sun *not* to rise and the stars *not* to shine (sealing them up, as if he were putting them in an envelope and sealing it), in precise contradiction to his good commands in Genesis 1. This echoes Job's lament in 3:4–9.

Yes, he is the sovereign Creator who "stretched out the heavens" (v. 8) and indeed who "trampled the waves of the sea" (which may perhaps have the sense of walking on the back of the god of chaos, Sea). He made the constellations in the heavens (v. 9).[3] He does "great things . . . marvelous things . . ." (v. 10). But among these things are evil, disordered things. He is powerful, but it is not clear to Job that he is good. So what hope can Job have of bringing such a wild, almost manic, disordered God into the order of a courtroom?

He Is Invisible and Elusive (9:11–13)

> Behold, he passes by me, and I see him not;
>   he moves on, but I do not perceive him.
> Behold, he snatches away; who can turn him back?
>   Who will say to him, "What are you doing?"
> God will not turn back his anger;
>   beneath him bowed the helpers of Rahab. (vv. 11–13)

But there is another problem. God is invisible. And to be invisible means to be elusive; it gives the invisible one power over the visible ones (as in many science fiction novels and movies, from H. G. Wells's *The Invisible Man* onward). "He can pass me by, move on, come close to me, do me harm (snatching away my possessions and my children), and I can't even see him. What chance have I to challenge such an elusive God? I am no match for him. Even 'the helpers of Rahab,' storybook monsters of evil, were no match for him.[4] And what is more, he seems to be treating me as one of the evil 'helpers of Rahab'; in the cosmic battle, he seems to think I am on the enemy's side."

He Is Too Strong for Me (9:14–20)

> How then can I answer him,
>> choosing my words with him?
> Though I am in the right, I cannot answer him;
>> I must appeal for mercy to my accuser.
> If I summoned him and he answered me,
>> I would not believe that he was listening to my voice.
> For he crushes me with a tempest
>> and multiplies my wounds without cause;
> he will not let me get my breath,
>> but fills me with bitterness.
> If it is a contest of strength, behold, he is mighty!
>> If it is a matter of justice, who can summon him?
> Though I am in the right, my own mouth would condemn me;
>> though I am blameless, he would prove me perverse. (vv. 14–20)

Job vividly portrays the absurdity of even thinking he might win a court case—*Job v. God*. It doesn't matter that Job is actually "in the right" (v. 15), which he is, as we know from 1:1; 1:8; 2:3. In this chaotic courtroom, might is right. He can't argue but can only beg for "mercy" (v. 15). "Even if God answered my subpoena [v. 16], I don't think he would bother actually listening to me. He would be more like a mugger or street fighter than a lawyer [vv. 17, 18]; he would knock the wind out of me so I had no 'breath' [or "spirit," which is the same word] (v. 18). Indeed he would crush me 'with a tempest' (v. 17) [the storm from which God does eventually speak in 38:1 and 40:6, where the ESV translates the same word as "whirlwind"]." To be in court against God would be like trying to make a rational speech facing a hurricane. And he would do all this "without cause" (v. 17b), with no moral justification. We, the readers, know that God has indeed said to the Satan that the enemy has incited God against Job "without reason" (2:3, same phrase). So this is true.

"I cannot face him because he is too strong [v. 19a] and cannot be summoned into court [v. 19b]. Even though I am in the right, in that terrible courtroom I would find myself admitting my guilt [v. 20a, "my own mouth would condemn me"], although my confession would be extracted under torture."

He Is Unjust (9:21–24)

> I am blameless; I regard not myself;
>> I loathe my life.
> It is all one; therefore I say,
>> "He destroys both the blameless and the wicked."
> When disaster brings sudden death,
>> he mocks at the calamity of the innocent.

The earth is given into the hand of the wicked;
   he covers the faces of its judges—
   if it is not he, who then is it? (vv. 21–24)

The climax of Job's phalanx of problems is that the wild, chaotic, elusive, mighty God is not fair. "I am blameless," says Job, and we know this is true (1:1, 8; 2:3). "I regard not myself" (v. 21) may mean "I am so distraught that I don't even know what I'm saying. I am beside myself with confusion and grief."

In verse 22 Job comes right out with a terrible accusation: "therefore I say, 'He destroys both the blameless and the wicked.'" This is in direct contradiction to what Bildad has so firmly asserted in chapter 8. Job is saying, "I am blameless, and yet he is destroying me." If we could prove this of a human judge, we would call for his resignation. Job is effectively calling for the resignation of God. "Shall not the Judge of all the earth do what is just?" asked Abraham (Genesis 18:25). Job wishes it were true, but he is reaching the conclusion that it is not.

He goes on (v. 23) to suppose that when a disaster brings "sudden death" to both blameless and wicked people alike (disasters are no respecters of virtue), God actually "mocks at the calamity of the innocent." There he is, laughing away in Heaven like some cruel tyrant. And it is happening all over the world: "The earth is given into the hand of the wicked" (v. 24)—a statement as true today as then. There is injustice everywhere. People with power to decide the destinies of others ("judges") do not judge justly. Their faces are covered; the idiom "covering the faces" speaks of distorting judgment, for example by bribes: "a bribe blinds the clear-sighted" (Exodus 23:8).

But when this happens, who is causing it? Answer: the sovereign God, for if something happens, he does it. "He covers the faces of its judges—if it is not he, who then is it?" (v. 24). This is a significant comment. Job knows there is something terribly wrong about saying that God actively brings injustice on earth. But if he is to hold on to the sovereignty of God, he cannot see what other conclusion he can reach. Who else can act sovereignly on earth?

It is a terrible thing that Job says, but we can see why he says it. From his viewpoint it is hard to see what else he can say. There is an honesty about him that is lacking in the comforters.

Three Possible Ways Out (9:25–35)

My days are swifter than a runner;
   they flee away; they see no good.
They go by like skiffs of reed,
   like an eagle swooping on the prey. (vv. 25, 26)

The prime of Job's life is running away from him, like an Olympic 100 meter runner (v. 25), like a paper-light boat made of papyrus skimming down a fast-flowing river (v. 26a), or like an eagle swooping with lightning speed on its prey (v. 26b). "Any second now my life will be gone." There is an urgency in Job's voice. "What am I to do?"

He comes up with three possible strategies.

Move On and Cheer Up (9:27–29)

> If I say, "I will forget my complaint,
>   I will put off my sad face, and be of good cheer,"
> I become afraid of all my suffering,
>   for I know you will not hold me innocent.
> I shall be condemned;
>   why then do I labor in vain? (vv. 27–29)

First, how about a bit of cheerful denial: "I will forget my complaint, I will put off my sad face, and be of good cheer" (v. 27). "Things have been bad. But I have moved through the stages of grieving, and now it is time to move on, cheer up, and look forward to a new day." That would be an entirely reasonable, indeed healthy movement for human grief. All of us do that eventually after suffering loss. Why can Job not do that? Because what he is suffering is not at root the loss of his possessions and his children; it is the judgment of God against sinners. If he pretends it is just human suffering, he will be in denial about the true nature of what he endures. "I become afraid of my suffering, for I know you will not hold me innocent. I shall be condemned . . ." (vv. 28, 29a). His suffering is deeper than a present-tense suffering. It is a present-tense suffering that is the harbinger of a future condemnation. So he concludes, "why then do I labor in vain?" (v. 29)—"why do I keep seeking to be in the right before God when there is no point and I am chasing after a dream that will never be realized?"

Wash Myself (9:30, 31)

> If I wash myself with snow
>   and cleanse my hands with lye,
> yet you will plunge me into a pit,
>   and my own clothes will abhor me. (vv. 30, 31)

Second, Job considers the pointlessness of making renewed efforts to make sure he really is clean, examining his conscience afresh, searching his heart for any secret sins that he can confess. The penitent King David prays, "Purge me with hyssop, and I shall be clean; wash me, and I shall be whiter than snow" (Psalm 51:7). Job may be echoing that kind of thought. To "wash myself with snow" cannot be literal, for snow will not wash any better than water on its own (Job 9:30); it is presumably an idiom meaning "wash myself so that I am as white as snow."

But Job is convinced that however clean he may be, God is determined to prove him dirty. "God is like some malicious enemy who will kidnap me after a shower and 'plunge me into a pit,'" the disgusting smelly pit being an image of the underworld (v. 31; as in 17:14; 33:18). "God will so tar me with the stench of death that 'my own clothes will abhor me' (v. 31). It is not just that I will feel terrible in my smelly clothes—my clothes will feel terrible to be clothing *me!*" If we ask Job how he knows this, he would answer that his sufferings prove that this is what God is doing.

So he reaches out for his final hope.

Find a Mediator (9:32–35)

> For he is not a man, as I am, that I might answer him,
>   that we should come to trial together.
> There is no arbiter between us,
>   who might lay his hand on us both.
> Let him take his rod away from me,
>   and let not dread of him terrify me.
> Then I would speak without fear of him,
>   for I am not so in myself. (vv. 32–35)

The root problem is that God "is not a man" (v. 32), not a mortal, not a human being. The problem is that he is the transcendent God. So there is no chance of a fair trial with equally-matched contestants. What Job really needs is an "arbiter" (v. 33), a mediator, someone "who might lay his hand on us both" to make sure they both keep the rules of the courtroom and justice is done (v. 33). Whether Job is lamenting the absence of a mediator or expressing a wish that there might be a mediator (NIV, "If only there were someone to mediate between us" [v. 33]), this is a deep longing of his heart. "There is no mediator, as far as I can see, but how I wish that there were." It is a "mediator between God and men" (1 Timothy 2:5) that Job so badly needs.[5] Once Job has raised this question of a mediator, "it cannot simply be left. It is here a forlorn wish, and after the next passages he slips back into near despair. But each time the impossible hope becomes stronger"[6] as he comes back to this hope in 16:21 and 19:23–27. Job's yearning for reconciliation with God shines brightly in this hope.[7]

Job longs for God to "take his rod [of punishment] away," so that Job need no longer be terrified (v. 34) and will be able to "speak without fear of him" (v. 35a). At the moment he cannot do this ("for I am not so in myself" means something like "as things stand, there is no way I can do it" [v. 35 MESSAGE]).

Four Agonized Questions for God (10:1–22)

In chapter 10 Job asks four agonized questions to the God he longs to see.

Why Are You against Me? (10:1–3)

> I loathe my life;
> I will give free utterance to my complaint;
>   I will speak in the bitterness of my soul.
> I will say to God, Do not condemn me;
>   let me know why you contend against me.
> Does it seem good to you to oppress,
>   to despise the work of your hands
>   and favor the designs of the wicked? (vv. 1–3)

Please "let me know why you contend against me" (v. 2b). "Why have you set yourself against me?" It seems clear to Job that God is against him, but he cannot understand why. In verse 3 he calls himself "the work of your hands"; he will develop this theme in verses 8–16.

Why Do You Watch Me? (10:4–7)

> Have you eyes of flesh?
>   Do you see as man sees?
> Are your days as the days of man,
>   or your years as a man's years,
> that you seek out my iniquity
>   and search for my sin,
> although you know that I am not guilty,
>   and there is none to deliver out of your hand? (vv. 4–7)

At the end of chapter 7 Job has accused God of being a hostile surveillance watcher (7:17–21). He comes back to this now. Verses 4, 5 make the point that God is not human and doesn't have eyes that only see the exterior (v. 4) and have limited time for action (v. 5). If God were human, then Job could understand how he might need to look carefully at Job to assess what kind of person he really is. He could understand how a human might need to "seek out my iniquity and search for my sin" (v. 6). "But you are not human, and 'you know' perfectly well 'that I am not guilty'; furthermore, you know that you have absolute power over me—'there is none to deliver out of your hand' [v. 7]. So it seems both unnecessary and unfair for you to treat me like this."

Why Did You Create Me? (10:8–17)

> Your hands fashioned and made me,
>> and now you have destroyed me altogether.
> Remember that you have made me like clay;
>> and will you return me to the dust?
> Did you not pour me out like milk
>> and curdle me like cheese?
> You clothed me with skin and flesh,
>> and knit me together with bones and sinews.
> You have granted me life and steadfast love,
>> and your care has preserved my spirit.
> Yet these things you hid in your heart;
>> I know that this was your purpose.
> If I sin, you watch me
>> and do not acquit me of my iniquity.
> If I am guilty, woe to me!
>> If I am in the right, I cannot lift up my head,
> for I am filled with disgrace
>> and look on my affliction.
> And were my head lifted up, you would hunt me like a lion
>> and again work wonders against me.
> You renew your witnesses against me
>> and increase your vexation toward me;
>> you bring fresh troops against me. (vv. 8–17)

In verses 8–17 Job comes back to being "the work of your hands" (v. 3). It is at the same time a beautiful and a pathetic passage. In verses 8, 9 he pictures the hands of God (the personal intimate action of God) carefully putting him together, as he did with Adam (Genesis 2:7), taking incoherent disconnected matter ("dust") and organizing it into a living organism of wonderful complexity. "What is the point of making me," asks Job, "if you only did it to 'destroy me altogether' (v. 8), to 'return me to the dust'(v. 9)?"

Verses 10, 11 are a vivid and moving poetic picture of the creative action of God. Just as liquid milk can be made to curdle and turn into cheese, so the semen and ovum can be, as it were, curdled into a living being and then "clothed . . . with skin and flesh" (v. 11) on the outside and "knit . . . together with bones and sinews" on the inside. What a wonderful creative act is each conception, gestation, and birth![8]

Verse 12 presses this further. Not only did God knit Job together, but further "You have granted me life and steadfast love [*chesed*]," and his provi-

dential "care has preserved my spirit." All this was in the past. But not now.
"Now," says Job in the bitterness of his soul, "I realize why you did all this
["this was your purpose," v. 13b]. All this time you gave the appearance of
a loving Creator, but 'you hid in your heart' [v. 13b] the cruel intentions that
are now being worked out in my life. Now 'you watch me' [v. 14], you deem
me guilty, and you will not forgive. You are an implacable foe. 'If I am guilty,
woe to me!' [v. 15a]. But I am not. I am in the right. I am a genuine believer.
But still 'I cannot lift up my head' [v. 15b] with dignity, for my suffering tells
the world that I am a guilty sinner. 'I am filled with disgrace' [v. 15c] for all
to see. And I have no hope of escape. Even if, by some miracle I were to lift
up my head, you would hunt me down and crush me again [v. 16]."

Verse 17 is the climax. God does three things. First, he renews his witnesses against Job (v. 17a). Every suffering is a testimony to the wisdom of
the watching world that Job is a sinner. Every fresh disaster says, "This man
is under the judgment of God." Second, he increases his "vexation" (that is
to say, his anger) against Job (v. 17b). Far from being slow to anger, God is
quick to anger and implacable in his anger. Third, he brings wave upon wave
of "fresh troops" against Job (v. 17c). Like a siege army sweeping through a
breach in Job's skin or wall, God pours in trouble upon trouble.

Why Don't You Kill Me? (10:18–22)

> Why did you bring me out from the womb?
>   Would that I had died before any eye had seen me
> and were as though I had not been,
>   carried from the womb to the grave.
> Are not my days few?
>   Then cease, and leave me alone, that I may find a little cheer
> before I go—and I shall not return—
>   to the land of darkness and deep shadow,
> the land of gloom like thick darkness,
>   like deep shadow without any order,
>   where light is as thick darkness. (vv. 18–22)

So Job comes back to his lament of chapter 3 and asks, "Why don't you
just kill me? Why did I have to be born and be born alive? Why could I not
have been stillborn? Then at least I could be still and at peace. Just leave me
alone for a moment's peace [v. 20], for very soon I shall go 'to the land of
darkness and deep shadow, the land of gloom like thick darkness, like deep
shadow without any order, where light is as thick as darkness' [vv. 21, 22]."
Job piles up anti-creation themes. His world has been disordered by God, and

he feels himself heading to a land "without any order" (v. 22). But life on earth is so terrible that he feels he can hardly get there quickly enough.

And yet deep in his heart the question "why?" is addressed to the God who seems such a monster. And in that question and that address there lies hope. Whatever Job says, the fact that he says it to God and says it with such vehemence suggests that he knows he has not reached the end of his quest for meaning. There is in Job the inner energy of faith, the mark of a real believer. Job may be wrong in his perception of God and of the reality of his situation, but he is deeply right in his heart and the direction of his turning and his yearning. Thank God for that.

10

Zophar's First Speech:
The Cruelty of the System

JOB 11

ONE OF THE MOST frightening things about Job's comforters is how beautiful their speeches are (at times) and how very close they are to the kinds of things we often say to one another in our churches. Jesus' strongest words were reserved for the Pharisees, perhaps because, to the casual observer, they were the most like him and most easily confused with him. In the same way we need to be warned most forcefully against Job's comforters because they are so like us.

We love to hear Paul exclaim, "Oh, the depth of the riches and wisdom and knowledge of God! How unsearchable are his judgments and how inscrutable his ways!" (Romans 11:33). What a wonderful thing to say and how beautifully expressed! But Zophar says something similar when he says that the deep things of God's wisdom and the limits of his power extend higher than Heaven, deeper than Sheol, further than the earth, and wider than the sea (Job 11:7–9). We love to hear Jesus promise us life in all its fullness (John 10:10). And yet Zophar offers Job something not dissimilar in verses 15–19 of this speech.

So what is going on? After all, God says that Zophar has "not spoken . . . what is right" about him (42:7). Are we to conclude that Paul and the Lord Jesus have not spoken rightly? Surely not! When we hear a teacher or preacher speaking words that sound right, how are we to tell if he is a Paul or a Zophar? The same concepts and remarkably similar words may have different implications and alternative meanings depending on the contexts in which they are spoken.

Let us bear this in mind as we listen to Zophar in his first contribution to the debates. He begins with a cruel accusation against Job, continues with a barbed challenge, and concludes with a deceptive offer.

A Cruel Accusation (vv. 1–6)

Then Zophar the Naamathite answered and said:

> "Should a multitude of words go unanswered,
>   and a man full of talk be judged right?
> Should your babble silence men,
>   and when you mock, shall no one shame you?
> For you say, 'My doctrine is pure,
>   and I am clean in God's eyes.'
> But oh, that God would speak
>   and open his lips to you,
> and that he would tell you the secrets of wisdom!
>   For he is manifold in understanding.
> Know then that God exacts of you less than your guilt deserves."
>   (vv. 1–6)

In verses 2, 3 Zophar essentially says in four ways, "You ought to shut up and listen to me!" He describes Job's speeches as "a multitude of words," with the sense that although there are lots of them, they don't have much substance (v. 2). He describes Job as "a man full of talk," a verbose man, a glib, empty-headed man who likes the sound of his own voice much too much (an endemic danger for preachers) (v. 2). He calls Job's talk "babble" (v. 3) or empty chatter, much as Paul does of the false teachers in Ephesus (2 Timothy 2:16). He lines Job up with those who "mock," (Job 11:3). Augustine said that ultimately there are only mockers (of God) and praisers (of God). Some of what Job has said about God and to God amounts to mockery and insult. We may think particularly of when Job says that God "destroys both the blameless and the wicked" (9:22).

It is, thinks Zophar, outrageous that Job should get away with saying these things. He must not and cannot have the last word; if he reduces the others to silence, then he is presumed to have won his case. So these words must not "go unanswered . . . be judged right . . . silence men" (vv. 2, 3). Somebody must "shame" Job (v. 3) into admitting he is wrong, and Zophar thinks he is the man to do it!

There are two parts to Zophar's accusation. The first is in verse 4: "For you say, 'My doctrine is pure, and I am clean in God's eyes.'" Actually that is not what Job says. Far from claiming that his "doctrine" (what he says about

God) is "pure," Job is the first to admit that his thinking is in a state of great confusion. Zophar treats statements like 9:22 as if they were the calm and rational conclusion of a heretic's doctrinal statement rather than the agonized thoughts of a desperate man. And Job does not claim to be "clean in God's eyes." He claims to be "blameless," which indeed we know him to be, but the two are not the same. To be "clean" suggests sinless perfection, whereas to be "blameless" means to have integrity, to be genuine, to be the same on the inside as appears on the outside. Zophar accuses Job of being a Pharisee when in fact he merely claims to be a believer.

Eliphaz says that Job may call for all he is worth, but no one will answer (5:1). Zophar wishes someone would answer. He wants God to answer, and he is pretty confident as to what God would say—"the secrets of wisdom" because God "is manifold in understanding"(vv. 5, 6). The word translated "manifold" is literally "twofold" (NIV, "true wisdom has two sides"), but the sense seems to be that God's understanding is full or total, as opposed to Job's partial grasp of reality. Pope suggests that "twofold" may suggest a revealed side of God's wisdom discernible in creation and a hidden side that God keeps to himself.

But verse 6c gives us the telltale sentence. This is the second part of Zophar's accusation: "Know then that God exacts of you less than your guilt deserves" (v. 6). That is, "I want you to grasp that making you go bankrupt, killing your household and farm servants, killing your children, and destroying your health—all that is only paying you back for a part of your unforgiven sin. It would have been much worse had God paid you for it all." While it is hard to imagine what could have been worse for Job (in this life), this telltale statement reveals both a cruelty and an arrogance in Zophar. It is, of course, a deeply cruel thing to say to a man in extremis. But it is also arrogant. It is all very well for Zophar to say that God's wisdom is secret and "manifold" and to imply that Job cannot grasp it all; both of those statements are true. But this final line shows that however secret God's wisdom may be, Zophar is pretty confident that *he* knows what it all means! This arrogance colors what would otherwise be a beautiful description of God's wisdom in verses 7–9.

A Barbed Challenge (vv. 7–12)

> Can you find out the deep things of God?
>> Can you find out the limit of the Almighty?
> It is higher than heaven—what can you do?
>> Deeper than Sheol—what can you know?
> Its measure is longer than the earth
>> and broader than the sea.

> If he passes through and imprisons
> and summons the court, who can turn him back?
> For he knows worthless men;
> when he sees iniquity, will he not consider it?
> But a stupid man will get understanding
> when a wild donkey's colt is born a man! (vv. 7–12)

Verse 7 speaks of "the deep things of God" and "the limit of the Almighty." If the first of these designates the heart or center of God, the second points to the outer limits of his authority and power. Between them they speak eloquently of the fullness of Godhead. This fullness is "higher than heaven," "deeper than Sheol," "longer than the earth," and "broader than the sea" (vv. 8, 9). In all the dimensions of the cosmos, God fills all in all. So the challenge to Job is that he cannot hope to "do" (v. 8a) or "know" (v. 8b) enough; that is, he cannot hope to know in such a way as to be able to act on his knowledge, to have the kind of knowledge that is power (as in our expression "knowledge is power").

This would be a beautiful and appropriate challenge if Zophar applied it to himself as well. But it is clear that he does not. In verses 10–12 he speaks of God "passing through" (that is, passing by, coming by) and then putting someone in prison and calling together a courtroom (v. 10). When he does that, no one can or ought to challenge him because "he knows worthless men" (v. 11); that is, he can see into the heart of a man and detect when someone is empty and valueless. So "when he sees iniquity" (v. 11) in someone, he will act, he will imprison, he will summon the court for sentencing. The implication is simple: Job is the "worthless" man; God has come along and imprisoned Job and is about to sentence him. To challenge God's knowledge and judgment is stupid; it is the kind of incorrigible stupidity that is inherent in the fool, in the way wild animality is inherent in "a wild donkey's colt" (v. 12). Zophar is sure that when God arrested Job and imprisoned him, he knew what he was doing. Zophar says to Job not only "You don't understand God" but also "You need to grasp that I, Zophar, do understand God!"

But we must let Zophar continue. Since he is so sure he understands God, he is confident in making Job an offer on God's behalf. The offer is simple and runs as follows.

A Deceptive Offer (vv. 13–20)

The offer begins with a condition to be satisfied (vv. 13, 14), continues with a description of the blessings offered (vv. 15–19), and concludes with a word of warning (v. 20), should Job not fulfill the conditions.

If you prepare your heart,
> you will stretch out your hands toward him.

If iniquity is in your hand, put it far away,
> and let not injustice dwell in your tents.

Surely then you will lift up your face without blemish;
> you will be secure and will not fear.

You will forget your misery;
> you will remember it as waters that have passed away.

And your life will be brighter than the noonday;
> its darkness will be like the morning.

And you will feel secure, because there is hope;
> you will look around and take your rest in security.

You will lie down, and none will make you afraid;
> many will court your favor.

But the eyes of the wicked will fail;
> all way of escape will be lost to them,
> and their hope is to breathe their last. (vv. 13–20)

The condition is simple: repent and pray. In verse 13a to "prepare your heart" means to turn the heart. The same idiom is used in 1 Samuel 7:3: "If you are returning to the LORD with all your heart . . ." To "stretch out your hands" (v. 13b) means to pray. So Job is to repent in his heart and to express this repentance in prayer for forgiveness. Verse 14 emphasizes the repentance. When Zophar says, "*If* iniquity is in your hand" he implies that it is. Job is to turn away from his sin. The words "iniquity" and "injustice" in this context suggest sins like acquiring property through wrongdoing, extortion, and other sins of which Zophar suspects Job. So Job is to repent of the sin that he has presumably been keeping secret until now.

The incentive is beautifully described in verses 15–19. The man who cannot lift up his head at the moment (10:15) will lift up his face spotless, innocent, dignified. He will be safe and free from the paralyzing fear of God's judgment that is Job's experience now. Sure, he has been miserable, but he will look back on that "misery" as water under the bridge (in our idiom) or as a torrent that flooded for a while but has now passed (11:16). The darkness of his life (so vivid in chapter 3) will be changed into light (much as in Psalm 37:6 or Isaiah 58:10) (v. 17). Insecurity and restlessness will be replaced by safety and "hope" (v. 18). At the moment when he "lies down" to sleep he is afflicted by nightmares (7:13, 14), but then he will "lie down" in peace (v. 19a) and be restored to dignity and a great place in society (11:19b).

All of which does happen to Job at the end of the book. There are two problems with what Zophar says, however. The first is that Job has no secret sins of which he needs to repent, so Zophar's counsel is irrelevant to him. The second—and this one is even more serious—is that the motivation Zophar gives to Job for repentance is precisely the motivation of the Satan's accusation. The Satan thinks that Job has only been pious *in order that* his piety will win him prosperity. If Job repents *in order to* regain these blessings, he will prove the Satan right![1]

But then, according to Zophar, if he doesn't repent, worse is in store for him. Verse 20 piles up three terrible pictures. First, his "eyes" will grow dim, a vivid picture of the loss of vision and joy that accompanies approaching death. Second, he will have no "escape" from the judgment of God, which will be his terrible and inescapable fate. Third, his "hope" will, paradoxically, be just a dying wheeze or the last gasp of a dying man.

What a terrifying end to Zophar's speech, addressed (as we know) to a blameless believer facing the loss of his greatness, the destruction of his property, the death of his children, and the breakdown of his health! Here is what happens when partial and distorted "truth" is applied with arrogant confidence by those who ought to know better—or ought to know that they do not know what they think they know. Let us take great care not to be like Zophar!

By contrast, H. H. Rowley writes:

> By insisting that there is such a thing as innocent suffering the author of Job is bringing a message of the first importance to the sufferer. The hardest part of his suffering need not be the feeling that he is deserted by God, or the fear that all men may regard him as cast out from God's presence. If his suffering may be innocent it may not spell isolation from God, and when he most needs the sustaining presence of God he may still have it.[2]

11

Job's First Reply to Zophar: A Longing for Resurrection

JOB 12—14

WE CONTINUE OUR STUDY of the book of Job with a look at Job's next reply.

Why Are We Told What Job Does Not Know?

One of the most significant features of the book of Job is that from beginning to end we, the readers, know something that Job, the main human
character, does not know. Twice in chapters 1, 2 we are given a divine prophetic insight into what has happened in Heaven. We know what God has
said to the Satan, what the Satan has said to God, and what God has decreed
for Job. We know that Job's sufferings are not because he is an impenitent
sinner but precisely because he is a real and faithful believer. We know that
Job is not the story of everyman but the story of the faithful and obedient
believer. We know that the sufferings of Job are in some strange and deep
way necessary for the glory of God and the well-being of the universe. But
Job knows none of these things.

So the question is, why are we told what we are told, and what are we to
learn from the drama? For what purpose are we, the readers, privileged as Job
was not? Presumably the book is not just told for us to enjoy as spectators,
watching from the comfort of our armchairs. I think there are at least two
answers to these questions. First, we gain from the sufferings of Job a deep
insight into the sufferings of Jesus Christ. The Gospels are quite sparing in
what they tell us of the inner workings of Jesus' heart and soul. We know that
his soul was sometimes troubled (e.g., John 12:27), that he shrank from the
darkness of the cross in horror (e.g., Luke 22:39–46), and that he felt the pain

of living in a godless world ("O faithless and twisted generation, how long am I to be with you?" Matthew 17:17). We know from the Psalms of lament (perhaps especially Psalms 22 and 69) something of the horror of the wrath of God. But the speeches of Job give us a unique insight into what it feels like for a believer to experience God-forsakenness. And therefore they help us to understand and feel the darkness of the cross.

But I think there is a second reason. We are naturally prone to keep slipping into not knowing what we know. We know, because God has told us, that there is such a thing as undeserved and redemptive suffering, and that as believers walk in the footsteps of Jesus and the shadow of the cross we too are called upon to suffer. We know that as forgiven sinners none of our sufferings are God's punishment for our sins, for that has already been paid. We know that some of our sufferings are God's loving fatherly discipline for those he loves. But we also know that some of our sufferings are the filling out of what was lacking in the sufferings of Jesus, undeserved and with no disciplinary purpose. We know these things because God has told us.

But because our hearts shrink from this darkness, we naturally forget that we know these things and behave as if we do not know them. We slip into a practical not knowing of what we know. The System of the comforters is the default assumption of all of us if we are morally serious. We naturally expect blessing for godliness and grief for sin. An immersion in the speeches of Job will help us really and deeply to know what we know, to remember that our default system is not true, and so to prepare us for the realities of discipleship.

Summary of Job 12—14

Job 12—14 is by far the longest of all Job's speeches to his comforters. It brings to a close the first cycle of speeches. In it we shall see Job make significant progress. He speaks first to his friends (12:1—13:19[1]) and then to God (13:20 onward).

To his friends he clarifies in his own mind that The System of thought that he and they have shared in the past does not work. It is cruel (12:1–6), shallow (12:7–12), tame (12:13–25), and deceitful (13:1–12). As a result, Job resolves that he must take his case to God himself (13:13–19).

And so he does. He expresses his deep longing to deal with God (13:20–22) but recognizes that the problem of sin (13:23–27), with consequent mortality (13:28—14:6) and death (14:7–12), must be overcome by resurrection (14:13–17) if his search is not to end in despair (14:18–22).

Job Rebukes His Friends (12:1—13:19)

Although formally Job is replying to Zophar (who spoke in chapter 11), practically he is replying to his friends with his reflections on what all three of them have said thus far. What he says here is a wide-ranging and comprehensive exposé of the bankruptcy of The System. It was a system that Job himself had shared, along with religious and morally-serious people of all ages. But it is a system he now sees to be a failure.

The System Is Cruel (12:1–6)

The first feature of The System that Job identifies is its cruelty.

> Then Job answered and said:
>
>> "No doubt you are the people,
>>   and wisdom will die with you.
>> But I have understanding as well as you;
>>   I am not inferior to you.
>>   Who does not know such things as these?
>> I am a laughingstock to my friends;
>>   I, who called to God and he answered me,
>>   a just and blameless man, am a laughingstock.
>> In the thought of one who is at ease there is contempt for misfortune;
>>   it is ready for those whose feet slip.
>> The tents of robbers are at peace,
>>   and those who provoke God are secure,
>>   who bring their god in their hand." (vv. 1–6)

There is heavy and bitter irony in verse 2. The word used for "the people" denoted the upper class, the landed nobility, the kind of people who really matter in the world's eyes.[2] "Oh," says Job, "I have not the slightest doubt that you are the only really significant people in the world, and I'm really worried that when you die, there will be no wisdom left in the world because you are the only really wise people (or so you seem to think)!"

Zophar has implied that Job must be a fool (11:12), but (12:3) Job insists that he is just as well qualified in wisdom and "understanding" as they are. He is not in the least "inferior." He knows The System as well as they do. "Who does not know such things as these? You haven't told me anything I didn't already know. But here's the problem [v. 4]: I 'called to God and he answered me'—I was in right relation with him, so he heard my prayers. I am a just and blameless man [like Noah in Genesis 6:9]. But I have become 'a laughingstock,' the object of mockery."

Why? Verse 5 answers this. Those who are "at ease" (everything is going well for them) despise those who are suffering misfortune because, according to The System, misfortune "is ready for those whose feet slip," that is, for sinners. Misfortune is evidence of unforgiven sin. So when others suffer misfortune, we despise them; their misfortune exposes their sin. This attitude goes deeper than Shakespeare's "He jests at scars that never felt a wound."[3] It is more like "They despise those with scars, for their scars evidence their rottenness." The NIV makes this connection explicit: 'Those who are at ease have contempt for misfortune *as the fate of* those whose feet are slipping."

"But," says Job essentially in verse 6, "the reality is that while I, a just and blameless man, am despised by those who follow The System, all the while robbers and ungodly people 'are at peace' and 'secure'" (v. 6). Something doesn't fit.[4]

So The System cruelly mocks and despises those who suffer misfortune, for according to The System this misfortune necessarily proves the despicable character of the sufferers.

The System Is Shallow (12:7–12)

It would seem that in verses 7–12 Job is quoting or parodying what his friends had said, or would have said, to him. The pronouns "you" in verses 7, 8 are singular, suggesting that these words were addressed to Job rather than to his three friends.[5] If this is correct, then Job's parody shows up the shallowness of The System.

> But ask the beasts, and they will teach you;
>   the birds of the heavens, and they will tell you;
> or the bushes of the earth, and they will teach you;
>   and the fish of the sea will declare to you.
> Who among all these does not know
>   that the hand of the LORD has done this?
> In his hand is the life of every living thing
>   and the breath of all mankind.
> Does not the ear test words
>   as the palate tastes food?
> Wisdom is with the aged,
>   and understanding in length of days. (vv. 7–12)

"You say to me," says Job, "that even subrational creatures like wild beasts, birds, and fish know that what has happened to me is God's doing [vv. 7–9]. Just pay attention to them, you say again and again, 'and they will teach you' [notice the repetition of this clause]. We know this because he holds all living creatures in his hand [v. 10]. We have the wise discernment to 'test words,' just as a good tongue can taste food [v. 11]; we know when words are right and when they are wrong. After all, we are senior people ('the aged' having 'length of days' [v. 12]); we have been around for a long time, and what we say is in line with the traditions of the elders. It's obvious we are right."

In putting it so trivially Job exposes the shallowness of The System and its complete inadequacy in the face of the realities of what has happened to Job.

So The System is cruel and shallow. Even worse, it is tame.

The System Is Tame (12:13–25)

The theme of verses 13–25 is God's wild sovereignty. As Job understands it, "the God he has encountered is no placid governor of a universe of order" but is "inapprehensible and untameable."[6] In fact, he is positively dangerous. "From what I have seen of God's activity," says Job, "there can be no tame, systematic (as in your system) assurance that moral order will be upheld. Far from it."

Job paints a vivid picture of this scary God by reference first to natural disasters (vv. 13–15), then to leaders (vv. 16–21), and finally to nations (vv. 22–25).

> With God are wisdom and might;
>   he has counsel and understanding.
> If he tears down, none can rebuild;
>   if he shuts a man in, none can open.
> If he withholds the waters, they dry up;
>   if he sends them out, they overwhelm the land. (vv. 13–15)

The combination of "wisdom and might" (v. 13) includes both knowing what to do and having the power to do it. Both of these lie "with God" and not at all with human beings. But what does God do? Often, says Job, he "tears down" and "shuts a man in" (v. 14)—in a prison, as he has with Job in his grief. He is a destructive god, the god of "nature red in tooth and claw," as Tennyson put it, the god of the tsunami. Think about water, says Job. Sometimes he gives too little, and there is drought (v. 15a); at other times there is too much, and we have floods (v. 15b). Far from being the God of a reliable natural order, he is the god of natural disasters. Job's friends' system could not account for that.

And then what about the fate of great human leaders?

> With him are strength and sound wisdom;
>   the deceived and the deceiver are his.
> He leads counselors away stripped,
>   and judges he makes fools.
> He looses the bonds of kings
>   and binds a waistcloth on their hips.
> He leads priests away stripped
>   and overthrows the mighty.
> He deprives of speech those who are trusted
>   and takes away the discernment of the elders.
> He pours contempt on princes
>   and loosens the belt of the strong. (vv. 16–21)

Verse 16 begins similarly to verse 13: "With God are wisdom and might . . . With him are strength and sound wisdom." What follows is a catalog of the undoing of human power and wisdom. In verse 17 the "counselors" or "judges" are wise ministers of state, like Ahithophel with David. They are "stripped" naked of their mental powers and are made into fools. This is the fate of human traditional wisdom like that of Job's "comforters." In verse 18 kings may have put "bonds" on people, but God undoes the power of the kings, releases their prisoners, and "binds a waistcloth [or possibly a captive's belt] on their hips." He undoes the order of human power. It is the same with religious leaders (v. 19a, " priests") and with all human power (v. 19b). But it is especially true of human attempts at wisdom (v. 20): trusted counselors, senior wise leaders, are rendered speechless by the sheer arbitrariness of what this dangerous god does.

And what he does with leaders, he does with peoples:

> He uncovers the deeps out of darkness
>   and brings deep darkness to light.
> He makes nations great, and he destroys them;
>   he enlarges nations, and leads them away.
> He takes away understanding from the chiefs of the people of the earth
>   and makes them wander in a trackless waste.
> They grope in the dark without light,
>   and he makes them stagger like a drunken man. (vv. 22–25)

To "uncover the deeps out of darkness" (v. 22) is to bring evil and chaos into an ordered world. God does this with nations (v. 23); he plays with them, raising them up and casting them down. He "enlarges" their borders in great empires, and then he "leads them away" (v. 23) into exile (as happened later with Israel under David and Solomon and then to exiles in Assyria and Babylon). And in verses 24, 25 we again see this emphasis on God's blinding human wisdom. He "takes away understanding"; he makes people "wander in a trackless waste" (the word "trackless" indicates that they have no clue where they are or where they are going). They "grope in the dark without light" and "stagger" as if they were drunk. This god is wild and dangerous. He is dangerous in nature, dangerous with leaders, dangerous with nations, and especially dangerous to all human beings who think—as Job's friends did with their system—that they have the universe sorted out and have attained wisdom. "In short," says Job, "your system is tame and cannot cope with the real God who is dangerous."

Not only is The System cruel, shallow, and tame—it is also deceitful. It misrepresents God.

The System Is Deceitful (13:1–12)

> Behold, my eye has seen all this,
>   my ear has heard and understood it.
> What you know, I also know;
>   I am not inferior to you.
> But I would speak to the Almighty,
>   and I desire to argue my case with God.
> As for you, you whitewash with lies;
>   worthless physicians are you all.
> Oh that you would keep silent,
>   and it would be your wisdom!
> Hear now my argument
>   and listen to the pleadings of my lips.
> Will you speak falsely for God
>   and speak deceitfully for him?
> Will you show partiality toward him?
>   Will you plead the case for God?
> Will it be well with you when he searches you out?
>   Or can you deceive him, as one deceives a man?
> He will surely rebuke you
>   if in secret you show partiality.
> Will not his majesty terrify you,
>   and the dread of him fall upon you?
> Your maxims are proverbs of ashes;
>   your defenses are defenses of clay. (vv. 1–12)

Job essentially says in verses 1, 2, "What I am talking about (the wildness of God) is from eyewitness evidence. I have 'seen all this,' and not only in my own life. Furthermore, I know The System [v. 2] as well as you do. And I know The System doesn't work. Which is why 'I would speak to the Almighty, and I desire to argue my case with God' [v. 3]." This is a very important decision by Job, one he comes back to in verses 13–19.

But before he does, he has one last thing to say about The System: it is not true. "'You 'whitewash with lies' [v. 4a], painting over the messy reality of the world with a shallow coat of systematic white paint to make it look tidy. You are 'worthless physicians' [v. 4]; your medicine for my condition is at best a placebo and at worst something that makes my condition harsher. It is certainly not the gospel medicine I need. So I wish you would just shut up; that is the nearest you will get to wisdom [v. 5]!" This reminds us of the fool who is counted as wise if he remains silent (Proverbs 17:28). "I wish you would shut up and really listen to me [v. 6]. But instead you 'speak falsely for God and speak deceitfully for him' [v. 7]. You claim to be standing up for God, but you do so without truth. Indeed you show favoritism ['partiality'] toward God [v. 8], doing your best to paint him in a good [read systematic or tidy] light.

"But ironically God himself doesn't want you to do that. When God finds you have been using untruth to make him look good, he will be angry with you [vv. 9–11]. It's not me who's in danger from God, it is you! When you are confronted by the real 'majesty' of this untamable God, you will be terrified [v. 11], and your system will be no defense at all. In summary all your supposedly wise 'maxims' and 'defenses' (that is, defenses of God) are utterly worthless, like burnt-out ashes or useless clay [v. 12]."

In response to a system that is cruel, shallow, tame, and deceitful, Job reaches his conclusion: "I must take my case to God."

I Must Take My Case to God (13:13–19)

> Let me have silence, and I will speak,
>> and let come on me what may.
> Why should I take my flesh in my teeth
>> and put my life in my hand?
> Though he slay me, I will hope in him;
>> yet I will argue my ways to his face.
> This will be my salvation,
>> that the godless shall not come before him.
> Keep listening to my words,
>> and let my declaration be in your ears.
> Behold, I have prepared my case;
>> I know that I shall be in the right.
> Who is there who will contend with me?
>> For then I would be silent and die. (vv. 13–19)

Job knows that what he is about to do is deeply dangerous (v. 13): "Let me have silence"—that is, silence from the three friends—"and I will speak" to God himself (cf. v. 3: "But I would speak to the Almighty . . ."), "and let come on me what may" (v. 13). "I am going to take the risk of addressing this dangerous God. In doing so 'I take my flesh in my teeth [which may mean something like "I bite my tongue" to brace myself for danger[7]] and put my life in my hand' [v. 14]." In our contemporary idiom, this means "I take my life in my hands."

Job goes on in essence, "God may kill me, but even if he does, I must put my hope in him [v. 15a].[8] I know that godless people cannot stand in his presence and live [v. 16b, "shall not come before him"], and I know in my heart that I am not godless; so I believe that this dangerous gamble (as it must seem to others) will pay off and 'be my salvation' [v. 16a]." The expression "this will be my salvation" (v. 16) may lie behind Paul's saying, "this will turn out for my deliverance" in Philippians 1:19 (this phrase in verse 16 in the Greek of the Septuagint is identical to the text in Philippians 1:19).

In verses 17–19 Job prepares to make a public appeal to the Almighty. But he wants his friends to continue to listen (v. 17). He has thought hard about this (v. 18a) and is confident that he will be vindicated as a true believer (v. 18b). If not, then he would shut up and abandon all hope (v. 19).

Job is about to do something hugely significant. It is worth pausing to ask why. After all, he knows it is dangerous. The System of his friends tells him he must be a secret sinner because he is suffering. He knows this is not true. The evidence of his eyes tells him that God is dangerous, random, and unpredictable. The faith in his heart tells him that God is righteous and that he, Job, is a believer who is in the right before God. Knowing The System is not true, and despite the evidence of randomness and danger, Job's decision goes with Job's faith. This is why he appeals to God.

Job Pleads with God (13:20—14:17)

Job's comforters are (momentarily) silenced and listen as Job takes his life in his hands and speaks to God.

Job Longs to Deal with God Himself (13:20–22)

> Only grant me two things,
>   then I will not hide myself from your face:
> withdraw your hand far from me,
>   and let not dread of you terrify me.
> Then call, and I will answer;
>   or let me speak, and you reply to me. (vv. 20–22)

He pleads two closely related requests. First, he asks the dangerous Almighty to "withdraw your hand far from me, and let not dread of you terrify me" (v. 21). Job pleads for a brief pause in his misery. His grief and pain is so deep that he is paralyzed and weakened by it. If only God will take away his hand of judgment for a moment, then Job could speak.

And then, second, "call, and I will answer; or let me speak, and you reply to me" (v. 22). Like Esther with the Persian king, Job longs for the golden scepter of God's grace to be extended to him. Job longs to enter the dwelling place of God and speak face-to-face. This longing to speak with the God who is responsible for all Job's loss and misery (of this Job has no doubt) is very remarkable. It is a sign of faith that Job in his heart of hearts so loves this God that he must speak with him.

And yet the moment Job says this, he is deeply aware of the problem, which he expounds in sequence.

Job Recognizes That Sin Is the Root Problem (13:23–27)

> How many are my iniquities and my sins?
>   Make me know my transgression and my sin.
> Why do you hide your face
>   and count me as your enemy?
> Will you frighten a driven leaf
>   and pursue dry chaff?
> For you write bitter things against me
>   and make me inherit the iniquities of my youth.
> You put my feet in the stocks
>   and watch all my paths;
>   you set a limit for the soles of my feet. (vv. 23–27)

Job knows that at the root of his pain lies not mortality but sin. He piles up the words—"iniquities . . . sins . . . transgression . . . sin" (v. 23). Sin in all its variety and depravity is the heart of Job's problem, as it is the heart of all human problems. God is treating Job as an unforgiven sinner, and Job wants to know in detail and in all its enormity what exactly the problem is: "How many . . . Make me know . . ." God is hiding his face of favor from Job and is treating Job as a sinner under wrath, as his "enemy" (v. 24). Job is like a dry "leaf" blowing around in an autumn gale or a piece of "dry chaff" tossed to and fro in the wind (v. 25), because God is writing down in his book of judgment "bitter things against [him]" (v. 26a). Indeed, these bitter things include "the iniquities of my youth" (v. 26b). Job feels he is being treated as a sinner whose guilt has been piling up ever since childhood; now he is entering into the terrible inheritance of sin. God has put his feet in the stocks (v. 27a, exposing him to public disgrace), watching his paths (like a prisoner doing forced labor), and imprisoning him (v. 27c), so that his feet cannot walk free. All this is because of his sins.

And yet Job thought those sins had been covered by sacrifice (1:4, 5). He thought he was in the right with God, a blameless believer. He cannot now understand what is going on.

What is more, sin leads to mortality.

Job Feels Deeply the Misery of Mortality, the Result of Sin (13:28—14:6)

> Man wastes away like a rotten thing,
>   like a garment that is moth-eaten.
> Man who is born of a woman
>   is few of days and full of trouble.
> He comes out like a flower and withers;
>   he flees like a shadow and continues not.
> And do you open your eyes on such a one
>   and bring me into judgment with you?
> Who can bring a clean thing out of an unclean?
>   There is not one.
> Since his days are determined,
>   and the number of his months is with you,
>   and you have appointed his limits that he cannot pass,
> look away from him and leave him alone,
>   that he may enjoy, like a hired hand, his day. (13:28—14:6)

These verses pile up vivid images of the misery and transience of mortality. "Man who is born of woman" (14:1) mortal man, man who inherits the original sin of Adam, conceived in sin (Psalm 51:5), is like (1) some organic material going rotten (13:28a), (2) a moth-eaten piece of clothing (13:28b), (3) a short-lived flower (14:2a), and (4) a fleeting shadow (14:2b). A piece of fresh fruit, a new piece of clothing, a fresh flower, and a sharp shadow all seem so definite; but in a moment they are gone. Perhaps there is a progression from things that last slightly longer to things that last almost no time at all (the shadow is most fleeting of all). Ironically man is "few of days and full of trouble," with a terrible concentration of troubles squeezed into the short years of his life on earth (v. 1). Writing toward the end of World War II, the German Lutheran pastor Helmut Thielicke wrote:

> Goethe . . . once said in his old age that he could hardly think that he had been really happy for more than a month in his whole life. And I believe that proportion would hold true in history as a whole: the happy times are like tiny islands in an ocean of blood and tears. The history of the world, taken as a whole, is a story of war, deeply marked with the hoofprints of the apocalyptic horseman. It is the story of humanity without a Father—*so it seems.*[9]

Job would have agreed.

What hope is there, asks Job, for such a rotting creature to stand clean before God (vv. 3,4)? He is so transient (v. 5), with his lifespan so tightly defined according to God's decision, that the best he can hope for is some brief respite from pain (v. 6), like a tea break for "a hired hand" (v. 26). Unless sin is dealt with, human beings can hope for no better than this. Here is a healthy realism about the human problem and the human predicament.

But worse is to come: mortality leads to death.

Job Feels Despair in the Face of Death, the Entailment of Sin (14:7–12)

> For there is hope for a tree,
>> if it be cut down, that it will sprout again,
>> and that its shoots will not cease.
> Though its root grow old in the earth,
>> and its stump die in the soil,
> yet at the scent of water it will bud
>> and put out branches like a young plant.
> But a man dies and is laid low;
>> man breathes his last, and where is he?
> As waters fail from a lake
>> and a river wastes away and dries up,
> so a man lies down and rises not again;
>> till the heavens are no more he will not awake
>> or be roused out of his sleep. (vv. 7–12)

The theme of this section is the finality of death, which is the end of mortality and the entailment of sin. In vivid imagery Job speaks of a tree (vv. 7–9) when it is cut down. Think of a beautiful tall tree, perhaps a Californian redwood. Then see, in your mind's eye, lumberjacks cutting it down. Down it falls, and that's the end of it. Except that it isn't. Even after a long time, if the conditions are right, "it will bud and put out branches like a young plant" (v. 9). As long as its roots are intact, there is hope for it. But for man there is no such hope (v. 10). When a man is cut down, he is destroyed root and branch (in our idiom). He "breathes his last," and there is no more hope for him (v. 10). Like a lake or riverbed going permanently dry (v. 11), there is no hope for him—ever (v. 12): "so a man lies down and rises not again; till the heavens are no more he will not awake or be roused out of his sleep."

If sin is not dealt with, mortality leads to death; and death really is the end of life (and hope and light) on earth. Job is utterly realistic about this. Which is why he hopes against hope for a resurrection that will prove that sin is dealt with and forgiven.

Job Longs for Resurrection to Prove That Sin Is Dealt with (14:13–17)

Job now contradicts what he has just said. He has just contrasted a dead human being with a cut-down tree. Now he ventures to hope that a dead human being may in fact have a hope for the future. Deep down he knows that only resurrection can be the answer to the human condition.

> Oh that you would hide me in Sheol,
> > that you would conceal me until your wrath be past,
> > that you would appoint me a set time, and remember me!
> If a man dies, shall he live again?
> > All the days of my service I would wait,
> > till my renewal should come.
> You would call, and I would answer you;
> > you would long for the work of your hands.
> For then you would number my steps;
> > you would not keep watch over my sin;
> my transgression would be sealed up in a bag,
> > and you would cover over my iniquity. (vv. 13–17)

This is a wonderful passage. It is very personal. This is one on one, the believer speaking to the God he loves. "I know I am heading for Sheol, the place of the dead," says Job. "And we all know that Sheol is the place of no return [7:9]. But what I wish is that you would 'hide me' there, 'conceal me until your wrath be past' [v. 13], and that the day would come, your 'set time,' when you would 'remember me' and summon me back into life [v. 13]. This would be completely against what we know to be the case: 'If a man dies, shall he live again?' [v. 14a]. Not in the normal run of affairs, he won't. But I would be willing to 'wait, till my renewal should come' [v. 14b]." Renewal is a lovely word for resurrection, a word that combines newness (re*new*al) with continuity (*re*newal).

The most wonderful thing about this "renewal" (v. 14) is the personal relationship: "You would call, and I would answer you" (v. 15a). And the one who calls Job back from the dead would be the one who "would long for the work of your hands" (v. 15b). There is an anticipation here of the love of the resurrecting God. Furthermore, this God would now watch over Job for good rather than keeping watch over his sin (v. 16), for his sin would be dealt with once and for all: "my transgression would be sealed up in a bag, and you would cover over my iniquity" (v. 17). These are beautiful and final pictures. All Job's transgressions are finally tied up in a garbage bag and thrown away, never to be reopened. Although Job would not have known about this, the idea of iniquity being "covered over" (v. 17b) reminds us of the propitiation foreshadowed for Israel in the mercy seat over the Ark of the Covenant.

Job knows that if his sin is dealt with, then—and only then—can he hope to come back from Sheol into relationship with the God he loves. It is a wonderful glimpse of the gospel. But it is very quickly replaced by misery at the end of his speech.

If There Is No Resurrection, There Is No Hope (14:18–22)

> But the mountain falls and crumbles away,
>   and the rock is removed from its place;
> the waters wear away the stones;
>   the torrents wash away the soil of the earth;
>   so you destroy the hope of man.
> You prevail forever against him, and he passes;
>   you change his countenance, and send him away.
> His sons come to honor, and he does not know it;
>   they are brought low, and he perceives it not.
> He feels only the pain of his own body,
>   and he mourns only for himself. (vv. 18–22)

It is characteristic of Job's speeches that honest misery and lament is interrupted from time to time with glimpses of hope and gospel, just as an April day in England can have mostly rain but also occasional glimpses of the sun. At the end of this speech Job goes back to lamentation as he faces up to the misery of the judgment of God. Verses 18, 19a use the imagery of irreversible erosion to help us feel the hopelessness of life under sin and judgment. The winds, the rain, and the floodwaters wear away even rocks and mountains; they cause landslides. And they are irreversible. No process known to man can put erosion into reverse. So it is with God's judgment; it destroys "the hope of man" (v. 19b). Just as the hardest granite on earth cannot resist the waters of erosion, so the proudest man on earth cannot prevail against the judgment of God: "You prevail forever against him, and he passes" away (v. 20a); his face is changed and becomes lined with age and is finally frozen in death. God sends him away from his presence into Sheol (v. 20b). And when that happens he becomes isolated from his nearest and dearest (v. 21); his sons may meet with honor and success, or they may meet with humiliation, but in neither case will he be aware of it. He is all alone under the judgment of God (v. 22), feeling his own pain and grieving for himself.

Conclusion

Such is the misery of life on earth if sin is not dealt with. Job knows and faces this truth head-on. He shows here two marks of the believer. The first is a resolute realism about sin. There is no pretending, no denial, no minimizing of the seriousness of sin. Job knows that sin is the reason for our fragile mortality, and sin is the cause of death (Romans 5:12–21). And yet—and this is the second mark—he cannot keep himself from holding on to the hope of resurrection, the hope that one day sin will be so decisively dealt with that even death will not be final, that even though he dies, yet he will live and see his Maker.

In his suffering Job foreshadows the man who will enter fully into the misery of being identified with sinners in life and death, who will feel in his own body the fragility of mortality, who will experience in all its horrors the final penalty for sins, and who will taste death on behalf of sinners, but not because he himself is a sinner. Job foreshadows the one who will be raised from the dead to prove that in his death he has decisively paid the penalty for sins, so that the sins of all who trust in him will be "sealed up in a bag" (v. 17) and covered over by his blood.

What is more, Job foreshadows all men and women in Christ, who experience in their own bodies something of the misery of living in a world under judgment, who will know what it is in life to be surrounded by death, and who, because they are in Christ, will suffer not because they are sinners (though they are) but because they are blameless and because in some way their sufferings are a sharing in the sufferings of Christ. They too will discover the utter bankruptcy of The System of religion, its cruelty to sufferers, its shallowness and banality in the face of the realities of life, its pathetic tameness in the presence of a sovereign and dangerous God, and above all its false witness about God, its deceptiveness. They too will know what it is to pin all their hopes not on any system of religion but on the God they love and long to meet. They will experience mortality in all its transience and misery, death as their last enemy, and finally resurrection to eternal life.

The Second Cycle of Speeches

Job 15—21

12

Eliphaz's Second Speech: On the Scandal of Redemptive Suffering

JOB 15

WHY DOES THE WORLD HATE THE GOSPEL? On the face of it, that question is a million miles away from Job's debates with his friends. And yet, strangely and paradoxically, those debates help us grasp the answer to this contemporary question. The controversy in these heated cycles of speeches is between what I have called The System and Job's anguished discovery that The System doesn't work. The System represents the default understanding of all morally serious men and women, which is that the universe is moral and that whoever or whatever power (or powers) there may be in the universe rewards good behavior and punishes bad behavior. This seems obvious to us by nature and utterly necessary if we are not to be cast adrift into the theatre of the absurd.

In casting doubt on the validity of The System, Job is opening up two complementary possibilities. The immediate possibility is that his own sufferings are not God's punishment for his unforgiven sin. The other possibility, which is an entailment of the first, is that there is such a thing as sins that are not punished in the sinner because in some way they have been visited on an innocent substitute. The relatively innocent sufferings of Job foreshadow the utterly innocent sufferings of Jesus Christ, and those sufferings make grace possible in human experience. In principle, therefore, the story of Job is the story of redemptive suffering, the suffering of one that makes redemption possible for others. That is to say, the sufferings of Job, in anticipating the agony of the cross, speak ultimately of the gospel of Jesus Christ. And the hostility of Job's friends foreshadows and helps us understand the hostility of the world today to the gospel of free grace.

We move now to the start of the second cycle of speeches. Job has wound up the first cycle with a long and significant speech (chapters 12—14) in which he has pointed the way ahead, toward the forgiveness of sins and the resurrection of the believer. It is Eliphaz's turn to lead the second cycle, as he led the first. And he is not impressed. As in the three speeches of the first cycle, he begins with a personal word to Job and continues with a description of the fate of the wicked. But unlike the speeches in the first cycle, he does not conclude with a further personal address to Job. This change signals a darkening of the tone. The sympathetic Eliphaz of chapters 4, 5 is gone; now we have a much angrier and hostile Eliphaz who is losing patience with his friend Job. His tone is "much less courteous and conciliatory."[1]

Redemptive Suffering Is a Disgraceful Idea (vv. 1–16)

In verses 1–16 Eliphaz speaks directly to Job. He rebukes him in no uncertain terms for what he has said in his speeches so far. Eliphaz says at least six things about Job's words.

Job, Your Words Are . . . Empty (vv. 2, 3)

Then Eliphaz the Temanite answered and said:

> "Should a wise man answer with windy knowledge,
>   and fill his belly with the east wind?
> Should he argue in unprofitable talk,
>   or in words with which he can do no good?" (vv. 1–3)

Eliphaz thinks Job has been spouting a lot of hot air. His so-called "knowledge" is just a wind blowing around and achieving nothing (v. 2). The "east wind" is the hot sirocco blowing in off the desert, a wind that is both unpleasant (being very hot) and unfruitful; coming from the desert, it brings no rain (v. 2). In the same way Job's words are "unprofitable," useless, and doing "no good" to anybody (v. 3). Bildad has said something similar (8:2), as has Zophar (11:2). As far as The System is concerned, the idea of undeserved suffering has no correspondence to reality; it is therefore insubstantial talk, the kind of thing idle academics might do in the seminar room, but of no use in giving wisdom for actual life. This is not the kind of talk for "a wise man," he says to Job (14:2).

But it is worse than this. His words are not only empty—they are dangerous.

Job, Your Words Are . . . Dangerous (v. 4)

> But you are doing away with the fear of God
> and hindering meditation before God. (v. 4)

The word "meditation" in this context means a proper reverence for and devotion to God.[2] "The fear of God" is a normal definition of healthy religion, especially used by those who consider themselves "wise"; it is used in the context of the proper reverence and worship of the Lord in Proverbs. The accusation here is that what Job has been saying is undermining proper religion and piety. This may simply mean that Job is himself being impious in challenging God like this. But more likely it means that if Job's ideas were to catch on, all the usual incentives to be virtuous and pious would be removed. After all, if blessing does not necessarily follow virtue, why bother to be virtuous? And if God's curse does not necessarily follow vice, why restrain yourself? Why not eat, drink, and be merry? If we live in a world in which blessing and suffering are not predictable or explicable, what point is there in any morality or religion? Job's ideas about undeserved suffering are profoundly subversive.

Job, Your Words Are . . . Crafty/Self-Justifying (vv. 5, 6)

> For your iniquity teaches your mouth,
>   and you choose the tongue of the crafty.
> Your own mouth condemns you, and not I;
>   your own lips testify against you. (vv. 5, 6)

Having accused Job of speaking words with no substantial content (vv. 2, 3) and dangerous effects (v. 4), Eliphaz goes on to accuse Job of bad motives. He claims to be able to deduce why Job is saying what he does. It is an old and well-tried strategy to undermine what someone says by psychoanalyzing them and accusing them of evil motives ("You're only saying that because . . .").[3] "Job, you are only saying these things because you know you are guilty and you want to cover it up. Your absurd claims of undeserved suffering are no more than a mask for a guilty conscience," says Eliphaz in verse 3. But God is a match for such crafty talk (v. 5), for "he catches the wise in their own craftiness" (5:13).

How does Eliphaz know this and claim such access to Job's heart? Verse 6 tells us: "it is by the words of your mouth that I know you are guilty. You are self-condemned."

Job, Your Words Are . . . Arrogant (vv. 7–10)

> Are you the first man who was born?
>> Or were you brought forth before the hills?
> Have you listened in the council of God?
>> And do you limit wisdom to yourself?
> What do you know that we do not know?
>> What do you understand that is not clear to us?
> Both the gray-haired and the aged are among us,
>> older than your father. (vv. 7–10)

Next Eliphaz accuses Job of sheer brazen arrogance. "You seem to think you were a kind of primeval man, born of God before the creation of the world!" "The hills" (v. 7) are a way of speaking of the oldest part of creation, as in our expression "as old as the hills." "You are speaking as if you had security clearance for God's cabinet chamber." The word "council" (v. 8) signifies the place of intimate, confidential conversation; it is where the false prophets of Jeremiah 23 claimed to have been. "You are claiming among human beings 'a monopoly on wisdom' [NIV, v. 8b]; you are like the soldier who is out of step but insists he is the only one in step! You seem to think you know something that none of us knows [v. 9], and yet we are much older and senior than you [v. 10]."

So Eliphaz pulls rank on Job. But he also implies that the long-established tradition of morally serious people cannot be lightly challenged. The word group "know" appears more than seventy times in Job. It is a vital question: how do we know what we claim to know? For Eliphaz and his friends, tradition is the best we can do.

Then Eliphaz changes tack.

Job, Your Words Are . . . Hurtful (vv. 11–13)

> Are the comforts of God too small for you,
>> or the word that deals gently with you?
> Why does your heart carry you away,
>> and why do your eyes flash,
> that you turn your spirit against God
>> and bring such words out of your mouth? (vv. 11–13)

Now Eliphaz says in effect, "I feel hurt by your reaction." He and his friends had come to bring Job "comfort" (2:11). In his first speech Eliphaz has been sympathetic and considerate; he has given Job "the comforts of God" by means of "the word that deals gently with you" (15:11), that "word" being the message of The System, and perhaps in particular the "word" revealed to

Eliphaz in that spooky vision (4:12: "Now a word was brought to me . . ."). "We have applied The System to your wounds as gently as we could," says Eliphaz, "and you are being hurtful by not being grateful. Why are you so angry? You used to be one of us, a devotee of The System. Why not now?"

Finally, Eliphaz comes back to the main point he has made in his first speech.

Job, Your Words Are . . . Unrealistic (vv. 14–16)
> What is man, that he can be pure?
>   Or he who is born of a woman, that he can be righteous?
> Behold, God puts no trust in his holy ones,
>   and the heavens are not pure in his sight;
> how much less one who is abominable and corrupt,
>   a man who drinks injustice like water! (vv. 14–16)

Eliphaz has already insisted that human beings cannot be pure or in the right before God (4:17). Job has as good as admitted it himself (9:2). Bildad will echo it later (25:4).

Here he says much the same, but with a twisting of the knife. In chapter 4 the reason was our mortality (we "dwell in houses of clay," 4:19); now it is that we are actively disgusting to God. "You are not the first man, Job; you are 'born of a woman,' a normal mortal (15:14). God is so pure and holy that even the holiness of the angels is not clean to him [v. 15, echoing 4:18]. There is moral pollution even in the upper levels of the cosmos.[4] So what hope have you who are by nature 'abominable' (disgusting, vile, repulsive to God) and 'corrupt' (filthy to God)? To you, as to all human beings by nature, it is as natural to do 'injustice' as it is to drink a glass of water [v. 16]. You have to do wrong, just as you have to drink water to stay alive. Doing wrong is not something you do on special bad days; it is something you do every day."

Reflections on Eliphaz's Accusation

It is worth taking a step back and asking how Eliphaz's accusations against Job foreshadow later accusations leveled against the gospel of grace. Eliphaz says that to claim undeserved suffering is empty, dangerous, self-justifying, arrogant, hurtful, and unrealistic. The same accusations are leveled against the claims of undeserved grace. It is said to be empty, having no correspondence with moral realities. It is said to be dangerous, undermining the necessary incentives to behave well; what is the point, after all, if free grace forgives all my sin? This was the objection made to Paul's gospel of grace, as if he were saying, "And why not do evil, that good may come?" (Romans 3:8).

This is one reason why the gospel of free grace is continually leaking away from churches: the religious mind-set hates it. Grace is also said to be self-justifying, something we only believe because we want people to think better of us, a crafty and deceptive means of getting people to think we're OK when we're not. Those with assurance of forgiveness by grace are often accused of being arrogant. "You seem to think you're better than everybody else. How else could you claim to be sure of going to Heaven?" Grace is said to be an emotional crutch for those who cannot cope with the moral realities of life, the perfectly adequate comforts of the simple system of moral reward. You only believe in grace, they say, because you are not prepared, having made your bed, to lie on it. Above all, grace is said to be unrealistic: how can a sinful human being really hope to be in the right before God?

Ultimately, because the book of Job is about undeserved suffering, it is about undeserved grace too. The undeserved suffering of this righteous man foreshadows the undeserved suffering of the One who knew no sin, and his suffering makes possible the amazing grace of undeserved forgiveness to sinners.

The Indentikit Portrait of the Wicked (vv. 17–35)

Eliphaz continues with a vivid description of the miseries experienced by a generalized and anonymous wicked man. Although this wicked man is not named, there are hints that connect him with Job, who is, or so Eliphaz implies, "abominable and corrupt . . . who drinks injustice like water" (v. 16). Again and again Eliphaz describes the wicked man in language that Job has already used of himself.[5]

It is a clever portrait, for Eliphaz focuses on the fears and the fate of the wicked man, and not on any particular crimes.

This Portrait Is Based on Pure Tradition (vv. 17–19)

> I will show you; hear me,
>   and what I have seen I will declare
> (what wise men have told,
>   without hiding it from their fathers,
> to whom alone the land was given,
>   and no stranger passed among them). (vv. 17–19)

Eliphaz begins his portrait by an appeal to pure tradition. "'I will show you' a picture of a wicked man, and then you can put two and two together and see where it points. So listen in—'hear me'—and I will tell you 'what I have seen' (v. 17)" (perhaps in the spooky vision of chapter 4). This is wise tradition (v. 18),[6] and it is pure tradition, a tradition begun in some pristine age when "no stranger" with strange unorthodox teaching "passed among them" in the land (v. 19). This tradition is pure; anything else is heterodox.

We will now look at the portrait.

The Fears of the Wicked (vv. 20–24)

The first focus is on the fears of the wicked, what we might call the terrors of a bad conscience.

> The wicked man writhes in pain all his days,
>> through all the years that are laid up for the ruthless.
> Dreadful sounds are in his ears;
>> in prosperity the destroyer will come upon him.
> He does not believe that he will return out of darkness,
>> and he is marked for the sword.
> He wanders abroad for bread, saying, "Where is it?"
>> He knows that a day of darkness is ready at his hand;
> distress and anguish terrify him;
>> they prevail against him, like a king ready for battle. (vv. 20–24)

Although there are a few places where the exact meaning is uncertain, the overall picture is clear: the wicked man has a miserable life full of dread, distress, and anguish. Verses 20–24 focus on the anticipation of his doom, for "the wicked man is forever plagued by an awareness of his doom; he lives continually with the signs of Death and his attendant forces waiting to consume" him.[7]

So he "writhes in pain" (v. 20) like a woman in hard labor. Job has used the same word root of himself (6:10, "pain unsparing"). He keeps hearing "dreadful sounds" (15:21); he is full of fears, and even when things seem to be going really well "in prosperity" suddenly "the destroyer will come upon him" (v. 21). This is exactly what has happened to Job in chapters 1, 2; he has said of himself, "what I dread befalls me" (3:25). In his heart the wicked man knows he is on a one-way street to darkness and that the sword (like the sword of Damocles) is hanging over him (15:22). Job feels this about himself—he is heading for Sheol and will not return (7:9, 10).

The translation of verse 23 is uncertain. The word translated "Where?" may be revocalized as "vulture," and the sense may be that this wicked man is wandering around scavenging for food like a vulture or that he is wandering around like a piece of carrion about to be eaten by a vulture. Whichever way we take it, it is a picture of vulnerability and anxiety. His life is full of "distress and anguish" (v. 24), like "the anguish of my spirit" that Job has spoken of (7:11); these will "terrify" him (15:24), just as God terrifies Job with nightmares (7:14).

It is a frightening picture of the subjective anxiety and terror that haunts the wicked man. And it fits so frighteningly well with how Job has described his own state of mind. "Put two and two together," says Eliphaz. "If you have these feelings, what does that say about your morality and standing before God? Bad feelings are a sure indicator of bad character."

Then Eliphaz moves on from the subjective terror of the wicked to the objective ruin that awaits them.

The Fate of the Wicked (vv. 25–35)

The focus now shifts to the fate of the wicked, from the subjective terrors of a bad conscience to the objective ruin they deserve.

> Because he has stretched out his hand against God
>   and defies the Almighty,
> running stubbornly against him
>   with a thickly bossed shield;
> because he has covered his face with his fat
>   and gathered fat upon his waist
> and has lived in desolate cities,
>   in houses that none should inhabit,
>   which were ready to become heaps of ruins;
> he will not be rich, and his wealth will not endure,
>   nor will his possessions spread over the earth;
> he will not depart from darkness;
>   the flame will dry up his shoots,
>   and by the breath of his mouth he will depart.
> Let him not trust in emptiness, deceiving himself,
>   for emptiness will be his payment.
> It will be paid in full before his time,
>   and his branch will not be green.
> He will shake off his unripe grape like the vine,
>   and cast off his blossom like the olive tree.
> For the company of the godless is barren,
>   and fire consumes the tents of bribery.
> They conceive trouble and give birth to evil,
>   and their womb prepares deceit. (vv. 25–35)

This wicked man suffers because he has arrogantly challenged God to a fight (vv. 25, 26). He has "stretched out his hand against God," giving God the finger or shaking his fist at God (v. 25). He is like a foolhardy warrior running against God; a Don Quixote tilting at windmills is not more stupid.

And this, according to Eliphaz, is what Job is doing when he insists on an audience with God.

Furthermore, in his prosperity he has "covered his face with his fat and gathered fat upon his waist" (v. 27); he has the double chin and the heavy belly of a rich man who has indulged himself in too many donuts. He thinks he is a warrior, but in fact his self-indulgence has weakened him. Just as an obese man is in no physical condition for a fight, so a selfish man is in no moral condition for a contest with God.

Verse 28 is more naturally translated with a future tense: "he *will* live in desolate cities and in houses that none should inhabit."[8] However rich he is, as Job was, his riches will not last (v. 29); just like Job, he will go bankrupt because of his wickedness. He is on a one-way street to "darkness" (v. 30a), and the fire of God's judgment "will dry up his shoots" (v. 30b), so that he has no hope, just as the fire (lightning) of 1:16 had destroyed Job's property.[9]

If he trusts in "emptiness" (vanity, idols, anything but God), then "emptiness will be his payment" (v. 31), as Job is discovering (7:3: "so I am allotted months of emptiness"). No matter how fruitful he looks in the early days of his prosperity, he will not actually bear fruit (15:32, 33) but will be like a vine that sheds its grapes before they ripen or an olive tree whose blossom blows away and never becomes fruitful.

In his wickedness he keeps company with godless people (as in Proverbs 1:10–19 or Psalm 1), with people who love bribery and injustice; but he will find their company "barren" and ready to be consumed by the "fire" of God's judgment (v. 34). That is the destiny of these wicked people who "conceive . . . and give birth to evil" (v. 35). The word "trouble" in verse 35 has been used by Eliphaz in his first speech (4:8; 5:6, 7) and by Job of himself (3:10). Eliphaz's point is that no one reaps trouble without first sowing trouble. "So if you are reaping trouble, Job, what does this prove about what you must have sown?" That's what The System teaches us.

Conclusion

This is a terrifying picture of the fears and the fate of the wicked. Both the subjective fears and the objective fate are closely paralleled in Job's own dark experience. The lesson of The System is simple: this proves you are a sinner. Wherever grace is denied, cruelty follows.

It is this harsh, grace-free system that Job is challenging with his insistence that his sufferings are undeserved. Let us learn from Eliphaz to recognize the natural man's objections to grace and take great care not to let the grace leach out of our teaching and our convictions. It is frightening how you and I can hear ourselves saying what the comforters say and how close they are not only to religions like Islam but also to some so-called Biblical Christianity. The more we find ourselves in sympathy with the comforters, the less we have really grasped the gospel of grace.

13

Job's Second Reply to Eliphaz: Drinking the Cup of God's Wrath

JOB 16, 17

WHEN JAMES AND JOHN asked Jesus if they could sit in the places of honor at his right and his left hand in the kingdom, Jesus asked them, "Are you able to drink the cup that I drink . . . ?" When they said they could, Jesus replied, "The cup that I drink you will drink" (Mark 10:38, 39). This surprises us. We would expect Jesus to say, "No, you cannot drink this cup of God's judgment; that is why I am going to drink it for you." But he says they can and will. Not in the sense of dying as a substitute for sins, but nevertheless in real experience they will know, as disciples of Christ, in some measure what it is to taste the wrath of God against sinners, even though their own sins are forgiven. Job tastes this cup in anticipation. Jesus Christ drinks it to the dregs on the cross. Christian disciples today continue to drink from this cup in their experience of redemptive suffering.

In Job 16, 17 we get another glimpse into the taste of this cup. In it we learn about Job, we learn in anticipation about Jesus Christ, and we learn in some measure about the experience of Christian discipleship.

Job Has a Deep Longing to Receive and to Give Comfort (16:1–6)
The first facet of Job's experience that we meet in this speech is a deep longing in his heart, or—to be more accurate—two deep longings.

Then Job answered and said:

"I have heard many such things;
    miserable comforters are you all.

> Shall windy words have an end?
>   Or what provokes you that you answer?
> I also could speak as you do,
>   if you were in my place;
> I could join words together against you
>   and shake my head at you.
> I could strengthen you with my mouth,
>   and the solace of my lips would assuage your pain.
> If I speak, my pain is not assuaged,
>   and if I forbear, how much of it leaves me?" (vv. 1–6)

The effect of the friends' speeches upon Job is deeply depressing. "Oh," he says in essence, "I have heard this kind of thing many times before" (v. 2a). Job knows the religious system well. But its effect on him is "miserable," (v. 2). His friends had come to bring him "comfort" (2:11), but the paradoxical effect of their attempts to comfort him is to make him all the more miserable. They are, in what has been called "the ultimate oxymoron,"[1] "miserable comforters" (v. 2b). Job has previously described the diet they offer him as disgusting (6:5, 6) and compared them to disappointed parched travelers coming to a dry wadi (6:14–23).

Although Eliphaz implies that they have offered him "the comforts of God" (15:11), comfort is not what Job experiences through their grace-free words. The word "miserable" comes from the word "trouble." Eliphaz has said that Job's troubles must be because he himself has sown "trouble" (4:8). Job replies that his friends have simply amplified his troubles.

They think Job is a windbag (8:2; 15:2). But it is their words that are "windy" (16:3a), that is, long-winded and empty. "Why must you go on and on arguing with me?" asks Job (v. 3b). "Let's think about what it would be like if our roles were reversed, if you were suffering and I had come to comfort you. Sure, I could play your game and feed you with The System [v. 4]. I could put together eloquent and confident system speeches and shake my head against you with disapproval.[2] But in fact I would hope to 'strengthen you with my mouth, and the solace of my lips would assuage your pain' [v. 5]." Job has not one longing (to be comforted himself) but two longings; he would also love to be able to comfort others in pain. It is not yet clear how he could do this. But by the end of the book he will indeed be in a position, like Paul, to "comfort those who are in any affliction, with the comfort with which we ourselves are comforted by God" (2 Corinthians 1:4).

At the moment, however, nothing he says seems to make any difference to his pain. Speech doesn't help, nor does silence (v. 6). The narrator has told us that Job's pain was "very great" (2:13); he was not exaggerating. It is an inescapable pain.

It is worth reflecting on these longings for comfort. It is natural that Job should long for comfort. It is sobering that no system of grace-free philosophy or religion can bring true comfort. But it is wonderful that in the heart of every true believer longing for comfort, there is also a longing to comfort others. What is more, only those who have known the longing for God's comfort and then felt that comfort are able to comfort others.

These two longings, to receive and to give comfort, are wonderfully fulfilled in the Lord Jesus who, even as he hung dying, cared for his mother (John 19:26, 27). It is a mark of a disciple of Jesus and an heir and successor to Job that even as we long to be comforted, our hearts contain a matching longing to bring comfort to others in pain. Faith turns us outward even in pain.

Job Endures a Terrible Experience of God's Wrath (16:7–14)

The root reason why Job is suffering so intensely is not, contrary to what we might expect, because of his bankruptcy, his bereavements, or his bodily emaciation; it is because he is experiencing the felt hostility of God. God is the actor, the agent, and the attacker in verses 7–14.

First, God has shriveled Job up.

> Surely now God has worn me out;
>   he has made desolate all my company.
> And he has shriveled me up,
>   which is a witness against me,
> and my leanness has risen up against me;
>   it testifies to my face. (vv. 7, 8)

In three parallel statements of climactic intensity, Job says God has "worn me out" (that is, debilitated me), "made desolate all my company" (v. 7; that is, my social world, from my wider reputation in the community to my intimate family), and "shriveled me up" (v. 8) into "a pathetic wrinkled wretch."[3] Chapters 1—3 have used the idea of a skin or "hedge" around Job, first a protective hedge (1:10, "a hedge around him and his house and all that he has, on every side") and then an imprisoning hedge (3:23, "whom God has hedged in"). Every human being has not only a physical skin to protect a healthy body, but wider skins or hedges of intimate relationships of hearth and home and wider family and a place in society. God has invaded each of these until all that is left is this pathetic, wrinkled, miserable apology of a man.

We see this so vividly in the Lord Jesus. In his incarnation the protective hedge of Heaven is taken away, he lives with nowhere to lay his head, his natural family does not believe in him, and even when he accumulates a large band of disciples, these too are whittled down so that most leave him (John 6:66), and even those who remain desert him at the end, and on the cross he hangs deeply alone, his skin shriveled.

Second, this attack has been very personal and violent.

> He has torn me in his wrath and hated me;
>> he has gnashed his teeth at me;
>> my adversary sharpens his eyes against me. (Job 16:9)

God has acted toward Job like a wild predatory beast tearing at its prey with cruel claws and sharp teeth, full of personal hatred, and with sharp, evil, hostile eyes. God has, as it were, given Job the evil eye, watching with hostile intent his every move, waiting to pounce upon him. Astonishingly, we must see this too fulfilled upon the cross when the Lord Jesus was "made . . . sin" (2 Corinthians 5:21) and the Father's hostility against sinners was poured out upon him.

Third, this attack has left Job abandoned and exposed.

> Men have gaped at me with their mouth;
>> they have struck me insolently on the cheek;
>> they mass themselves together against me.
> God gives me up to the ungodly
>> and casts me into the hands of the wicked. (vv. 10, 11)

Evil people, like a pack of scavengers, have gathered around Job, delighted that God's attack has given them easy pickings. They "have gaped at me" with mouths wide open, not aghast, but open and ready to devour his substance (v. 10). They have "struck me insolently on the cheek," confident that God would no longer protect him (v. 10). They have come together unitedly—"they *mass* themselves together against me" (v. 10). But the only reason they can do this with impunity is that "*God* gives me up to the ungodly and casts me into the hands of the wicked" (v. 11). "After mauling his prey, God, the savage beast, leaves his victim for the gathering packs of the wicked and hurls Job, like a piece of meat, helpless into their midst."[4]

Yet again we see this terrible loneliness of Job fulfilled in the mockery of Jesus—the Roman soldiers abusing him (Matthew 27:27–31), the strange alliance of the Gentiles with Pontius Pilate and the Jewish leaders (Acts 4:5, 6, 27, fulfilling Psalm 2:1, 2) all massing together against him, free to do so with impunity because the Father has forsaken his Son and abandoned him to the mockery of people.

Fourth, this attack is relentless and unceasing.

> I was at ease, and he broke me apart;
>> he seized me by the neck and dashed me to pieces;
> he set me up as his target;
>> his archers surround me.
> He slashes open my kidneys and does not spare;
>> he pours out my gall on the ground.
> He breaks me with breach upon breach;
>> he runs upon me like a warrior. (vv. 12–14)

The imagery here is visceral in its power. "I was at ease" (v. 12; cf. 1:1–5), not a guilty "ease" but the ease of a virtuous man enjoying the blessings of God. And what did God do? Habel's paraphrase picks up the force of verse 12a, b well: "I was at ease but he smashed and smashed me, seized my neck and bashed and bashed me."[5] And then God "set me up as his target" (v. 12), using him as target practice for his "archers," who leave him for dead on the ground with his blood and vital juices spilling out on the ground (v. 13).

Finally, he treats Job like a city under siege (v. 14), making "breach upon breach" in his walls (the skin or hedge idea again) and running upon him again and again like a mighty "warrior" (v. 14). All the hosts of Heaven seem to be arrayed against him. Eliphaz has accused Job of "running stubbornly" against God "with a thickly bossed shield" (15:26). "The reality is that God is running against me," Job says. "I did not choose to attack God; God has taken the terrible initiative to attack me."

We will meet some of these violent images again in chapter 19. They anticipate the image of Leviathan in chapter 41 and will help us when we come to understand that enigmatic chapter.[6]

All this is Job's experience. All his protective skins, hedges, and walls have been breached. He is shriveled up so there is hardly anything of him left inside. He has been attacked violently by God and left exposed to the mockery of people, and all of this relentlessly. Job experiences the violent, incessant hostility of God. And yet all the time we the readers know that Job is actually God's "servant," the man God approves of, the man God singles out for his exceptional piety and morality (1:1, 8; 2:3).

All this and more was Jesus' experience. The reality was that he was the beloved Son, in whom the Father's heart was well pleased (Mark 1:11; 9:7). And yet in his experience he was God-forsaken (Mark 15:34). And his experience created its own reality, as it does with every sufferer. He knew a real God-forsakenness at the same time he was the Father's beloved Son.

This feeling of God-forsakenness is also an authentic part of Christian experience. It is possible to be—objectively—a dearly beloved son or daughter of God while also experiencing—subjectively and in part—all the ingredients of Job's experience here.

And Yet Job Has a Clear Conscience (16:15–17)

> I have sewed sackcloth upon my skin
> > and have laid my strength in the dust.
> My face is red with weeping,
> > and on my eyelids is deep darkness,
> although there is no violence in my hands,
> > and my prayer is pure. (vv. 15–17)

It is vital to the paradoxes of Job's experience that alongside this felt hostility of God he should have a clear conscience. Verses 15, 16 paint for us a terribly vivid picture of a man in extremis. Because his "skin" is so damaged and punctured, he has to sew "sackcloth" on it (v. 15a). His "strength" (v. 15b; literally, his "horn") is laid "in the dust" like a defeated ox or rhinoceros putting down its horn. His "face," the mirror of his soul, "is red with weeping" (v. 16a), and there are dark rings around his eyes (v. 16b), the shadow of death visible in his grief-stricken face.

But all this has happened "although there is no violence in my hands" (he has not been the agent of violent acts), "and my prayer is pure" (v. 17). This does not mean that Job claims sinless perfection; it does mean that he believes his sin has been forgiven. He has "clean hands and a pure heart" (Psalm 24:4) and therefore ought to have access to God (as Psalm 24 teaches). This conscious awareness that there is no unconfessed and unforgiven sin in his life is of enormous importance for the book. It is the trigger, under God, for the wonderful hope toward which Job now begins to reach.

Job Reaches Toward a Wonderful Hope of a Mediator (16:18–21)

> O earth, cover not my blood,
> > and let my cry find no resting place.
> Even now, behold, my witness is in heaven,
> > and he who testifies for me is on high.
> My friends scorn me;
> > my eye pours out tears to God,
> that he would argue the case of a man with God,
> > as a son of man does with his neighbor. (vv. 18–21)

Verses 18–21 are a significant development in Job's heart. It begins with a cry that can be offered only from the clear conscience of a believer and follows directly on from his assertion of innocence in verse 17: "O earth, cover not my blood, and let my cry find no resting place." Like Abel in Genesis 4, he was being murdered! When Cain murdered Abel, God said to Cain, "The voice of your brother's blood is crying to me from the ground" (Genesis 4:10). Abel, the innocent man of faith (Matthew 23:35; Hebrews 11:4), is dead, but his blood cries out for vindication. He is buried in Sheol, but his cry finds "no resting place" (v. 18) in Sheol.[7] In the same way, the "blood" shed by violent acts in the Jerusalem of Ezekiel's day is, as it were, "set on the bare rock . . . that it may not be covered" (Ezekiel 24:7, 8). Isaiah looks forward to the day when "the earth will disclose the blood shed on it, and will no more cover its slain" (Isaiah 26:21). Shed blood cries to God for justice. The Christian martyrs of a future day cry to God to bring justice because of their shed blood (Revelation 6:10). These cries as it were echo around the universe until God hears and answers them. In the same way Job believes that his cry from a clear conscience will echo around the universe until justice is done. It will not, it cannot be hushed up.

So Job continues, "Even now, behold, my witness is in heaven, and he who testifies for me is on high" (16:19). Job's emaciated body witnesses against him to all believers in The System that Job is an unforgiven sinner (e.g., v. 8); but somehow there is—there must be—a higher witness who will give testimony to the truth.

Who is this witness who gives testimony in Heaven and on high? Consistently in Scripture it is God himself who avenges innocent blood. He does so in Genesis 4. In Isaiah we read, "For behold, the LORD is coming out from his place to punish the inhabitants of the earth for their iniquity, and the earth will disclose the blood shed on it, and will no more cover its slain" (Isaiah 26:21). The uncovered cry of innocent blood calls upon the Lord to bring justice. Despite the skepticism of many scholars,[8] this witness must be no less than God himself. Job is appealing to God against God, and in so doing he foreshadows the gospel of grace in Jesus Christ. Jones rightly says this "expresses daring faith and remarkable insight," an insight that is proved true at the cross of Christ.[9]

Job has no other helper, for his friends scorn him;[10] so he "pours out tears to God" and cries to him "that he would argue the case of a man with God, as a son of man [a mortal] does with his neighbor" (v. 21; that is, with a fellow human being). Job is appealing to one who has the status to argue the case with God as an equal. He appeals to God against God. This appeal was foreshadowed back in chapter 9, where Job wished there was a mediator, lamenting that there is not (9:33). But here "the fierce conviction that there is a witness in heaven is far stronger than the desperate hope of chapter 9."[11]

But Job Still Has to Face the Last Enemy (16:22—17:16)

But there is more to the picture. Despite the wonderful hope for which Job rightly reaches out, the reality is that he is staring into the jaws of death. Death pervades the final section of the speech. This section is bracketed by the prospect of death: in 16:22—17:1 "the graveyard is ready for me" (17:1), and in 17:13–16 all that he has to look forward to is "Sheol," the grave.

> For when a few years have come
>   I shall go the way from which I shall not return.
> My spirit is broken; my days are extinct;
>   the graveyard is ready for me. (16:22—17:1)

The eyes of faith have been wonderfully opened, but now Job looks around and sees the reality. Very soon, "when a few years have come," he will have to take the one-way ticket to the grave and Sheol (16:22). In his mind's eye he sees the gateway with its inscription "Abandon hope, all ye who enter here."[12] His "spirit" (17:1), his vital energy, his desire for life, is "broken," his "days are extinct," which means cut short. All that lies ahead is "the grave-yard." There is an emotional intensity in these short lines. Essentially Job is saying:

> My spirit is broken.
> My days are cut short.
> The grave awaits me.

He goes on:

> Surely there are mockers about me,
>   and my eye dwells on their provocation. (17:2)

Job is surrounded by mockers (as in 16:10). All he can see is their "provocation," that is, their hostility. Even Job's so-called "comforters" have become mockers of his pain.

Verses 3–5 appear to be a renewal of Job's plea to God against God from 16:18–21.

Lay down a pledge for me with you;
    who is there who will put up security for me?
Since you have closed their hearts to understanding,
    therefore you will not let them triumph.
He who informs against his friends to get a share of their property—
    the eyes of his children will fail. (vv. 3–5)

The translation of verse 3 is uncertain. Who is Job asking to lay down a pledge and with whom? The NIV translates this, "Give me, O God, the pledge you demand." Although the words "O God" are not in the Hebrew, they interpret this correctly as an appeal to God. Some suggest that Job is offering himself as a pledge for himself, but this makes no sense.[13] Much more in tune with the flow of the speech is to suppose that Job is crying to God to lay down a pledge before God on Job's behalf.

To give a pledge means to take responsibility for someone else, perhaps for their debt, to "put up security," to give a guarantee for one's well-being (v. 3). If I am deeply in debt and you graciously pledge on my behalf, it means you will guarantee the payment of my debt, if necessary by paying it yourself. So in Genesis 43:9 Judah says to Jacob about Benjamin, "I will be a pledge of his safety." In Proverbs 11:15 we read, "Whoever puts up security [a pledge] for a stranger will surely suffer harm"; it is a costly thing to do. In Isaiah 38:14 when King Hezekiah is sick he prays, "O Lord, I am oppressed; be my pledge of safety." This is what the psalmist asks for in Psalm 119:122: "Give your servant a pledge of good." Calvin paraphrases this, "Lord . . . since the proud cruelly rush upon me to destroy me, interpose thyself between us, as if thou wert my surety." [14]

Verses 4, 5 warn his friends that if they are disloyal they will face the judgment of the God who will vindicate Job.

But again we return from hope to reality:

He has made me a byword of the peoples,
    and I am one before whom men spit.
My eye has grown dim from vexation,
    and all my members are like a shadow. (vv. 6, 7)

Job has become a "byword" for a disgraced, impenitent sinner under the judgment of God (v. 6). People spit in his face.[15] His "eye," the indicator of interior spirit and life, "has grown dim" (v. 7), like Isaac's in his old age (Genesis 27:1), but unlike Moses (Deuteronomy 34:7). All Job's "members" (his limbs, his frame) are "like a shadow" (Job 17:7); he has become a shadow of his former self.

The upright are appalled at this,
   and the innocent stirs himself up against the godless.
Yet the righteous holds to his way,
   and he who has clean hands grows stronger and stronger. (vv. 8, 9)

While it is possible that "the upright" here is a sarcastic reference to his friends, the self-righteous who are appalled to see this sinner getting his comeuppance, it is more likely Job is appealing to genuinely righteous people who would be sympathetically appalled at Job's plight (v. 8). In some way Job affirms again his confidence in final vindication.

But you, come on again, all of you,
   and I shall not find a wise man among you.
My days are past; my plans are broken off,
   the desires of my heart.
They make night into day:
   "The light," they say, "is near to the darkness."
If I hope for Sheol as my house,
   if I make my bed in darkness,
if I say to the pit, "You are my father,"
   and to the worm, "My mother," or "My sister,"
where then is my hope?
   Who will see my hope?
Will it go down to the bars of Sheol?
   Shall we descend together into the dust? (vv. 10–16)

In the final section Job challenges his friends again: "But you, come on again, all of you" (v. 10). The verb "come on again" is literally "turn back"; it may be an appeal for them to repent and relent. More likely it is a sarcastic challenge for them to attack him again. But he has no expectations of wisdom from them. "I shall not find a wise man among you" (v. 10) contrasts with the sarcasm of 12:2 when Job said he is worried that when they die, wisdom will die with them!

But for Job there is no hope (v. 11). As in chapter 3 he has nothing to which to look forward. He used to make plans ("the desires of my heart," [17:11]) but no longer.[16] The key issue is hope (notice that "hope" appears three times in verses 13–16). And the denial of hope leads to Sheol. The only home Job can see ahead is Sheol, the place of "darkness" (v. 13), "the pit," the place of corruption and disintegration ("the worm," v. 14). There can be no hope there (v. 15), for if his hope descends with him to Sheol, it will be in the prison with unbreakable "bars" (v. 16), in the place of utter disintegration ("the dust" [v. 16]).

And yet even in the gloom there is a ray of hope. Why else does Job ruminate about what will happen to his hope that there will be in Heaven a mediator, the hope that God will speak to God for him? Why keep speaking if there is no hope? Those who really have no hope fall silent in despair. There is a paradox of faith in Job's eloquent expressions of despair; in their very reasonings there is hope. Job has in his heart both the universal longing for comfort and the believer's longing to bring comfort to others. Although he experiences the felt hostility of God, he knows he is innocent; his clear conscience testifies that to his heart. And he cannot believe that a clear conscience will ultimately not be vindicated. So he deduces, with the wonderful logic of faith, that God who will intercede for him before God. Yes, he gazes into the jaws of death itself, and all the voices of the world proclaim to him the death of hope in his imminent death. But the voice of faith appeals to God to put up a pledge for Job's life.

The foreshadowing of the experience of the Lord Jesus Christ is awesome. He too felt the longings both to be comforted and to comfort. He too knew in all its fullness what it was to be identified with sinners, from his baptism to his cross. He experienced in its unadulterated intensity the holy hatred of God against sinners. He too knew that he had a clear conscience, in fact that every moment of his life he did what pleased the Father (John 8:29), that his life and his death were the expression of a perfect obedience. And even as he gazed with holy terror into the jaws of death he at the same time knew that he had been given authority both to lay down his life and to take it up again (John 10:18).

It is in Christ alone that Christian disciples may expect to experience some echo of Job's trials, to feel in our hearts the longing to be comforted and to comfort others with the comfort with which we ourselves have been comforted, to tremble as we live in a world under the judgment of God and experience in some measure that judgment in our bodies and hearts, to appeal to our divine Mediator to speak for us before our divine Judge, with the appeal of the perfect obedience of the one man who has made us righteous (Romans 5:19), an appeal offered from a clear conscience. When the day comes for us to gaze into the terrible jaws of death, we may know with a confidence greater than Job's that our hope will not die with us and that we will rise with Jesus to life eternal.

14

Bildad's Second Speech: The Road to Hell

JOB 18

JOB 18 IS AN OUTSTANDING SERMON ON HELL. In its structure, its theology, its rhetoric, and its persuasive force it is an exceptional sermon. It is said that Jonathan Edwards's sermon "Sinners in the Hands of an Angry God" was one of the most frightening sermons ever preached. Bildad's can certainly rival that. I run a training course for preachers. Had I heard Bildad preach this one, I would have had to give him high marks—on every count except one. Those who preach know well that the proper application of a sermon is perhaps the most difficult part to get right. Bildad gets this part horribly wrong. His sermon is so fundamentally misapplied that it needs to be consigned to the incinerator of failed sermons. It is not an edifying sermon; and yet to understand why is it unedifying will, paradoxically, be deeply edifying for us.

So let us hear Bildad. Job has just spoken of his "house" and his "bed" and asked where he is going and how he can hope to live in the place of death (17:13–16). Bildad answers and says in summary, "I know where you are going. You are on the road to Hell."

Bildad's sermon has two parts. First (vv. 1–4) he opens up the core issue, which is the moral stability of the world as somewhere in which everything and everyone has its or their place. Then most of the sermon is a description of the place in the created order where the wicked dwell. The idea of place runs through the sermon, whether it be "place" (vv. 4, 21), "tent" (vv. 6, 14, 15), "habitation" (v. 15), or "street" (v. 17).

The Issue: A Tidy World Where Everything Has Its Place (vv. 1–4)

Some homes are a mess, and some homes are tidy. Some homeowners are constantly tidying, fighting against the Second Law of Thermodynamics, keeping things in their right places. But what is the world like? What kind of homeowner is God? That is a trivial example. But it illustrates the issue that Bildad introduces.

> Then Bildad the Shuhite answered and said:
>
>> "How long will you hunt for words?
>>   Consider, and then we will speak.
>> Why are we counted as cattle?
>>   Why are we stupid in your sight?
>> You who tear yourself in your anger,
>>   shall the earth be forsaken for you,
>>   or the rock be removed out of its place?" (vv. 1–4)

Bildad begins angrily accusing Job of playing word games (v. 2a). The address "you" is plural here; perhaps Bildad implies that Job is just one of a larger class of wicked people. He challenges him to come to his senses (ESV, "Consider"; NIV, "Be sensible") and let the friends speak (v. 2b). In his last speech Bildad challenged Job to listen to the wisdom of tradition (8:8). Job has rudely suggested he might as well ask advice from cattle (12:7). "Are you calling us cattle? Do you think we're stupid?" asks Bildad in effect (18:3).

Job has accused God of tearing at him (16:9). Bildad says that what is really happening is self-harm (18:4a : "you . . . tear yourself"), which is as pointless for Job as it would be for the prophets of Baal in a later age (1 Kings 18:28, 29). He is aggravating his grief by getting hot under the collar, and it won't do any good. The reason it won't do any good—and this is the nub—is that the creation order cannot be disturbed (v. 4b). "The earth" and "the rock" are pictures of the stability of the world (v. 4). They picture not just the physical predictability of the physical sciences but also moral order. When Hannah rejoices that God puts wrongs right, she says, "For the pillars of the earth are the LORD's, and on them he has set the world" (1 Samuel 2:8b).[1]

In Bildad's view, by Job's suggesting that his suffering is undeserved, he is challenging the well-ordered nature of the world. To ask God to bless a sinner like him is like asking God to move the mountains around just for him, so that, uniquely in Job's case, an exception can be made! Ironically, Job has already accused God of doing this kind of thing, calling him "he who removes mountains . . . overturns them . . . shakes the earth . . . and its pillars tremble" (9:5, 6).

The word "place" (18:4b) is significant. Bildad and his friends inhabit a conceptual universe that is like a tidy house in which everything has its place and everything is in its place. Or if it isn't, we may be sure it will soon be put back. They are the moral equivalent of the very house-proud person who will not abide things being out of place. Job, they think, is like a rude guest who comes in and wants to trash the place.

The Place of the Wicked in a Tidy World (vv. 5–21)

We still use the idea of *place* in a metaphorical sense when we say things like "I'm not in a good place at the moment." In the descriptions that follow, the "place," "tent," or "habitation" of the wicked is a vivid way of speaking of their "total world."[2]

Instead of wanting to remove the rock "out of its place" (v. 4), disrupting creation order, Bildad invites Job to come and see the place where wicked people dwell. In his tidy world, if a person is in that place, they must be wicked. Job is invited to draw his own conclusions.

Bildad paints a terrifying picture in five stages.

Hell Is the Place of Total Darkness (vv. 5, 6)

> Indeed, the light of the wicked is put out,
> and the flame of his fire does not shine.
> The light is dark in his tent,
> and his lamp above him is put out. (vv. 5, 6)

When a man is "wicked," he is destined for darkness. The fourfold repetition of words for light (v. 5a, "light"; v. 5b, "flame of his fire," that is, a light-giving burning torch; v. 6a, "light"; v. 6b, "lamp") builds an emphatic picture of life extinguished in death. In Hell there is not even a glimmer of light.

At the end of his previous speech Job spoke of Sheol as the place where he must "make [his] bed in darkness" (17:13). At the end of a previous speech he also spoke of having a one-way ticket "to the land of darkness and deep shadow, the land of gloom like thick darkness, like deep shadow without any order, where light is as thick darkness" (10:21, 22). Bildad agrees but states that the only people who suffer this fate are the wicked. "Draw your own conclusions, Job."

Hell Is the Place of Inescapable Punishment (vv. 7–10)

> His strong steps are shortened,
> and his own schemes throw him down.
> For he is cast into a net by his own feet,

and he walks on its mesh.
A trap seizes him by the heel;
    a snare lays hold of him.
A rope is hidden for him in the ground,
    a trap for him in the path. (vv. 7–10)

In verses 7–10 the dominant metaphor is the trap. Six times, once in each half-verse of 8–10, there is a word for trap ("net," "mesh," "trap," "snare," "rope" (a noose), and "trap" again). Verse 7 is the key. Here is a man with "strong steps," vigorous strides, a man with power and confidence. He is a wicked man in prosperity. But as he walks along his way, these confident "steps" will be "shortened"; he will come to a standstill. Why? Because "his own schemes," the craftiness and twistedness of his wickedness, will "throw him down." He is "hoist with his own petard."[3] And being "throw[n] down" he finds himself heading to the underworld. His sin is the cause ("his own schemes"), and death is the result (Romans 5:12).

Verses 8–10 draw a vivid picture of this man. We see him tripped up by his own trap (v. 8), seized by the heel and gripped by the snare (v. 9), entangled in his own noose (v. 10). The point is that his fate is inescapable. All the skill of the hunter's art stands against him, and he cannot escape. Hell is the place of inescapable punishment.

Job feels himself hunted and trapped by God. God has hunted him (10:16) and has put his feet in the stocks (13:27). He knows what it is to be "hedged in" (3:23), trapped and unable to escape. Precisely, says Bildad. Hell is that place. And the only people in Hell are the wicked. "Draw your own conclusion, Job."

The next image presses forward from being trapped to being terrified.

Hell Is the Place of Insatiable Terror (vv. 11–14)

Terrors frighten him on every side,
    and chase him at his heels.
His strength is famished,
    and calamity is ready for his stumbling.
It consumes the parts of his skin;
    the firstborn of death consumes his limbs.
He is torn from the tent in which he trusted
    and is brought to the king of terrors. (vv. 11–14)

Terror brackets verses 11–14.[4] The word "terrors" has overtones of the demonic; it is associated with darkness and Sheol.[5] Terrors are almost like evil spirits bringing the fear of Sheol into human hearts. We might think of the Black Riders in the Lord of the Rings trilogy.

In verse 12a ("His strength is famished") the reference is not to Job's hunger but to the appetite of "the king of terrors" (v. 14). "Calamity" (v. 12b) is ready and waiting for him to stumble into his trap. And when he does, it will start to consume him (v. 13), both his "skin," the outer protection of his existence, and his "limbs." The expression "the firstborn of death" (v. 13) probably does not refer to a god other than death but to death himself as the firstborn, the one with supreme authority in the realm of the dead, "the king of terrors." He tears the wicked man away from his "tent," which he thought was secure (that "in which he trusted"), and drags him off to face "the king of terrors" (v. 14).

This is a terrifying picture of death as the Grim Reaper with an insatiable appetite for living beings, with the right to consume and devour the wicked. Hell is the place of insatiable terror, of terror that goes on and on and is never satisfied. Job's skin and bones have been cruelly attacked (2:4, 5). Job feels that "the terrors of God" are arrayed against him (6:4); he cannot sleep at night, and his fear is incessant (7:4); he is in a constant state of terror (9:34), terrified by God's angry majesty (13:11, 21). Precisely, says Bildad. Hell is the place being described. And the only people in Hell are the wicked. "Draw your own conclusion, Job."

Hell Is a Place of Total Dissolution (vv. 15, 16)

> In his tent dwells that which is none of his;
> > sulfur is scattered over his habitation.
> His roots dry up beneath,
> > and his branches wither above. (vv. 15, 16)

Next incessant terror is accompanied by total dissolution of self. The dominant image here is fire. Eliphaz has introduced this idea in 15:30. Bildad develops it vividly.

Verse 15a should probably be translated "Fire resides in his tent."[6] "Sulfur" is also called brimstone, the hot-burning substance that gives us our expression "fire and brimstone" (as in Sodom and Gomorrah). The wicked man's "tent" and "habitation" is utterly destroyed. Here is a fire that erupts from below, as the fires of Sheol did for Nathan and Abiram (Numbers 16; Psalm 106:17, 18). The destruction is total and irreversible because it burns up both his "branches" and his "roots" (Job 18:16).

Jesus used just this frightening image when speaking of Hell. Just as "fire and sulfur" rained down from Heaven on Sodom and Gomorrah in Lot's day, "so will it be on the day when the Son of Man is revealed' (Luke 17:29, 30). Hell is the place where "the fire is not quenched" (Mark 9:47, 48); it is "the eternal fire" (Matthew 25:41).

The point of this hot fire is that it dissolves the organic orderings that create and sustain life. It reduces the wonderful complexity and potentialities of organic life to a few lifeless inorganic molecules, or even atoms of carbon. Job used to be at the heart of a bustling organic society. But "the fire of God" (lightning) fell, and his society has been destroyed (1:16). Yes, says Bildad, Hell is the place of total dissolution. Only the wicked go there. "Draw your own conclusion, Job."

Hell Is the Place of Terrible Separation (vv. 17–20)

His memory perishes from the earth,
and he has no name in the street.
He is thrust from light into darkness,
and driven out of the world.
He has no posterity or progeny among his people,
and no survivor where he used to live.
They of the west are appalled at his day,
and horror seizes them of the east. (vv. 17–20)

In his last image Bildad paints Hell as the place of a terrible separation from this world of life and light. The wicked are a blot on the landscape; they will and must be taken away into another place. And this will be complete; not a speck of their dust will be left behind. Bildad conveys this in the images of their "memory" or "name" (v. 17; their reputation) and of their descendants ("posterity or progeny" [v. 19]). We read elsewhere that in judgment God has "blotted out" the "name" of the guilty "forever and ever" (Psalm 9:5). The psalmist prays that God "may cut off the memory" of the wicked "from the earth" (Psalm 109:15). This is the judgment of God.

When the family name is gone and there is no home on earth where there are any memorabilia of a man, any photos or drawings, anyone to say, "That was my great-granddad," and when historical records have faded so that they have slipped from being front-page news to being a footnote in history books, and finally even the footnote is deleted, when that happens they have no more existence on earth. It is a terrible thing to be extinguished and obliterated from life on earth. But that is the fate of the wicked.

The paradox of Hell is that it is the place that is not a place. It is a place with no stability, no center, no location in the universe. The new heavens and new earth will have no place for Hell. It will be, in an absolute sense, outside of reality. There is a partial analogy with the way Babylon in Bible imagery became the place symbolizing scattering, the place that is not a place.[7]

When a wicked man is trapped by his own evil, sucked down into death and darkness, his whole personality dissolved in eternal flames, there will be nothing left of him on earth. This is an appalling fate (v. 20), just as Job's friends were astonished to see Job's condition (2:12, 13). With the death of his children, Job feels he is well on the way to being wiped off the face of the earth. Precisely, says Bildad. That is Hell. And only the wicked go to Hell. "Draw your own conclusion, Job."

Conclusion: Hell Is the Place for the Wicked (v. 21)

> Surely such are the dwellings of the unrighteous,
>   such is the place of him who knows not God. (v. 21)

Bildad rests his case by asserting that this terrible place of total darkness, inescapable punishment, insatiable terror, total dissolution, and terrible separation, Hell, is the dwelling place of all unrighteous people who do not know God.[8] He invites Job to draw his own conclusion.

Bildad's Application: Hell Is Where You Are Going, Job

Bildad does not spell out the application of his sermon, but it is clear. Job is already experiencing in anticipation the terrors of Hell. This is evidence of his wickedness and proves he is going to Hell. There is no appeal here to Job for repentance. Bildad seems to feel that it is too late for that.

Where Does Bildad Go Wrong?

Bildad and his friends are absolutely right that the cosmos is an ordered place. From Genesis 1 onward it has an order in which different beings have different places. The proper place of any component of the cosmos expresses something of its function in the government of the universe. The "waters that were above the expanse [firmament]" (Genesis 1:7) stay above the firmament, the fish stay in the sea, the dry land stays dry, and so on. The universe is a cosmos, not a place of chaos. Bildad's portrait of Hell is terribly accurate and powerfully persuasive; Hell is all the things that Bildad says it is. The day will come when the Creator will tidy up the universe once and for all, and in that day the wicked will indeed be swept away into that place that is no place.

So where does Bildad go wrong? He goes wrong because Job is not wicked. Job is "blameless and upright . . . [he] fears God and turns away from evil" (1:1, 8; 2:3). A blameless and upright believer is enduring the torments of Hell. But Bildad's System has no place for this. The way Bildad thinks of creation order is pretty much a perfect order undisturbed by the earthquake of man's disobedience. The reality is that wicked people do sometimes prosper, and blameless believers do sometimes suffer undeserved grief.

Supremely Job's experience of Hell is fulfilled by the Lord Jesus Christ's entering into Hell for us on the cross. When Jesus went to Hell for us, the land was cast into supernatural "darkness" (Mark 15:33). He felt himself dragged down into the inescapable punishment of sinners, the insatiable terrors of Hell, and the total dissolution of his relationship with his Father; he endured the terrible separation from this world in public disgrace. And he did it to redeem sinners. He went to Hell that we might go to Heaven. The book of Job makes no ultimate sense without the cross of Christ.

Furthermore, Christ's disciples are called to live in a world on the road to Hell, in bodies as yet unredeemed (Romans 8:23). And therefore, although they are headed for the new creation and resurrection bodies, in this age they too must expect in some measure to drink the cup that Jesus drank. They must expect some darkness, some feeling of being trapped in a world under sin, some experiences that bring them terror, and some feelings of not belonging to this world. Because Jesus has drunk the cup of God's wrath to the dregs, we will never have to do that; but we cannot escape his words to James and John: "You will drink my cup" (Matthew 20:23).

15

Job's Second Reply to Bildad: Is God for Me or against Me?

JOB 19

AS WE HAVE LISTENED TO JOB, we have seen some paradoxical marks of a true worshipper. One of these is that he experiences deeply the pain of seeing a world he knows ought to be righteous but has become deeply unfair. Another is that in spite of this pain he does not become ultimately cynical but longs passionately for the God who is—or ought to be—running this troubled world. These two marks together, paradoxical as they are, issue in a life deeply marked by pain and by prayer. At the heart of the pain is the tension between the "god" who seems to be running this world and the God we hope and trust is actually doing so. The character of the one seems so puzzlingly at odds with the perfection of the other.

In a way the deepest question Job faces is, is God for me or against me? Ultimately nothing else matters. If God be for me, on my side, then ultimately nothing and no one can do me lasting harm, and I will come through it as more than a conqueror (Psalm 56:9; Romans 8:31–39). But if God is against me, then my despair is well grounded in objective reality.

This question lies beneath the question "Why?" that echoes in the book of Job (from 3:20, 23 onward) and on through the history of believers in pain. Glenn Chambers was a young Christian from New York. He had a lifelong dream of serving God in Ecuador. At last the opportunity came, and he was at the airport about to depart. Just before he left, he searched for a scrap of paper to write his mother a farewell note. All he could find was a scrap from a magazine, which happened to have an advertisement with the question "Why?" printed in large type. So he scribbled his farewell note around it, put it in an envelope, and mailed it. That night his airplane crashed into a mountain in Colombia, and he was killed. When his mother opened the letter a couple of days later, that question shouted at her from the page: *Why? Why did my son die?*

It is such a common question, but such a real one. "Why did she die?" asks a widower. "We had such plans for our retirement, and now I have nothing, and I am so alone." "Why did he get Alzheimer's?" asks the elderly wife. "From now on it will just be an agonizing weary, oh-so-gradual bereavement. Why did that have to happen? Why do I have to watch him whom I love fade away into absurdity and confusion?" "Why did I get into this job," asks another troubled Christian, "that is working out so badly, so full of frustration?" "Why was my childhood so difficult?" asks another. "Why did my parents split up, leaving such a long shadow of pain and insecurity in me? Why did that have to happen, so that I live with the consequences every day?" "Why was my son born handicapped," asks a weary mother, "so that all those childhood years were shot through with exhaustion and the bittersweet pain of caring for one who will never fulfill the potential of other babies? Why?"

Or to put all these questions another way, what was going on in Heaven to make this happen? Whose purpose was it, if there is a purpose? By whose doing, by whose agency did this thing happen? Whose hand did this? Or to put it most sharply, is God for me or against me? What kind of God does what he did to Job, trapping a believer in a prison of suffering, loneliness, pain, and misery?

You see, says the Christian, I read in the Bible that God loves me, that he cares about me, that he is for me. But if I'm honest it doesn't seem like that. There are times when it feels like God is against me. Perhaps he is.

Of all Job's laments, chapter 19 focuses most sharply on this crucial question. It leads us to the heart of the book.

The problem with the question, is God for me or against me? is that we all know the Sunday school answer. We know the answer we are supposed to give. Of course God is for us if we are in Christ (Romans 8:31–39). It is the answer we long to give. And yet . . .

Job is too honest just to let that pat answer trip off his tongue or to settle for the answer he is meant to give. He says, "I can't say that without being totally unreal."

Context

Bildad has just given an accurate and spine-chilling description of the fate of the wicked. He has implicitly invited Job to see how this matches up with his own experience and to draw the conclusion of The System that he himself must be deeply wicked.

Job is well able to do that. In some ways much of this next speech echoes that of Bildad. But the punch line does not!

Job says three main things here.

God Attacks Me as a Sinner (vv. 1–12)

First, Job freely admits that the way God is treating him is the way God treats God's enemies.

> Then Job answered and said:
>
> > "How long will you torment me
> >   and break me in pieces with words?
> > These ten times you have cast reproach upon me;
> >   are you not ashamed to wrong me?
> > And even if it be true that I have erred,
> >   my error remains with myself.
> > If indeed you magnify yourselves against me
> >   and make my disgrace an argument against me,
> > know then that God has put me in the wrong
> >   and closed his net about me." (vv. 1–6)

Job begins, as he has done before, by rebuking his friends. By their "words," the arguments of The System, they have broken him and tormented him (v. 2). This is strong language. To "torment," afflict, or inflict is what God did to Israel in the exile:

> Is it nothing to you, all you who pass by?
>   Look and see
> if there is any sorrow like my sorrow,
>   which was brought upon me,
> which the LORD *inflicted*
>   on the day of his fierce anger. (Lamentations 1:12)

It is their "words" or arguments that have caused this grief to Job. We might have thought his bankruptcy, bereavement, and broken health would be enough. But the deepest pain is their accusation that his sufferings prove that God is against him. It is this that drives an arrow right into his heart. They have "cast reproach" on him and wronged him by saying this, and they have done it repeatedly, "ten times" (v. 3).[1] Job is not claiming sinless perfection (v. 4): he may have "erred," but he has a clear conscience and no awareness of unforgiven sin such as might have caused his sufferings.[2] They see themselves as morally better than Job (they "magnify [themselves] against" him) and see his "disgrace" as proof of his guilt and hence "an argument against" him (v. 5).

But they need to understand that while they are right to imply that God is the author of Job's woes, "God has put [him] in the wrong" (v. 6). The verb "put . . . in the wrong" means here to pervert justice, exactly what Bildad has denied that God does (8:3).

Job is suffering the fate of sinners. Bildad can wax eloquent about that fate in theory, but Job can describe it from the inside, from his own agonizing experience. Here is Hell from the inside.

> Behold, I cry out, "Violence!" but I am not answered;
>   I call for help, but there is no justice.
> He has walled up my way, so that I cannot pass,
>   and he has set darkness upon my paths.
> He has stripped from me my glory
>   and taken the crown from my head.
> He breaks me down on every side, and I am gone,
>   and my hope has he pulled up like a tree.
> He has kindled his wrath against me
>   and counts me as his adversary.
> His troops come on together;
>   they have cast up their siege ramp against me
>   and encamp around my tent. (vv. 7–12)

In verse 7 Job is like a man being mugged in the street. He cries out "Violence!" but no one answers or helps. And the mugger is God! God ought to be the one who comes to the help of the afflicted. But he is the mugger, and "there is no justice."

The dominant image in verses 8–12 is that of being trapped like a city under siege. He blocks all escapes and shrouds Job's paths in "darkness" (v. 8). Like a king in a besieged city, Job is stripped of his "glory" and "crown," his capacity to rule as a man in the image of God (v. 9). The walls of his life are broken down on every side (v. 10a). Job has said that a cut-down tree has hope of growing again (14:7–9), but when God has attacked him, he has pulled him up by the roots so there is no hope for him (19:10b). God's attitude is hot and personal, his "wrath" has been kindled like a furnace against Job, and he counts Job "as his adversary" (v. 11). "I thought I was God's friend," says Job, "but God clearly thinks differently."

The climax is the massive overkill of verse 12. "His troops," all the armies of the Lord of hosts, "come on together"; they set up "their siege ramp." We can imagine this huge army setting up its armaments on all sides. But whom are they attacking? It is so pathetic: Job is on his own in his "tent," a picture of fragility and weakness. "What threat can I possibly be to God? It is as if I go for a night's camping on my own. I wake, peep out of the tent, and all around me are tanks and gun emplacements; overhead is the entire United States Air Force—all bent on attacking little old me."[3]

It is a terrible thing to have one's life invaded and broken down and to have no possible means of escape. The experience of being trapped in a city under siege is not one most of us have experienced. Later in the Bible story the inhabitants of Jerusalem experienced this more than once, by the Assyrians (that siege was lifted) and by the Babylonians (it ended in the sacking of the city). Job's whole life feels like that. It is the fate of sinners.

God Cruelly Isolates Me as a Sinner (vv. 13–20)

It is not enough that God has attacked him. God has also isolated him cruelly so that he has no human companionship, no fellowship, and no helper who can take his side. He is utterly alone.

> He has put my brothers far from me,
>   and those who knew me are wholly estranged from me.
> My relatives have failed me,
>   my close friends have forgotten me.
> The guests in my house and my maidservants count me as a stranger;
>   I have become a foreigner in their eyes.
> I call to my servant, but he gives me no answer;
>   I must plead with him with my mouth for mercy.
> My breath is strange to my wife,
>   and I am a stench to the children of my own mother.
> Even young children despise me;
>   when I rise they talk against me.
> All my intimate friends abhor me,
>   and those whom I loved have turned against me.
> My bones stick to my skin and to my flesh,
>   and I have escaped by the skin of my teeth. (vv. 13–20)

This is a terrible portrayal of the miserable loneliness of Hell. All the people whom Job had felt he could rely on have abandoned him. It is not just that he has discovered his Facebook friends to be shallow (that would be no surprise); those closest to him, those bound to him with ties of loyal friendship and fond love, have all failed him (vv. 13, 14). They have removed him from the equivalent of their Christmas card lists or their party invitations, for he is a public disgrace and as good as dead. They would as soon be associated with him as they would with a convicted criminal on death row.

In his own home he used to be honored master of the house. Now his former guests and his servants treat him like a dead man (v. 15). Verse 16 paints a pathetic picture of this great man calling to his servant. In the old days the moment the bell rang, the man would have scurried to Job's room and stood respectfully, awaiting his orders. Now he ignores Job, even though Job pleads with him for help. What a cruel reversal!

Job's ostracism extends even to his intimate family. His breath is repulsive to his wife and brothers, who cannot stand to have him near them (v. 17).[4] When little children come home from school, they poke fun at him (v. 18); we may perhaps imagine them throwing rotten fruit at this target for public ridicule. Even his closest friends have turned against him (v. 19); the word translated "intimate friends" appears in Psalm 55:12–14 ("familiar friend") in the experience of betrayal.

Job knows what it is to be attacked by God as a sinner, to be abandoned by all human help and devoid of all human love. Bildad has implied that this is what is happening to Job, and Job agrees. The difference is that Bildad assumes Job deserves it, and Job knows he does not. Bildad cannot cope with the idea of the innocent suffering, for it would challenge The System. Job is grappling honestly with the paradox of innocent suffering. What he now says is the logical and faith-inspired hope that arises from his clear conscience. We need to trace his inspired reasoning carefully.

And Yet God Will Be My Redeemer to Vindicate Me (vv. 21–29)

Job begins with a diagnosis, out of which arises a wish; this wish develops into a confident hope, which in turn is followed by a warning.

A Diagnosis: The Hand of God Has Touched Me (vv. 21, 22)

> Have mercy on me, have mercy on me, O you my friends,
> for the hand of God has touched me!
> Why do you, like God, pursue me?
> Why are you not satisfied with my flesh? (vv. 21, 22)

In this renewed rebuke of his "friends" (friends who are false friends), Job reasserts his diagnosis: "the hand of God has touched me!" (v. 21). To the question, is God for me or against me? there can be only one answer thus far: "Clearly he is against me. He regards me as his enemy and treats me as such, tearing viciously at my life and isolating me from all solace."

But we ought to pause a moment and consider Job's diagnosis. In verse 21 Job said, "The *hand* of God has touched me!" Is this true? Let us look back at something we know but Job doesn't. Is it true that the hand of God has struck him? Look back at 1:11, 12 where the Satan says to the Lord, "Stretch out your hand and touch all that he has. . . ." Does the Lord stretch out his hand against Job? No, he doesn't. In verse 12 we read, "And the Lord said to Satan, 'Behold, all that he has is in *your hand.*'" Again in 2:5, 6 the Satan asks the Lord to "stretch out your hand . . ."; but the Lord replies, "Behold, he is in *your* hand." The hands and fingers that destroyed Job's possessions and killed Job's children and wrecked Job's health were the hands of the Satan, not the hands of God. Yes, it was the hand of the Satan acting with the permission of the Lord and within the strict constraints given by the Lord; but it was the Satan's hand and not God's that actually did these terrible things.[5]

So whose are the monstrous hands that have attacked Job and ripped at him and isolated him and made his life a misery? Answer: the hands of the enemy, the Satan—acting with the permission of God and constrained by the strict limits given by God.

This is a very important insight. The Satan is fond of disguise; he "disguises himself as an angel of light" (2 Corinthians 11:14). Again and again in the book of Job the Satan masquerades as the Lord and persuades Job that it is directly the Lord who has turned against him. As when the Roman soldiers blindfolded Jesus and hit him—"Who is it that struck you?" (Luke 22:64)—Job cannot see whose hand is striking him.

We know this. But Job doesn't, and his friends certainly don't. They have no place in their theology for the Satan. Their world is a simple slot-machine world, with one slot-machine maker who has set the rules: put in a coin of goodness and out pops a canister of blessing; put in a coin of badness and out clunks a parcel of poison. Their God is not the Creator and Sustainer, but the clockmaker who sets the machine running and then just leaves it to run (an idea that was later shared by the eighteenth-century Deists). The idea that there might be real forces of evil in this world, forces with real personality and real influence, has no place in their thinking.

Although Job, like his friends, does not know what has happened in Heaven in chapters 1, 2, he is now beginning to wonder whose hand is behind his suffering. We have seen that in 9:24 he asks in perplexity, "If it is not [the Lord], then who is it?" Who treats his world so unfairly? These things are happening; God is in control; so presumably they are God's doing. If it is not God doing them, who is it?

Although most of Job's laments are just that—laments—somehow Job as a real believer cannot let go of the hope that ultimately the monster god is not the true God who has the last word. We find this longing hinted at in 9:33–35: "There is no arbiter between [me and God], who might lay his hand on us both . . ." (or possibly, "Would that there were an arbiter . . ."). However it is translated, the sense is that he wishes there were an arbiter, a just judge who would see that justice is done, as it were a God above the monster god.

In 16:18–21 we see this longing grow stronger: "O earth, cover not my blood" (v. 18); that is to say, "May my innocence and the unfairness of it all never be forgotten" (the idea being like the blood of *righteous* Abel in Genesis 4:10). May it not be that an innocent man is quietly buried and forgotten. "Let my cry [that is, my cry for justice] find no resting place. Even now, behold my witness [that is, the witness who speaks up for me in the law court] is in heaven, and he who testifies for me is on high" (16:18, 19). Somehow Job glimpses that there will be justice in the end, that a real believer will finally be vindicated and seen to be a real believer.

So we come to perhaps the pinnacle of Job's faith in the darkness.

A Wish—for Vindication (vv. 23, 24)

> Oh that my words were written!
>> Oh that they were inscribed in a book!
> Oh that with an iron pen and lead
>> they were engraved in the rock forever! (vv. 23–24)

Abandoned by all human helpers, Job yet longs to be proved to be in the right with God. He is still very glum. He has been fighting to prove his innocence. But it's a losing battle. He's pretty sure he's going to die. And he knows (v. 22b) that when he dies, his friends will not be satisfied with his death ("Why are you not satisfied with my flesh?"). They will malign his reputation forever. Under the banner heading "RIP (not)," they will put on his gravestone, "Here lies Job, who was a sinner with secret sins he refused to confess; he has paid the penalty for his sins at last, and the justice of God has been vindicated by his death. May he not rest in peace."

So with the repeated cry "Oh, that . . ."[6] he longs for his vindication to be written in a way that will survive his death. The issue is between "my words" (v. 23a) and their "words," with which they are breaking him in pieces (v. 2). Underneath, the contest is about the final verdict on his life. Their "words" say he is an unforgiven sinner paying the penalty for his sin; his "words" say he is a genuine believer who trusted God for forgiveness and walked with him.

The "words" that win will determine Job's destiny; this is why they matter so deeply.

There is a desperate crescendo here as he longs that his words may be recorded "in a book" (v. 23; or scroll), and then, as if he knows how impermanent a book can be, "with an iron pen and lead . . . engraved in the rock" (that is, on a stela) so that they will last "forever" (v. 24). Job's life is evanescent, like a cloud (7:9), or a lake (14:11, 12), worse than even a cut-down tree (14:7–10). A rock has the metaphorical solidity of God himself (e.g., Deuteronomy 32:4).[7] He yearns for a permanent and ineradicable vindication. (It is a lovely irony that we are still reading his words in his book so many centuries later!)

A Confident Hope—of Vindication by a Redeemer (vv. 25–27)
And yet. And yet. The longing for an eternal vindication ("forever") needs more even than an inscription on rock (v. 24). The steady erosion of the elements renders even that impermanent. So Job now makes the wonderful jump from a yearning ("Oh, that . . .") to a faith-filled hope ("I know . . .").[8]

> For I know that my Redeemer lives,
>   and at the last he will stand upon the earth.
> And after my skin has been thus destroyed,
>   yet in my flesh I shall see God,
> whom I shall see for myself,
>   and my eyes shall behold, and not another.
> My heart faints within me! (vv. 25–27)

What does Job "know" (v. 25)? By faith he knows three wonderful truths: he has a living Redeemer, this Redeemer will stand upon the earth, and Job will see him with his own eyes.

First, he has a living Redeemer. The "Redeemer" (*go'el*) was someone tied to you by covenant, usually a relative, whose calling was to stand for you when you were wronged (v. 25). If you were murdered, he saw to it that your murderer was punished;[9] if your share in the promised land was under threat, he safeguarded it;[10] if your widow was childless, he gave her a child. In every way he stood for you when you could not stand for yourself; he is your "Vindicator" (Pope, Fyall) and "Champion" (Clines). One of the most beautiful illustrations of this principle is in the book of Ruth, where Boaz acts as Naomi and Ruth's kinsman-redeemer, caring for them in their widowhood and becoming for Ruth the husband she needs. Job is confident he has a Redeemer who "lives" (v. 25), meaning "lives forever" in contrast with the impermanence even of an inscription on stone.

This Redeemer can be none other than God himself, the living God who often in the Old Testament stands as the Redeemer of his people. Many modern commentators reject this conclusion because they "find intolerable the logic . . . that God will help Job against God."[11] But their alternatives—perhaps that Job's "Redeemer" is his words, which he is confident will survive his death, or a sympathetic member of the heavenly council—are pathetically inadequate by comparison. This Redeemer must "live" in an absolute sense, and he must be able to stand for Job as an equal before God, who is Job's accuser. No one less eternal than God or of lower status than God will suffice.

This is not logical, by the sort of logic that the religious or philosophical systems can manage, but it is ultimately true. It is one of the deep ways in which the book of Job, like the whole Old Testament, ultimately does not make sense without Christ and without God, who is the Trinity. The sufferings of Job are a type and foreshadowing of the sufferings of Christ, in whom God is for us. As Luther put it, with his wonderful grasp of gospel paradox, God "loved us even as he hated us." It is not only that the believer is *simul iustus et peccator* (at the same time a justified man and a sinner); God is *simul Iudex et Redemptor* (at the same time Judge and Redeemer).

Second, Job knows by faith that this Redeemer will "at the last . . . stand upon the earth," literally "upon the dust," which may be a reference to Job's grave (v. 25). "Better than a fading tombstone inscribed with my vindication, there will be an eternally living vindicator standing on my grave, attesting my genuineness and right relationship with God." In this context the word "stand" refers to a witness standing in court to bear testimony.[12]

Third, Job knows that in the end he will see this Redeemer-God with his own eyes (vv. 26, 27). Although there is some uncertainty in translation, it seems that Job expects this to happen after his death ("after my skin has been thus destroyed" [v. 26]).[13] As he has longed, he will indeed be hidden in Sheol and then summoned in resurrection to meet his God (14:13–17). Far from death tearing off his "skin" and marching him off to "the king of terrors," as Bildad has asserted (18:13, 14), Job will be escorted to meet his God face-to-face.

To stand before God carries with it the meaning of having right relationship with God finally recognized and being vindicated. At the end of Psalm 17 David cries out, "As for me, I shall be vindicated and will see your face" (Psalm 17:15a NIV).[14] This anticipatory, faith-fueled confidence of Job anticipates his words "now my eye sees you" after God's final speech (Job 42:5).

It is all very personal, from the emphatic "*I* know" (v. 25) to the "whom I shall see for myself, and my eyes shall behold, and not another" (v. 27). Job's faith makes this future reality so vivid that it is almost as if he is already experiencing this longed-for vision of God. "My heart faints within me!" (v. 27). "Heart" is literally "bowels" or "kidneys," the seat of the emotions. We sometimes speak of having butterflies in our stomach; this was more like elephants.[15] The deepest longing of Job's heart is to stand before the God he loves and worships, and he believes that he will. He is a prophet, and the Spirit of Christ within him searches and inquires about what person and time is being indicated by these longings (1 Peter 1:10–12).

So Job says in effect, "I will not finally believe that the monster god is the God who made this world. I know that the God I have always feared and loved is related to me by covenant—I belong to him and his family and his people—and in the end, even if it is after my death, I will see him, and he will vindicate me so that it will be publicly seen that I have been a real believer with a clear conscience."

This is an extraordinary insight of faith. Even though Job then goes back into further chapters of lament, Christians read these words and rightly say, "Job spoke more truly than he realized!" There is a sovereign Redeemer who lives and who will one day vindicate every believer and declare him or her justified from all sin. The true God is the Father who sent his Son into the world to be the innocent believer who dies for sinners; and the true God is the Son who so loved us that he gave himself for us. So indeed every believer can say, "God is for me in Christ; and no power or death or demon in the present or the future can separate me from his love in Christ" (cf. Romans 8:31–39).

How can we be sure of this? Because there was once a real believer whom the monster god attacked with all his vicious terrors, a blameless believer who experienced a terrible death he did not deserve and whom the Redeemer God vindicated publicly on the third day when he raised him from the dead.

George Frederick Handel's librettist (Charles Jennens) was absolutely right when he set Job 19:25, 26 alongside the words "Now is Christ risen from the dead . . ." in that great aria in *The Messiah*. It is precisely the bodily resurrection of Christ that gives us the assurance that Job's confidence was not wishful make-believe but sure and certain hope. The Father stood upon Christ's tomb and acted as his Redeemer, to vindicate him by resurrection. This same God will stand upon the grave of every man or woman in Christ, to act as our Redeemer. And on the last day we will stand justified and vindicated before him by grace.

A Warning—to Those Who Do Not Believe in Grace (vv. 28, 29)

But we must not miss the final warning. Right at the end Job turns back to his friends to warn them.

If you say, "How we will pursue him!"
   and, "The root of the matter is found in him,"
be afraid of the sword,
   for wrath brings the punishment of the sword,
   that you may know there is a judgment. (vv. 28, 29)

They are saying they will "pursue" Job (v. 28). He has accused them of this in verse 22, and he comes back to it now. They pursue him because they believe the cause of his sufferings is his sin; this is what "the root of the matter is found in him" means (v. 28). They will not believe that his suffering can be innocent and even redemptive. There is no place in their system either for undeserved suffering or undeserved grace. Therefore they stand in great danger, for those who align themselves with "the accuser of our brothers" (Revelation 12:10) have hanging over them a "sword" (v. 29; like the sword of Damocles in Greek legend); they are under the wrath of God (Ephesians 2:3), and the day will come when they will "know there is a judgment" (Job 19:29).

The final word of this magnificent speech is not Job's awestruck confidence in his justification and resurrection; it is his warning to his friends in danger. There is nothing more important for them than to come to know the reality of undeserved suffering, for this will point them to the cross of Christ and thus to the undeserved grace without which they can have no hope.

Each of us who suffers or who cares for another who suffers ask, "Why has this happened? Why did this happen to me or to her or to him?" And we ask, perhaps in some desperation, "Is God for me or against me?" It sometimes feels as though God is a monster set on making our lives miserable, so that you or I or one for whom we care feels alone and deeply hurt.

As we hear Job's faith in these words, we can bring our pain to the Lord Jesus Christ. Even though our life may be ebbing away and our wick is burning low, we too may say, "I know that my Redeemer lives, and at the last he will stand upon the earth. And after my skin has thus been destroyed, yet in my flesh I shall see God, whom I shall see for myself, and my eyes shall behold, and not another. My heart faints within me!" (vv. 25–27).

16

Zophar's Second Speech: Another Portrait of Hell

JOB 20

THE INTERACTIONS CONTINUE with another speech by Zophar. The frustration of Job's "friends" is evident.

Why Go On Listening to the Comforters?

Why do we have to go on and on listening to these dreadful speeches? After all, God is going to tell us at the end of the book that they are wrong (42:7). So what is the point of listening to them? What benefit can they possibly have for us? Sure, we are told that "all Scripture" is "profitable" to us and points us to faith in Christ (2 Timothy 3:16, 17). But in what way are these interminable and repetitive speeches profitable, and how do they point us to faith in Christ?

This is a natural question. One general answer is presumably to warn us not to be like them when our natural pharisaism causes grace to be leeched out of our conversation and we lapse into the religious certainties of grace-free philosophy or religion. These speeches stand as a warning to us to guard grace jealously.

But the question is intensified after we have heard Bildad's spine-tingling description of Hell in chapter 18 and when we are about to hear Zophar's equally terrifying description of judgment in chapter 20. What specifically is the benefit to us of having to listen to these detailed and deeply evocative descriptions of Hell?

To answer this question we need to acknowledge that the fault with these sermons is not only in their content but in their misapplication (as we saw with Bildad in Job 18). They describe life under the judgment of God and then implicitly note the parallels with Job's experience before drawing the conclusion that Job is under the judgment of God. Their deduction is false. Their sin lies in maligning God's chosen servant Job. But their descriptions of Hell are entirely accurate. And in that we have the clue we need.

These sermons, like some of the laments in the Psalms, help us feel and experience through poetry just how dreadful it will ultimately be to fall under the wrath of God. In helping us enter into that experience through poetry, they benefit us in at least three ways.

First, they terrify us and move us to warn unbelievers that unless they repent, this will indeed be their destiny. Second, they help us grasp the depth of darkness and suffering that the Lord Jesus experienced on the cross. On the cross he was indeed under the wrath of his Father as he became sin for us (2 Corinthians 5:21). The narrative accounts of the crucifixion in the Gospels only go so far in helping us know what he suffered for us. Although the old hymn is right to say that ultimately "we may not know, we cannot tell, what pains he had to bear,"[1] nevertheless we are given these poetic insights, and they are enough to deepen our gratitude to "the Son of God, who loved me and gave himself for me" (Galatians 2:20).

But there is a third benefit. If it is true, as we have seen that it is, that disciples of Christ in this age do have in some measure to drink the cup that he drank, that we do suffer with him in order that in the end we may be glorified with him (Romans 8:17), then these descriptions describe in some measure what we may expect to be our experience in this age (though not in the next). In all three ways we may expect to profit by listening to this next speech by Zophar.

Context

In chapter 18 Bildad has described life under judgment and implied that Job himself must be under the judgment of God. Job has agreed, at the start of chapter 19, but insists that he does not deserve it and believes that in the end he will be vindicated as a believer. Zophar is furious. The main thrust of his riposte is a reaffirmation of what Bildad said, but the imagery is different.

Zophar describes the fate of the wicked in three main ways. The wicked person, he says, will be disappointed by fading joy, poisoned by sweet evil, and overwhelmed by inescapable wrath.

The Wicked Person Will Be Disappointed by Fading Joy (vv. 1–11)

Human happiness is terribly short-lived. Zophar begins with an angry reassertion of a core element of The System (vv. 1–5) before developing his point with vivid imagery (vv. 6–11).

Then Zophar the Naamathite answered and said:

"Therefore my thoughts answer me,
　　because of my haste within me.
I hear censure that insults me,
　　and out of my understanding a spirit answers me.
Do you not know this from of old,
　　since man was placed on earth,
that the exulting of the wicked is short,
　　and the joy of the godless but for a moment?" (vv. 1–5)

Zophar begins by telling Job that he is deeply upset by Job's assertions that he, Job, will be vindicated (19:23–27) and—perhaps even more—that Zophar and his friends are liable to judgment (19:28, 29). It is outrageous of Job to say this! Verse 2 may be paraphrased, "So—because you have said these outrageous things—my troubled thoughts prompt me to answer you, and quickly ["my haste"] because I am very disturbed by them." That is, "You have insulted me [v. 3], and I must respond." Verse 3b does not mean that Zophar hears some other "spirit," but that his own spirit or breath (*ruach*), which is a spirit of understanding, prompts him to give the answer he is about to speak.

And here it is, in essence: "Do you not know [or "Surely you know"] that right from the beginning of creation ["since man was placed on earth"] there has been an immutable spiritual law? This law is supported by the universal tradition of morally serious religious people" (vv. 4, 5). Bildad (8:8) and Eliphaz (15:18, 19) have already appealed to long tradition, and Zophar agrees.

So here is the law: "the exulting [the happiness, joy, mirth, laughter] of the wicked is short, and the joy of the godless but for a moment" (v. 5). The System understands that godless people may, and often do, have times of happiness, but it is very short-lived, "short . . . but for a moment."[2] It simply will not last. He now develops this theme:

Though his height mount up to the heavens,
　　and his head reach to the clouds,
he will perish forever like his own dung;
　　those who have seen him will say, "Where is he?"
He will fly away like a dream and not be found;
　　he will be chased away like a vision of the night.
The eye that saw him will see him no more,
　　nor will his place any more behold him.
His children will seek the favor of the poor,
　　and his hands will give back his wealth.
His bones are full of his youthful vigor,
　　but it will lie down with him in the dust. (vv. 6–11)

Wicked people are proud (v. 6). Their metaphorical "height" (that is, their self-regarding greatness) climbs up to Heaven, and their heads touch the clouds, like Adam in the garden (Genesis 3) or the builders of the Tower of Babel (Genesis 11:1–9). But however successful they may become for a while, it will not last. They came from dust, and they will become like excrement (Job 20:7a), buried or washed away (as we would say, washed down the sewer). They were visible, both to the watching eyes of people and to the watchful eye of God, but they will disappear utterly from this age (vv. 7b–9). People will look for him but will ask, "Where is he?" (v. 7). They will disappear just as a dream "dies at the opening day."[3] This closely echoes what Job has said of himself in 7:7–10. Any day now he will disappear. "Exactly," says Zophar, "and you need to understand that this is the destiny of the wicked!"

What is more, he will leave so little behind. This is the significance of "his children" in verse 10. There is some question as to whether verse 10a means that his children will be so poor that they have to beg from the poor (ESV) or that his children will have to pay back to the poor what their father stole from them.[4] But the thrust is clear: he leaves behind no lasting memorial. He may have been young and strong, but he will die prematurely (v. 11); he came from dust, and he will return to dust, just as Job lamented he would do (7:21).

All this is true. It is what Moses laments in Psalm 90:3–6. This terrible disappearance will be the fate of the wicked. When they look back with regret on their wasted lives, their happiness, however long it may have seemed at the time, will be seen to be just a passing moment (Job 20:5).

But the implication that Job is suffering this because of his own sin is false. When Jesus Christ suffered and died, the times of happiness he may have enjoyed, perhaps with Mary in childhood, must have felt like a short-lived joy. His life is summed up not as a man of happiness but as "a man of sorrows . . . acquainted with grief" (Isaiah 53:3). He was cut down in his prime, but for our sin, not his. Job foreshadows this redemptive suffering. Those who walk in Jesus' footsteps must expect to experience in some measure this same sadness of happiness cut short in this age.

Zophar goes on with this theme of judgment taking what was good and turning it to misery.

The Wicked Person Will Be Poisoned by Sweet Evil (vv. 12–19)

The image now is of food that tastes good but turns out to be poison. This is an unnatural image. In nature poison generally tastes horrible, to warn us not to consume it. But sin is an unnatural poison; its sweet taste belies its disgusting nature.

> Though evil is sweet in his mouth,
> > though he hides it under his tongue,
> though he is loath to let it go
> > and holds it in his mouth,
> yet his food is turned in his stomach;
> > it is the venom of cobras within him.
> He swallows down riches and vomits them up again;
> > God casts them out of his belly.
> He will suck the poison of cobras;
> > the tongue of a viper will kill him.
> He will not look upon the rivers,
> > the streams flowing with honey and curds.
> He will give back the fruit of his toil
> > and will not swallow it down;
> from the profit of his trading
> > he will get no enjoyment.
> For he has crushed and abandoned the poor;
> > he has seized a house that he did not build. (vv. 12–19)

The imagery is simple and hard-hitting; the theological point is powerful. Evil tastes good, but evil always leads to nausea and vomiting. Evil is so deliciously enjoyable that the wicked person rolls it around in his mouth, savoring its taste and making it last as long as he can (vv. 12, 13), as we might do with a tasty chocolate. But the delicious taste of evil belies its sting. The moment we swallow it, as we ingest it and it becomes a part of ourselves, we discover we have swallowed venomous snake poison (vv. 14–16). Verse 15 makes it clear that the delicious food Zophar has in mind is "riches" gained unjustly. The wicked person gets them, swallows them, and then "vomits them up again" because "God casts them out of his belly." God is "the ultimate emetic" for evildoers.[5] The man whose "tongue" savored evil (v. 12) will be killed by that same evil, which is the "tongue" (that is, fangs) of a viper (v. 16).

This is the wisdom of Proverbs ("Bread gained by deceit is sweet to a man, but afterward his mouth will be full of gravel," Proverbs 20:17) and reflects the language of Deuteronomy about the enemies of God's people, whose "grapes are grapes of poison; their clusters are bitter; their wine is the poison of serpents and the cruel venom of asps" (Deuteronomy 32:32, 33).

Although wickedness promises so much and dangles before us a land flowing with milk and honey, echoing and imitating the promises of God (e.g., Exodus 3:8, 17),[6] it will never deliver what it promises (Job 20:17). Just as poison is vomited up, so "the fruit of [the wicked man's] toil" is sure to be given back; he cannot "swallow it down" and keep it down (v. 18a). He trades (unjustly) and makes big profits, but he will never live to enjoy them for long (v. 18b).

The reason is that the riches he is trying to swallow are the result of oppression, crushing the poor and leaving them destitute (v. 19). Although Zophar only implicitly links Job to this oppression, his friend Eliphaz will soon do so to his face (22:5–9), and Job will defend himself vigorously against it (Job 29—31).

As with verses 1–11, Zophar's description of crime and punishment is ultimately true. Hell is the place where all evil enjoyment is turned to endless nausea. We must be warned by this that the lure of wickedness is deceitful. What is more, Job's sufferings do mirror this description. He was full of riches but is now emptied of those riches. But again the implication that Job is suffering this fate because of his wickedness is deeply flawed. We learn from this yet more of the depth of the sufferings of the cross, and we learn to expect that disciples of Jesus will experience in some measure this same sense of nauseous loss.

The Wicked Person Will Be Overwhelmed by Inescapable Wrath (vv. 20–28)

In Zophar's final section he becomes more blunt than ever. He has explicitly named God in verse 15 as the author of punishment. Now he emphasizes that these griefs are more than the inevitable results of evil; they are the hot personal wrath of God against sinners.

> Because he knew no contentment in his belly,
>   he will not let anything in which he delights escape him.
> There was nothing left after he had eaten;
>   therefore his prosperity will not endure.
> In the fullness of his sufficiency he will be in distress;
>   the hand of everyone in misery will come against him.
> To fill his belly to the full,
>   God will send his burning anger against him
>   and rain it upon him into his body.
> He will flee from an iron weapon;
>   a bronze arrow will strike him through.
> It is drawn forth and comes out of his body;
>   the glittering point comes out of his gallbladder;
>   terrors come upon him.
> Utter darkness is laid up for his treasures;
>   a fire not fanned will devour him;
>   what is left in his tent will be consumed.
> The heavens will reveal his iniquity,

and the earth will rise up against him.
The possessions of his house will be carried away,
    dragged off in the day of God's wrath. (vv. 20–28)

Here is a man with an insatiable appetite (vv. 20, 21). He is never content or satisfied with his riches; he is always coveting and grasping after more. How much money is enough? an interviewer asked a billionaire. A little bit more than you have, came the famous reply.[7] But however bloated he may be ("the fullness of his sufficiency," v. 22) he will be miserable with it. God will fill him not with satisfaction but with "his burning anger," which will "rain . . . upon him into his body" (v. 23; an awkward translation, having the sense of God pouring his anger down on this man so that it goes right into his body and heart).

The hot anger of God will be inescapable (vv. 24, 25). Job has complained of God's poisoned arrows (6:4). Zophar describes them with intense power. Here is a wicked man who flees from an iron-tipped arrow but is struck by a bronze-tipped arrow, which goes right into him. He pulls it out (this is the sense of "it is drawn forth," 20:25), and when he pulls it out of his body, "the glittering point comes out of his gallbladder," and the bile or gall (symbolic of the corruption within him) pours out of him as the "terrors" of the underworld "come upon him" and he is dragged down into Hell (v. 25).

The destiny for him and his ill-gotten gains is "utter darkness" (v. 26) where a flame that comes from the wrath of God, a flame so hot that it has no need to be "fanned" by human hands, "will devour him," and all that he is and has ("what is left in his tent") will be utterly consumed by fire (v. 26).

There will be no escape from this fate, and there can be no appeal. "The heavens" and "the earth" unite in witness "against him" (v. 27). In Zophar's view, there will be, and can be, no witnesses for the defense, despite what Job hopes and believes will happen for him (16:19; 19:25–27). His "possessions" will be taken away (20:28), indeed violently "dragged off in the day of God's wrath."[8]

Conclusion (v. 29)

This is the wicked man's portion from God,
    the heritage decreed for him by God. (v. 29)

Zophar sums up in verse 29, which ties back to verses 4, 5. It is very clear, very simple, very accurate, and completely misapplied. Yes, this is "the wicked man's portion from God"; this is ultimately what will happen to all who do not love and trust God; this is a description of Hell. But no, this does not mean that Job, who is suffering these things, is himself wicked. Job in his innocent suffering foreshadows the Lord Jesus Christ and his substitutionary and redemptive sufferings. Zophar's description helps us grasp more deeply what Jesus did for us. And furthermore it helps shape our expectations of what the Christian life will be like this side of the resurrection. "Through many tribulations we must enter the kingdom of God" (Acts 14:22). Zophar has described some of them. When the Christian experiences short-lived joy cut off by grief, he or she is following in the footsteps of Christ. When disciples of Jesus feel their life poisoned by the fruits of the wickedness of others, they are walking in the footsteps of Jesus. When we live as forgiven and justified men and women in a world under judgment, we remember that Job has walked there before us. And we are not surprised.

17

Job's Second Reply to Zophar: The Good Life

JOB 21

IN THE UK, WHERE I LIVE, there used to be a TV series called *The Good Life*. In it a young couple decide to break with the bourgeois conventions of their neighbors and live a radically eco-conscious lifestyle. It is a comedy. Part of its fun is the play on the double meaning of "good": is their life morally good or enjoyably good or some unpredictable combination of the two? Although it is a sitcom, it touches on an important question. Do those who live morally good lives also enjoy pleasurably good lives? The flip side of that is: do those whose lifestyle is bad have a miserably bad time in life? The System of the comforters says both answers will be yes.

One of the comforters' major themes in this second cycle of speeches has been that bad things happen to bad people. Eliphaz has insisted on this: "The wicked man writhes in pain all his days" (15:20). Bildad agrees: "Indeed, the light of the wicked is put out" (18:5). Zophar rams the message home: ". . . the exulting of the wicked is short, and the joy of the godless but for a moment" (20:5). We have seen that their descriptions of the fate of the wicked have many verbal echoes of the way Job has described his own condition. They thus imply that Job must be one of the wicked.

In his first two speeches in this cycle (16, 17; 19) Job has majored on his struggles with God and reached out in faith to his conviction that God is just and that there will be a mediator for him in Heaven. Now at the end of the cycle he answers the comforters head-on. In a nutshell his argument is this: "You say that bad things happen to bad people. I agree that ultimately bad things will happen to bad people. But you only have to look around to see that in this life very good things often happen to bad people. My implication is, if the wicked do not yet get the judgment they deserve, then is it not possible that the righteous may experience in this life bad things they do not deserve, before their ultimate vindication? And is it not therefore possible that I, Job, am righteous, and your deduction is utterly false?"

Job's argument is important for us in our pastoral engagement with others. We cannot deduce the spiritual state of a man or woman from their current happiness or prosperity or their present sufferings. The fact of this ignorance needs to be burned onto our consciousness, lest we slip into the errors of Job's comforters.

We may divide Job's argument into three main parts. After an introduction (vv. 1–6), he observes that wicked people are often happy (vv. 7–16) before noting the flip side—wicked people are rarely punished (vv. 17–26). Finally (vv. 27–33) he makes the point that they prosper even in death. Then he concludes (v. 34) with a final rebuke to his friends.

Introduction (vv. 1–6)

Then Job answered and said:

> "Keep listening to my words,
>   and let this be your comfort.
> Bear with me, and I will speak,
>   and after I have spoken, mock on.
> As for me, is my complaint against man?
>   Why should I not be impatient?
> Look at me and be appalled,
>   and lay your hand over your mouth.
> When I remember, I am dismayed,
>   and shuddering seizes my flesh." (vv. 1–6)

Verse 2 is ironic: "I wish you would shut up and be silent, as you were at the start [2:11–13]; anything would be better than the painful nonsense you are spouting at me [v. 34]!" The words "your comfort" (v. 2b) are ambiguous in English but clearly have the sense of the consolation that his friends give him rather than any comfort they might receive from Job. He pleads for a few moments of silence on their part to listen to what he has to say before, no doubt, they "mock on" (v. 3).

Job's complaint is not ultimately against them but against God (v. 4a), and for this reason it is not surprising he is "troubled" (v. 4b KJV; "impatient" ESV). If Job were engaged in a theological debate with human beings, it would be wrong for him to become so troubled and heated. But he is not. He is engaged in a life and death struggle for justification in the presence of God. The sense of verse 4 is: "As for me, is my complaint against human beings? No, it is against God. And *for that reason* it is understandable that I should speak in heat and distress."

Far from mocking him, his friends ought to grasp the seriousness of the issue, to "look at me and be appalled" (v. 5), to clap their hand over their mouth in silent "awe and stupefaction."[1] They ought to understand that the undeserved hell they are watching is an awesome thing, an event that prefigures the undeserved hell of the cross, the event that makes undeserved grace possible. But it is a terrible thing, and when Job thinks back to what has happened to him ("When I remember") he is "dismayed," so horrified that he physically shudders (v. 6). He shudders because he knows he is suffering the punishment that is due to the wicked. This horror is all the more shocking when contrasted with what often happens to wicked people in this life, which is the subject of the rest of his speech.

Wicked People Are Often Happy (vv. 7–16)

Job begins by observing the frequent happiness of evidently wicked people. This section has a headline (v. 7), a description (vv. 8–13), and finally the evidence that these people really are wicked (vv. 14–16).

A Headline (v. 7)

> Why do the wicked live,
> reach old age, and grow mighty in power? (v. 7)

This is "the nodal verse" of the speech.[2] Job is not asking God "why" this happens; he is saying to his comforters, "Why, if your system is valid, do the wicked prosper?" He asks the question because it invalidates The System. He says of wicked people that they "live" (rather than die), they "reach old age" (rather than die untimely deaths), and they "grow mighty in power," which includes both physical strength and virility and also material wealth and prosperity. Zophar has just said that "the exulting of the wicked is short, and the joy of the godless is but for a moment" (20:5). Job replies that it seems a pretty long "moment" to him!

This question is echoed elsewhere in the Old Testament. It may be asked from a standpoint of faith or of unbelief. The Jews of Malachi's day asked it in unbelief: "It is vain to serve God," they said. "What is the profit of our keeping his charge . . . ?" because "evildoers not only prosper but they put God to the test and they escape" (Malachi 3:14, 15). Others asked it in perplexity of faith, as did Jeremiah and Asaph (Jeremiah 12:1, 2; Psalm 73:3ff.). One mark of faith is not to let go of the truths we do know, even as we grapple with what seems to be their contradiction. Commenting on the fact that Jeremiah begins his complaint with the words "Righteous are you, O Lord," Derek Kidner writes, "It was wise of Jeremiah (and an example worth remembering) to precede what he could not grasp with what he could not deny," namely the righteousness of God.[3] In a similar spirit, Job asks his question in faith. Like Jeremiah and Asaph, he was deeply perplexed by moral disorder, but his faith was not finally shaken. One commentator says that Job's implied answer to this question is, "Because there is no moral order in the universe, no principle of retribution and no justice."[4] But this is not correct. Job believes that ultimately there is moral order. It is just that he observes that this order is not yet established. It is this "not yet" that distinguishes him from his friends.

To strengthen his headline, he now expands with a vivid description.

Description (vv. 8–13)

> Their offspring are established in their presence,
>   and their descendants before their eyes.
> Their houses are safe from fear,
>   and no rod of God is upon them.
> Their bull breeds without fail;
>   their cow calves and does not miscarry.
> They send out their little boys like a flock,
>   and their children dance.
> They sing to the tambourine and the lyre
>   and rejoice to the sound of the pipe.
> They spend their days in prosperity,
>   and in peace they go down to Sheol. (vv. 8–13)

"First," he says in effect, "I notice that they have children, and their children grow up, pass exams, get jobs, have families, and are 'established' [v. 8]," the very opposite of what Bildad has claimed: "He has no posterity or progeny . . . no survivor" (18:19) and the opposite of Job's own sad experience of being bereft of his own children (1:19).

Next, "their houses are safe from fear," their estates prosper, and no disciplinary or punishing "rod of God" beats them (v. 9), unlike Job himself who pleaded, "Let [God] take his rod away from me" (9:34). Later covenant blessings of farm animals multiplying all fall on the wicked (21:10; Deuteronomy 28:4; Psalm 144:13, 14). In a lovely (but ironic) picture, he sees their big families with many children jumping happily out of the SUV and racing around happily like a flock of gamboling lambs (Job 21:11). Their family life is filled with happy music, "the tambourine and the lyre" (v. 12), associated in Bible imagery with joy and celebration.[5]

To sum it up, their lives are characterized by "prosperity" (v. 13a), and they die quickly and painlessly in their sleep (v. 13b). The words "in peace" are literally "in an instant," the sense being that they are spared a long and painful decline due to illness or dementia.

What a wonderful life they lead! Ah, but The System says that all this prosperity proves they must be good people. "So what have you to say to that, Job?" Job goes on to prove that these people are not good.

Evidence of Their Wickedness (vv. 14–16)

> They say to God, "Depart from us!
>   We do not desire the knowledge of your ways.
> What is the Almighty, that we should serve him?
>   And what profit do we get if we pray to him?"
> Behold, is not their prosperity in their hand?
>   The counsel of the wicked is far from me. (vv. 14–16)

We know from their words that these are wicked people. They want nothing to do with God: "Leave us alone!"[6] they say. "We don't want to know your ways of living; we want to be autonomous, to make our own laws, choose our own lifestyles, sing with Frank Sinatra, 'I did it my way.'" Bildad has already described the wicked man as "him who knows not God" (18:21). This is the polar opposite of the godly piety of the Psalms: "Make me to know your ways, O LORD; teach me your paths" (Psalm 25:4).

In verse 15 they ask the Satan's question: "Who is this supposedly 'Almighty' God, and what is it about him that makes him *worth* serving? What is in it for us? What '*profit* do we get if we pray to him'?" Right at the start of the book, the Satan said that this motive (what's in it for me?) was Job's motive. It is the motive of wicked religion, of prosperity religion, and of the health, wealth, and prosperity gospel (which is not the gospel at all).

The meaning of verse 16a is unclear. It may mean that they are claiming their prosperity to be their own doing and under their own control ("in their hand") and that they do not need God to become rich ("Our happiness is certainly not his doing!"[7]). The ESV takes it this way. Or it may be Job's critical judgment that the wicked are being foolish in thinking their prosperity is under their own control, because it isn't.[8]

In verse 16b Job distances himself from their thinking: "The counsel of the wicked"—these wicked things they say—"is far from me."

So, says Job, these people who are self-evidently wicked, condemned by what comes out of their own mouths, are also self-evidently prosperous. And that contradicts The System. But let's look at the other side: his friends say the wicked will suffer the punishments of God. Do they?

Wicked People Are Rarely Punished (vv. 17–26)

> How often is it that the lamp of the wicked is put out?
>> That their calamity comes upon them?
>> That God distributes pains in his anger?
> That they are like straw before the wind,
>> and like chaff that the storm carries away?
> You say, "God stores up their iniquity for their children."
>> Let him pay it out to them, that they may know it.
> Let their own eyes see their destruction,
>> and let them drink of the wrath of the Almighty.
> For what do they care for their houses after them,
>> when the number of their months is cut off?
> Will any teach God knowledge,
>> seeing that he judges those who are on high?
> One dies in his full vigor,
>> being wholly at ease and secure,
> his pails full of milk
>> and the marrow of his bones moist.
> Another dies in bitterness of soul,
>> never having tasted of prosperity.
> They lie down alike in the dust,
>> and the worms cover them. (vv. 17–26)

Bildad is sure that "the light of the wicked is put out" (18:5). Zophar says there is a "day of God's wrath" (20:28). But "How often" does this happen observably in this age (21:17)? Not very often! The comforters say that they are worthless creatures, weightless before God, blown away by the wind of God's judgment like chaff and straw (v. 18). Psalm 1 says much the same: "The wicked are . . . like chaff that the wind drives away" (Psalm 1:4). But it doesn't look like it! We will see that Job does believe, as the Bible teaches, that ultimately the wicked are indeed like chaff and that God will send his angels to separate the righteous from the wicked like wheat from chaff (Matthew 13:24–30), but not yet. And that is the point.

Job anticipates that they will defend themselves by saying that God's judgment hangs over the families of these people and that their families will suffer (v. 19). God "stores up" their sin in secret and is ready to "pay it out" to their families (v. 19).

Job agrees with Ezekiel 18 that it would be unjust for final judgment not to fall on those who deserve it. After all, wicked people, by definition, don't really care for the destiny of their families (vv. 20, 21). The words "their *houses* after them" has the sense of their families being left behind (v. 21). "It's no skin off my nose if trouble comes to my family after I die, as long as I'm okay!"

In verses 23–26 Job compares two deaths. In verses 23, 24 he pictures a wicked wealthy man who is healthy to the end (he dies "in his full vigor" [v. 23]), having enjoyed a restful and refreshing retirement before dying quietly in his sleep.[9] In verse 25 we see one who "dies in bitterness of soul" (as Job himself expects to do, 3:20), never having known "prosperity" (21:25b). When they die, they are "laid out side by side in the cemetery" (v. 26 MESSAGE). As far as we can observe, the one has had a long and happy life, the other a miserable life, and that is the end of the story. Who had the better life? Answer: the person who cared nothing for God, kept his distance from God, and lived a wicked life. Is that the whole story? It is as far as we can observe. And therefore observation and expectations in this life cannot be the whole story. The religious system that governs expectations in this life cannot be correct.

But there is one final stage in Job's argument. He observes that even in death the wicked prosper!

Even in Death the Wicked Prosper (vv. 27–33)

> Behold, I know your thoughts
> and your schemes to wrong me.
> For you say, "Where is the house of the prince?
> Where is the tent in which the wicked lived?"
> Have you not asked those who travel the roads,
> and do you not accept their testimony
> that the evil man is spared in the day of calamity,
> that he is rescued in the day of wrath?
> Who declares his way to his face,
> and who repays him for what he has done?
> When he is carried to the grave,
> watch is kept over his tomb.
> The clods of the valley are sweet to him;
> all mankind follows after him,
> and those who go before him are innumerable. (vv. 27–33)

"I know what you are thinking," says Job (v. 27). They say (a) wicked people come to ruin, (b) Job has come to ruin, and therefore (c) Job must be a wicked person. That is their "scheme," and it wrongs him (v. 27).

Part of their "scheme" is that powerful, wicked people completely disappear from the earth under the judgment of God (v. 28). Their "tent" is uprooted, as Bildad has insisted (18:15–21), and their "house" is destroyed (not only their palaces, but their dynasties). There is no more trace of them on earth (v. 28).

But is it true? In verses 29, 30 Job challenges them to ask for the eyewitness "testimony" of "those who travel the roads"—that is to say, anybody who takes the trouble to walk around a bit (v. 29)! Instead of staying cocooned in your religious system, just open your eyes and walk around. If you take the trouble to do that, you will notice that the wicked do not die violent deaths (v. 30), nobody dares tell them "to their face" how evil they are, for they are too frightened of them (v. 31a), and they are not called to account for their evil deeds (v. 31b). Oh, sure, in the end they do die (peacefully, in their sleep). But even then (vv. 32, 33) they are given grand funerals, people build fine memorials for them that are guarded so they will not be desecrated, and they rest peacefully in "the valley" (the traditional place for burials).[10] And they are popular (v. 33b, c). Lots of people follow not only their coffin (in the funeral procession) but their examples of prosperous wickedness ("all mankind follows after him" [v. 33]). These men and women lead an evil life that they call "the good life"; but they are in a huge company, with many having gone that way before and crowds wanting to follow them afterward.

Concluding Rebuke (v. 34)
> How then will you comfort me with empty nothings?
>> There is nothing left of your answers but falsehood. (v. 34)

At the start Job asked them to shut up because this would give him "comfort" (21:2); he comes back to this at the end. Their system is a lot of nonsense. It just doesn't fit with the clear observations of any honest man with his eyes open. Anyone can see that wicked people often prosper and are rarely punished in this life. It is utterly stupid, and deeply hurtful, to suppose that we can deduce from someone's situation in this age the true state of his or her heart. A bad person may enjoy a good life, and a good person may suffer the pain of a bad life. Only the end will reveal the heart.

The Third (Truncated) Cycle of Speeches

Job 22—28

18

Eliphaz's Third Speech:
Repent and Prosper

JOB 22

"REPENT!" MAY BE A GRACIOUS INVITATION, but it may also be a cruel and manipulative imposition. The final section of Eliphaz's final speech is, on the face of it, a beautiful exhortation and invitation to repent (vv. 21–30). I well remember a leader at a Christian youth event choosing this as a passage for a Bible study and how our hearts warmed to the invitation to make God our gold, to find delight in him, and to enjoy his blessings. But when we read this text in the context in which Eliphaz says it, we will see that it is not a spiritual invitation to intimacy but rather the pastoral equivalent of rape. But that is to jump ahead of ourselves.

Eliphaz begins not with an invitation but with an accusation. He says to Job in effect, "You have definitely sinned." He goes on to say, "and don't think God can't see you," along with a warning that God will most definitely punish sinners. Only then does he give his invitation to repent.

You Have Definitely Sinned (vv. 1–11)

This is an extraordinarily blunt section. In it Eliphaz explicitly charges Job with gross sin. He does it face-to-face, up close and personal. He begins with a doctrinal presupposition (vv. 1–4), continues with a general accusation (v. 5), and expands this with particular charges (vv. 6–9) before drawing his conclusions (vv. 10, 11).

The Doctrinal Presupposition: God Is Dispassionate
and Consistent (vv. 1–4)

Then Eliphaz the Temanite answered and said:

> "Can a man be profitable to God?
>> Surely he who is wise is profitable to himself.
> Is it any pleasure to the Almighty if you are in the right,
>> or is it gain to him if you make your ways blameless?
> Is it for your fear of him that he reproves you
>> and enters into judgment with you?" (vv. 1–4)

While the rest of this speech is not difficult to understand, the opening verses seem puzzling to us. In verse 2 Eliphaz asks whether anything human beings can do can be of benefit to God. The word for "man" (*geber*) emphasizes a strong man or warrior. In parallel with "he who is wise" Eliphaz is asking if even the strongest and wisest people, those with the most to offer, can benefit God (and, by implication, if any human being can benefit God). He is asking whether we can ever put God in our debt, so that God is in some manner obligated to behave toward us in a certain way. He implies that we cannot. Verse 3 takes this and applies it specifically to human virtue: however righteous (v. 3a) or "blameless" (v. 3b) we may be, we cannot give any gift to God in a way that means he owes us one.[1] The thought is that God is dispassionate; he reacts to human virtue or wickedness with entire consistency. He is not *affected* by our piety or our sin.

It therefore follows that the reason for the blessing or suffering we experience must lie entirely with us. If we are blessed, it is because we are virtuous; if we are cursed, it is because we are sinful. It is unthinkable (v. 4) that God would be punishing Job because of, or in spite of, his piety ("your fear of him").

So runs Eliphaz's logic. It seems very orthodox. The problem is that we—the readers—know that in some strange, deep, and wonderful way the glory of God is dependent upon Job's continuing piety. If Job is shown to be wicked, or only superficially pious, a man who worships God only for what he can get out of God, then the honor of God is impugned. The perseverance of this saint will bring glory to God!

But Eliphaz does not know this, and so he continues to follow his logic to its terrible conclusion.

The General Accusation: You Are a Gross Sinner (v. 5)

> Is not your evil abundant?
>> There is no end to your iniquities. (v. 5)

Back at the start of his first speech, Eliphaz had made the charitable assumption that Job is pious (4:3, 4). Now, for the first time in the book, he explicitly accuses him of being an impenitent and guilty sinner. This has been heavily hinted at but never spoken aloud. It has been the elephant in the room; now it is publicly named. Not only is Job a sinner—he is an "abundant" sinner with "no end to [his] iniquities." He is a massive, gross, overwhelming, guilty sinner. Eliphaz points the finger with no ambiguity, like a prosecuting attorney in a courtroom drama.

Particular Charges: The Abuses of Power (vv. 6–9)

> For you have exacted pledges of your brothers for nothing
>   and stripped the naked of their clothing.
> You have given no water to the weary to drink,
>   and you have withheld bread from the hungry.
> The man with power possessed the land,
>   and the favored man lived in it.
> You have sent widows away empty,
>   and the arms of the fatherless were crushed. (vv. 6–9)

Eliphaz expands on this general accusation by spelling out some of the sins Job has *supposedly* committed. They focus on the abuse of power. According to verse 6 he has demanded security from his own kith and kin (the meaning of "brothers") without any valid cause (the meaning of "for nothing"), strong-arming them into parting with things that are vital to their daily life and well-being; this is the meaning of "stripped the naked of their clothing," taking from them the outer clothing that is necessary to keep them warm (as forbidden for Israel in Exodus 22:26, 27 and Deuteronomy 24:6, 10, 11). According to verse 7 he has refused to share the basic necessities of existence ("bread" and "water") with the destitute (cf. Matthew 25:42, 43). Verse 8 portrays Job as "the man with power" who is a landowner ("possessed the land"), a privileged man ("the favored man"). He holds all the cards in his hand, which makes his refusal to help others and his abuse of privilege all the more despicable. According to verse 9 he has pushed around the most vulnerable people in society, "widows" and "the fatherless" who have no one to defend them. (To crush "the arms" means to destroy their strength.)

What a despicable picture of tyranny and despotism this is. Here is Job, "the greatest of all the people of the east" (1:3), throwing his weight around, enjoying his privileged position, riding roughshod over the weak, and exploiting his power for his own enjoyment. So it is not surprising that God is punishing him.

Conclusion: This Is Why You Are Suffering (vv. 10, 11)
> Therefore snares are all around you,
>> and sudden terror overwhelms you,
> or darkness, so that you cannot see,
>> and a flood of water covers you. (vv. 10, 11)

"Therefore"—this is why, here is very good reason to explain why—"snares are all around you" (v. 10). "No wonder you find yourself in God's trap and unable to escape. It is small surprise you are experiencing the 'terror' (v. 10) of Hell sweeping over you, that your light is turned to 'darkness' (v. 11) and the floods of chaos and disorder are washing over the solid ground you had thought was so secure. Of course these terrible things are happening to you. What else could you expect in light of your abundant evil?" It is all so obvious, or is it? It would be, if we did not know from the narrator (1:1) and twice from God himself (1:8; 2:3) that it is not true. When Job defends himself vigorously against these accusations (chapter 31) he is telling the truth.

But Eliphaz is in full flood, and we must not interrupt him further.

God Will Definitely Punish Sinners
(So Don't Identify with Them) (vv. 12–20)

Eliphaz piles up his arguments with two more that stress God's certain punishment of sinners.

Don't Think God Can't See You (vv. 12–14)
> Is not God high in the heavens?
>> See the highest stars, how lofty they are!
> But you say, "What does God know?
>> Can he judge through the deep darkness?
> Thick clouds veil him, so that he does not see,
>> and he walks on the vault of heaven." (vv. 12–14)

Eliphaz now compares two different ways of understanding the transcendence of God. His own understanding (v. 12) is that God is supremely high, right up at the zenith of the sky, above the highest stars. He is so high that he can see everything, rather as we might climb a tall building or a high mountain to get a good view. God has a perfect view of the world. He is "a God of seeing" (Genesis 16:13).

"But you say . . ." Job's understanding of transcendence (or so Eliphaz suggests, vv. 13, 14) is that because God is above this world, with "the deep darkness" (v. 13) and "thick clouds" swirling around him, the clouds that veil his presence from us also veil our actions from him, "so that he does not see," (v. 14). He cannot know what is going on upon earth, for he is separate from earth, too far away to see or know. There he is, walking around "on the vault of heaven," wandering to and fro in the clouds, unaware of what happens on earth (v. 14). He is a distant god, like the watchmaker god of the eighteenth-century Deists. "I expect he set things ticking at the beginning, but he has no knowledge of it or interest in it now."

This is exactly the view of the wicked in Psalm 73: "And they say, 'How can God know? Is there knowledge in the Most High?'" (Psalm 73:11). Eliphaz says this is Job's view. He continues by warning Job not to line himself up with these wicked people, these practical atheists who live as if God cannot see them.

Don't Team up with Those on Death Row (vv. 15–20)

> Will you keep to the old way
>   that wicked men have trod?
> They were snatched away before their time;
>   their foundation was washed away.
> They said to God, "Depart from us,"
>   and "What can the Almighty do to us?"
> Yet he filled their houses with good things—
>   but the counsel of the wicked is far from me.
> The righteous see it and are glad;
>   the innocent one mocks at them,
> saying, "Surely our adversaries are cut off,
>   and what they left the fire has consumed." (vv. 15–20)

"Job, what you are doing is nothing new! You are joining 'the old way,' but not the good old way [cf. Jeremiah 6:16]; this is the well-worn path trodden by the wicked [v. 15]. And what happened to them? They died young, 'snatched away before their time' [v. 16]; even if they thought their lives rested on firm foundations, the floods washed them away. Don't think you will do any better. People who behave like this are on death row; how stupid to line yourself up with them."

The description of the wicked in verse 17 closely echoes the way Job himself has described them (21:14). You know they are wicked by what they say to God, even though all their good things in life come from him (22:18a). Eliphaz had determined to steer well clear of their words and their ways (v. 18b, "the counsel of the wicked is far from me"). In terms of the bipolar choice of Psalm 1, "I, Eliphaz, am not going to walk in the counsel of the wicked. Not me!"

And, in Eliphaz's view, when God does punish the wicked, those who are "righteous" will rejoice (vv. 19, 20). We will be "glad" (v. 19); we will mock them and laugh them to scorn (as God does in Psalm 2). We will see them "cut off" and all they are and have "consumed" by "fire," and we will shout for joy. "So if I were you, Job, I would steer well clear of them" (v. 20).

Eliphaz feels he has made his case against Job. Since God is dispassionate, Job's sufferings must indicate that Job is a very serious sinner, walking in the old path of sinners heading for judgment. Eliphaz has warned Job in no uncertain terms. If Eliphaz were giving Job a good cop, bad cop interview, he has played the bad cop; now it is time for the good cop part of the routine, the soft appeal.

If You Repent, God Will Abundantly Bless You (vv. 21–30)

Eliphaz's appeal begins with an exhortation and condition (vv. 21–24) before waxing eloquent about the blessings (vv. 25–30).

The Exhortation and Condition: If You Repent . . . (vv. 21–24)

> Agree with God, and be at peace;
>   thereby good will come to you.
> Receive instruction from his mouth,
>   and lay up his words in your heart.
> If you return to the Almighty you will be built up;
>   if you remove injustice far from your tents,
> if you lay gold in the dust,
>   and gold of Ophir among the stones of the torrent-bed . . . (vv. 21–24)

To "agree with God" (v. 21a) means to "come to terms"[2] with him or to submit or "yield"[3] to him in a way that leads to "peace" with God rather than pitting yourself against him, as Eliphaz thought Job was doing. Peace with God is the key issue. Job longs to be at peace with God (and will in due course discover that he is at peace with God). If you do that, says Eliphaz, then "good will come to you" (v. 21b), the blessings expounded in verses 25–30. Again this is very close to the Satan's motivation: submit to God for the good things you will get from him. But it is very subtle and subversive. The language of verse 22 is of a man learning wisdom. Instead of being an obstinate fool, be humble and receptive. Be receptive to his instruction (*torah*), and take his words to heart.

Verse 23 explicitly uses the language of repentance: "If you return [*shub*, repent] to the Almighty . . ." and specifically "if you remove injustice far from your tents" ("injustice" refers to all the abuses of power of which Eliphaz has accused him, vv. 6–9). If verse 23 speaks of repentance from unjust deeds, verse 24 speaks to the heart, using the language of idolatry. "Gold" has been Job's god, or so Eliphaz implies. To "lay gold in the dust"—even the very finest gold, the legendary gold of the ancient east, "gold of Ophir"—is to take those things, people, and projects that are most dear to us, the things we value most, and lay them in the dust from which they came (v. 24). "With such a gesture a person makes a statement that the wealth of this world has no claims on his affections."[4]

So there is the condition: repent, turn from your wicked ways, dethrone the evil idols in your heart, and turn back to God, submitting to his word and his ways. If you do that, then countless blessings will be yours.

The Blessings: Then God Will Abundantly Bless You (vv. 25–30)

> Then the Almighty will be your gold
>   and your precious silver.
> For then you will delight yourself in the Almighty
>   and lift up your face to God.
> You will make your prayer to him, and he will hear you,
>   and you will pay your vows.
> You will decide on a matter, and it will be established for you,
>   and light will shine on your ways.
> For when they are humbled you say, "It is because of pride";
>   but he saves the lowly.
> He delivers even the one who is not innocent,
>   who will be delivered through the cleanness of your hands. (vv. 25–30)

The blessings may be divided into four. First, there is the delightful presence of God (vv. 25, 26). When the idols have been dethroned, the Almighty God will be Job's treasure, his "gold and . . . precious silver" (v. 25). His relationship with God will be one of "delight" rather than terror (v. 26). To "lift up [the] face" is an idiom (v. 26). The expression is used by Abner when he says to Asahel that if he were to kill him, "How then could I *lift up my face* to your brother Joab?" (2 Samuel 2:22), or as we would say, "I wouldn't be able to look him in the eye." Zophar has spoken of this as parallel with being secure and without fear (Job 11:15). So Job will be able to stand in the presence of God safely, without fear, in right relationship with God. This is of course what Job so deeply longs for.

Second, as a consequence of this right relationship Job's prayers will be heard (v. 27). God will not only hear his prayer in the sense of being aware of what he has asked, but in the sense of hearing to respond (along the lines of the old word *heed*). To "pay your vows" (v. 27b) means to fulfill vows of thanksgiving after answered prayer, as Jonah says: "But I with the voice of thanksgiving will sacrifice to you; what I have vowed I will pay" (Jonah 2:9). So if Job repents, his life will be a succession of answered prayers.

But the blessing is not only presence and prayer—it is also prosperity (v. 28). When Job makes a decision about something, it will happen (v. 28a). God's light will shine on his ways (v. 28b); wherever he goes will be filled with light and life and will be free from darkness and death.

The final blessing is that Job will become a source of blessing to others through his intercessory prayers (vv. 29, 30). The translation of the last part of verse 29a is difficult. When people are "humbled" or brought low, what will Job say? Some commentators translate Job's words with the sense of "Lift them up!" (NET), i.e., a prayer for them to be rescued, and this fits with verse 30. Job prays for people who are brought low, and through his prayers God's salvation comes to them (v. 29b). God rescues those who were guilty (v. 30a) through Job's innocence and right relationship with God (v. 30b). Job will be a patriarchal mediator, like Abraham for Sodom (Genesis 18:20–33). Ironically this is precisely what Job will end up doing for guilty Eliphaz and his friends (Job 42:7–10)!

Taking Stock of Eliphaz's Speech

What are we to make of this final speech by Eliphaz? It is a tour de force of logic and rhetorical power. As with all the comforters' speeches, it does contain truth. God does see what happens on earth. God does want men and women to turn to him in humble repentance. God does bless the penitent with right relationship with him.

So what is the problem? The problem is that Job is already penitent. He is a believer walking morally in the light. And yet he is experiencing deep darkness. Just as the wicked often prosper in this age (Job 21), so the righteous sometimes suffer in this age, with a suffering they do not deserve. To call on a penitent believer to repent of sins he is not aware of is to pressure him to compromise his integrity. The well-calibrated conscience, informed and convicted by the Spirit of God, will prompt the believer to repent day by day of the sins of which he or she is made aware. But to press this believer to repent of sins he has not committed is a grotesque rape of his integrity.

In an even greater way no one could convict the Lord Jesus of sin (John 8:46), and yet he suffered for sinners.

19

Job's Third Reply to Eliphaz: Your Kingdom Come

JOB 23, 24

WHEN JESUS TAUGHT US TO PRAY, "Your kingdom come, your will be done, on earth as it is in heaven" (Matthew 6:10), he taught us at least three things—a recognition, a hope, and a desire. First, we recognize that although God is sovereign and nothing happens on earth outside of his will, nevertheless his will is not done on earth in the same way as it is done in Heaven. It is done on earth completely, for there is no dualism, no power that rivals God's authority; but it is not done perfectly. There is a difference between God's will as he commands (which always happens) and God's will as he desires (which will not happen fully until the end).

Second, the fact that Jesus authorizes us to pray this prayer teaches us the sure and certain hope that one day God's will will be done on earth exactly and perfectly as it is in Heaven.

And, third, because Jesus tells us to pray this prayer, we know that our desires and affections ought strongly and consistently to be directed toward that day. There are two complementary sides to this longing. On the one hand believers groan for the day when we will finally be vindicated, waiting eagerly for our adoption as God's heirs, the day when our bodies will be redeemed (Romans 8:23). On the other hand God's people cannot but long for the day when evil will be punished and the world cleared of wickedness. This too is part of the gospel. In Revelation 14 John sees an "angel . . . with an eternal gospel to proclaim." When he listens to this "eternal gospel" he hears, "Fear God and give him glory, because the hour of his judgment has come . . ." (Revelation 14:6, 7). The last judgment is the gospel, for it is the day when his people will finally be rescued.

245

In the speech we are about to hear, Job longs for both sides of gospel hope. He longs first for the vindication of the righteous (and specifically himself) (chapter 23) and then for the punishment of the wicked (chapter 24). He "is perplexed, first by God's ways with the righteous—namely himself—and then by God's ways with the wicked."[1]

I Long for the Vindication of the Righteous (23:1–17)

Job pours out his heart's desire, gives voice to his heart's confidence, and expresses his heart's fears.

Job's Heart's Desire, the Vindication for Which He Longs: To See God Face to Face (vv. 1–7)

Then Job answered and said:

> "Today also my complaint is bitter;
>> my hand is heavy on account of my groaning.
> Oh, that I knew where I might find him,
>> that I might come even to his seat!
> I would lay my case before him
>> and fill my mouth with arguments.
> I would know what he would answer me
>> and understand what he would say to me.
> Would he contend with me in the greatness of his power?
>> No; he would pay attention to me.
> There an upright man could argue with him,
>> and I would be acquitted forever by my judge." (vv. 1–7)

The words "Today also" (v. 2) do not necessarily imply that the debates have taken place on different days (though it does not exclude that possibility). More likely it has the sense of "Even now."[2] Job is still suffering deeply. His complaint is "bitter" (v. 2); "the bitterness of my soul" of which he spoke earlier (7:11) is still his experience. Almost everything in his life tastes horrible still. In verse 2b he may say "my hand is heavy" (ESV, Hartley) or "his hand is heavy" (Pope, Habel). Either he is saying that God's hand of judgment is heavy upon him or that his own hand (his ability for action) is heavy—he is weighed down. Either way his life is still miserable.

Verse 3 is remarkable. The expression of this explicit and daring wish is deeply significant.[3] The longings of the heart are vividly expressed in Job by the words "Oh, that . . . ," which occur more often in Job than in any other Biblical book. In chapter 6 he longs that God would crush him before he denies him ("Oh that . . . it would please God to crush me . . . ," 6:8–10).

In chapter 14 he yearns that God would hide him in Sheol "until your wrath be past" and then remember and renew him ("Oh that you would hide me in Sheol . . . ," 14:13–17). In chapter 19 he uses this phrase three times to express his desire that his defense testimony will be preserved ("Oh that my words were written. Oh that they were inscribed in a book! Oh that with an iron pen . . . ," 19:23, 24). In this speech his heart aches to meet with God ("Oh, that I knew where I might find him," 23:3). Finally, at the climax of his last speech he longs for vindication before God ("Oh, that I had one to hear me! . . . Oh, that I had the indictment . . . ," 31:35).

Job longs deeply to "find" God, to "come even to his seat" (23:3). The word "seat" may have the sense of his fixed place, his throne. Like Philip many centuries later, Job longs to see the God whom he will one day know as Father (John 14:8). Job knows by faith (since 19:25–27) that he has a heavenly mediator, and this steels him to express this desire.[4]

In verses 4–7 he talks through the longed-for meeting with God. "I would tell him about myself, my trust, my love, my integrity [v. 4], and I know how he would answer me [v. 5]. He would not crush me unfairly [v. 6a]; he would 'pay attention to me' [v. 6b]. I would stand before him 'upright' and 'be acquitted forever by my judge' [v. 7]." Job speaks these words with faith and awe. If we ask him what is the longing of his heart, he will answer that deeper than the desire for his riches to be restored or his children to be given back to him is the heart-yearning to stand before God righteous.

But how can he dare to long for this?

Job's Heart's Confidence, the Vindication He Anticipates:
The Fruit of a Clear Conscience (vv. 8–12)
In this section Job speaks of a problem (vv. 8, 9) and a confidence in spite of the problem (vv. 10–12).

> Behold, I go forward, but he is not there,
>   and backward, but I do not perceive him;
> on the left hand when he is working, I do not behold him;
>   he turns to the right hand, but I do not see him.
> But he knows the way that I take;
>   when he has tried me, I shall come out as gold.
> My foot has held fast to his steps;
>   I have kept his way and have not turned aside.
> I have not departed from the commandment of his lips;
>   I have treasured the words of his mouth more than my portion of food.
>   (vv. 8–12)

Job's problem—not surprisingly—is that God is invisible. The words translated "forward . . . backward . . . on the left hand . . . to the right hand" (vv. 8, 9) are traditionally spoken from the standpoint of someone facing east and so may mean "east . . . west . . . north . . . south." The north (Zaphon) is traditionally the place of the mountain of the gods, and the imagery was taken over by Jewish monotheism (e.g., Psalm 48:2, where Zion is spoken of as being in the "north"—symbolically, if not geographically). This may be why the north ("on the left hand") is the place where "he is working" (v. 9). The repeated point is that in whatever point of the compass Job searches, wherever he goes on the outer fringes of the cosmos, he cannot "perceive . . . behold . . . see him" (v. 8, 9). God is invisible, and therefore Job can have no control over God (since knowledge of someone's whereabouts is akin to power over them). He longs to "find" God (v. 3).

But although he cannot as yet find God, he has a confidence in final vindication. This confidence is expressed in verses 10–12 in terms of a clear conscience. Notice the repetition of the word "way" (vv. 10a, 11b): although Job does not know where God is, he does know and follow "his way" of life (morally), and he is confident that God knows Job's "way" and that God knows that Job's "way" is in line with God's own "way."

Job is steadfast ("My foot has held fast" [v. 11]), single-hearted ("[I] have not turned aside" [v. 11][5]), and motivated by love ("I have treasured the words of his mouth" [v. 12]). He is a believer walking the walk of faith. Without having seen God, he loves him and loves his words (cf. 1 Peter 1:8). His conscience is clear before God. This is why he can say that when God has "tried" him, he will come forth "as gold" (v. 10b). This trying may refer to refining or purification;[6] or it may simply be a confidence that when tested he will be found to be genuine, that "the tested genuineness of [his] faith," which is "more precious than gold," will be seen in the end (cf. 1 Peter 1:7).

So Job longs for final vindication before God, and he is confident of final vindication before God. But this confidence is not a shallow or trite thing, for Job is also afraid.

Job's Heart's Fear, the Awe That Is Mixed with His Confidence: God Is Frighteningly Sovereign (vv. 13–17)

But he is unchangeable, and who can turn him back?
What he desires, that he does.
For he will complete what he appoints for me,
and many such things are in his mind.
Therefore I am terrified at his presence;
when I consider, I am in dread of him.

God has made my heart faint;
    the Almighty has terrified me;
yet I am not silenced because of the darkness,
    nor because thick darkness covers my face. (vv. 13–17)

It is all very well to have a clear conscience, says Job, "[b]ut . . ." And what a "[b]ut" this is! But God is "unchangeable." This word is literally "he is one." He is unique, incomparable; he is the One later celebrated in the Shema of Deuteronomy 6:4. The particular aspect of his unique deity here is that he does what he chooses to do, and no human being can "turn him back" (v. 13). As C. S. Lewis so famously said of Aslan in the Chronicles of Narnia, he is not "tame." "I am suffering," says Job in essence, "and I can have no confidence that my sufferings are yet at an end" (v. 14). So Job is "terrified at his presence . . . in dread of him" (v. 15). God has made Job's heart "faint" and "terrified" him (v. 16). The words "at his presence" (v. 15) are literally "to/before his face." The same Hebrew word is used in verse 4 ("before him"). Job longs to stand before God face-to-face (v. 4), and yet he is also terrified at the prospect (v. 15). Job knows that God is "a consuming fire" (Deuteronomy 4:24). He is right. Even under the new covenant, believers are warned that "our God is a consuming fire" (Hebrews 12:29). The hope of final justification before God is not a light or shallow hope; we will never breeze into God's presence to talk with him face-to-face. Always there will be awe in the presence of the God who is the one and only, utterly unlike us mortals.

The translation of verse 17 is uncertain. The word translated "not" may mean "surely," which changes the sense. It is possible that it is a word of final hope and confidence (as in the ESV), but it is equally possible that it is another lament, saying something like "Indeed, I am *surely* destroyed before the darkness; before me gloom covers all."[7]

In summary, chapter 23 expresses the longing for final vindication, a measure of confidence in final vindication, but a residue of terror in the presence of the sovereign and unpredictable God. Job now turns his focus from his own vindication to the punishment of the wicked.

I Long for the Punishment of the Wicked (24:1–25)

Are There Dislocations in the Text?

We do not have to spend long with the commentators to find that most of them think the text of the remainder of the cycles of speeches has been dislocated. In *The Anchor Bible* Pope says that chapters 24—27 "are thoroughly scrambled." There are two main reasons why they think this. The first is that the tidy symmetry of the first two cycles of speeches is broken in the third. In the first two we have decent-length speeches in the sequence: Eliphaz—Job—Bildad—Job—Zophar—Job. But in the third we have Eliphaz (chapter 22) and Job (chapters 23, 24) followed by a pathetic little word from Bildad (chapter 25) and no contribution from Zophar at all. It is assumed that this is a mistake and that the text we have is a distortion of the tidy original. So, for example, Pope supplements Bildad's short speech with 26:5–14 and supplies a speech from Zophar from 27:8–23. But this is an unwarranted assumption. There is no a priori reason why the third cycle should not stutter to an untidy end and no manuscript support for any rearrangement.

The second reason carries more weight. Critics note that there are times when Job seems to say things that more or less echo and agree with his friends, despite having been hammer and tongs in dispute with them thus far. So, for example, in 24:18–24 he agrees that the wicked come to a sticky end and are "no longer remembered," which seems to contradict what he has claimed in chapter 21. So, for example, Pope suggests that most of 24:18–25 "belong in the mouth of one of the friends."

What are we to make of this? We may make three observations. First, it is hard to imagine what process could plausibly have dislocated the text in the complicated way supposed by the critics. Pope, for example, has to suggest that 24:18–20 and 24:22–25 belong in the mouth of one of the friends but verse 21 in the middle does not! The complexities of the rearrangements count against the likelihood that this is the true explanation.

Second, it is possible that in some places Job is quoting the view of the friends, either in their own words or in his paraphrase of their view. There are no speech marks in the Hebrew, and we have seen that this is likely what he has done in 12:7–12. This is why the ESV (following the RSV) inserts the words "You say . . ." at the start of 24:18, even though they are not in the Hebrew. In a similar way, in the Greek New Testament we take it that in several places in 1 Corinthians Paul is quoting from his opponents (e.g., 1 Corinthians 7:1, "It is good for a man not to have sexual relations with a woman," a view with which Paul immediately and categorically disagrees). So it may be on occasion that this is the explanation. If it is, we will expect Job to say something to indicate his disagreement with this position.

But third, and in my view this is the most important observation, we must not impose on highly charged and emotional speeches the cool logical consistency we might expect in an academic seminar paper. Job is being tossed to and fro in his feelings, his hopes, his fears, and his faith. We must not be surprised when he changes his mind. And in particular we must allow for the possibility that as the speeches progress, Job may progress in his understanding and that his great insight of faith in 19:25–27 may have informed his grasp of truth. After all, we have seen Eliphaz change from the charitable view that Job is righteous (4:6) to an out-and-out conviction that Job is thoroughly wicked (22:5–9).

As far as chapter 24 is concerned, Habel has argued carefully and persuasively that the chapter has "a basic unity and coherence"; he writes of "the unity and coherent lyrical beauty of this closely argued speech."[8]

In chapter 24 Job argues that the punishment of the wicked is necessary because of the victims of their wickedness (vv. 1–12), necessary because they reverse creation order (vv. 13–17), and therefore certain in the end (vv. 18–25).

The Punishment of the Wicked Is Necessary Because of the Victims of Their Wickedness (vv. 1–12)

Job begins by asking a question (v. 1). He follows this with a picture alternately of crimes (vv. 2–4, 9) and victims (vv. 5–8, 10–12).

The Question (v. 1)

> Why are not times of judgment kept by the Almighty,
>   and why do those who know him never see his days? (v. 1)

This is the question that drives the chapter. It concerns "times" and "days," when Almighty God will judge the wicked. "Those who know him" (the righteous by faith, like Job) long for that judgment, but they do not see it. Eliphaz has spoken of "a day of darkness" for the wicked (15:23) and Zophar of "the day of God's wrath" (20:28). But where is it? After all, it is necessary.

The Crimes (vv. 2–4)

> Some move landmarks;
>   they seize flocks and pasture them.
> They drive away the donkey of the fatherless;
>   they take the widow's ox for a pledge.
> They thrust the poor off the road;
>   the poor of the earth all hide themselves. (vv. 2–4)

Here are crimes against the poor, the orphan, and the widow. Their boundary markers (v. 2) are moved by the strong, who appropriate their land (forbidden later in the Law, e.g., Deuteronomy 19:14). The strong seize their flocks, take away the farm animals on which they rely, and use their power to squeeze the poor out of society ("off the road") so that the poor have to "hide themselves" from the depredations of the powerful (v. 4). It is a picture of cruelty repeated all over the world and all through human history.

The Victims (vv. 5–8)

>Behold, like wild donkeys in the desert
>   the poor go out to their toil, seeking game;
>   the wasteland yields food for their children.
>They gather their fodder in the field,
>   and they glean the vineyard of the wicked man.
>They lie all night naked, without clothing,
>   and have no covering in the cold.
>They are wet with the rain of the mountains
>   and cling to the rock for lack of shelter. (vv. 5–8)

These abuses of power lead to a pathetic and moving picture of human distress. Here are men and women, made in the image of God, but driven out of civilized society, marginalized, wandering, lost and wild like wild donkeys in the wilderness(v. 5a), slaving away to find food (v. 5b, where "game" just means food), and having to send their children out to find scraps of food on the rubbish tips of society, as in some Third-World slums (v. 5c). The "wicked man" has a big, beautiful, prosperous vineyard, but all these marginalized people can do is hope to catch a few gleanings from it (v. 6). They lack the basic clothing and protection needed for life (v. 7), and you can see them, drenched to the skin on the hills, clinging pathetically to the rock "for lack of shelter" (v. 8). The picture of them clinging to a rock for support may allude to the image of God as the Rock, the reliable one who can be trusted (e.g., Deuteronomy 32:15); but these people have no help from him.

These are not people who are comfortably well off and yet envious of those richer than they are; they are destitute. And they are destitute because of the selfish greed of the rich and their abuses of power. When will God act to punish the greedy? "Come now, you rich, weep and howl for the miseries that are coming upon you. . . . Behold, the wages of the laborers who mowed your fields, which you kept back by fraud, are crying out against you . . . You have lived on the earth in luxury and in self-indulgence . . ." (James 5:1–5).

More Crimes (v. 9)

>(There are those who snatch the fatherless child from the breast,
>   and they take a pledge against the poor.) (v. 9)

The ESV puts verse 9 in parentheses, but there is no need to do so. Here is a crime that is climactic. Here is the most heartless crime of all. Not only do they steal property and reduce people to poverty by the abuse of power, but when poor people become sufficiently poor, they force them to sell their children as wage-slaves. As collateral for the loans they need for survival, they have to "pledge" a defenseless orphan. Children are sometimes conscripted as child soldiers (as in so many twentieth- and twenty-first-century wars) or forced into slave-labor factories (as in the Third World). The word "snatch" is repeated from verse 2 (ESV, "seize"): not only do they "snatch" flocks and property, they "snatch" defenseless human beings too.

More Victims (vv. 10–12)
> They go about naked, without clothing;
>> hungry, they carry the sheaves;
> among the olive rows of the wicked they make oil;
>> they tread the winepresses, but suffer thirst.
> From out of the city the dying groan,
>> and the soul of the wounded cries for help;
>> yet God charges no one with wrong. (vv. 10–12)

We have here another moving portrayal of the marginalized. Notice the irony: they slave away carrying sheaves and treading winepresses, surrounded by plenty of food and drink, but they themselves are hungry and thirsty. It is reminiscent of Steinbeck's descriptions of those migrating to California in *The Grapes of Wrath* or Woody Guthrie's song "Do Re Mi." These people are dying and groaning, crying out for help; but the God who would later be the God of the exodus, who heard his people's cry (Exodus 2:23, 24), does nothing and charges no one with wrong (Job 24:12c). Why not? Job comes back to the question of verse 1. Judgment of the wicked is so necessary because of the human misery they cause all over the world. When will God act? *Your kingdom come!*

Then the imagery changes from crime and victims to darkness and light.

The Punishment of the Wicked Is Necessary Because
They Reverse Creation Order (vv. 13–17)
> There are those who rebel against the light,
>> who are not acquainted with its ways,
>> and do not stay in its paths.
> The murderer rises before it is light,
>> that he may kill the poor and needy,
>> and in the night he is like a thief.
> The eye of the adulterer also waits for the twilight,
>> saying, "No eye will see me";
>> and he veils his face.

> In the dark they dig through houses;
>> by day they shut themselves up;
>> they do not know the light.
> For deep darkness is morning to all of them;
>> for they are friends with the terrors of deep darkness. (vv. 13–17)

The abuses of power portrayed in verses 2–12 could in many countries be done more or less within the letter of the law. They are the kind of respectable sins that don't seem too bad until they are exposed. But other sins are flagrant breaches of right behavior in any culture. Murder and adultery, for example. You don't need the sixth and seventh commandments to tell you that those are wrong.

The language of this next section is dominated by the imagery of light (vv. 13, 14, 16) and twilight, darkness, or night (vv. 14, 15, 16, 17). Daytime, or light, speaks of deeds that are done in the open with a clear conscience, things we are happy for anyone to see. To "rebel against the light" (v. 13) is to adopt a lifestyle characterized by actions we want to remain secret. So the murderer gets to work "before it is light" and like a thief breaks in upon "the poor and needy" to kill them (v. 14). So does "the adulterer," breaking what God has joined together, but doing it covertly (v. 15). This is a lifestyle of people who shut themselves away by day, lest their actions be exposed (v. 16), to whom "deep darkness" (a spiritual as well as a literal darkness) is like "morning to all of them" (v. 17). The punch line is verse 17b: by befriending dark deeds they befriend "deep darkness," and "darkness" is inseparably associated with "terrors," the terrors of Hell. God has so ordered creation that life is tied to light, morality, and virtue, and evil is inseparably tied to darkness, death, and Hell. Those who blatantly reverse the ordering of creation are making friends with Hell. Their punishment is necessary and inevitable.

So Job has moved his argument forward from the horror of the victims to the stupidity of the wicked. This leads naturally to his conclusion: the wicked will certainly be punished in the end. Their dark deeds lead to a dark destiny.

The Punishment of the Wicked Is Certain in the End (vv. 18–25)

It is not easy to be sure exactly what Job's argument is here, but it would seem to follow three stages. First, a summary or quotation of the view of the friends that evil will always be punished swiftly (vv. 18–20), then a reminder of how evil is their evil (v. 21), and finally Job's own conclusion that the wicked will be punished, but not yet (vv. 22–25).

You Say the Wicked Will Be Punished Immediately (vv. 18–20)

You say, "Swift are they on the face of the waters;
    their portion is cursed in the land;
    no treader turns toward their vineyards.
Drought and heat snatch away the snow waters;
    so does Sheol those who have sinned.
The womb forgets them;
    the worm finds them sweet;
they are no longer remembered,
    so wickedness is broken like a tree." (vv. 18–20)

Job piles up images of disaster and judgment. Like foamy bubbles or "flotsam"[9] being blown away on top of the water, they will be blown away, swiftly (v. 18a). Their "portion" (their family and possessions, their estate) will be "cursed" (v. 18b) and their vineyards abandoned, so that no farm laborer will go there to tread the grapes (v. 18c). Just as waters from melting snow evaporate and soak away quickly in a time of drought and hot sunshine, so the wicked will be here today but gone tomorrow (v. 19a). That is what Sheol does with impenitent sinners; it devours them. Even their mother, who of all people was most deeply aware of them, for they grew in her womb, will utterly forget they ever existed (v. 20a). The worm will enjoy devouring them in their graves (v. 20b). No one will remember them (v. 20c); they will be broken like a tree with no hope for the future.

It is possible that Job is actually affirming that he now believes this. But the absoluteness and impression of rapidity contradicts what he has argued so forcefully in chapter 21. So it may be that he is quoting the view of his friends (notably Bildad in 8:12–15) in order to correct it in verses 22–24. The ESV takes it this way and inserts the words, "You say . . ." at the start (v. 18).

Never Forget How Cruel the Wicked Are (v. 21)

They wrong the barren, childless woman,
    and do no good to the widow. (v. 21)

Verse 21 simply reminds us of the cruelty of these wicked people. "The barren . . . woman" (v. 21a) has no children to look after her in her old age and to protect her when she is widowed (v. 21b). The powerful wicked people "wrong" her, which has the sense of feeding or preying on her. They treat this vulnerable defenseless woman with heartless cruelty. But even if they are not punished immediately, they will most certainly be punished.

The Wicked Will Be Punished but Not Yet (vv. 22–25)

> Yet God prolongs the life of the mighty by his power;
>   they rise up when they despair of life.
> He gives them security, and they are supported,
>   and his eyes are upon their ways.
> They are exalted a little while, and then are gone;
>   they are brought low and gathered up like all others;
>   they are cut off like the heads of grain.
> If it is not so, who will prove me a liar
>   and show that there is nothing in what I say? (vv. 22–25)

The translation of verse 22 is difficult. Verse 22a probably means that God "prolongs" (or causes to continue) the life of these wicked mighty people. They are not destroyed immediately, whatever the friends may say. They "rise up" or "rise high" in pride (v. 22b), but the time will come when they will "despair of life." By putting the word "when" in the middle of verse 22b, the ESV disguises this flow, which might be better translated "they rise up, yet they despair of life" (Habel: "They may rise high, *but* they have no stability in life"). Yes, they will often prosper, and sometimes for quite some time. But in the end they will "despair."

While they prosper, God does indeed "give them security" (v. 23a), or at least the feeling and impression of security. But all the while God's "eyes are upon their ways" (v. 23b). He does see, and he does care. So while indeed they "are exalted," it is only for "a little while," and after that they "are gone" (v. 24a). There will be a harvest (v. 24b, c), and when God's time is ripe they will be "cut off like the heads of grain."

The whole time they are doing their wicked and oppressive deeds, God is watching and waiting. Just as in the time of Abraham "the iniquity of the Amorites" was "not yet complete" (Genesis 15:16), so these wicked in the days of Job, and the wicked in our day, by their "hard and impenitent hearts" are "storing up wrath" for themselves "on the day of wrath when God's righteous judgment will be revealed" (Romans 2:5). As in the Parable of the Weeds, the farmer says, "Let both grow together until the harvest" (Matthew 13:30), so it was in Job's age, and so it is today.

Job's concluding challenge (v. 25) shows how confident he now is that the wicked will eventually be punished. It is arbitrary of scholars to say that Job could not have said these things. He is not echoing exactly what the comforters have said when they spoke of the destiny of the wicked. He stresses the delay, the period when God prolongs the life of these people, gives them a feeling of security, and exalts them; only when their iniquity is complete will the stored-up wrath be poured out upon them. Just as Job has glimpsed the confidence of faith that believes in his final justification, so he has grasped the certainty of the final destruction of the wicked.

Conclusion: Your Kingdom Come!

So Job prays for God's kingdom to come. He knows full well that it has not yet come, that in his own terrible experience and in the prosperity of the wicked God's will is not yet done on earth as it is in Heaven. But in praying this he believes that one day he himself will be vindicated and the wicked will be destroyed. And he longs with every fiber of his being for that day. Job's speech is a wonderful prayer and one we can echo in Christ.

20

Bildad's Third Speech: A Mortal Cannot Hope to Be Right with God

JOB 25

BILDAD'S THIRD SPEECH is the last we hear of any of the three comforters. Although scholars say it is "far too short,"[1] this is a purely subjective judgment. They often add in other passages, notably 26:5–14, to fill it out.[2] But we have no manuscript support for this arbitrary rearrangement. Indeed the shortness of Bildad's speech (and the absence of any word from Zophar) points up nicely the bankruptcy of the comforters. They stutter into silence, beaten by Job's perseverance, integrity, and faith.

In this final word Bildad reiterates one point (v. 4) that has been eloquently made already by Eliphaz twice (4:17; 15:14–16). He prefaces this point by praising God for his sovereignty (vv. 2, 3) and follows it by praising God for his purity (vv. 5, 6).

The Sovereignty of God (vv. 2, 3)

Then Bildad the Shuhite answered and said:

> "Dominion and fear are with God;
>   he makes peace in his high heaven.
> Is there any number to his armies?
>   Upon whom does his light not arise?" (vv. 1–3)

The word "fear" in verse 2a has the sense of awe or "reverence."[3] God is so great that he has won the absolute victory over the highest powers in the heavens, thus making "peace" (v. 2b). He has countless heavenly warriors in his "armies" (v. 3a, as in the title "The Lord of hosts," used many times in the Old Testament), and the "light" of his omnipresent greatness is everywhere (v. 3b). There is no dark corner of the universe where his writ does not rule. We ought therefore to bow in reverence and awe before him rather than seeking to be justified in his presence.

Human Beings Cannot Be Justified before God (v. 4)

How then can man be in the right before God?
How can he who is born of woman be pure? (v. 4)

Repeating what Eliphaz has said before, Bildad's central point is that Job's desire and hope to stand before God face-to-face is absurd and arrogant. The word for "man" (*enosh*) and the phrase "born of woman" emphasize human frailty and mortality. It is not possible for impure human beings to stand "pure" and clean "before God."

Job has come close to admitting this, twice. He has asked, "How can a man be in the right before God?" (9:2), and he has reasoned, "Who can bring a clean thing out of an unclean? There is not one" (14:4). And yet he clings in hope to the belief that there will be for him a mediator who will stand for him in Heaven and enable him to be justified before God.[4]

The Purity of God (vv. 5, 6)

Behold, even the moon is not bright,
and the stars are not pure in his eyes;
how much less man, who is a maggot,
and the son of man, who is a worm! (vv. 5, 6)

Bildad contrasts the pure shining light of the Middle-Eastern "moon" and "stars" with the dirtiness of mortals, who have about them the smell of death, like maggots and worms (v. 5). Far from seeing man as "a little lower than the heavenly beings" (Psalm 8:5), he regards humans as little better than maggots.

Bildad thus reiterates the denial of grace and unbelief that there could be a heavenly mediator and prefigures those whose enemy is the cross of Christ. It is his final word, and a tragic mistake.

21

Job's Third Reply to Bildad: The Difference between Religion and Wisdom

JOB 26

ONE OF THE MOST interesting observations about the cycles of speeches is that Job is inconsistent, whereas his friends are essentially consistent. Sure, their tone shifts from the sympathetic (especially Eliphaz in his first speech) to the downright brutal. But their theological system is intact, as tidy and precise at the end as it was at the beginning. Job, however, is not at all consistent. He begins by taking their system for granted; this is his starting point, as it is theirs. But his understanding has been shaken to the core by his experience of undeserved suffering. His speeches lament his pain, and they rage with pathetic frustration at the God he cannot understand. And then gradually, so gradually, his longing for the heavenly mediator becomes clearer (9:33–35; 16:18, 19; 19:25–27). So in the end the inconsistency of Job is wiser than the consistency of his friends. It is an inconsistency of integrity and faith.

This is one of the reasons why many scholars find chapters 24—27 so difficult. They expect Job to be consistent, like his friends; so when they find him saying things that they do not expect him to say, and that he has not said earlier, they assume the text has been dislocated and assign these sections to others. But it seems that toward the end of the cycles Job begins to grasp some deep truths and indeed to teach them to his friends. Job's speeches have a prophetic character (James 5:10, 11); so it should not surprise us to find in them pointers to the wisdom of God.

Although chapters 26, 27 are both spoken by Job, they are separate speeches and are differently introduced. Chapter 26 is introduced in the same way as all the speeches in the three cycles, with the words, "Then Job answered and said . . ." But chapter 27 is introduced with the words, "And Job again took up his discourse, and said . . ." So we will consider these speeches separately rather than lumping them together.

Chapter 26 is Job's final answer to Bildad. In it Job speaks as a teacher. He says one negative truth (a rebuke) and two positive truths. The negative (vv. 1–4) is that the friends' theological system offers no saving wisdom. The two positives are, first, that real wisdom is to be found in God's absolute sovereignty, even above the order of creation (vv. 5–13), and finally that God has an even deeper wisdom (v. 14).

The System Offers No Saving Wisdom (vv. 1–4)

Then Job answered and said:

> "How you have helped him who has no power!
>   How you have saved the arm that has no strength!
> How you have counseled him who has no wisdom,
>   and plentifully declared sound knowledge!
> With whose help have you uttered words,
>   and whose breath has come out from you?" (vv. 1–4)

Job begins with biting sarcasm. He has already lamented that when the friends die, there will be no wisdom left in the world (12:2)! More explicitly, he has said that there is not a wise man among them (17:10). Now he takes sarcasm to new heights. He says in essence, "I am so grateful that I, who am powerless and weak, have found such lifesaving help and salvation from your lips [v. 2], that I, who have no wisdom and never say anything right, have been privileged to listen to your plentiful, health-giving ['sound'] 'knowledge' [v. 3]! What a lucky man I am! But just tell me from where you obtained such saving wisdom [v. 4]. Someone wonderful must have helped you. You must have been inspired by some wonderful 'breath' [or 'spirit,' v. 4]!"

It is almost as if Job posts on Facebook, "Just been listening to eight wonderful speeches from the wisest men on earth. I've been having some difficulties and sadnesses recently, and they've really helped me so much. Not!"

The key point is to note that the words for wisdom ("wisdom," v. 3a; "knowledge," v. 3b; "words," v. 4a) are—or ought to be—linked with words for salvation ("helped," v. 2a; "saved," v. 2b). The true wisdom of God the Savior will not only instruct but actually help and rescue the suffering and the needy. The proof that the theological system of the comforters is bankrupt is precisely that it has no power to save. Human religion and philosophy has never had power to save, and it never will. Only the message of the cross, which undergirds the messages of undeserved suffering and unmerited grace, has the power to help the helpless.

True Wisdom Is Found in the Absolute Sovereignty of God, Even over Creation Order (vv. 5–13)

Job now launches into a powerful and beautiful hymn of praise to God the Creator. There are similarities between this and what the friends have sometimes said (which is why, for example, Habel adds verses 5–14 to Bildad's short speech in chapter 25). But we will see that Job actually praises God for something that lies outside the theological tidiness of The System.[1]

God Is Sovereign over Death (vv. 5, 6)

> The dead tremble
> > under the waters and their inhabitants.
> Sheol is naked before God,
> > and Abaddon has no covering. (vv. 5, 6)

Job begins with the lowest extreme of creation. In the deep, "under the waters" of the deepest sea, lies "Sheol," the place of the dead (vv. 5, 6). "Abaddon" (v. 6) means "Destruction" and in Greek later was translated "Apollyon," who is "the angel of the bottomless pit" (Revelation 9:11). The parallel of "Sheol" and "Abaddon" in verse 6 speaks both of the place of the dead and the supernatural spiritual power who stands guard over that place. Abaddon will reappear in 28:22. In this place are "the dead" (v. 5a). Literally this is "the *Rephaim*." This word can refer to supernaturally strong human beings (as in Genesis 14:5; 15:20), but the context here suggests that the translation "the dead" for Sheol and Abaddon is correct; the word conjures up shadowy images of the shades, ghostly figures wandering around Sheol.

In the three references to "the dead," "Sheol," and "Abaddon" there is a crescendo. Dead people cannot escape the sovereignty of God. The realm of the dead provides no protection from the searching eyes of God. And, climactically, the supernatural power guarding this prison "has no covering" before the eyes of God (v. 6). The point would seem to be that God's sovereignty extends to the dead, the realm of the dead, and the guardian of the realm of the dead. There is no second god, no evil supernatural power who has an independent existence or realm where he or it can escape the searching presence of God.

God Maintains the Created Order (vv. 7–10)

> He stretches out the north over the void
>   and hangs the earth on nothing.
> He binds up the waters in his thick clouds,
>   and the cloud is not split open under them.
> He covers the face of the full moon
>   and spreads over it his cloud.
> He has inscribed a circle on the face of the waters
>   at the boundary between light and darkness. (vv. 7–10)

Job now moves from under the sea to over the ground. The governing idea in verses 7–10 is the creation as a place of order. The reference to "the north" (Hebrew *zaphon*) in verse 7 is probably to Mount Zaphon, the cosmic mountain or the mountain of the gods in ancient religious thought. This very high mountain was where the gods and goddesses dwelt, rather like Mount Olympus in Greek mythology in later centuries. Isaiah describes the pride of the King of Babylon in these terms: "You said in your heart, 'I will ascend to heaven; above the stars of God I will set my throne on high; I will sit on the mount of assembly in the far reaches of the north [*zaphon*]'" (Isaiah 14:13).

The Old Testament takes this polytheistic language and appropriates it to describe the sovereignty of the one true God. So Psalm 48:2 describes Mount Zion as being "in the far north [*zaphon*]," which it is not geographically, but it is theologically; it is the place from which the one true God governs the world. In verse 7 "the north" is presented in parallel with "the earth," which suggests that "the north" is the equivalent of "the heavens" (as in the usual pairing of the heavens and the earth). God "stretches out" (as a builder) both the high and heavenly part of creation ("the north") and the low and earthly part. And he does so "over the void" or "on nothing," a pair of images that remind us of the state of the earth before Genesis 1 ("without form and void," Genesis 1:2).

So Genesis 1 is in our minds as we read this hymn of praise. Verse 8 reminds us that in the poetic cosmology of Genesis 1 there are waters above the ceiling or firmament of the sky, and these waters are kept up there. As verse 8 puts it, in spite of the great weight of these waters, the clouds form a barrier, and only some waters get through. It is a lovely, vivid picture—the clouds holding up the waters and not splitting. In our idiom a split cloud would give a cloudburst. In the language of Genesis 6—8, ultimately burst clouds will lead to a flood of chaotic waters that would destroy the earth. But God prevents this. He maintains order.

In verse 9 "the full moon" can be translated "his throne" (by different vocalization), in which case the reference to being covered by clouds may be about the inaccessibility of the throne of God.

In verse 10 "circle" is literally a "limit" or "statute" (*choq*). It refers to the horizon, in the poetic sense of a circle that limits the extent of the sea. In this sense it divides "light" (the dry ground, the place of order) from "darkness" (the sea, the place of chaos and danger). Personified Wisdom speaks poetically of this in Proverbs: "When he established the heavens, I was there; when he drew a circle on the face of the deep . . ." (Proverbs 8:27).

The overall picture, reminiscent of Genesis 1, is of creation as a place of order and boundaries, upheld by the power of God. But now there is a surprise.

God Shakes the Created Order When He So Chooses (v. 11)
> The pillars of heaven tremble
> and are astounded at his rebuke. (v. 11)

In Old Testament poetic cosmology, "the pillars of heaven" are the distant mountains on which the firmament or platform of Heaven rests. These solid mountains are like pillars holding up the firmament, which in turn protects the earth from being destroyed by a flood. But here, after the reassuring language of creation order in verses 7–10, the Creator's "rebuke" actually shakes the creation order! We imagine the Creator speaking in judgment and the most solid parts of creation shaking in terror. The point is that The System of the comforters is not God. Yes, there is creation order, but creation order is not the ultimate reality. The ultimate reality is the Sovereign God who can and does shake the ordered predictability of creation when he so chooses. But why? Verses 12, 13 give us a hint.

It Is Only by Shaking the Created Order That
He Will Subdue Evil (vv. 12, 13)
> By his power he stilled the sea;
> by his understanding he shattered Rahab.
> By his wind the heavens were made fair;
> his hand pierced the fleeing serpent. (vv. 12, 13)

These verses speak, in storybook language that would be recognized all over the ancient Near East, of the conquest and subjugation of supernatural evil. "The sea" is a picture of all the forces of chaos and disorder that threaten to swamp the moral order of creation with injustice (v. 12). "Rahab" (v. 12), also called "the fleeing serpent" (v. 13), is a storybook name for the gigantic sea monster or sea serpent that lives in the sea and embodies all the anti-God forces of evil in the universe. We meet this "fleeing" [or possibly "gliding"] serpent" in Isaiah 27, where we meet Rahab's other name, Leviathan: "In that day the LORD with his hard and great and strong sword will punish Leviathan the fleeing serpent, Leviathan the twisting serpent, and he will slay the dragon that is in the sea" (Isaiah 27:1). We will meet this monster again in chapter 41.

The voice of God that rebukes "the pillars" (v. 11) now blows as a "wind" (or "breath," "spirit") to subdue the chaotic waters ("stilled the sea" [v. 12]) and to end the storms of moral disorder ("the heavens were made fair" [v. 13]) by subduing cosmic evil.

In all this Job understands that the sovereignty of God does not simply mean the upholding of moral order in creation, as the comforters believe. He has grasped that the problem and threat of evil is of such a magnitude that its destruction will involve a shaking that goes to the core of creation, a shaking that is embodied and anticipated in his own innocent sufferings, a shaking that will finally be fulfilled only when the earth quakes at the cross of Jesus Christ and there is darkness at noon. Job sees this only hazily, of course, but this is the prophetic logic of his words.

Because Job is reaching out in faith for a truth that lies beyond his grasp (like the prophets in 1 Peter 1:10–12), he concludes by affirming that there is a wisdom of God deeper than anything that can be discerned by observation of creation and providence.[2]

God Has an Even Deeper Wisdom (v. 14)

> Behold, these are but the outskirts of his ways,
> and how small a whisper do we hear of him!
> But the thunder of his power who can understand? (v. 14)

The phrase "his ways" in the context of creation language means more than just God's actions; it refers to the structures or laws of the cosmic order, to "a law or principle of God's cosmic design."[3] The hymn has ranged from the realm of the dead below to the upholding of the firmament of Heaven above and to the subjugation of cosmic evil. It is not narrow in its scope! And yet it describes only "the outskirts of his ways"; it is no more than "a whisper" of God in the fullness of his wisdom and "power." There is something more. There is, as we have the privilege of knowing now, the wisdom and power of the cross of Christ, which is both wiser and more powerful than all human wisdom and power (1 Corinthians 1:18–31).

Putting Job's argument together we can see how it answers Bildad and his friends. They have a tidy theological and cosmic system, in which creation order is undisturbed and invulnerable. This system has no power to save because it has no place for the subjugation of evil. Evil can, and will, only be defeated by a wisdom that comes from the God who is sovereign over Sheol, Abaddon, and the serpent; it is a wisdom as yet, in Job's day, unrevealed, but a wisdom that will finally be made known in the wisdom of the cross of Christ. Job speaks well, and he speaks more truly than he knows. It is a fine and final answer to Bildad.

Job's Two Summary Speeches (Job 27—31)

At the start of chapter 27 and again at the start of chapter 29 we have the new introductory words, "And Job again took up his discourse, and said . . ." This form of words is also used about Balaam at the start of each of his four formal public pronouncements about Israel (Numbers 23:7, 18; 24:3, 15). It is used in the prophets to introduce a formal pronouncement of woe. So Isaiah says the day will come when Israel "will take up this taunt against the king of Babylon . . ." (Isaiah 14:4), where the word the ESV translates "taunt" is the same word translated "discourse" here in Job 27:1 (the word *mashal*). In Micah 2:4 the ESV translates this "taunt song."[4]

So in its context here in Job, at the end of the cycles of speeches, this probably has the sense of introducing a formal and weighty public pronouncement. Before Elihu and then the Lord answer Job, Job makes two great formal pronouncements or summary speeches. The first consists of chapter 27 and possibly chapter 28 and is addressed primarily to his friends.[5] The second, in chapters 29–31, is addressed primarily to God.

Because chapter 28 is very different from everything that has come before, we shall consider it separately from chapter 27.

Job's
Two Summary Speeches

Job 27—31

22

Job Begins to Sum Up: The Danger of Opposing the Gospel

JOB 27

IT IS A DANGEROUS THING to speak against a man or woman whom God has justified. To illustrate this with a very inadequate example, imagine a bully taking it out on a boy on the school playground. Then a huge hulk of an older boy appears, rippling with muscles and nearly seven feet tall. As he picks up the bully by the scruff of the neck and the bully cowers before him, the older boy says to him, "How dare you treat my kid brother like that!" In an awful shock of realization the bully grasps that he has made a big mistake. He has spoken and acted against a boy with a strong protector, and now he is in big trouble.

When God sets a man or woman in right relationship with himself, he commits himself to him or her and guarantees that on the last day he will publicly vindicate him or her before the universe and will say, "This man (or this woman) is mine." How terrible it is to speak and act against such a man or woman. To do so is to line ourselves up with the one called "the accuser of our brothers" (Revelation 12:10), the Satan who speaks against the people of God, accusing justified people of having unforgiven sin, challenging the verdict of God that they stand clean in his sight.

Ultimately this invites the frightening words, "You killed him, but God raised him." That message was given by the apostles about those who killed Jesus the Messiah (e.g., Acts 2:23, 24). But similar words will be spoken on the judgment day to all who have hated the people of Christ: "You hated them, you opposed them, you vilified them; but God has raised them with Christ."

For twenty-three chapters now Job has been in bitter controversy with his so-called friends. They have, perhaps unwittingly but with increasing confidence, lined up their judgments with that of the Satan. They have been the accusers of Job. In chapter 27 Job addresses them in the plural. He is no longer speaking just to Bildad, as he was in chapter 26; the "you" in verse 11 is plural, and also the "all of you" in verse 12.

Job shows us how the believer ought to respond to such accusers. His speech consists of a boast, a prayer, and a warning.

The Believer Boasts in His Right Status with God (vv. 1–6)

And Job again took up his discourse, and said:

> "As God lives, who has taken away my right,
>   and the Almighty, who has made my soul bitter,
> as long as my breath is in me,
>   and the spirit of God is in my nostrils,
> my lips will not speak falsehood,
>   and my tongue will not utter deceit.
> Far be it from me to say that you are right;
>   till I die I will not put away my integrity from me.
> I hold fast my righteousness and will not let it go;
>   my heart does not reproach me for any of my days." (vv. 1–6)

With the formal words, "As God lives . . ." Job introduces what is in effect an oath.[1] He swears by the God who is the author of his sufferings (v. 2), for there can be no higher authority for his oath. And he swears this with every breath in his lungs (v. 3a); this is his consistent testimony. The expression translated "the spirit of God" (v. 3b) could also be translated "the breath of God," which may indeed catch the sense more clearly. The word *ruach* here clearly refers to his breath, the physical and natural life given to him by God (as in Genesis 2:7). The point of verses 2, 3 is that what Job is about to say he testifies on the authority of God and with all his being. This is going to be no light boast! Verse 4 stresses the absolute truthfulness of this boast.

So what is the boast? It begins "Far be it from me . . ." (v. 5a), a form of words that implies calling down God's judgment upon him if he is not telling the truth. Our colloquial expression "I'll be damned" gets the sense of it, although Job uses it with deep seriousness and not the shallow blasphemous manner in which it is usually used in our culture. Verses 5, 6 spell out Job's boast, negatively (v. 5a) and then three times positively (vv. 5b, 6a, 6b). Negatively, they are wrong in their accusations and assessment of him. They accuse him of being an impenitent and unforgiven sinner, but they are wrong. Positively Job hugs tightly to his "integrity" (v. 5b), his "righteous-ness" (v. 6a), and the testimony of a clear conscience (v. 6b). His "integrity" is closely tied to being "blameless," a man who is genuine, who is on the inside what his piety proclaims him to be on the outside (1:1, 8; 2:3). His "righteous-ness" or innocence is his right standing before God. He holds tightly to these; they are all he has to hold on to in his desperate suffering. "I know I am right with God." All this is backed up by a "heart" that does not "reproach" him (v. 6b); in this context "heart" means his "conscience" (NET). He knows the assurance of a clear conscience.

Job is not being arrogant in clinging to this boast. He is not glad about what he is in himself, but he is deeply joyful about what God has made him. In the midst of the most terrible grief and suffering he clings to this. Did not the Lord Jesus in his suffering hold on by faith to the fact that he was the beloved Son of God in whom his Father was well pleased? And have not countless believers since, when they have nothing in this world to hold on to, held tightly to the only thing the world cannot take from them, their righteous-ness in Christ?

This is the first part of Job's response. But he cannot rest while his accus-ers continue to direct their accusations toward him. So he prays for judgment.

The Believer Prays for God to Judge His Accusers (vv. 7–10)

Many assign part or all of verses 7–23 to one of the comforters (perhaps Bildad or Zophar), in spite of the fact that "There is no version of *Job* extant, in Hebrew or any other language, that locates 27:7–23 in any other place."[2] There is no objective reason to relocate this passage. Besides, while it is true that the spine-chilling description of the fate of the wicked has a striking number of points of contact with similar descriptions in the speeches of the comforters, the context is different. They described the torments of the wicked because these sufferings parallel Job's sufferings, and they thus implied that he is wicked. He describes them because this terrible fate is what will befall his friends if they continue to accuse and malign him.

> Let my enemy be as the wicked,
>> and let him who rises up against me be as the unrighteous.
> For what is the hope of the godless when God cuts him off,
>> when God takes away his life?
> Will God hear his cry
>> when distress comes upon him?
> Will he take delight in the Almighty?
>> Will he call upon God at all times? (vv. 7–10)

Job prays, "Let my enemy be as the wicked" (v. 7a). He is praying very specifically against those who "rise up against" him (v. 7b).[3] He is praying against his accusing friend, and ultimately against the Satan who inspires their accusations. Wonderfully, those friends are in the end forgiven (42:9), and by their repentance they cease to be his enemies. But as long as they remain his accusers, they must necessarily be the objects of this prayer. They will face judgment (being "cut off," v. 8a), and when they do, their prayers will be in vain (vv. 9, 10). By opposing Job they place themselves in terrible danger.

The Believer Warns His Accusers of Their Danger (vv. 11–23)

Job now warns them of their danger. He first offers to be their teacher (vv. 11, 12) before becoming their watchman (vv. 13–23).

> I will teach you concerning the hand of God;
>   what is with the Almighty I will not conceal.
> Behold, all of you have seen it yourselves;
>   why then have you become altogether vain? (vv. 11, 12)

We may imagine that the offer "I will teach you" was not well received by the friends, who reckoned it ought to be the other way around (v. 11)! Nevertheless Job offers to teach them "concerning the hand of God," which means not only his power but what he does with his power (v. 11). Similarly "what is with the Almighty" is a slightly awkward expression meaning how the Almighty uses his power, what he does with his power (v. 11). In verse 12 Job tells them they have seen the evidence they need, that he is innocent and yet is suffering. He therefore challenges them about why they are persisting in talking nonsense (why they are "altogether vain" or empty) about him and his supposed guilt. This is a foreshadowing of what we call the wisdom of the cross, which is placarded in front of us when we see the only perfectly innocent man in history being crucified.

As their teacher Job now warns them of the fate not just of the wicked in general but specifically of those who malign God's innocent and justified suffering servant.

> This is the portion of a wicked man with God,
>   and the heritage that oppressors receive from the Almighty:
> If his children are multiplied, it is for the sword,
>   and his descendants have not enough bread.
> Those who survive him the pestilence buries,
>   and his widows do not weep.
> Though he heap up silver like dust,

and pile up clothing like clay,
he may pile it up, but the righteous will wear it,
    and the innocent will divide the silver.
He builds his house like a moth's,
    like a booth that a watchman makes.
He goes to bed rich, but will do so no more;
    he opens his eyes, and his wealth is gone.
Terrors overtake him like a flood;
    in the night a whirlwind carries him off.
The east wind lifts him up and he is gone;
    it sweeps him out of his place.
It hurls at him without pity;
    he flees from its power in headlong flight.
It claps its hands at him
    and hisses at him from its place. (vv. 13–23)

The main thing Job wants to say is in verse 13: "I am about to describe the fate that the Almighty God will allocate to those who wickedly oppress the righteous" (paraphrase). Verse 13 is almost verbatim the same as how Zophar introduced his description of judgment in 20:29. But as we have seen, the context is different.

Job then elaborates on this in five stages, each described by a pair of verses. First (vv. 14, 15), their families will be destroyed. Even if a wicked man has lots of children, they will be killed in war or die through famine and plague.[4] The awkward translation "his widows do not weep" does not imply polygamy (v. 15); it means there will be no one to mourn for these wicked people since the whole family will have suffered disaster.

Second, the righteous will inherit their wealth (vv. 16, 17). The word "clay" (v. 16b) suggests a pile of clay as parallel with a heap of dust (v. 16a). The pictures conjure up massive accumulations of excess but also a worrying association with death (the dust of death, the clay from which human beings were formed and to which they will return). We look at their abundance and notice, with the eyes of faith, that although it is like a *big* pile of dust, it is also like a big pile of *dust*!

This pair of verses is a neatly fashioned chiasm: silver (v. 16a)—clothes (v. 16b)—clothes (v. 17a)—silver (v. 17b). Whether it be luxurious riches (silver) or ostentatious fashion and fashion accessories (clothing piled up), it will end up being enjoyed by "the righteous" (those who are so by faith), "the innocent" (v. 17; those justified by God). Those who oppose God's justified servant cannot enjoy their prosperity forever. As Proverbs puts it, "A good man leaves an inheritance to his children's children, but the sinner's wealth is laid up for the righteous" (Proverbs 13:22).

Third, what they think is their security will turn out to be insecure fragility (vv. 18, 19). Their houses no doubt look enormously impressive. I suspect that Eliphaz, Bildad, and Zophar, along with so many of history's most vigorous opponents of Christianity, lived in large and solid houses. And yet, with the eyes of faith, Job knows that this solidity is only apparent. The images that come to his mind are a moth's cocoon or the makeshift temporary shed quickly built for temporary shelter for the watchman guarding a field at harvesttime (v. 18). This "booth" (*sukka*) is a fragile and temporary dwelling. How fragile is the security of the enemies of the people of God! It is, in the language of an even greater teacher later, a house "built . . . on the sand" (Matthew 7:26). So this rich and powerful enemy of the people of God "goes to bed" one night the proud possessor of a huge estate and a magnificent portfolio on Wall Street or the London Stock Exchange. And then, when "he opens his eyes," it is no longer there (v. 19)! As Proverbs puts it, "When your eyes light on" your big pile of wealth, "it is gone, for suddenly it sprouts wings" (Proverbs 23:5).

Fourth, their destiny is to be swept away from this world by the "terrors" of death (vv. 20, 21). We have met the terrors of death before several times. They will come upon the enemies of the people of God and overtake them "like a flood" of chaotic tsunami waters (v. 20a) or a tornado taking them by surprise in the middle of the night (v. 20b). The "whirlwind" (v. 20) is a common symbol of destructive judgment (e.g., Proverbs 1:27; 10:25), most famously in Hosea's words, "For they sow the wind, and they shall reap the whirlwind" (Hosea 8:7). The fierce "east wind" from the desert will sweep in, lift him up, and carry him away so that he is swept "out of his place" (v. 21), the "place" where he thought was so secure and in which he invested so so much time and energy. Hosea calls "the east wind" "the wind of the LORD" (Hosea 13:15; cf. Jeremiah 18:17).

Finally, the wicked man will be mocked and laughed at by the demonic agent of God's judgment (vv. 22, 23). "The east wind" (v. 21) here seems like "a vivid personification" of "a destructive demon"[5] as it throws itself at him with no pity and "claps its hands at him and hisses at him" (v. 23). We can imagine the wild wind whistling about the ruins of his house and his nameless pauper's grave, mocking his proud autonomy and his arrogant hostility to the people of God.[6]

Here is a terrifying picture of the danger in which we stand if we set ourselves as accusers and enemies of the man or woman whom God has justified. We can have no future, no security, but only desolation and destruction to which to look forward. We must not be like that! This is the loving warning of Job to his friends and to us.

23

Why God Won't
Answer My Question

JOB 28

JOB HAS SCREAMED OUT an urgent existential question: "Why?" (3:20, 23).
This is not the question of the armchair religious or philosophical dilettante,
enjoying a stimulating debate. This is the agonized question of the wheelchair sufferer who feels he or she desperately needs an answer. In chapter 28
we stand back from the pain and the debates to ask why God will not answer
the question "Why?"

Job has asked the question "Why?" His friends have answered it with a
simple answer: "because you are an impenitent sinner." But Job knows this
answer is not true. The debates have raged to and fro, with increasingly heated
tones, but no satisfactory answer has been forthcoming. We have seen that Job
27 is Job's final word to his friends. After chapter 28 he makes his wonderful
final speech in his defense before God. In between stands chapter 28.

Who Speaks in Chapter 28?

Who is speaking in chapter 28? This is a very different chapter from all that
has gone before and all that follows. It is a unique chapter in the book. It has
no smooth literary connection with the immediate contexts before or after;
it is not explicitly addressed to any of the participants; it contains no accusations, no complaints, and no responses to anything said previously. And it
has a reflective tone, which contrasts with the passionate arguments on either
side.[1] Here is a tranquil, contemplative pause for thought. If Job were read
aloud, this chapter would be read in a quieter tone of voice. In a Greek tragedy
it might be read by a chorus standing at the back of the stage.[2]

For this reason most scholars assume that this chapter is an interlude inserted by the writer/compiler of the book.[3] Others assume, since there is no explicit indication of a change of speaker, that this is the continuation of Job's speech that began in chapter 27; certainly the connecting word *ki*, which begins verse 1, suggests a connection with the preceding chapter. But it probably does not matter much. Either way it stands as an inspired prophetic poem that speaks to us with the authority of God. If it is the second part of Job's speech that began in chapter 27, then the burden of it is to challenge the friends about the arrogance that thinks it can understand the wisdom of God. This makes perfect sense: Job the teacher (27:11, 12) is teaching them—and us—about God's wisdom.

This profound and beautiful poem comes in three parts.

A Costly Search for a Valuable Object (vv. 1–11)

The poem begins, with no explanation, by inviting us to tour around and marvel at the wonders of human mining exploration. Two motifs interweave—on the one hand an object of great value, on the other a search of great difficulty and cost. "Think about the miner," says our poet. "He has an immensely dangerous and difficult task. But it is worth it, for the objects of his search are of such wonderful value."

As we read this passage, we note all sorts of ways in which this poem prompts us to make links with the drama of the book.

> Surely there is a mine for silver,
>   and a place for gold that they refine.
> Iron is taken out of the earth,
>   and copper is smelted from the ore.
> Man puts an end to darkness
>   and searches out to the farthest limit
>   the ore in gloom and deep darkness.
> He opens shafts in a valley away from where anyone lives;
>   they [the miners] are forgotten by travelers;
>   they hang in the air, far away from mankind; they swing to and fro
>   [perhaps swinging dangerously from ropes or in suspended cages
>   while working in a vertical shaft].
> As for the earth, out of it comes bread,
>   but underneath it is turned up as by fire.
> Its stones are the place of sapphires,
>   and it has dust of gold.
> That path no bird of prey knows,
>   and the falcon's eye has not seen it.
> The proud beasts have not trodden it;

the lion has not passed over it.
Man puts his hand to the flinty rock
    and overturns mountains by the roots.
He cuts out channels in the rocks,
    and his eye sees every precious thing.
He dams up the streams so that they do not trickle,
    and the thing that is hidden he brings out to light. (vv. 1–11)

"A mine" (v. 1a) is a deep mysterious "place." Chapter 27 ended with two eerie references to "place": "the east wind lifts" the wicked "out of his place" (27:21) and then mocks and "hisses at him from its place" (27:23). The place of the wicked and the place of the demonic east wind are terrible places. But here is another place, a place under the ground, a place of loneliness and potential suffering. We are immediately drawn in to a world with puzzles and hidden perplexities, things we cannot find and cannot understand, and yet that are of value and worth searching out. And yet these valuable things have been placed here, which obliquely suggests that maybe someone has deliberately placed these valuable things in such a way that they are hard to find.

And yet they are worth finding, which reminds us of Job's longing, "Oh, that I knew where I might find" God (23:3).[4] This search is dangerous, lonely, and difficult (28:4). These precious jewels are not easily found or extracted. So Job is not just suffering; he is searching desperately and in great loneliness to understand the answer to the question, "Why?"

Whereas agriculture is relatively easy (v. 5a), the search for this hidden treasure is hard and violent (vv. 5b, 9). This is no light or airy matter, a matter of casual interest. Here is a search that is characteristic of humankind alone (vv. 7, 8). Neither the falcon with his matchless eyesight nor the lion with his unparalleled strength is engaged in this particular costly search. So the poet has drawn us into a search for something of matchless value, a search only embarked upon by those prepared for pain and loneliness and therefore by those (that is, human beings) who truly appreciate the matchless value of the object of the search.

Why has he drawn us into this search and caused us to meditate upon its necessity and its cost? He answers that in verse 12: "But where shall wisdom be found?"

This poem celebrates the wonders of human technology, of what we sometimes call know-how; but the deeper question is not know-how but know-why. Here in this poem about mining we see a parallel between the natural domain and a greater and deeper search in the cosmic domain, the search for wisdom (which is synonymous with understanding). In the imagery of the Old Testament this wisdom means something like the Architecture of the Universe: "The LORD by wisdom founded the earth; by understanding he established the heavens" (Proverbs 3:19).

When God built the universe, he did so according to the blueprint called wisdom. Wisdom is the fundamental underlying order according to which the universe is constructed. This is deeper than just an order in its material composition (which is the subject of the study of the material sciences); this order extends also to the moral and spiritual dimensions of existence. It is metaphysical as well as physical. For the idea that this world might just have order in its material aspect (the subject of the physical sciences) but not in its moral aspect would be unthinkable to the ancient (or modern) believer. Just as the physical scientist pursues the project of science in the belief that there is order to be discovered (which is why so much of the modern scientific enterprise has roots in Christian soil), so the believer lives on this earth in the conviction that it is not a chaotic universe but one built upon a fundamental underlying and majestic order. It is this conviction that is being so sorely challenged in the life and experience of Job.

Sometimes we speak of the architecture of a piece of hardware or software. By this we mean the underlying structure, such that, if we understand it, we will grasp why it behaves and responds as it does. There are times when it feels to me as if my laptop has been demonized; what is happening to it seems to me utterly illogical and unintelligible! If only I can find somebody who really understands its architecture, how it works, then—and only then—can I hope to see it cured.

In a similar way the poet knows that if we can grasp the architecture or structure of the Universe, then we will know the answer to the question, "Why?" (cf. 3:20, 23). And we will know the answer not only for our personal pain but also for every person and event in history.

We might imagine that the book of Job is primarily about arguments, philosophies, and debates. It is not: it is about the search of a believing sufferer for wisdom, the longing to understand *why* this world is as it is. And implicit therefore in this as yet unexplained start to the poem is the invitation to us as readers to be not just philosophers, thinkers, or debaters but honest seekers after wisdom.

So the poet moves to a meditation on the most deeply frustrating tension of Job's existence. He simply must know the answer to the question, "Why?" and yet he absolutely cannot find this out.

Wisdom Is Priceless and Unobtainable at the Same Time (vv. 12–22)

Two motifs interweave in verses 1–11. On the one hand, jewels are valuable (e.g., v. 10, "precious"); on the other hand, they are inaccessible. The poet now turns to "wisdom" or "understanding" (v. 12), which are synonymous, and develops these two themes of value and inaccessibility in parallel.

In verses 15–19 he majors on its matchless value. But he brackets this praise with two parallel laments of its inaccessibility (vv. 12–14, 20–22). Here is something that cannot be found (vv. 12–14) and yet simply must be found if life is to be worth living (vv. 15–19), and yet it really cannot be found (vv. 20-22). This is the sandwich structure of verses 12–22.

12–14	Wisdom cannot be found.
15–19	Wisdom is so valuable that it simply must be found.
20–22	Wisdom cannot be found.

But where shall wisdom be found?
    And where is the place of understanding?
Man does not know its worth,
    and it is not found in the land of the living.
The deep says, "It is not in me,"
    and the sea says, "It is not with me."
It cannot be bought for gold,
    and silver cannot be weighed as its price.
It cannot be valued in the gold of Ophir,
    in precious onyx or sapphire.
Gold and glass cannot equal it,
    nor can it be exchanged for jewels of fine gold.
No mention shall be made of coral or crystal;
    the price of wisdom is above pearls.
The topaz of Ethiopia cannot equal it,
    nor can it be valued in pure gold.
From where, then, does wisdom come?
    And where is the place of understanding?
It is hidden from the eyes of all living
    and concealed from the birds of the air.
Abaddon and Death say,
    "We have heard a rumor of it with our ears." (vv. 12–22)

The incomparable value of wisdom is spelled out with poetic vigor in verses 15–19. The poet wants us to be in no doubt of the priceless value of gaining a grasp of how this world fits together, how it works, what its foundational structure is (moral as well as material). And no one so longs to grasp what this order is as the suffering believer.

If any search is worth pursuing, surely this is it, for wisdom lies, as it were, at the root of the whole created order, underpinning it, set in place before the world was made (cf. Proverbs 8:22–31). If only Job, or any believer, can gain access to this understanding, then the question "Why?" will be answered. Job will know why all this has happened to him. At last he will not be suffering in the dark. So in verses 15–19 the poet piles up images of the most precious things this world affords. Pile up all the gold and silver, he implies (v. 15), the very best gold (v. 16a), onyx and sapphire (v. 16b), wonderful jewels, coral, crystal, topaz (vv. 17–19)—collect together all the riches of the whole wide wonderful world—and still you will not have sufficient wealth to purchase wisdom or gain access to this understanding for which you yearn.

Here in the eloquent language of poetry motivation is piled upon motivation to pursue this search. And yet we know from verses 12–14 that this search is bound to fail. Wisdom "is not found in the land of the living" (v. 13), and even if we were to venture into "the deep," the lowest part of the sea, the place where the entrances to the place of the dead were in the poetic cosmology, even there our inquiries would be met with blank looks ("It is not in me," v. 14).

So in verses 20–22 the poet dumps us back on the ash-heap of frustration. He says, "Where does this search that seemed so passionately worth pursuing end?" It ends with lonely Job on his heap of rubbish screaming the question, "Why?" (3:20, 23). No living creature can find wisdom (28:21). Even if we were to go to the guardians of the most desperate extremities of the cosmos, Abaddon ("the angel of the bottomless pit," Revelation 9:11) and death (Job 28:22), even these terrible personified powers would have to shrug their shoulders and say, "Well, yes, if you press me, I think I did once hear a thirdhand rumor that somewhere wisdom exists. I had a second cousin who once worked for a man who seemed to think he had heard a conversation in a pub where someone was talking about it. But I have no idea where to find it."

Since the start of humankind, men and women have wanted to find the source of wisdom, the tree of the knowledge of good and evil, so that we might become like God (Genesis 2, 3), so that we might be able to build a tower that reaches up to the heavens (Genesis 11), so that the hidden things might be revealed to us (Deuteronomy 29:29). But we can't.

What is the poet doing? He is giving us pause for thought. We have been caught up in an awesome and terrible human tension. Job longs to know why. Is he right to long to understand? Yes, he is, for to understand this would be to understand the radical structure of the universe, and no greater goal can be possible for the human mind. Yes, he is right to search. But is his search doomed to failure? Yes, it is. He must seek and yet he will never find wisdom.

If the poem ended at verse 22 it would indeed be a theatre of the absurd, a poem to breed despair and nurture the living death of nihilism. But it does not end in verse 22. And in verses 23–28 the poet offers us a paradoxical but profound resolution.

The Humbling Resolution (vv. 23–28)

With one voice the poet has sung the praises of wisdom and extolled the value of understanding. With a parallel voice he has lamented the utter inaccessibility of wisdom. He has asked, "But where shall wisdom be found? And where is the place of understanding?" (v. 12) and "From where . . . does wisdom come? And where is the place of understanding?" (v. 20).

In verses 23, 24 he almost answers himself, but not quite.

> God understands the way to it,
>   and he knows its place.
> For he looks to the ends of the earth
>   and sees everything under the heavens. (vv. 23, 24)

We are not told the location of wisdom, but our eyes are directed to the One who alone knows that "place" (28:12, 20, linking back to 28:1b), for he has set it in place, and therefore he alone understands the way.

In anticipation of the Lord's speeches at the end of the book, the poet presses home his point by directing our wonder to one of the most uncontrollable and seemingly random facets of the created order—the weather (vv. 25, 26). My fellow Englishmen love this, for our weather is peculiarly random! But there are further nuances of meaning here. "Wind," "rain," "thunder," and "lightning" are not only elusive and intangible, they are also ambivalent, bringing destruction (as they did for Job in 1:19) but also sometimes bringing the blessing of rain to make the crops grow.

> When he gave to the wind its weight
>   and apportioned the waters by measure,
> when he made a decree for the rain
>   and a way for the lightning of the thunder,
> then he saw it and declared it;
>   he established it, and searched it out. (vv. 25–27)

Even today with supercomputers, satellites, and a myriad of weather sensors, we struggle to make sense of the world's weather systems. Here is a wild, unpredictable, and uncontrollable random force on the margins of the ordered world; here, breaking in to our ordered lives day by day, is chaos and threat.

And yet God

- "gave to the wind its weight" (v. 25; telling it when to blow hard and when soft),
- "apportioned the waters by measure" (v. 25; telling the floodwaters and river waters and seas to go here but not there, to stop at this point, etc.; cf. 38:8–11),
- "made a decree for the rain" (v. 26; telling it when, where, and how much to fall), and
- "made . . . a way for the lightning of the thunder" (v. 26; controlling every rumble of thunder and each lightning bolt).

And, says our poet, when God ordered the weather systems of the cosmos, he also "saw . . . declared . . . established . . . searched . . . out" wisdom (v. 27). The imagery may be of a skilled jeweler seeing a jewel (he "saw"), examining it (to declare its worth), preparing it (establishing), and probing it for flaws ("searched . . . out"). Wisdom is the centerpiece of God's crown jewels, utterly flawless and of infinite value. And God alone knows its place.

There the poem ends. Verse 28 is a prose postscript not sharing the meter of verses 1–27. And as the poem ends, our hopes may be raised, for surely if God knows the way to wisdom, maybe he will take us there and open our eyes so we too may grasp wisdom and find the answers to all our agonized questions.

Not so! We have listened to the voices of "the deep" and "the sea" (v. 14) and of "Abaddon and Death" (v. 22). Now let us listen to the voice of God. Verse 28 is the first time God has spoken in the book since the drama of Job 1, 2 and the first time in the whole book that he has spoken to human beings.

And he said to man,

"Behold, the fear of the Lord, that is wisdom,
and to turn away from evil is understanding." (v. 28)

How we respond to this verse is a litmus test for our hearts. In a saying that is crucial to the whole book, God directs our attention away from our agonized questions and toward himself. He does not take us by the hand and lead us to the answers; rather he beckons us to bow before the Lord himself, who knows the answers but chooses not to tell us. Our eyes are directed away from the search for the architecture and toward the person of the Architect. We ask, "Why doesn't God answer *my* question?" To which he replies, "Turn your gaze and your inquiry away from the answer you want and toward the God you must seek." If you want to live in this world as a wise person, a man or woman of understanding, rather than a fool, do not seek wisdom for its own sake, for if you were to find it you would become a puffed-up know-it-all (cf. 1 Corinthians 8:1). So do not seek wisdom; seek the Lord.

This is deeply humbling. Neither the marvels of human technology nor the insights of human philosophy yield the ultimate goal, the theory of everything. And yet the truth of verse 28 is also profoundly reassuring. Right at the start we saw Job fearing God and turning away from evil (1:1). The heavenly courtroom knows that God approves of this (1:1, 8; 2:3). But now Job himself, and every other human being, knows for sure that what Job was doing at the start is precisely what he ought to have been doing, and it is what he—and we—ought to continue to do. We should not expect to find wisdom (to know the answers to all our questions) but rather to bow in humble worship before the One who does and therefore to turn away from evil.

In verses 12, 20 in the original Hebrew "Wisdom" is written with the definite article (literally "*The* Wisdom"), whereas in verse 28 it lacks this (simply "wisdom"). So there does seem to be a distinction between the wisdom and understanding that are the subject of the poem (vv. 1–27) and the wisdom and understanding that are the calling of human beings in verse 28. To find the former would be to grasp the hidden order at the heart of the universe, whereas to find the latter is to live by faith, not by sight, bowing before the Creator and looking to him alone.

What has this wonderful poem achieved? More than anything else it has made us stop and think. We must pause when we read this. Why this curious and seemingly irrelevant poem interrupting the passionate ebb and flow of debate? Answer: we must ponder and consider again the biggest issues of the book. What are the really big questions? And where have we arrived in unraveling them? Not far!

Indeed Job 28 may be seen as implicit criticism of the sterile arguments of Job's three friends, whose speeches have achieved so little. In this respect (and some others) Job 28 anticipates the speeches of God at the end of the book.

But why have we not made more progress? It is not only because Job's friends are foolish. At a deeper level this poem teaches that although the questions Job asks are big and significant (wisdom is indeed of priceless value), the search for wisdom *as an object in itself* is doomed. The seeking required of us is not ultimately the seeking for philosophical answers or even for practical wisdom; it is seeking after God himself. This is, we remember, one of the great marks we have noted of Job the believer. While he cannot make head or tail of his perplexities, in his heart and with his voice he longs passionately for God. And in so doing, in continuing to fear God and turn from evil, he is precisely on the right track. Job 28:28 gives divine affirmation to Job (and to us) that we need no secret of the higher life, no mysterious spiritual law to raise us to a deeper level of spirituality or godliness, no answers achieved only by some spiritual elite. We are called, as was Job, to begin our lives of discipleship with the fear of God and repentance from evil and to continue our walk with God exactly the way we started it (cf. Colossians 2:6).

When the apostles were guided by the Holy Spirit to reflect on Jesus Christ, one of the Old Testament categories they found themselves drawn to was that of wisdom. In his blameless life, his undeserved death, and his vindication on the third day, Jesus Christ was and is the Wisdom of God, the Christ, "in whom are hidden all the treasures of wisdom and knowledge" (Colossians 2:2, 3). Jesus Christ himself was and is the wise man par excellence. He supremely, more even than Job, feared God and turned away from evil. And in his life and death and resurrection, the fundamental structure of the universe, wisdom, is revealed as in no other way. All the treasures of wisdom are to be found in him.

Job's Final Defense (29—31)

"And Job again took up his discourse, and said . . ." (29:1).

Echoing the start of chapter 27, Job begins the second of his weighty final speeches with this same formula, "took up his discourse, and said."[5] In chapter 27, and perhaps also chapter 28, Job has made his final statement to his friends. He has insisted on his right standing with God and has prayed for God's judgment on those who persist in contradicting God's verdict on him, warning his friends not to set themselves against God. In chapter 28 we have been drawn into the search for wisdom and have heard that a life of repentance and reverence is what wisdom means for Job and for us (28:28). Chapters 29—31 grow naturally out of 28:28, for we will now hear the words of a man who fears God and turns away from evil.[6]

In chapters 29—31 Job sums up his case before God in three parts. In chapter 29 he longs for the wonderful old days before his sufferings. In chapter 30 he laments the misery of his present sufferings. And in chapter 31 he protests before God his innocence. The shape of this final speech is like that of the Psalms of lament.

Although chapters 29—31 are one speech, we will consider the longing, the lament, and the protestation in turn to make sure that we dwell on each part and mine from it the riches within.

Job's
Final Defense

Job 29—31

24

The Longing:
A Nostalgia for Paradise

JOB 29

IT IS A MARK OF GRACE when a desperate longing for a lost happiness turns out to contain within itself the seeds of a future destiny. This is what we will see in Job. We will hear him expressing a yearning that he feels now to be hopeless, and yet it points to a coming joy. He will speak with what is, on the face of it, a desperate, even bitter nostalgia for a treasured past. And yet this memory will turn out to be a "nostalgia for paradise," a paradise that will yet be his.[1]

What Job longs for is something he has already partially experienced. This kind of longing, lit up by an experience in this world and yet point- ing beyond, has been called *sehnsucht* by the eighteenth-century German Romantic writers. In the twentieth century C. S. Lewis expressed it like this:

> Most people would know that they do want, and want acutely, something that cannot be had in this world. There are all sorts of things in this world that offer to give it to you, but they never quite keep their promise. The longings which arise in us when we first fall in love, or first think of some foreign country, or first take up some subject that excites us, are longings which no marriage, no travel, no learning, can really satisfy. . . . There was something we grasped at, in that first moment of longing, which just fades away in the reality.[2]

A Speech of Longing

Job begins, "Oh, that . . ." (v. 2) with the sense, "Oh, how I wish or long for . . ." What Job is about to say is not a mere description of his past; it expresses a deep longing. We have heard and felt Job's longings before, in chapter 19 ("Oh that my words were written! Oh that they were inscribed in a book! Oh that with an iron pen and lead . . . ," 19:23, 24) and in chapter 23 ("Oh, that I knew where I might find him . . . ," 23:3). We shall hear and feel them again near the end of this speech ("Oh, that I had one to hear me! . . . Oh, that I had the indictment . . . ," 31:35). Indeed, this whole speech is bracketed by heartfelt yearning. This is important. Mere description can be dispassionate, but longings reveal the heart. So as we trace the lines of Job's desires, we prepare ourselves to see how this sweet and painful nostalgia points forward to a greater fulfillment to come.

The Structure of Job 29

The two main facets of Job's nostalgia relate to his fellowship with God (vv. 1–6) and his dignity and stature in his society (vv. 7–25). But it will be helpful to subdivide the latter into his dignity (vv. 7–10), the reason for his dignity (vv. 11–17), his hopes (vv. 18–20), and then in conclusion his dignity again, repeated for climactic emphasis (vv. 21–25). I have chosen headings that deliberately point forward to the fulfillment of Job's longings.

Job Longs for the Friendship of the Son (vv. 2–6)

> Oh, that I were as in the months of old,
>> as in the days when God watched over me,
> when his lamp shone upon my head,
>> and by his light I walked through darkness,
> as I was in my prime,
>> when the friendship of God was upon my tent,
> when the Almighty was yet with me,
>> when my children were all around me,
> when my steps were washed with butter,
>> and the rock poured out for me streams of oil! (vv. 2–6)

What Job longs for first and foremost is very revealing of his heart. When he begins "Oh, that I were as in the months of old" (v. 2a) and then starts the parallel with "as in the days . . ." (v. 2b), we naturally want to complete the poetic parallelism by saying something like "as in the days when all was well with my life, my family, and my business." Of course Job would love to be back in those good old days. But when Job completes the parallelism of verse 2 he says, "as in the days when God watched over me." It was the loving watchfulness of God over his life that meant everything to him, not because of the blessings that were consequent upon that watchfulness, but because of the fellowship with God that lay at its heart.

Fellowship with God is often, and beautifully, expressed with this language of God watching with a smiling face. The priests would later bless Israel by saying, "The LORD bless you and keep you; the LORD make his face to shine upon you and be gracious to you; the LORD lift up his countenance upon you and give you peace" (Numbers 6:24–26). And yet for Job, God's watching has become a hostile, unforgiving intrusion: "If I sin, you watch me and do not acquit me . . ." (Job 10:14); "You put my feet in the stocks and watch all my paths . . ." (13:27). Above all else, Job longs for restored fellowship with God.

This fellowship had meant that although Job "walked through darkness" (29:3), in a world of sin and sadness, he could see where he was going and could be confident of life as he walked by the "lamp" and "light" of God's presence (v. 3). He looks back to those days as his "prime" (v. 4a), which means days of ripe maturity,[3] the days when "God's intimate friendship" (NIV) was at the heart of his life, his family, and his farm. The word translated "friendship" is a warm and strong word; in 19:19 the ESV translates it "intimate friends." It has the sense of one in whom one confides and has confidence (as in Psalm 25:14; Proverbs 3:32). Like Abraham whom God called "my friend" (Isaiah 41:8), Job had been one who confided in God and in whom God confided his will. This had meant so much to Job and made the pain of having God as his enemy all the more distressing (13:24–26; 16:9–14; 19:6–12), for he had known what it was to have "the Almighty . . . with me" (29:5a), God both with him and for him in every way.

When Job had walked with God (like Enoch in his day, Genesis 5:24), it was no surprise that he experienced blessing. This is described in terms first of his "children" (or "boys/youths") being all around him (v. 5b), perhaps an allusion not only to his own children but to the groups of servant boys killed in the successive disasters as well (1:15, 16, 17, 19).[4]

The imagery of verse 6a needs translation into a contemporary idiom, not least because having steps "washed with butter" conjures up for us absurd visions of slipping and sliding. The word "butter" is literally the "curds" from the milk of the herd (as in Deuteronomy 32:14). It speaks of plentiful food and drink, so much that it overflowed all around Job. We might speak of a carpet of bank notes, cream with strawberries, or icing on cakes.

The "oil" of verse 6b is olive oil, used for cooking, fuel for lamps, and the anointing of skin. To have "streams of oil" is again an idiom expressing plentiful abundance of all that is needful for life (v. 6). This oil is poured out for Job from "the rock" (v. 6), an unpromising source, but one that God delights to use, as he would later when he "suckled" Jacob "with honey out of the rock, and oil out of the flinty crag" (Deuteronomy 32:13). In that same song Moses speaks of God himself as "the Rock" (Deuteronomy 32:4, 15). Paul will later teach that this provision was a foreshadowing of the gracious provision of God for his people through Christ ("the Rock was Christ," 1 Corinthians 10:4).

So Job headlines his longing with the desire for the God in whose fellowship he used to delight. In this primary longing he foreshadows the one who walked with God as the Son with the Father, dwelling in the bosom of the Father from all eternity (John 1:18) and for whom being forsaken by the Father was the ultimate and unbearable pain (Mark 15:34).

What comes next may also be a surprise, for when Job turns to expand on the nature of the blessing he experienced through fellowship with God, it turns out that this blessing is not at all the blessing that a hedonist might describe. It is not, in our terms, his exotic holidays, his swimming pool, his designer clothes, or his fast car that fill his thoughts. The blessing he now describes is a long way from the blessings promised in the prosperity gospel or even the self-centered subjective blessings promised in the therapeutic gospel. It is a blessing that consists in being a blessing to others. Those who walk in fellowship with the God of grace will themselves become embodiments of that grace to a needy world. It is very striking that "[f]ive verses are devoted to describing [Job's] life at home, as opposed to twenty about his social service!"[5] which is what follows.

Job Longs for the Dignity of the Savior (vv. 7–17)

This next section begins with a vivid description of Job's former dignity (vv. 7–10):

> When I went out to the gate of the city,
>   when I prepared my seat in the square,
> the young men saw me and withdrew,
>   and the aged rose and stood;
> the princes refrained from talking
>   and laid their hand on their mouth;
> the voice of the nobles was hushed,
>   and their tongue stuck to the roof of their mouth. (vv. 7–10)

Picture the scene: "the gate of the city" with its associated "square" is the open space by the city gate where merchants buy and sell, where business is transacted, where the elders make judicial decisions, where government is transacted (v. 7). It is the place that matters, where people of substance and significance attend. At the periphery there are men smoking, chatting, chilling; at the heart there are all the important people of the region, "the aged" (elders, senior people), "the princes" (people of influence), "the nobles," all the people who really count. Picture a blend of the Supreme Court, the White House, both houses of Congress, and the most significant news media and websites in society, all merged into one melee of power and influence.

And then, in the midst of this busy hubbub, see one man enter (v. 7). He walks in and takes his seat (the phrase "I prepared my seat" [v. 7] means here "I took my seat"). The moment he is spotted, a hush descends on the assembly. The youths pull back (v. 8a); this man does not have to elbow or shoulder his way through the throng, asking politely, "Excuse me, do you mind if I squeeze through?" A respectful path opens. The senior people stand up in his honor (v. 8b).[6] And everybody—everybody!—stops talking (vv. 9, 10). The princes put a hushing finger to their mouths. Even the tongues of the really really important people, the people who are usually so full of themselves and cannot stop talking, stick to the roof of their mouths (a strong idiom, used, for example, in Ezekiel 3:26 or Psalm 137:6 of the absolute inability to speak). They are struck dumb at the presence of this great man. We are left in no doubt that this Job is—or was—a very great man in his region. Job is not imagining these things or exaggerating his former greatness. We have already been told that he was indeed "the greatest of all the people of the east" (1:3).

But why was he so honored? Verses 11–17 tell us.

> When the ear heard, it called me blessed,
>   and when the eye saw, it approved,
> because I delivered the poor who cried for help,
>   and the fatherless who had none to help him.
> The blessing of him who was about to perish came upon me,
>   and I caused the widow's heart to sing for joy.
> I put on righteousness, and it clothed me;
>   my justice was like a robe and a turban.
> I was eyes to the blind
>   and feet to the lame.
> I was a father to the needy,
>   and I searched out the cause of him whom I did not know.
> I broke the fangs of the unrighteous
>   and made him drop his prey from his teeth. (vv. 11–17)

Whenever people heard Job's words or the report of Job's actions and decisions, whenever they saw what Job did, they "approved" and called him a "blessed" man (v. 11) "because . . ." (v. 12a)—well, not because of his wealth or his prosperity! They called him "blessed" because of the blessing he brought to the society he governed.

Verses 12, 13 give four descriptions of men and women who cannot help themselves—the "poor" (v. 12a), the "fatherless" (v. 12b), "him who was about to perish" (that is, the destitute, the one about to perish from lack of food or shelter, v. 13a), and "the widow" (v. 13b). These are four ways of describing essentially the same helpless people. Job rescued them (v. 12), and as a result they blessed him and sang for joy (v. 13).

Verses 15, 16 mirror verses 12, 13. "The blind" cannot see, so Job does their seeing for them (v. 15a). "The lame" cannot walk, so Job acts as "feet" for them (v. 15b). "The needy" have no father to protect them and provide for them, so Job is "a father" to them (v. 16a). The stranger, the immigrant, the visitor from elsewhere is vulnerable to exploitation in court and to xenophobia in society, but Job takes great pains to research the rights and wrongs of their case and make sure justice is done (v. 16b).[7]

At the heart of Job's dignity lies the truth at the core of verses 12–16—his justice. The significance of verse 14 is shown by its being framed by verses 12 and 13 before and the balancing verses 15 and 16 after.[8] When Job takes his seat in the city gate, he puts on ceremonial dress. The "robe" is a mantle worn on formal dress occasions, and the "turban" signifies the status of a ruler (v. 14).[9] This outward dress indicates that Job is a judge or ruler.

The point of verse 14 is that, in Job's case, the outward dress of a judge matches his inward character and his judicial actions, which are precisely those of "righteousness" and "justice." The reason Job is called "blessed" (v. 11a) is that he is the righteous judge who brings the blessing of justice to his society. It is a terrible thing when wicked men rage around in a society like wild beasts with sharp fangs, with predatory behavior exhibited by their unchecked abuse of power. What a blessing to have Job as the ruler and judge, for he "broke the fangs of the unrighteous and made him drop his prey from his teeth" (v. 17). Such a leader will be the savior of his society. No wonder they treated him with dignity! So, derivative from his fellowship with God like a son, Job longs for the dignity of being the leader-savior of his people.

In all this Job is not being proud or self-righteous. I think it was Matthew Henry who said that if a great man be also a good man, his goodness will be much more his satisfaction than his greatness. It is so with Job; the thing he remembers with most gratitude is the virtue with which God had endued him.[10]

Job's memory in his region foreshadows the day when another man will walk in another region, will silence the voices of his critics (Matthew 22:46), and will bring "justice to victory" (Matthew 12:20) by being eyes to the blind and feet to the lame, by restoring a dead son to his widowed mother (Luke 7:11–17), by bringing blessing to Gentile outsiders (as in Mark 7:24–30), and by being in his own self the King proclaiming the kingdom of God.

Job Longs for the Eternity of the Savior (vv. 18–20)

The third facet of Job's longing relates not so much to memory of past greatness as to the expectations that accompanied that greatness. In verses 18–20 we learn what Job used to think.

> Then I thought, "I shall die in my nest,
>   and I shall multiply my days as the sand,
> my roots spread out to the waters,
>   with the dew all night on my branches,
> my glory fresh with me,
>   and my bow ever new in my hand." (vv. 18–20)

First, Job expected to die in his "nest" (v. 18a). This means with his family around him. The image is used in Deuteronomy 32:11 of the place where the eagle has its young and in Isaiah 16:2 of the place where the chicks are. Job had expected to die surrounded by his stable family; he did not expect his children to predecease him, as they have done. Second, he expected a long life, to "multiply my days" as the number of grains of "sand" on the seashore (v. 18b).[11] Third (v. 19) he expects both his "roots" and his "branches"—that is, his whole being, both in its sources and in its fruit—to be well-watered and full of life both day and night, as the righteous will be promised later in Psalm 1 and Jeremiah 17:7, 8. Fourth (v. 20), he expects his "glory" (literally "liver," in the sense of his inner being, as in Psalm 16:9) to remain "fresh" and his "bow" (an image speaking of masculine strength and power[12]) to be effective to the end. He does not anticipate a decline into powerlessness or impotency of any kind.

These expectations of Job arise from a conviction that the world is a well-ordered place, that God's justice will prevail, that goodness will be accompanied by greatness, and that greatness will not be transient. Job expresses these expectations in terms of a long life rather than eternity, for such are the only expectations that could readily be understood in that day; but they point to a right and natural longing that the rule of such a good man will last forever.

Later in the history of Israel the memories and longings of Job will be echoed very closely in the prayer for the perfect king that we find in Psalm 72, where the people pray for the king to have "justice" and "righteousness" as the "royal son" who walks in fellowship with the covenant Father (Psalm 72:1, 2). This prayer includes, quite naturally, the desire that this king will rule forever (Psalm 72:5, 7, 15, 17).

Job Longs for the Sovereignty of the Savior (vv. 21–25)

Finally Job comes back to the memory of his former dignity.[13] It is this that will provide the sharpest contrast in chapter 30 with his present plight.

> Men listened to me and waited
>   and kept silence for my counsel.
> After I spoke they did not speak again,
>   and my word dropped upon them.
> They waited for me as for the rain,
>   and they opened their mouths as for the spring rain.
> I smiled on them when they had no confidence,
>   and the light of my face they did not cast down.
> I chose their way and sat as chief,
>   and I lived like a king among his troops,
>   like one who comforts mourners. (vv. 21–25)

Verse 21 picks up where we left off in the dramatic scene in the city gate (vv. 9, 10). The nobles and others fall silent; they wait expectantly to hear what Job will say. When he has spoken, no one will try to top what he says, to add to it, to correct it, to think they need to supplement or change it (v. 22). I remember once, when preaching, how the man leading the meeting added a few minutes of extra comment at the end of my sermon; clearly he felt it needed improving, and he may well have been right! But no one did that for Job. Job's words were life-giving words (v. 23), gracious words, anticipating the one who would say, "The words that I have spoken to you are spirit and life" (John 6:63). Just as the spring rains ensured the crops would mature to life-giving harvest, so Job's wise counsel and just judgments brought life to his society. His smile and "the light" of favor in his face brought wonderful blessing to them (v. 24).[14] The expression "the light of my face" is usually used of God and his favor (e.g., Numbers 6:25; Psalm 4:6). Job is not using it arrogantly but soberly; his face was the image of God's face, for he was the image and likeness of God to his people.

Verse 25 sums up Job's great status. It was Job who made good decisions for the community as their leader and military commander[15] and one who brought comfort to those in grief.[16]

Taking Stock of Job 29

I said at the start that it is a mark of grace when a desperate longing for a lost happiness turns out to contain within itself the seeds of a future destiny. Job has painted for us in primary colors his yearning for the good old days, when he knew friendship with God like a son and dignity among people like a savior. But in what sense may we read these outpourings of Job's heart as containing the seeds of a future destiny? Would we not be wiser to say that those days were gone forever? No, for several reasons.

First, and most immediately, because Job himself experiences this fellowship and honor again at the end of the book, when God affirms him as his honored servant and restores his greatness (Job 42).

Second, because the longings of Job's heart chime and resonate with other typological longings and expectations in the history of Israel. In particular, the promises of the covenant to the kings in David's line, the expectations of the king, and the prayers for the king all follow the same contours as Job's memory. The king too will walk in fellowship with God as God's son, and the king, like Job, will rule in justice and bring blessing to the people of God; the king also and ultimately will reign forever.[17] Had Job longed and yearned only for material or psychological blessing (as promised in the prosperity gospel and the therapeutic gospel), we would be wise to see his longings as a hopeless wistfulness; but because he yearns supremely for friendship with God and then for justice in leadership, we may see in his longings the shadow of the same longings in the prophecies and covenants of Israel's kings.

Third, because all such longings are rooted in creation. The delight of walking in fellowship with God and the dignity of ruling God's world are precisely what was given in creation to Adam. To remember experiencing an echo of that human delight and dignity is to remember experiencing something that approximated on a local scale to what Adam had been promised on a global scale.

Fourth, because all these longings find their "Yes" in Jesus the Messiah (2 Corinthians 1:20), who incarnated such a life of fellowship with the Father and blessing to people in his earthly ministry and who experiences just such a leadership in his resurrected and exalted standing at God's right hand. Christ is the second Adam, who will do for the renewed creation what Adam was to do for the now fallen creation, keeping and guarding it from evil (Genesis 2:15).

And finally, because the Bible teaches that all who are in Christ by grace through faith may expect to be raised to rule and govern the new creation in Christ: "Do you not know that the saints will judge [rule] the world?" (1 Corinthians 6:2). What Job had experienced in a local sense, Adam had been given before the fall and Christ will fulfill in a cosmic sense. And what Christ fulfills in a cosmic sense, all who are in Christ will experience and enter into, in Christ. It is precisely because Job's longings are in tune with creation order and redemption promise that his longings contain within themselves the seed of future hope. We too should long, as Job did, for the joy of intimate fellowship with our heavenly Father in Jesus and for the final joy of governing the cleansed and renewed creation in Christ. Such longings, experienced at best in part in this age, are the yearnings of Spirit-filled hearts. They will not be disappointed.

To sum up these five reasons:

1. Job is, at the simplest level, Job and will experience these things again at the end of the story.
2. Job is a king-like man, foreshadowing King David and his covenant heirs.
3. Job is a great human being following in the pattern of Adam.
4. Job is therefore a type of Jesus Christ himself, the Son of David and the Second Adam.
5. Job, as a believer, anticipates the man or woman in Christ today.

But we have jumped ahead of ourselves, for Job is still in the depths, and chapter 30 will provide a cruel contrast to the delightful memories of chapter 29.

25

The Lament:
The Stripping of Dignity

JOB 30

ONE OF THE MOST painful facets of the judgment of God is that it dehumanizes people. Men and women are created with infinite dignity and honor in the image and likeness of God. The judgment of God strips them of this dignity and reduces them to creatures with the status of beasts. It is this that Job laments at the head of the second part of his closing speech. In chapter 29 he began with the supreme joy of fellowship with God (29:1–6) and went on to describe his consequent dignity (29:7–25). Here in chapter 30 he begins with the experience of indignity (30:1–15) before reflecting on the perceived hostility of God (30:16–31). The structure of chapter 30 therefore reflects and balances the structure of chapter 29. If chapter 29 described life under the smile of God, chapter 30 throbs with the drumbeat of the terrible wrath of God.

If the tone of chapter 29 was yearning and longing, the experience described in chapter 30 is emphatically that of being trapped in the present tense. The words "But now . . ." or "And now . . ." appear, almost as a refrain, in verses 1, 9, and 16. "I long for a paradisal past, but all I can experience is a hellish present." The hope that comes from the memory of the past and hope for the future is removed and replaced by the prison of now. This is what it is to undergo redemptive suffering. The experience of Job only makes ultimate sense when it is understood as a foreshadowing of the redemptive suffering of Jesus Christ.

Redemptive Suffering Turns God's Good Order Upside Down (vv. 1–15)

Job begins with a description of mockery: "But now they laugh at me . . ." (v. 1). The word translated "laugh" here is the same as that translated "smiled" in 29:24. When Job "smiled" at his people, he expressed a pleasure that conveyed and promised blessing to them; but when they "smile/laugh" at him, they express a cruel pleasure enjoyed at his expense.[1] He begins with a description of the mockers and continues with the nature and effects of their mockery.

A Portrait of the Mockers (vv. 1–8)

> But now they laugh at me,
>   men who are younger than I,
> whose fathers I would have disdained
>   to set with the dogs of my flock.
> What could I gain from the strength of their hands,
>   men whose vigor is gone?
> Through want and hard hunger
>   they gnaw the dry ground by night in waste and desolation;
> they pick saltwort and the leaves of bushes,
>   and the roots of the broom tree for their food.
> They are driven out from human company;
>   they shout after them as after a thief.
> In the gullies of the torrents they must dwell,
>   in holes of the earth and of the rocks.
> Among the bushes they bray;
>   under the nettles they huddle together.
> A senseless, a nameless brood,
>   they have been whipped out of the land. (vv. 1–8)

The headline fact about the mockers is that they are "younger" than Job (v. 1b). There is a proper ordering in human society, in which wise elders ought to be respected by those younger than they are. In chapter 29 Job remembers how "the young men saw me and withdrew" in humble respect (29:8); here this order is turned upside down, and they mock Job mercilessly.

But so that we feel the full force of the disorder experienced by Job, he is not content just to describe them as "younger" than him. In verses 1b–8 he gives a vivid and chilling description of their family, their usefulness, their reputation, and their character.

First, in verse 1b Job describes their family: dogs—even useful sheepdogs (which is the meaning of "the dogs of my flock")—were utterly despised creatures, "symbols of filth and baseness."[2] When Goliath accuses David of not treating him with respect, he says, "Am I a dog . . . ?"[3] Job would not have given the fathers of these men jobs on his estate, even as shepherds in charge of his sheepdogs. These men are junior to men who are more despised than shepherds. Such is their family.

Second, in verses 2–4 Job speaks of their usefulness, which is zero: these young men[4] are unemployable. They have no "vigor" (v. 2) because they are undernourished, reduced to eating revolting salty vegetation and other wild stuff of a kind consumed only in dire extremity.[5] They are reduced to being feral creatures picking out scraps on rubbish heaps. You would not want to give them even the most despised and servile job on your estate because they are utterly useless; they have no energy, no stamina, no concentration, no skills, and no sense. If you took them on your payroll, they would be on permanent sick leave.

But it is not only their uselessness that causes Job to despise them; it is also their reputation, described in verses 5–7. They are the kind of people you don't want near your property or your family. When they come near, you shout at them to go away, as you do for disreputable and potentially danger-ous people (v. 5). So they are reduced to living in terrible places, in wadis that suddenly flood and drown people when the rains come (v. 6a), in caves (v. 6b), in the wild (v. 7).[6] Here are men excluded from civilized society.

But supremely the horror of this mockery is focused on the character of the mockers. They are a "senseless, a nameless brood" (v. 8a). This is criti-cally important to understanding Job's lament. Clines is very critical of Job and accuses him of mocking the weak; he finds Job's description deeply dis-tasteful and inconsistent with having a healthy social conscience. Job ought to take pity on these poor destitute men, not to look down on them, Clines says. Commenting on the words "what could I gain" in verse 2, Clines says Job speaks "like the coarsest of nineteenth-century mill owners, for whom people have no value apart from their productivity." But this is entirely to miss the point of the description, the key and climax of which is in verse 8. When Job describes them as "senseless" and "nameless" he makes it clear that he is not describing the virtuous poor; he paints a picture of men who are poor because they deserve to be poor (v. 2). The word "senseless" means they have the character of fools (literally, "sons of a base fool"[7]), men whose problem is not intellectual limitation but moral wickedness. The word "name-less" may just mean people who are not known, people who do not fill in a census form; but more likely it includes the idea that they have no "name" in the sense of no deserved reputation for worthiness. These are men who are destitute and unemployable not because they are victims of a cruel society but because they never worked at school, never took the opportunities offered them, never showed honesty or reliability because they are thieves and violent men, because they are foolish and wicked. That is why they are—or ought to be—at the bottom of the heap, excluded from any healthy society. And yet, surprise and shock, they are not right at the bottom of the heap; there is one lower than they are.

How terrible to be laughed at by *these*, of all people! Job is "an outcast even among the outcasts";[8] he is laughed at by thieves and robbers. He is like a sex offender in a high-security prison full of serial murderers who regard him as worse even than they are. Here is a man who by character ought to be right at the top but experiences the indignity of being right at the bottom. In his indignity he foreshadows one who will be cursed and mocked by a violent robber under capital punishment (cf. Luke 23:39).

The Substance and Significance of Their Mockery (vv. 9–15)

Having described the mockers, Job repeats the refrain "And now" and describes the substance and significance of their mockery.

> And now I have become their song;
>   I am a byword to them.
> They abhor me; they keep aloof from me;
>   they do not hesitate to spit at the sight of me.
> Because God has loosed my cord and humbled me,
>   they have cast off restraint in my presence.
> On my right hand the rabble rise;
>   they push away my feet;
>   they cast up against me their ways of destruction.
> They break up my path;
>   they promote my calamity;
>   they need no one to help them.
> As through a wide breach they come;
>   amid the crash they roll on.
> Terrors are turned upon me;
>   my honor is pursued as by the wind,
>   and my prosperity has passed away like a cloud. (vv. 9–15)

Verse 9 is the headline and echoes verse 1a ("they laugh at me"). He has become one of their jokes, a laughingstock among them (their "song" in the sense of a taunting song[9]). To "become a Job" is now an idiom or "byword" among them to refer to someone utterly cursed and worthless.

In verses 10–14 the substance and the significance of their mockery alternate. First, in verse 10 the substance is that they regard Job as utterly despicable. These men who are despised and rejected by society in their turn utterly despise and reject Job. There may be camaraderie among outcasts, but this does not extend to Job. They keep their distance from him and "spit" when they see him (or, more likely, spit in his face[10]).

How can they get away with this? Verse 11 uncovers the significance of their mockery. It happens because God has "loosed" Job's "cord" and brought him low. The idiom to "loose the cord" may refer to human life as a fragile tent (so that when the tent cord is loosed, the tent collapses, as in 4:21) or to human strength as being like a bow (so that when the bow is unstrung, human strength becomes weak). Either way it is God who has done this. He has unleashed the dogs of war, so that the proper order of human society is removed and God's "restraint" is taken away.

As a result in verses 12–14 Job's mockers become his attackers. In vivid imagery of a siege, this "rabble" rises against him, trips him up, and builds siege ramps against him (this is the meaning of "cast up against me their ways of destruction"). Verses 13, 14 use wild metaphors to portray their crashing in on Job's life to destroy him.

Verse 15 points back to the significance of all this, with the evocative word "terrors." This word speaks of the terrors of death and has supernatural connotations. Bildad has said of the wicked man, "terrors frighten him on every side, and chase him at his heels. . . . He is torn from the tent in which he trusted and is brought to the king of terrors" (18:11, 14). Job himself has said that "terrors overtake" the wicked man (27:20). The indignities suffered by Job speak of a creation order disordered and therefore of death breaking into the world. The effect of this mockery is not just to hurt Job's feelings but to take away Job's "honor" (30:15), his reputation, his name as God's servant. All is blown away.

The two words "God" and "terrors" are the key to verses 9–15. Job rightly understands that the disorder he experiences is God's doing and that it has a supernatural dimension, the unleashing of death into a world that he had known as a world of order and life. He is experiencing the judgment of God. He cannot understand why this should be so. But this side of the cross of Christ, Job's indignity begins to make sense when we see that it foreshadows the redemptive suffering of the cross, when one greater than Job endured indignities even deeper than Job's. And it makes sense too when we grasp that Christian people are called to fill up in their own sufferings what is lacking in the sufferings of Christ, that in the unfair sufferings of Christian believers are felt the aftershocks and in their sufferings are heard the echoes of the sufferings foreshadowed in the indignities of Job.

But if redemptive suffering turns God's order upside down, the remainder of Job's lament takes us deep into the heart and pain of this suffering, for it is a suffering that is so necessary that God will not heed the calls of the sufferers until it is accomplished. So Job moves from the experience of indignity in his relations with his fellow human beings to reflection on what this must mean for his relations with God.

Redemptive Suffering Is Absolutely Necessary (vv. 16–31)

In the remainder of Job's lament he focuses on two facets of his pain: there is no answer from God, and there is no justice in his sufferings. Each of these, in their shock and surprise, point to a deep and divine necessity.

Redemptive Suffering Is So Necessary That There Must Be No Answer from God to Job's Cries (vv. 16–23)

> And now my soul is poured out within me;
>   days of affliction have taken hold of me.
> The night racks my bones,
>   and the pain that gnaws me takes no rest.
> With great force my garment is disfigured;
>   it binds me about like the collar of my tunic.
> God has cast me into the mire,
>   and I have become like dust and ashes.
> I cry to you for help and you do not answer me;
>   I stand, and you only look at me.
> You have turned cruel to me;
>   with the might of your hand you persecute me.
> You lift me up on the wind; you make me ride on it,
>   and you toss me about in the roar of the storm.
> For I know that you will bring me to death
>   and to the house appointed for all living. (vv. 16–23)

Verses 16, 17 press home how long Job's suffering lasts. The miserable "And now" extends to "days of affliction" (v. 16b) and "the night" of bone-racking agony, with gnawing pain that "takes no rest" (v. 17); it goes on so long that his "soul" (v. 16), his whole inner being, is poured out, drains away, ebbs away until there will be nothing of Job left to lament . Verse 18 seems to describe the experience of being strangled by his own shirt and verse 19 the slippery deathly mud so familiar from the laments in the Psalms.

So in verses 20–23, in verses right at the heart of chapters 29—31,[11] Job addresses God directly for the only time in chapters 29—31. Trapped in this seemingly eternal "now" misery, Job cries out to God for help, but God gives no answer (v. 20a). Job stands (v. 20b) in the posture of urgent and earnest petition,[12] but God just looks at him with silent inaction. Here is a man who prays as he has never prayed before, and his prayers are met with silence from Heaven. He experiences God as "cruel" (v. 21a), as one with a persecuting hand (v. 21b). He sees God as one who lifts him up, exalting him to a great position, and yet it turns out he has only done this as a tornado might sweep a man up high in the air, only to dash him to the ground; this is what has happened to Job. In a parody of Psalm 18, God has been a cruel storm-god to him.[13]

And so (v. 23) Job concludes that God has in mind bringing him right down to death. The silence of Heaven in response to Job's prayers must mean that God intends to kill him. What are we to make of this? At one level Job turns out to be not quite right, for God does not—quite—kill him. He is restored without going right down to death, although he has endured a kind of living death for a while. And yet at a deeper level Job is right, for his sufferings foreshadow the pain of a man who had to go right down to death, even death on a cross, before his cries would be answered. There is a terrible divine necessity about redemptive suffering. God is doing something so ultimately wonderful that unanswered prayer is the necessary price of achieving it, and Job begins to experience this. His prayers will be answered, but only when his sufferings have achieved that for which God purposes them. In a deeper way it was the same for Jesus Christ. In a similar way it is yet the same for Christian people today; when God remains silent in answer to our urgent cries, it is not that he does not hear, but rather that it is somehow necessary for us to cry in vain and wait in hope until he achieves in us, and in his world, what he wills to achieve.

Redemptive Suffering Is So Necessary That Job Needs
to Endure Unjust Suffering (vv. 24–31)
At the heart of verses 16–23 is the pain of unanswered prayer. At the heart of verses 24–31 is the misery of injustice.

> Yet does not one in a heap of ruins stretch out his hand,
>   and in his disaster cry for help?
> Did not I weep for him whose day was hard?
>   Was not my soul grieved for the needy?
> But when I hoped for good, evil came,
>   and when I waited for light, darkness came. (vv. 24–26)

The main point of verses 24–26 is that God has not treated Job as Job has treated others. When Job, as a regional ruler, came across sufferers ("him whose day was hard . . . the needy"), he wept for them, his soul was "grieved," and he took pity on them (v. 25). That is the right and, one might suppose, the godly thing to do, because it is the response we expect from God. And yet when Job's day was hard and Job was needy, God did not seem to weep for him or to take pity on him. On the contrary, God sent him yet more evil and deeper darkness (v. 26). In these three verses Job is contrasting how decent people generally behave with how God has behaved toward him.

> My inward parts are in turmoil and never still;
>> days of affliction come to meet me.
> I go about darkened, but not by the sun;
>> I stand up in the assembly and cry for help.
> I am a brother of jackals
>> and a companion of ostriches.
> My skin turns black and falls from me,
>> and my bones burn with heat.
> My lyre is turned to mourning,
>> and my pipe to the voice of those who weep. (vv. 27–31)

So in verses 27–31 Job continues to describe the depth and the endurance of his misery. He is all churned up inside (v. 27a), with day after day of affliction as it were coming to meet him; each morning he wakes to another day of affliction. He is "darkened" by grief (v. 28a), "cry[ing] for help" (v. 28b), lonely and mournful like the jackal or the ostrich (or possibly the owl).[14] He is outwardly decaying (v. 30a, "skin") and inwardly fevered (v. 30b, "bones"). His whole life is consumed by mourning and weeping (v. 31).

There is a divine necessity about the sufferings of Job. There is something so deeply necessary that it justifies injustice and the unanswered prayer of a righteous man. Centuries later it will justify the most unjust action in human history, when a man without sin is falsely accused, unfairly condemned, and unjustly stripped of his dignity, excluded from society, and submitted to the utterly disgraceful death of sinners. It will justify this righteous man's "loud cries and tears" going unanswered until his task is completed (Hebrews 5:7). And if this was ultimately necessary for Jesus Christ, it remains necessary that Christian people should know what it is to have their prayers for rescue unanswered in the present ("But now . . .") as they suffer unjustly in this age.

Ultimately we shall see that there is a good purpose and a great purpose achieved by these sufferings. But not now, not yet.

26

Job's Last Word

JOB 31

WHAT WOULD YOU SAY as your last words about yourself? You might wish to speak about others or, best of all, about God. But what would you say about yourself? It is of course likely that you and I will not have the time, the clarity of mind, or the strength to speak the last words of our choice. But supposing you could, what would you like to say about yourself? What would be the most important final statement to make about yourself before you meet your Maker? Or, to put it another way, what would be your first word about yourself to your Maker when you stand before his judgment throne? What is the most important thing you would want to say to God the Judge about you as a person? What words will sum up what is most deeply on your mind and in your heart concerning yourself?

This is a searching question. When the Apostle Paul speaks of his certainty that there will be a resurrection and a judgment, he says, "So I always take pains to have a clear conscience toward both God and man" (Acts 24:16). The final thing he wants to be able to say about himself before he dies, and the first thing he wants to be able to say to God at the judgment, is, "My conscience is clear. I have no unforgiven sin on my mind or in my heart. And therefore I can face my Maker with confidence."[1]

In Job 31 we read the third and final part of Job's final speech. At the end of it we read the dramatic statement, "The words of Job are ended" (v. 40b). And ended they are, apart from a couple of very brief exclamations after God's speeches. Chapter 31 is therefore the final thing Job wishes to say about himself as he prepares to meet his God. We need to consider these words very carefully to see what exactly Job is claiming about himself and what the implications are for us as Christian people.

It is easy to skim Job 31 and get the impression that Job is a self-righteous Pharisee, thanking God that he is not sinful like other people. On the face of it Job essentially says in chapter 31, at some length, "If I had done anything wrong, then I would have deserved to be punished by God. But I have not done anything wrong. So God ought to vindicate me." Again and again the structure seems to be along the lines of "If I had done this particular sin, it would have been wrong, and I would have deserved punishment, but I haven't." So we almost instinctively want to dismiss this speech as cant and hypocrisy.

If it were as simple as that, it would be very hard to make sense of God's affirmation of Job at the end of the book (42:7). It would also be very hard to make sense of God's rejection of Job's three friends (also in 42:7), who have said that Job is a hypocritical, self-righteous sinner who refuses to admit his guilt. No, says God, he is not. So what exactly is Job saying?

In chapters 29, 30 Job has spoken about his experience and has reflected on what these experiences seem to mean for his standing before God. Now he speaks about himself, his character, his actions, his desires, and his heart.

The Structure of Job 31

The most glaring puzzle in the structure of the chapter is why, after Job's dramatic and climactic appeal to God in verses 35–37, we then have the seemingly odd little paragraph at the end about his land (vv. 38–40). This feels like an afterthought, as though Job is saying, "Oh, and I've just remembered another sin I might have committed but haven't; here it is." While this is possible (and, after all, Job is a man in extremis[2]), it seems more likely that this last section has a particular function. While we ought not to be too dogmatic about the precise intended structure, there seems merit in the chiastic structure below.[3]

> A. covenant made (vv. 1–3)
> > B. challenge given (vv. 4–6)
> > > C. catalog of covenant faithfulness (vv. 7–34)
> > B'. The challenge repeated (vv. 35–37)
> A'. The covenant attested (vv. 38–40)

The key to the beginning and end (A and A') is covenant. This is mentioned explicitly in verse 1 ("I have made a covenant with my eyes") and alluded to implicitly at the end, since to any Israelite reader the references to the "land" being blessed or cursed will remind them of the covenant blessings and curses (e.g. Deuteronomy 27, 28). Job is not an Israelite; so we need to ask what sort of covenant is involved here. But it does seem that the motif of covenant ties the beginning and end of the speech together and helps explain the function of verses 38–40.

The two challenges, first in verses 4–6 and then repeated in verses 35–37, are tied together by the Hebrew root *spr* and the word "steps." In the ESV the *spr* root appears as "number" (v. 4), "indictment" (v. 35), and "account" (v. 37).

We shall follow this chiastic structure in our exposition.

A. The Nature of the Covenant: The Commitment to a Clear Conscience (vv. 1–3)

> I have made a covenant with my eyes;
>   how then could I gaze at a virgin?
> What would be my portion from God above
>   and my heritage from the Almighty on high?
> Is not calamity for the unrighteous,
>   and disaster for the workers of iniquity? (vv. 1–3)

Job headlines this final climactic section of his defense, the last word of his last words, by saying he has made a covenant with his eyes. He has entered into a solemn and binding commitment with himself, specifically in the aspect of his desires, his affections, the longings of the heart. The eyes express the desires of the heart. This is not a covenant given to him from outside, as the covenant with Abraham will later be; it is a covenant with himself. We might say he has solemnly bound himself to keep a clear conscience.

The particular desire he speaks of is to "gaze at a virgin" (v. 1b). The word "virgin" means in this context an attractive and desirable young woman who is not his wife. To "gaze" means to eye up with a view to sex.[4] This goes beyond the recognition that she is attractive, for there is no sin in that, and this recognition can be turned to thankfulness to God for making such beauty. Rather, this is to indulge in the imaginative fantasy of having sex with her, to allow desires to grow in his heart that, in the absence of outward restraint, will lead to adultery or sexual immorality. This he has solemnly bound himself not to do.

To many of us this verse is familiar as the motto verse of one of the well-known and excellent Internet filtering and accountability websites (www.covenanteyes.com). But its demands are deeper than that and point to self-control in the area of desire as well as in the actual practice of what we see with our eyes.

There is a puzzle here. Why does Job headline this particular desire? Is he sex-obsessed? Besides, he is going to include adultery in his list of sins a little later anyway (vv. 9–12). I think it is likely that he begins with this not because it is worse than the sins he will list later or because it is the supreme temptation in his life, but because in its heart-searching demands it can symbolize and sum up a life of inner purity. As any man can attest, the calling to inward sexual faithfulness is a searching demand. To adapt the language of James 3:2, any man who can keep his sexual desires under full control is able to control his whole body. No doubt women can say something similar, with due regard for gender differences in this area.

Furthermore, there is a strong connection in the Bible between sexual faithfulness and religious faithfulness.[5] To be faithful in the area of sex is closely connected with the avoidance of idolatry. It would therefore be a mistake to take this as the first in Job's list of possible sins. Rather, it headlines his commitment to purity of the heart. He agrees entirely with his friends that impurity and wickedness in his heart would bring upon him "calamity" and "disaster" as his "portion" and "heritage" (vv. 2, 3).

The covenant Job has made is to keep a clear conscience before God on high. We do not know just how much he knows about God and God's standards, but he knows something, and he has pledged himself to keep his conscience clear.

B. The Keeping of the Covenant: By Faithfulness in the Heart (vv. 4–6)

> Does not he see my ways
>   and number all my steps?
> If I have walked with falsehood
>   and my foot has hastened to deceit;
> (Let me be weighed in a just balance,
>   and let God know my integrity!) (vv. 4–6)

Job knows that his covenant with his conscience is not merely a commitment to do what seems right to him. He is no postmodern, and he has no illusions about conscience having an autonomous authority in his life. He is committed to purity in the sight of God who sees the heart. Verses 4, 5 use the language of walking—"steps," feet, and "ways." He knows that God sees his "ways"—his life, actions, words, and thoughts—and "numbers" or keeps an accounting, a record, of all his "steps" (v. 4). He knows how easy it would be to "walk with falsehood" or "deceit" (v. 5), to become an empty idolater, following the desires and imaginations of his own heart. But he knows—unlike Belshazzar who was "weighed . . . and found wanting" (Daniel 5:24–28)— that when he is weighed by the God of justice, he will be seen to be a man of "integrity" or blamelessness (Job 31:6), as indeed we know he is (1:1, 8; 2:3).

In 2010–2011 the British Museum in London presented an exhibition of the Egyptian Book of the Dead, the long-lasting tradition of books, writings, and drawings that accompanied corpses on their supposed journey to the afterlife. One of the most striking images is the judgment scene, showing the heart of the dead person being weighed against a feather. The feather symbolizes the Egyptian concept of *ma 'at*, which means something like truth or justice. A heart that is too heavy has contravened *ma 'at* and cannot pass through to the blessings of the afterlife, unless the gods can be fooled by magic spells.

So this idea of being weighed in the judgment is a very old one. Job shares the idea, but the clarity of his conscience enables him to face the judgment with confidence. "Surely," he says in essence, "when I am face-to-face with my Maker, he will see that I really am on the inside what I have seemed to be on the outside."

C. The Outworking of Covenant Faithfulness in Heart and Life (vv. 7–34)

A general claim to a clear conscience is all very well, but if it is to carry conviction it will need to be fleshed out in heart and life. What does Job mean by saying he has integrity or blamelessness, that he has been faithful to his covenant with his eyes?

As with the various lists of sins, virtues, or spiritual gifts in the New Testament, it would be a mistake to view this list of Job's as comprehensive. Rather it is illustrative of the kinds of guilt he has avoided.

The examples he cites generally include the first and second, and sometimes the third or fourth, of the following four elements:

- (a) **Sin:** "If . . ." followed by a description of the sin.
- (b) **Judgment:** "Then . . ." followed by an acknowledgment of appropriate punishment.
- (c) **Reason:** "For . . ." followed by a reason why this sin is a sin and why this judgment is appropriate.
- (d) **Innocence:** "But . . ." followed by an affirmation that Job is not guilty of this sin. The exact word "but" is not found in this passage, but that is the sense of it.

Because the list follows verses 4 and 6, all of them carry the implicit claim of innocence.

1. Turning Aside in the Heart (vv. 7, 8)

The list begins with what is really a continuation of verse 5.[6]

> **Sin:** If I have walked with falsehood
> and my foot has hastened to deceit . . . (v. 5)

Verse 7 continues with the language of walking ("my step"):

> if my step has turned aside from the way
>   and my heart has gone after my eyes,
>   and if any spot has stuck to my hands . . . (v. 7)
>
> **Judgment:** . . . then let me sow, and another eat,
>   and let what grows for me be rooted out. (v. 8)

The sin described in verses 5, 7 is quite general, but it is described in three ways. First, it is a turning aside from the right "way"; second, it consists in the "heart" going after the "eyes"—that is to say, what the eye sees leads to and stirs up evil desires in the heart; third, it involves a "spot" or stain of impurity sticking to the "hands," as a way of describing actions that are impure.[7] While the first and third of these are about action (the foot and the hand), the middle one is about the heart, and it is this that causes the actions. Job has made a covenant with his eyes, and the sin for which he claims innocence is that of his heart being led astray by his eyes. Centuries later the Apostle John would write of "the desires of the flesh and the desires of the eyes and pride of life" (1 John 2:16).

Job describes the appropriate punishment (v. 8) in terms of the frustrated farmer, in language that Israel will later recognize as describing covenant curses (e.g., Deuteronomy 28). He will sow in tears but never reap, for others will have invaded his land and will enjoy his produce. What grows on his land will "be rooted out" by terrorism, natural disaster, and war (v. 8). All this is just what has happened to Job (Job 1, 2), even though he does not deserve it.

2. Adultery (vv. 9–12)

> **Sin:** If my heart has been enticed toward a woman,
>   and I have lain in wait at my neighbor's door. (v. 9)
>
> **Judgment:** then let my wife grind for another,
>   and let others bow down on her. (v. 10)
>
> **Reason:** For that would be a heinous crime;
>   that would be an iniquity to be punished by the judges;
> for that would be a fire that consumes as far as Abaddon,
>   and it would burn to the root all my increase. (vv. 11, 12)

If Job's first example is general, his second is very specific: adultery. It is described in verse 9. The first half of the parallelism (v. 9a) speaks of a "heart . . . enticed" toward a woman who is not his wife. Although Job is speaking of the action of adultery, he knows that the action of adultery begins with an adulterous heart, as Jesus will also spell out many centuries later (Matthew 5:28). The second half of the parallelism speaks of the action, both literally as a secretive lying in wait, ready to creep through his "neighbor's door" when he is away to have sex with his wife, but also perhaps figuratively, lying in wait at the "door" of her sexual intimacy.

The punishment Job describes fits the sin; it is for another man to do to Job what he has done to his neighbor in stealing the sexual intimacy of his wife. The words "grind for" may refer to his wife being taken from him and now doing domestic duties for his neighbor, grinding his grain (v. 10). But the words "bow down on her" are unambiguously and brutally sexual (v. 10).

Job describes both the sin and the punishment from the man's point of view. This does not necessarily imply a sexist lack of concern for women and their point of view. It simply says that if Job steals his neighbor's wife, causing him pain and loss, it will be an appropriate punishment for Job also to suffer the theft of his own wife, with the pain and loss that would cause him. Of course there are also all sorts of pains and griefs for the women who are caught up in the misery of these sins of their husbands.

This is a terrible punishment for a terrible sin. Job gives a reason why this terrible punishment would be appropriate. He agrees that this is a terrible and culpable crime that ought to be punished in court (v. 11), but not only in court, for it would light a "fire" of judgment that will burn all the way to "Abaddon" (destruction or Hell personified) and will consume in the fires of Hell "all my increase"—that is, all Job's property, family, possessions, and well-being (v. 12). This again is just what has happened to Job (cf. 1:16, "the fire . . . from heaven"), although he is innocent of this sin.

3. Injustice to Servants (vv. 13–15)

Sin: If I have rejected the cause of my manservant or my maidservant, when they brought a complaint against me. (v. 13)

Judgment: what then shall I do when God rises up?
When he makes inquiry, what shall I answer him? (v. 14)

Reason: Did not he who made me in the womb make him?
And did not one fashion us in the womb? (v. 15)

The third example Job gives concerns the way he treated those over whom he had power, his servants. The slightly archaic expression "rejected the cause" means to deny justice (v. 13). The question of justice between a master and his servants will always be a vexed one in human affairs, because where there is a mismatch of power, justice will always depend upon the fairness of the more powerful party. This is the problem Job has been having with God, who is much more powerful than Job, his loyal servant (9:1–20). Had Job treated his servants the way God has treated him, it would have been wrong.

He does not specify the punishment but simply says that he would have no answer in court when God "rises up"—that is, stands up in court[8]—and "makes inquiry" into what has happened (v. 14).[9]

The reason it would be wrong for Job to have denied justice to his servants is given in verse 15: God the Judge is the Maker of both Job and his servants. Job shares with his servants a common humanity and a common answerability to God. This reason is precisely the reason given in another wisdom book, the book of Proverbs: "Whoever mocks the poor insults his Maker" (Proverbs 17:5a); "The rich and the poor meet together; the LORD is the maker of them all" (Proverbs 22:2).

4. Lack of Generosity to the Needy (vv. 16–20)

Sin: If I have withheld anything that the poor desired,
　　or have caused the eyes of the widow to fail,
or have eaten my morsel alone,
　　and the fatherless has not eaten of it. (vv. 16, 17)

Innocence: (for from my youth the fatherless grew up with me as with a
　　　　father,
　　and from my mother's womb I guided the widow). (v. 18)

Sin: if I have seen anyone perish for lack of clothing,
　　or the needy without covering,
if his body has not blessed me,
　　and if he was not warmed with the fleece of my sheep . . . (vv. 19, 20)

In verses 16–20 Job describes two closely related sins, both of which concern lack of generosity to the needy. They are described as "the poor" (v. 16a), "the widow" (v. 16b), "the fatherless" (v. 17b), and "the needy" (v. 19b), all of which describe weak and defenseless people in need.

The sin is described first in general terms, as withholding "anything that the poor desired" or causing "the eyes of the widow to fail" (v. 16). In context this must refer to things that defenseless people need for life and that the wealthy Job is able to supply. There is a contrast between "the eyes" of the widow here, which desire necessities, and the "eyes" of Job in verse 1 or verse 7, which might be tempted toward what he does not need and ought not to have. The widow's "eyes" express a right and natural desire, and Job has helped satisfy it.

Then in verse 17 we focus in on food necessary for survival, what Job calls "my morsel." Unlike the lonely miser, Job's table has been generously shared with the fatherless. And in verse 18 he explicitly claims that he has been consistently generous to the poor, from his—presumably rich—youth onward. His wealthy home has been an open home and a place of plenty for the needy. Verses 19, 20 shift from food to the other essential of survival, clothing. This is not a matter of luxury designer clothes but of clothing without which people "perish" (v. 19a). Job's flocks of sheep have provided warm clothing not only for him and his family but for many needy people.

5. *Violence against the Defenseless (vv. 21–23)*

Sin: if I have raised my hand against the fatherless,
because I saw my help in the gate. (v. 21)

Judgment: then let my shoulder blade fall from my shoulder,
and let my arm be broken from its socket. (v. 22)

Reason: For I was in terror of calamity from God,
and I could not have faced his majesty. (v. 23)

Next, Job moves from not being generous to being actively hostile and violent against the defenseless. The idiom to "raise the hand" (v. 21) means publicly to condemn and act in judgment. It is used of God's judgment in Isaiah 19:16 and Zechariah 2:9. For Job, with his position as a regional judge, it would mean abusing his legal power falsely to condemn the defenseless. The strange expression "because I saw my help in the gate" (v. 21) may mean that Job sees his friends in or near the court ("the gate" is the place of business and judgment for the city) and is intimidated by them so that he gives a wrong judgment against defenseless people. Or it may just mean that Job knows he has "help," that is to say influence, in court. Either way Job has not abused his position and power.

Had he done so then it would be appropriate for his own shoulder blade (which supported his upraised "hand" [v. 21]) to be dislocated, so that his "arm" (power in action) would be "broken" (v. 22). The one who raises a hand to harm the innocent and defenseless will find his arm broken and his shoulder dislocated by the God of judgment. In verse 23 Job expands on this: the reason he has not done this is that he fears God and knows that God will bring "calamity" (as in v. 3) to those who do this. Job fears the "majesty" of God the Judge.

Again this terrible experience of having his arm broken and his shoulder dislocated—vivid ways of speaking of a man's broken power—has been Job's experience, even though he has not deserved it.

6. Trust in Wealth (vv. 24, 25)

Sin: If I have made gold my trust
or called fine gold my confidence,
if I have rejoiced because my wealth was abundant
or because my hand had found much . . . (vv. 24, 25)

Job moves now from his social behavior, toward his servants and toward the defenseless, to his heart and his faith. He had been a very rich man, but he denies putting his trust in his riches, which is always a danger for the rich. "If riches increase, set not your heart on them," says the psalmist (Psalm 62:10). Job has heeded this counsel. He knows that "whoever trusts in his riches will fall" (Proverbs 11:28), and he has resisted this temptation. Throughout his time of prosperity he has continued to put his trust in God alone. There is no judgment explicitly stated for this because Job moves directly on to another sin. But the clear implication is that this sin also is serious and would render Job liable to judgment.

7. Idolatry of Heavenly Bodies (vv. 26–28)

Sin: . . . if I have looked at the sun when it shone,
or the moon moving in splendor,
and my heart has been secretly enticed,
and my mouth has kissed my hand. (v. 26, 27)

Judgment: this also would be an iniquity to be punished by the judges,
for I would have been false to God above. (v. 28)

The theme of trust continues in the next sin, which speaks not of trust in human riches but of faith in the gods of the heavenly bodies, the sun and the moon. In this context to "look at" the sun or the moon means to worship it (v. 26). The words "when it shone" and "moving in splendor" remind us of the wonder of the sun and moon and the reasons why they have been worshipped (v. 26). Job's heart might have been "enticed" by these false gods (v. 27). The expression "my mouth has kissed my hand" suggests something like throwing or blowing a kiss at the sun or the moon as an expression of worship (v. 27). In 1 Kings 19:18 we read of "every mouth that has not kissed" Baal.

Job agrees that to worship the sun or moon would deserve punishment because it would be "false to God above" (v. 28). There is one God above, and only one, and Job has worshipped him and has not been an idolater.

8. Vindictiveness toward Enemies (vv. 29, 30)

Sin: If I have rejoiced at the ruin of him who hated me,
   or exulted when evil overtook him. (v. 29)

Innocence: (I have not let my mouth sin
   by asking for his life with a curse) . . . (v. 30)

Job moves back to his social behavior and speaks now of his attitude toward his enemies. There has been no *schadenfreude* with Job. He has not cheered with selfish, vengeful delight when his enemies got their comeuppance (v. 29). He has not even cursed them (v. 30). "Do not rejoice when your enemy falls," says Proverbs, "and let not your heart be glad when he stumbles, lest the LORD see it and be displeased, and turn away his anger from him" (Proverbs 24:17, 18). Although the imprecations in the Psalms are righteous, there is no place in Biblical righteousness for selfish, vengeful delight. The joy of the righteous is in seeing wrongs righted, but never in seeing enemies punished, however good and right this may be.

9. Lack of Hospitality to Strangers (vv. 31, 32)

Sin: if the men of my tent have not said,
   "Who is there that has not been filled with his meat?" (v. 31)

Innocence: (the sojourner has not lodged in the street;
   I have opened my doors to the traveler) . . . (v. 32)

Because of verse 32, it would seem that verse 31 refers to "the sojourner . . . the traveler." What is in view here is showing proper hospitality, an important moral obligation in the world of the ancient east. Unlike the terrible stories of Sodom (Genesis 19:1–11) and Jebus (Judges 19:16–26), where hospitality was refused, leading to terrible violence, no traveler in Job's region had to rough it. Job's doors were always open.

10. Hypocrisy (vv. 33, 34)

Sin: . . . if I have concealed my transgressions as others do
   by hiding my iniquity in my heart,
because I stood in great fear of the multitude,
   and the contempt of families terrified me,
   so that I kept silence, and did not go out of doors— (vv. 33, 34)

Job's first example was a general one concerning the faithfulness of his heart and life; his final example also searches the heart. Job denies being a hypocrite, pretending to be one thing while in reality being another. His claim before God is to be blameless or to have "integrity" (v. 6); it is therefore fitting that he ends his list with hypocrisy.

The words "as others do" (v. 33a) may read "as Adam did" (ESV footnote). Right at the start of human disobedience Adam hid himself and his sin, and so did Eve. Hiding sins from God has been the human default ever since. But Job has not been a sin-concealer.

He does not deny committing "transgressions" and having "iniquity"; he does deny concealing them (v. 33), as David had done before writing Psalm 32. This is a particular danger for prominent godly people, who would naturally fear the damage to their reputation when they admit their sin. "The multitude" and the "families" (or "clans") might think less well of him, and for fear of this he might hide his iniquity in his heart, keep silence, and do his best to conceal his sin (v. 34). But like David in later years after his adultery with Bathsheba, Job lives a life of open confession before God and, when appropriate, before people. He never claims to be sinless; he does claim to be consistently penitent.

This is a remarkable list of examples. In each one Job describes a sin. In most of them he explicitly acknowledges that the sin would deserve punishment; in several of them the punishment tallies frighteningly closely with what Job himself has actually experienced. In some of them he backs this up with a reason for the judgment. In some he explicitly claims innocence, and in all of them he implicitly denies guilt. In the first and last he goes to the heart of the matter, claiming to have a heart, and therefore a conscience, that is right before God.

B'. The Challenge Repeated (vv. 35–37)

> Oh, that I had one to hear me!
>> (Here is my signature! Let the Almighty answer me!)
>> Oh, that I had the indictment written by my adversary!
> Surely I would carry it on my shoulder;
>> I would bind it on me as a crown;
> I would give him an account of all my steps;
>> like a prince I would approach him. (vv. 35–37)

Right near the start Job has asked, "Does not [the Almighty] see my ways and number [or count or account for] all my steps?" (v. 4). He has asked to be "weighed in a just balance" so that his "integrity" may be known and acknowledged by God (v. 6). Now he comes back to this challenge. With that deep sighing and longing with which he began his final speech (29:2), he says, "Oh, that . . ."[10] He longed at the start for the dignity of a son of God; he yearns now for the vindication, the justification before God, that will make this sonship sure. "Oh, that I had one to hear me!"—that is, a just judge to hear his case in the court of the universe (31:25).

Continuing the law-court language, he goes on, "Here is my signature! Let the Almighty answer me!" (v. 35). The word "signature" is the last letter of the Hebrew alphabet (*taw*), and in this context it indicates not only that Job is signing off on his final defense, but also that he is claiming innocence.[11] Job is challenging the just Judge to give convincing evidence of his guilt and is confident that he will not and cannot do so.

Job has run out of patience. He has challenged his accuser to make his case in court (e.g., 13:22), but instead he has had to endure the tediously repetitive accusations of his supposed friends, none of which has hit the mark. He says at last, "I lay down my final case for the defense. I append my signature, and I challenge the Almighty, no less, to answer me. If I am guilty, then I challenge him to punish me as I deserve, with death. And if he does not, then I will be declared righteous by default, for if an opponent is silenced and remains silent, he is defeated in court. And all the world will know that I have been falsely accused."

This is a moment of electrifying tension. In our human affairs it is a moment of high drama when a President or Prime Minister is summoned to appear before a tribunal. Here it is as if the Creator of the Universe is summoned to appear before what is in effect an impeachment tribunal. Job implies, "God has treated me as guilty, and if in fact I am not guilty, then God stands guilty of injustice! Or so it appears."

In a wonderfully surprising court scene, Job longs for "the indictment [or accounting] written by my adversary" (v. 35) and imagines himself proudly carrying it around on his shoulder as a mark of status[12] or on his head as a crown (v. 36). Imagine walking around with the charge sheet that lists all my crimes, tied to my shoulder or prominently placed on my head; that would be strange behavior for a guilty person! But Job is not a guilty person; he is confident that he can "give . . . an account of all my steps" (v. 37) to the one who keeps an account of all his steps (v. 4) and that when that accounting is done, he will be able to walk boldly into the presence of the Almighty. It is a bold and wonderful scene: when this suffering servant, who bears in his person all the marks of being accursed by God, finally receives the charge sheet of his sins, it will turn out to be a glorious vindication of his integrity!

A'. The Covenant Attested by Creation (vv. 38–40)

"If my land has cried out against me
    and its furrows have wept together,
if I have eaten its yield without payment
    and made its owners breathe their last,
let thorns grow instead of wheat,
    and foul weeds instead of barley."

The words of Job are ended. (vv. 38–40)

And so we come to Job's final paragraph, where he calls creation to witness to his having kept his covenant (v. 1). Creation appears here represented by Job's "land." His farmland has seen how he has treated his tenant farmers. Had he defrauded them, eating the harvest without paying them fairly, and thus causing them harm[13] (v. 39), then the land itself would have "cried out against" him, and the plowman's furrows would have "wept together" (v. 38). Job is here doing something much deeper than just adding a postscript to his list of sins; he is claiming that the covenant he has kept with his conscience is a covenant in the sight of the God who is the Maker of Heaven and earth. It is a covenant to live in tune with creation order.[14] Later, when there is a covenant with Israel, the promised land bears witness to this covenant (e.g., Deuteronomy 30:19; Isaiah 1:2; Micah 6:2) and laments when Israel is unfaithful (e.g., Jeremiah 12:4). Alienation from the ground goes right back to the beginnings of the curse (Genesis 3:18). Job echoes this when he calls upon himself the curse of "thorns" and "foul weeds" if he has broken this covenant (v. 40a).

What Are We to Make of This Final Speech?

And so "the words of Job are ended." But what are we to make of him and of this final speech? Sure, it is very fine and bold, but is it true? And if it is true, how can it be true for a sinner to say these things? This is the critical question, and it can only be answered by reading this speech in the light of the doctrines of justification and of union with Christ from the rest of Scripture.

First, we note that, as so often in the book, Job is a foreshadowing of a man who will fulfill these things perfectly. There will come a man whose perfect obedience will extend both to his single-hearted worship and love for his Father and to his perfectly sinless and utterly good treatment of all his fellow human beings. When we read these protestations of innocence as the words of this sinless man, we can read them with no awkwardness, for he fulfills the innocence of Job in the perfection of his obedient life.

But this still leaves the question of how the historical man Job can say these things and expect God to take him seriously. And clearly he does expect God to take him seriously, and we shall see that God does indeed take him seriously and will—in chapter 42—affirm Job as his faithful covenant servant. But how can a sinner—and Job is a sinner—claim such innocence without opening himself to the accusation of pharisaical cant? And how can he conclude his list of sins precisely by denying the sin of hypocrisy, which was the trademark pharisaical sin?

Essentially this question is the same, doctrinally, as the puzzle of how the adulterer and murderer David can so often claim innocence in the Psalms. Psalm 17 is a paramount example, where David claims not just innocence in one particular matter but a deep and wide innocence: "You have tried my heart, you have visited me by night, you have tested me, and you will find nothing" (Psalm 17:3). For David the answer is given explicitly in Romans 4. David has appropriated "the blessing of the one to whom God counts righteousness apart from works" (Romans 4:6). A righteousness from God, an alien righteousness (as Luther called it), is counted, imputed, or reckoned to him, so that when his steps are "counted" they are counted righteous. David in his faith foreshadows all who are righteous by faith in Christ today. And so does Job.

Job is a man—a remarkable man, for he has so little revelation—who in his heart of trust in the Almighty is credited with a righteousness not his own. But it is more than that; like all men and women who are truly justified today, Job's justification has life-changing consequences. This is why his actual life begins to conform to the righteousness credited to him by grace. This is why he walks with a clear conscience. This is why, when he sins, he offers sacrifice, as we saw him do for his children in chapter 1. The innocence Job claims in chapter 31 is an innocence reckoned to him perfectly by grace, through the perfect obedience of the Lord Jesus Christ, and it is an innocence beginning to be worked in his actual life, also by grace, in an anticipatory working of the Holy Spirit in his heart. Job 31 is true by grace, both in Job's status and in Job's life. He is, as the Apostle John would later put it, a man who is "walk[ing] in the light" (1 John 1:7).

And yet he is about to be rebuked, first by Elihu and then, climactically and twice, by the Lord himself! The end of chapter 31 is the high point of Job's positive portrayal in the book, but it is not the end of the book. Before the book can be concluded, there is more to be said about Job, and it will begin with sustained rebuke.

Part 3

THE ANSWERS
TO JOB

Job 32:1—42:6

27

Elihu and the
Justice of God

JOB 32:1–5

THE ACCUSATION "IT'S NOT FAIR!" is common and deeply felt. We are hard-wired with a sense of what justice is and an expectation that justice ought to be done. Watch a football crowd when the referee makes a wrong call! We overturn governments because they are unjust or corrupt. We expose corruption and injustice in high places and expect it to be put right.

Job has made the accusation, "God is not fair!" He is not merely speaking of corruption in high places but of corruption in the Most High Place. If there is not justice in the universe, what hope is there for us? On a personal level, if I feel that God has not treated me right, in my health, my upbringing, my abilities, my relationships, my work, or in a failed relationship, a bereavement, a sickness, or a psychiatric disorder, then my faith will be harmed, my obedience will become reluctant, my hope will be destroyed, and my joy will be poisoned. The very first temptation in the garden in Eden was to believe that God is not fair. We are reminded as we meet Elihu that the justice or fairness of God lies at the heart of the book of Job.

> So these three men ceased to answer Job, because he was righteous in his own eyes. Then Elihu the son of Barachel the Buzite, of the family of Ram, burned with anger. He burned with anger at Job because he justified himself rather than God. He burned with anger also at Job's three friends because they had found no answer, although they had declared Job to be in the wrong. Now Elihu had waited to speak to Job because they were older than he. And when Elihu saw that there was no answer in the mouth of these three men, he burned with anger. (vv. 1–5)

We come now to the third and final section of the book of Job. Three times the author introduces a new character or characters. First he introduced Job himself (1:1–5). Next he introduced Eliphaz, Bildad, and Zophar (2:11–13). Now, many chapters later, he introduces a final human character, Elihu. This introduction, like the other two, is in prose.

The Central Issue of Elihu's Speeches Is the Justice of God

Two themes dominate this carefully worded introduction: answers and anger. The three friends "ceased to *answer*" Job (v. 1); Elihu is angry with Job's friends "because they had found *no answer*" to Job's protestations of innocence (v. 3); and it was "when Elihu saw that there was *no answer* in the mouth" of Job's comforters that he spoke (v. 5). Each of his speeches begins with the words "Elihu . . . *answered* and said." Elihu believes there needs to be an answer to Job. The lack of a satisfactory and persuasive answer has made him deeply angry: "Elihu . . . burned with anger. He burned with anger. . . . He burned with anger . . . he burned with anger" (vv. 2, 3, 5). He is a very angry man![1] And when he comes on stage, we begin to hear the answers to Job. Up until now we have heard three men who have failed to answer Job, but now the answers begin. Elihu begins the answers; the Lord will complete them.

It is important to feel the force, and the surprise, of the central issue here. The force of it is quite simply that to accuse God of injustice is a terribly serious matter. Elihu is angry first with Job "because he was righteous in his own eyes" (v. 1) and "because he justified himself rather than God" (v. 2); he is angry that a mortal man should claim—and persistently claim—to be in the right in a way that suggested that God must be in the wrong for causing him to suffer. That is a good and right anger. Elihu is right to be hotly indignant on the behalf of the name and reputation of the good and just God of all the earth when he is accused of injustice by a human being. It seems that "Elihu's anger is in measure akin to the anger of the Lord. . . . God's zeal for his own glory translated itself into Elihu's jealousy for God's glory."[2] It would be good if we too shared Elihu's indignation more deeply than we do. The expressions "righteous in his own eyes" (v. 1) and "justified himself" (v. 2) remind us of the introduction to Jesus' parable about the Pharisee and the tax-collector, which he told "to some who trusted in themselves that they were righteous" (Luke 18:9–14). Job does here sound very like the Pharisee in that story! But here's the surprise: God affirms Job's godliness (42:7), and so we are wrong if we lump Job in with the Pharisees. Elihu is right to be indignant, and yet Job is right to claim his righteousness!

Furthermore, Elihu is angry with Eliphaz, Bildad, and Zophar (vv. 3–5) "because they had found no answer" (v. 3) and "there was no answer in the mouth of these three men" (v. 5). Oh, sure, they had "declared Job to be in the wrong" (v. 3), repeatedly and at some length. So in what sense was there "no answer" in their mouths? In the sense that Job was not persuaded—Job persisted in claiming he was in the right with God, and Job had the last word (Job 29—31).[3] So although they had spoken a lot, they had not shut Job's mouth, which is what Elihu reckons is necessary if the honor of God is to be maintained, "so that every mouth may be stopped, and the whole world may be held accountable to God" (Romans 3:19). Elihu is right. And yet Job is right. So what are we to make of this?

What Are We to Make of Elihu?

Before we immerse ourselves in the flow and the detail of Elihu's speeches, it is worth asking how we are supposed to listen to them. Are we to listen attentively, expecting to hear wisdom, even authoritative wisdom from God? Are we to listen scornfully, expecting to hear folly? Or are we to expect a mixture of the two?[4]

For perhaps a couple of centuries, it would be fair to say that Elihu has not been in fashion with commentators. Older commentators have often regarded chapters 32—37 as a secondary insertion into the book. More recent commentators have been more inclined to respect their place as integral to the book but have regarded Elihu's role as essentially negative, perhaps a clown or jester to provide comic relief after the intensity of chapters 29—31[5] or as one whose protestations are undermined by the author of the book.[6] Almost every commentary is skeptical about Elihu, critical of his views, his tone, and his character. Such a widespread agreement among critics ought not to be lightly jettisoned, and yet I think it is wrong. Let us consider some of the arguments.

There is no mention of Elihu elsewhere in the book, which encourages some to see his speeches as a secondary insertion; but this is a fragile argument, for an actor in a drama may have only one appearance, and yet that appearance can be significant, intentional, and positive.

It is said that his speeches interrupt the flow from the end of chapter 31 to the start of the Lord's speeches in chapter 38. This again is a weak argument, for as we shall see, chapters 32—37 can also be read as flowing very naturally into chapters 38—41. At one fairly obvious level, a public reading of chapter 37 would need no great change of musical key when we move into chapter 38; the one moves very easily into the other.

It is often said that Elihu's style is diffuse, verbose, bombastic, and pretentious.[7] But this is a very subjective argument and one that betrays a certain cultural arrogance. Who are we, with our particular cultural canons of style, to pronounce on Elihu's style? How are we to know if his culture would have regarded him as bombastic or impressive, as pretentious or significant? No doubt some of us might find the style of some canonical prophets, such as Ezekiel, not to be to our taste, but the problem lies with us rather than with the text. If we find Elihu repetitive, this may reflect more on our impatience than on his inadequacy (and, besides, we might have said the same about Psalm 119 or the style of Deuteronomy).

It is true that the Lord does not engage with Elihu when he comes on stage with his own climactic speeches, whereas he does engage with Job and with Eliphaz, Bildad, and Zophar. It is suggested that God's ignoring of Elihu means that he is brusquely interrupting this silly fool. But the transition from the end of chapter 37 to the start of chapter 38 can be read in one of two ways. Does it mean that God is cutting Elihu off and indicating that he is wrong or insignificant and to be ignored? Or could it be that the Lord simply picks up where Elihu left off, regarding Elihu as a positive and preparatory speaker? It is said that Elihu's message is no different than the comforters; but as we shall see, that ignores some important nuances in his speeches.

Besides, a number of more objective factors ought to predispose us to take Elihu seriously and to listen attentively to his words. He is given a genealogy ("Elihu the son of Barachel the Buzite, of the family of Ram"), which tends to indicate weight and significance;[8] no genealogy is given for Eliphaz, Bildad, or Zophar. Elihu is given four speeches, more than any of the others. His speeches are not interrupted or answered, unlike the others'. His speeches come in a critical position in the book and may naturally be regarded as being preparatory for the Lord's speeches; perhaps Elihu is a kind of Elijah or John the Baptist figure.

Above all, the message Elihu brings is significantly different from that of the three friends. The Prologue to the 1560 Geneva Bible puts it like this: "In this story we have to mark that Job maintains a good cause, but handles it evil; again, his adversaries have an evil matter, but they defend it craftily." And yet it goes on, Job "bursts forth into many inconveniences"—that is, wrong ways of saying things—"both of words and sentences, and shows himself as a desperate man in many things, and as one that would resist God; and this is his good cause which he does not handle well."

It is Job's "inconveniences" that now become the focus of the book. Jones puts it succinctly: "[The friends] said that Job was suffering because he had sinned. Elihu says that Job has sinned because he was suffering."[9] As we shall see, this is a perceptive and helpful observation. In fact, both structurally and theologically the transition from the end of Job's words (at the end of chapter 31) to the start of Elihu's is a pivot point in the book. Structurally it is a pivot, for it is the beginning of the answers to Job. Theologically it is a pivot, for it marks the transition from the part of the book where Job is essentially on the front foot to the part where he is on the back foot. That is to say, in chapters 3—31 although Job is suffering deeply, he is very sure of his righteousness, and we know from 42:7 that his "comforters" are going to be rejected by God. So our default reading of Job's words is mainly positive. We have had no difficulty recognizing in Job a powerful and persuasive "type" of the Lord Jesus. In his sufferings, his innocence, his longings for vindication, and his yearning for restoration to lordship over (part of) God's world, he prefigures the Lord Jesus again and again.

However, again and again as we have listened to Job, we have had to gasp at his audacity in accusing God of injustice. However sympathetic we may be to his plight, and however strongly we believe his protestations of innocence (which we know to be true from 1:1, 8; 2:3), something in us hesitates when we hear him speaking of God with disrespect. It is not true that he is suffering because he has sinned. But it is true that because he is suffering he has said some sinful things. These will need to be corrected. Elihu begins the answering process that corrects him. Job may be a "type" of the Lord Jesus, but like all Old Testament types, he is conspicuous not only for the ways in which he is like Jesus, but also in the ways in which he falls short of Jesus.

There is a pastoral reflection here too. Job shows us a man with a clear conscience, walking a life of obedient faith and love for God, walking—as the Apostle John will put it—"in the light" (1 John 1). And yet when suffering comes there are residues of sin within him that come to light. The human heart is "deceitful" (Jeremiah 17:9), and a clear conscience is not a guarantee of sinlessness (cf. 1 Corinthians 4:4). Indeed, the human heart has been compared to a container of water with a residue of mud at the bottom. When all is calm, we see the clear water at the top and think there is just pure water within. But when the container is stirred and shaken, the mud swirls around and before long becomes visible, making it clear that all was not as pure as had been thought. It is therefore possible to have a clear conscience and to walk in daily repentance of known sin, while yet being a sinner at heart. This is the case for Job, and it explains how he can at the same time be affirmed and rebuked, indeed affirmed for speaking rightly of God while being rebuked for speaking wrongly about God! How wonderful it is that the Lord Jesus not only had a clear conscience but walked with an utterly clear heart, so that when suffering came he learned obedience, but not because he had been disobedient, and yet without sin in thought, word, or deed.

There is an inconsistency in our criticisms of Elihu. We do not like him taking Job on, although we are quite used to hearing the Lord take Job on in chapters 38—41. But if the Lord can confront and humble Job, why should he not begin to humble and confront him through the prophetic voice of Elihu beforehand? Of course, if it were true that Elihu's arguments were indistinguishable from those of the comforters, then we would be bound to be critical of him. But as we will see, they are not.

We will see that even Elihu's critics acknowledge that more than once Elihu implicitly claims divine inspiration for his words. If this is so—and I believe it is—then we are faced with a choice: either Elihu is a false prophet or he is a true prophet. Habel is the clearest example of a commentator who reads Elihu through the lens of a prior conviction that he is a false prophet. But it seems to me that without clear evidence of this—either through God's or the narrator's explicit indicators or through the un-Biblical nature of his doctrine—the natural reading of the text is that we should believe Elihu's claims and take his words at their face value, as true prophecy from God. It is this that we will do in the expositions that follow.[10]

28

Elihu's First Speech: The God Who Speaks

JOB 32:6—33:33

DOES GOD SPEAK TODAY? This question becomes a pressing one in times of suffering. When I cannot understand what God is doing, and when what he is doing seems to me not only incomprehensible but also desperately unjust, the longing for God to speak becomes unbearable. But does he speak, or is Heaven silent? This is one of the questions with which Job has been grappling. He longs to bring his case before God and for God to speak to him. Job has this longing because he is a believer. Were he an unbeliever, he would simply reject belief in God and go his own way. But he knows that it is with God he must deal, and he longs for some kind of answer from God to say what God is doing in Job's life.

Elihu comes like a preparatory prophet to bring God's word to Job and his friends. He will begin to bring an answer to Job in two senses, both in answering Job's protestations and in answering Job's longing to know if God speaks. Elihu makes four speeches. His first speech divides into the first part addressed to the three friends (chapter 32[1]) and the second part addressed to Job (chapter 33).

Human Religion Makes True Prophecy an Urgent Matter (32:1–22)

It is easy to read chapter 32 as a windy preamble, wasting our time before Elihu gets to the core of his first speech in chapter 33. That would be a mistake, for in chapter 32 Elihu goes to the heart of the difference between himself and the three friends, and the difference is the source and authority of his message. We will see that Elihu speaks with the voice of a prophet to three men whose only source of wisdom is the traditional worldview of morally serious religious people of every age. The difference is huge.

Prophecy Is Possible (vv. 6–10)

And Elihu the son of Barachel the Buzite answered and said:

> "I am young in years,
>   and you [plural] are aged;
> therefore I was timid and afraid
>   to declare my opinion to you.
> I said,[2] 'Let days speak,
>   and many years teach wisdom.'
> But it is the spirit in man,
>   the breath of the Almighty, that makes him understand.
> It is not the old who are wise,
>   nor the aged who understand what is right.
> Therefore I say, 'Listen to me;
>   let me also declare my opinion.'" (vv. 6–10)

Elihu begins with the question of authority: on what basis is he now speaking, and on what basis did the three comforters speak? The paragraph is bracketed by reference to "my opinion" (vv. 6, 10). Why should they, and Job, and we, listen to Elihu's "opinion"? What is it worth? He contrasts two possible sources of authority. The first, and in his culture most obvious, is seniority, age, experience. He speaks of this in verses 6, 7. The three comforters are "aged" (v. 6) in the sense of senior. They have been around for many "days," indeed "many years" (v. 7). They might naturally be expected to have accumulated a store of traditional wisdom over their long lives. But Elihu is "young in years"; he does not have that authority. So he is naturally "timid and afraid" to voice his opinion (v. 6). Like the younger men in Job's happier days, Elihu knows that society expects him to withdraw in the presence of his seniors (29:8). He naturally looks to these men to teach him wisdom, on the model of Proverbs 4:1–9.

And yet there is another possible source of understanding. Elihu calls this "the spirit [or breath] in man," "the breath of the Almighty" (v. 8). At one level this simply refers to "the breath of life," the human spirit (Genesis 2:7), and therefore the ability to speak, to breathe out words. But Elihu doesn't just mean that any old human being with breath in his or her lungs will have wisdom; he means that along with physical breath, the Almighty can, for some people at some times, also breathe into them his own "breath," his Spirit who will give them understanding and enable them to speak words of truth.

We shall see that Elihu claims to have been given this kind of breath; in other words, he claims divine inspiration, to be able to speak as a prophet of God.[3]

It is because prophecy is possible that tradition cannot claim ultimate authority. As Elihu puts it in verse 9, senior and experienced people do not necessarily have wisdom and a right understanding, and certainly not just by virtue of being senior. It is because of the possibility of prophecy that Elihu can say with confidence,[4] "Listen to me; let me also declare my opinion" (v. 10).

Prophecy Is Necessary (vv. 11–16)

But prophecy is not only possible—prophecy is necessary.

> Behold, I waited for your words,
>   I listened for your wise sayings,
>   while you searched out what to say.
> I gave you my attention,
>   and, behold, there was none among you who refuted Job
>   or who answered his words.
> Beware lest you say, "We have found wisdom;
>   God may vanquish him, not a man."
> He has not directed his words against me,
>   and I will not answer him with your speeches.
> They are dismayed; they answer no more;
>   they have not a word to say.
> And shall I wait, because they do not speak,
>   because they stand there, and answer no more? (vv. 11–16)

Elihu has been waiting and listening for quite a while (vv. 11, 12). During all the speeches from chapter 4 through chapter 31 he has waited and waited to see if anyone could answer Job with true wisdom. No one can say he has not been patient! He has given them plenty of time. But in spite of plundering the whole store of traditional wisdom, the worldview of the morally serious religious person, they have found no answer to Job's problem or pain. And it won't do (v. 13) to say, "Actually we have found wisdom, and we do know what we are talking about. But Job is hard-hearted and obtuse, and we're going to have to leave it to God to 'vanquish him' (v. 13) rather than doing it ourselves." "No," says Elihu, "that would be an abdication of your responsibility. If you don't have the resources and truth with which really and substantially to address Job's arguments, you cannot claim to be wise. So I'm going to come fresh into the arguments, as one who has just been a spectator so far, and I am going to say something new, not just a rehashing of 'your speeches'" [v. 14].

In verses 15, 16 Elihu looks around at whoever is listening, gestures towards the three supposedly wise men, and says in effect, "Look at them! They have been silenced. They have nothing to say. Am I supposed to wait around forever in this awkward silence?" What Elihu is doing is pointing up for them and for us the absolute necessity of a word from God. Human wisdom, earthly tradition, the understanding of senior people—these things have no answer to the predicament and perplexities of Job. Centuries later the Apostle Paul would say something similar about the wisdom of the cross and the emptiness of all human wisdom (1 Corinthians 1:18—2:5).

Prophecy Is Urgent (vv. 17–22)

Elihu now draws together the two strands of his argument. If (a) it is possible that God will put his truth into the mouth of any human being of his choice, young or old, and (b) human philosophy and understanding have no answer to the sufferings of a righteous man, then (c) there is an urgent necessity for the prophet to speak.

> I also will answer with my share;
> > I also will declare my opinion.
> For I am full of words;
> > the spirit within me constrains me.
> Behold, my belly is like wine that has no vent;
> > like new wineskins ready to burst.
> I must speak, that I may find relief;
> > I must open my lips and answer.
> I will not show partiality to any man
> > or use flattery toward any person.
> For I do not know how to flatter,
> > else my Maker would soon take me away. (vv. 17–22)

Elihu comes back to his "opinion" (cf. vv. 6, 10). In verses 18–20 he speaks eloquently of the divine necessity for him to speak. In imagery that is echoed by the prophet Jeremiah,[5] he speaks of himself as one into whom God has placed words that simply must be spoken. He cannot keep them to himself alone. He has such "spirit/breath" inside him that he feels like a man with a bloated stomach or a wineskin trying to contain the gases produced by new wine. His desire to speak is visceral. Here is a picture of divine necessity: "Woe to me if I do not speak to others what God has spoken to me!" This necessity arises not out of any self-importance on the part of Elihu (as commentators often suggest) but rather out of the dumbness of traditional wisdom in the face of the sufferings of Job.[6]

Verses 21, 22 emphasize the need for the prophet to speak words that are not shaped by the expectations or pressures of people; he must speak without partiality. He cannot be in the pay of anyone, like the prophets of Baal and Asherah in 1 Kings 18.

So Elihu begins by contrasting himself with the three friends. Implicitly he is saying that it is essential that someone should speak as the mouthpiece of God if the predicament and perplexities of Job are to be addressed. Elihu is right; the voice of prophecy is urgent. So let us hear what he says to Job.

The Prophet Appeals to the Suffering Seeker (33:1–33)
The Prophet's Voice Must Be Heeded (vv. 1–7)

> But now, hear my speech, O Job,
>   and listen to all my words.
> Behold, I open my mouth;
>   the tongue in my mouth speaks.
> My words declare the uprightness of my heart,
>   and what my lips know they speak sincerely.
> The Spirit of God has made me,
>   and the breath of the Almighty gives me life.
> Answer me, if you can;
>   set your words in order before me; take your stand.
> Behold, I am toward God as you are;
>   I too was pinched off from a piece of clay.
> Behold, no fear of me need terrify you;
>   my pressure will not be heavy upon you. (vv. 1–7)

Elihu begins his words to Job with an appeal. In verse 1 the appeal to "hear my speech" is heightened by the call to "listen to *all* my words." This is a formal summons, as one might be given to appear in court.[7] In verse 2 the declaration that "I open my mouth" is heightened by "the tongue in my mouth speaks." First the mouth opens, and then the tongue speaks. The effect is to call Job to urgent attention.

Elihu asks Job to listen because of his sincerity (v. 3), his being made by the Spirit (v. 4), his seriousness (v. 5), and his sympathy (vv. 6, 7). He is sincere, speaking from an upright heart; Job can trust his motives. He speaks with the Spirit of the God who made him; this is a play on the idea of being a living human (having the breath/spirit of God within) and being one in whom the Spirit of God has put the words of God, which is clearly Elihu's meaning here (as in 32:8, 18). And Elihu is serious; verse 5 calls Job to "answer . . . set your words in order . . . take your stand." These words of

Elihu are not to wash over Job (as the comforters' words have so often done) but to get under Job's skin and change his heart. And Elihu is sympathetic; that is the implication of verses 6, 7. God has accommodated himself to Job's mortality by putting his words in the mouth of a fellow human being, one "pinched off from a piece of clay" (v. 6; alluding to Genesis 2:7). This means that Job can hear the words of God without being terrified, as were the people of Israel when they cried to God for a mediator at Mount Sinai (Exodus 20:18, 19). Job has previously complained that he would be too frightened to hear the voice of God (e.g., 9:34; 13:21); he has no such excuse with Elihu.

This is the voice of prophecy, and it must be heeded.

Job's Accusation Must Be Answered (vv. 8–13)

Elihu now summarizes what Job has said, to make the point that these accusations are serious and must be answered.

> Surely you have spoken in my ears,
>   and I have heard the sound of your words.
> You say, "I am pure, without transgression;
>   I am clean, and there is no iniquity in me.
> Behold, he finds occasions against me,
>   he counts me as his enemy,
> he puts my feet in the stocks
>   and watches all my paths."
> Behold, in this you are not right. I will answer you,
>   for God is greater than man.
> Why do you contend against him,
>   saying, "He will answer none of man's words"? (vv. 8–13)

In verse 8 Elihu says he has been listening carefully not only to the empty words of the comforters but also to the words of Job in his speeches in chapters 4—31. In verses 9–11 he summarizes what he has heard in two points. First, Job says he is not guilty before God (v. 9). This is indeed what Job has repeatedly claimed, and Elihu reports it accurately.[8] Second (vv. 10, 11), Job accuses God of targeting Job unfairly and treating Job as his enemy, finding pretexts[9] to attack him. This again is just what Job has said (e.g., 13:24; 16:9–14; 19:6–12; 30:21). God has exposed Job to public ridicule and disgrace ("my feet in the stocks") and, like a hostile spy, has as it were tapped his phone, watching "all my paths" with a view not to providential protection but to satanic surveillance (v. 11). God has been to Job like the Stasi (the East German secret police) were to so many Germans before 1989. Job has said something very like this in 7:8, 20. And verse 11 is a quotation of Job's words in 13:27a.

The implication of these two points together is that God has treated Job unjustly, and this implication makes Elihu indignant. He says to Job, "In this you are not right," and that is why "I will answer you." The short headline reason he gives is that "God is greater than man" (v. 12); this will be a major theme in his speeches. But for the moment he focuses on Job's complaint that God will not "answer" his or anyone else's "words" (v. 13). Job has made this complaint, for example, in 9:3, 14–16. It seems to Job that God is treating him unfairly, and God will not and does not seem to speak to explain himself or to communicate in any way with Job or other sufferers. It is this complaint that Elihu will address in the remainder of the speech. It is important to note that, unlike the comforters, Elihu will not tell Job he is suffering because he has sinned; instead he will rebuke him for saying sinful and wrong things because he is suffering. Job does not have secret, undisclosed sins that have caused his suffering; but he is wrong in what he says about God in the midst of his suffering. In this Elihu is correct.

God Does Speak! (vv. 14–30)

> For God speaks in one way,
>> and in two, though man does not perceive it. (v. 14)

Job says God does not speak to human beings. Elihu says he does, and in more than one way. The idiom "one way, and in two . . ." means "in more than one way" and anticipates the similar idiom "twice, three times" in verse 29.[10] It also has the sense of God speaking repeatedly in his determination to be heard. The words "though man does not perceive it" are a way of saying that although God does speak—and speak repeatedly—people don't always realize it (v. 14).

Elihu expands on two of the ways in which he says that God speaks.

God Speaks through the Voice of Conscience (vv. 15–18)

> In a dream, in a vision of the night,
>> when deep sleep falls on men,
>> while they slumber on their beds,
> then he opens the ears of men
>> and terrifies them with warnings,
> that he may turn man aside from his deed
>> and conceal pride from a man;
> he keeps back his soul from the pit,
>> his life from perishing by the sword. (vv. 15–18)[11]

Although I have headed this "through the voice of conscience," this is not exactly what Elihu says. In verse 15 Elihu uses four words for dreams and visions. First, "dream" (cf. Genesis 20:3); second, "vision of the night" (as in Daniel 7:2); third, "deep sleep" when humans are totally passive (cf. Genesis 15:12); and fourth, "slumber" on the bed. These are all ways of speaking of times of human passivity, and it is in these times that God "opens the ears of men" and frightens them (v. 16). The open ear contrasts with the heavy or dull ear that will not hear (e.g., Isaiah 6:9, 10).

The emphasis is not on the precise experiences of dreams (it would be a mistake to try to define or categorize each kind) but on the fact that God frightens human beings about sin. It is what we would call the voice of a guilty conscience, that strange terror that afflicts us when we know we are guilty and unforgiven.

God speaks this way, says Elihu, with the purpose of verses 17, 18, to "turn man aside from his deed"—that is, to bring us to repentance and a changed life—"and conceal pride from a man"—which is a rather archaic way of saying to keep us from becoming proud.[12] In a similar way God gave the Apostle Paul "a thorn . . . in the flesh, a messenger of Satan to harass me, to keep me from becoming conceited" (2 Corinthians 12:7). By bringing us to repentance and guarding us from pride, God achieves his goal (v. 18) of keeping the life of a human being from "the pit" of decay and judgment, from that perishing from which there can be no rescue.

So God does speak, in that frightening conviction of our sins that turns us back and protects us from death and judgment. But there is a second way, and this will be Elihu's main emphasis.

God Speaks through Suffering (vv. 19–28)

What Elihu says here is in two parts. First he describes God speaking (vv. 19–22) and then the result (vv. 23–28).

Man is also rebuked with pain on his bed
    and with continual strife in his bones,
so that his life loathes bread,
    and his appetite the choicest food.
His flesh is so wasted away that it cannot be seen,
    and his bones that were not seen stick out.
His soul draws near the pit,
    and his life to those who bring death. (vv. 19–22)[13]

On the face of it, verses 19–22 are yet another description of suffering, and indeed of the suffering being endured by Job himself. But the key word here is "rebuked" (v. 19), for this suffering is a word to the sufferer from God; it is the second way in which God speaks. In his book *The Problem of Pain*, C. S. Lewis famously said:

> The human spirit will not even begin to try to surrender self-will as long as all seems to be well with it. Now error and sin both have this property, that the deeper they are the less their victim suspects their existence; they are masked evil. Pain is unmasked, unmistakable evil; every man knows that something is wrong when he is being hurt. . . . We can rest contentedly in our sins. . . . But pain insists upon being attended to. God whispers to us in our pleasures, speaks in our conscience, but shouts in our pains: it is His megaphone to rouse a deaf world.[14]

Lewis was not the first to see this truth. Elihu had seen it long before him. Here, according to Elihu, is a suffering that is also a "rebuke" or word from God. Just as in the first way of speaking the voice of God (vv. 15, 16) is followed by the gracious purpose of God to rescue (vv. 17, 18), so here the voice of God in suffering (vv. 19–22) is followed by an expanded description of the rescue that follows (vv. 23–28).

> If there be for him an angel,
>   a mediator, one of the thousand,
>   to declare to man what is right for him,
> and he is merciful to him, and says,
>   "Deliver him from going down into the pit;
>   I have found a ransom;
> let his flesh become fresh with youth;
>   let him return to the days of his youthful vigor";
> then man prays to God, and he accepts him;
>   he sees his face[15] with a shout of joy,
> and he restores to man his righteousness.
>   He sings before men and says:
> "I sinned and perverted what was right,
>   and it was not repaid to me.
> He has redeemed my soul from going down into the pit,
>   and my life shall look upon the light." (vv. 23–28)

The rescue begins with "an angel" or messenger of God, who is also called "a mediator" or advocate, one who will speak up for this sufferer in the court of Heaven (v. 23). We have met Job's longing for this mediator in chapters 9, 16, and 19 (9:33; 16:19; 19:25), and here he is, like the angel in Zechariah 3:1–5, who speaks against Satan when Satan accuses the high priest. He is "one of the thousand" (or perhaps "one out of a thousand"), which seems to be a way of indicating how rare and special he is (v. 23). His role is "to declare to man what is right for him" (v. 23), to tell him the right way to live, or possibly "to vouch for the person's uprightness."[16]

As a result of this mediation, "he"—that is, the mediator—shows mercy to the sufferer and speaks up for him in the court of Heaven, giving the word for him to be rescued from the pit (vv. 24, 25). This is because there is a "ransom" for the man, a redemption, a substitute to save him from danger (v. 24). This is something human beings can never do for themselves; God must do it for them (cf. Psalm 49:7). And so this sufferer is restored to health (v. 25). Here is an anticipation of the One who will be God's mediator and God's ransom to bring rescue from the pit of decay.

The result (vv. 26–28) is a prayer, a reconciliation with God accompanied by a shout of joy, a "righteousness" (v. 26) or justification in the presence of God, and a glad song before people celebrating God's great mercy and redeeming love.

In this way the "severe mercy" (in C. S. Lewis's famous phrase) of God in speaking to this sufferer through suffering has led to rescue and joy in God's salvation.

Conclusion: God Does Speak (vv. 29, 30)

Behold, God does all these things,
  twice, three times, with a man,
to bring back his soul from the pit,
  that he may be lighted with the light of life. (vv. 29, 30)

Elihu concludes that whether God speaks through the misery of a guilty conscience or through the pain of suffering, he does so repeatedly and persistently with the goal of rescuing people "from the pit" and giving them "the light of life."

Unlike the comforters, Elihu is not accusing Job of concealing his sins, nor does he "read" Job's sufferings as evidence of Job's sins. But he says that Job is wrong to accuse God of not speaking. This accusation has come from Job because of his sufferings; and yet Elihu says it may be precisely these sufferings that *are* the voice of God to him! I may think that because I am suffering, God is not speaking to me; but he is, and my sufferings may be his voice! And his purpose in my sufferings is gracious; it is that I may be rescued from death and restored to life.

The Prophet's Voice Must Be Heeded (vv. 31–33)

Pay attention, O Job, listen to me;
  be silent, and I will speak.

If you have any words, answer me;
    speak, for I desire to justify you.
If not, listen to me;
    be silent, and I will teach you wisdom. (vv. 31–33)

Elihu concludes by repeating his appeal to Job to heed his voice, the appeal with which he began (33:1–7). As well as speaking urgently and strongly to Job to listen, he says that his motive is "to justify you," to see Job stand tall and straight before God (v. 32). Elihu comes alongside Job; he is on Job's side. Even as he rebukes Job for speaking out of turn, he wants the best for Job.

Elihu's First Message: God Speaks, and He Speaks to Save

The core of Elihu's first speech is that God does speak. It is the silence of God that has troubled Job so deeply. Elihu comes to Job's comforters and tells them of the voice of prophecy, which will be the God-given and necessary voice to shed light on Job's sufferings. And he comes to Job and tells him of the voices of conscience and of suffering, by which God speaks to save. By implication he calls upon Job to listen to the voice of God coming to him in and through his sufferings and to let this voice do its gracious work of preserving Job from pride. Job needs to be humbled under the mighty hand of God. By grace he will be so humbled, but not just yet.

29

Elihu's Second Speech: Is God Fair?

JOB 34

NEITHER JOB NOR the three comforters speak after Elihu's first speech. We cannot know what they made of it, but it is perhaps not fanciful to imagine Job listening with care and storing these things up in his heart. It will be some time yet—and a greater voice must be heard—before he sees clearly, but there is a work of grace going on in his heart. Of that we may be sure. He foreshadows a greater man to come who will learn obedience through what he suffers (Hebrews 5:8). That man will learn obedience without sinning as he learns it. Job, however, needs to learn to bow in humble obedience before the God whom he cannot by nature worship perfectly.

In his second speech Elihu focuses on the central issue of the justice of God. We saw (when we studied 32:1–5) that this was the driving force that provoked him to speak in the first place. What he has said in the first address about God speaking is really preliminary to what he now says in the second. It goes to the heart of the book of Job: is God fair?

The address falls into two main parts. In verses 2–15 he speaks to a wider audience, and then from verse 16 onward he speaks directly to Job. This structure is similar to what we saw in his first address, in which chapter 32 was addressed to the comforters and chapter 33 to Job. In this address, as in the last, we are to picture Elihu at the microphone (as it were) with Job immediately in front of him, but the three comforters and probably other significant local people are also listening. Perhaps the community elders were there too to listen to this great ongoing debate. Elihu will say essentially the same thing in the first part as in the second, but in the second it becomes fuller and more personal, concluding with a heartfelt appeal to Job and a warning lest he not heed Elihu's words.

To a Wider Audience (vv. 1–15)

In this first part Elihu identifies the critical issue (vv. 2–4), then levels the most serious accusation against Job (vv. 5–9), before stating the central axiom (vv. 10, 11) and giving the key reason in support of this (vv. 12–15). Speaking, as it were, loudly and publicly, he puts on the table all the key elements of the debate. In the second part he will expand on these things to Job himself.

The Critical Issue Is the Justice and Goodness of God (vv. 2–4)
Then Elihu answered and said:

> "Hear my words, you wise men,
>   and give ear to me, you who know;
> for the ear tests words
>   as the palate tastes food.
> Let us choose what is right;
>   let us know among ourselves what is good." (vv. 1–4)

Elihu addresses the "wise men" and calls them "you who know" (v. 2), that is, men of learning. While he may be speaking just to the three comforters, his low opinion of them suggests he is speaking here to a wider audience, perhaps including the community elders. He is speaking potentially to any wise and knowledgeable listener. In verse 3 he uses an image Job himself has used in 12:11 ("Does not the ear test words as the palate tastes food?"). "See what these arguments taste like!" Elihu says in essence. It is an invitation not just to listen once but to turn the arguments over and over as one might with some unfamiliar food, working out which arguments taste good.

In verse 4 he states the one agenda item for discussion: "Let us choose [literally, decide or discern for ourselves] what is right . . . what is good." The word "right" or "justice" is a major theme of the speech, as is its opposite, to "do wrong" or "be wicked."[1] The word "good" has the sense of morally good.[2] Absalom puts the same two words together when he says to plaintiffs in the city gate, "See, your claims are good and right" (2 Samuel 15:3). We are to think together about God's government of the world and whether he governs it rightly and fairly and whether we can be happy and confident about the goodness of his government. There are few more important questions in the world.

The Most Serious Accusation Is That Job Has Accused God of Not Being Just and Good (vv. 5–9)

> For Job has said, "I am in the right,
> and God has taken away my right;
> in spite of my right I am counted a liar;
> my wound³ is incurable, though I am without transgression."
> What man is like Job,
> who drinks up scoffing like water,
> who travels in company with evildoers
> and walks with wicked men?
> For he has said, "It profits a man nothing
> that he should take delight in God." (vv. 5–9)

In verses 5, 6 Elihu sums up what Job has said in four claims.⁴ First (v. 5a), Job says he is "in the right" (v. 5); that is, he has justice on his side. Job has indeed said this, and repeatedly (see, for example, 10:15; 13:18). Second (v. 5b), he protests that "God has taken away my right"; that is, God has denied him justice. This is exactly what Job has said, for example in 27:2 ("As God lives, who has taken away my right . . ."). Third (v. 6a), Job laments that God counts him "a liar," branding him as self-evidently guilty by inflicting suffering on him. Job has said as much in 16:8 ("And he has shriveled me up, which is a witness against me"). Finally (v. 6b), he feels his "wound is incurable" and there is no hope for him. Although he will finally repent of this, at this point Job has believed the primal lie of the Satan—that God is not good but is a cruel and evil tormentor. The Satan has masqueraded as God and has persuaded Job of this.

Unlike the comforters, who accuse Job of secret sins for which they have no evidence, Elihu focuses on the public evidence of these things that Job has said. On the basis of Job's words he makes his accusation in verses 7–9. He is horrified by these things and accuses Job of drinking up "scoffing like water" (v. 7b); this metaphor would seem to mean that Job has scoffed or mocked at the goodness and justice of God because he has drunk in such views from others and has believed their lies, rather as Eve believed the snake's lie in the garden. In 15:16 Eliphaz had accused Job of drinking in "injustice like water." But whereas Eliphaz accused Job of making injustice his diet, Elihu accuses him of making mockery of God his diet. The former accusation is untrue, but sadly Elihu's is true, as Job himself will later admit.

By scoffing like this, Job has lined himself up with "evildoers" and "wicked" people (v. 8).⁵ Elihu is not saying that Job is himself wicked, just that by speaking like this he sounds as if he were (rather as Job himself had said to his wife in 2:10, "You speak *as* one of the foolish women *would* speak"). His keeping company with wicked men is defined in verse 9 as being because of what he has "said"—that "It profits a man nothing that he should take delight in [or seek to please] God." Job has indeed said or implied this. In 9:22 he accuses God of destroying "both the blameless and the wicked" (so what's the point of being blameless?). In 10:3 he accuses God of showing "favor" to the plans of the wicked (so why not be wicked to get the favor of God? Cf. Psalm 73:1–15). In 21:7–16 he has given an eloquent description of the prosperity of the wicked. Near the end of the Old Testament period unbelieving Jews will be saying much the same: "Everyone who does evil is good in the sight of the LORD, and he delights in them" (Malachi 2:17).

So here is Elihu's central accusation against Job. This is a good point to pause and ask ourselves about Elihu's tone. Critics often say he is harsh and unfeeling and shows no understanding of Job's predicament. But this is to take the viewpoint of our human-centered preoccupation with ourselves. We might do better to see Elihu as one who cares with overwhelming passion for the honor of God. To him anything that impugns God's honor is a terrible thing and eclipses any extenuating circumstances caused by human suffering. Perhaps this is why we find it so hard to accept the rightness of Elihu's concerns and arguments.

The Central Axiom Is That God Cannot Do Wrong (vv. 10, 11)

> Therefore, hear me, you men of understanding:
>   far be it from God that he should do wickedness,
>   and from the Almighty that he should do wrong.
> For according to the work of a man he will repay him,
>   and according to his ways he will make it befall him. (vv. 10, 11)

From verse 10 Elihu moves from his examination of Job's position to the exposition of his own position. With a renewed appeal to "you men of understanding" (any wise listeners), he states his central axiom, first negatively and then positively. Negatively (v. 10b, c), he cannot abide even the idea that the Almighty God might "do wickedness . . . do wrong." Positively (v. 11) he affirms the doctrine of just judgment: God repays people fairly and justly according to their works and "ways." It is precisely this that Job has denied, for example in 9:23, 24.

What Elihu says here sounds very like what the comforters have affirmed. For example, in chapter 8 Bildad has asked, "Does God pervert justice? Or does the Almighty pervert the right?" (8:3). But whereas Bildad's concern is narrowly with the punishment of the wicked, Elihu's is broader. He is arguing, not just for God's fair punishments, but for God's good and fair government of the world in every respect.

The Key Reason Is That God Is God! (vv. 12–15)

> Of a truth, God will not do wickedly,
>   and the Almighty will not pervert justice.
> Who gave him charge over the earth,
>   and who laid on him the whole world?
> If he should set his heart to it
>   and gather to himself his spirit and his breath,
> all flesh would perish together,
>   and man would return to dust. (vv. 12–15)

In verse 12 Elihu restates his axiom, prefaced by "Of a truth" for emphasis; he implies this idea is unthinkable. This raises the question of why it is unthinkable, why this axiom is true. In verses 13–15 Elihu gives perhaps the most deeply theological core of his answer: it is unthinkable because God is God! His government of the world is not a responsibility delegated to him by some superior deity (as Baal's by El in Canaanite religion); no one put him in charge of the world. Had they done so, we could conceive of him carrying out his responsibility in an unjust and irresponsible way, rather as a local governor might twist the justice of a fair emperor and administer his rule unfairly on a local level. But God is God; he is the supreme Governor of the world. If he is not just, then there can be no such thing as justice; but (by implication) the very existence of our ideas of justice mean that justice exists and must reside with the supreme God.

In verses 14, 15 he develops this thought by getting us to think about our absolute dependence upon God for life and breath.[6] We are utterly dependent upon him, and he is not one whit dependent upon us. To challenge the justice of his rule is to challenge his person, and that is a very foolish and dangerous thing to do.[7]

By challenging the goodness and justice of the Sovereign God, Job is challenging the very being of God, for goodness and justice inhere in his being and his power. In using this argument, Elihu is preparing the way for God's speeches in chapters 38—41.

So, having stated the issue, having summarized and accused Job, and having put his axiom and central reason on the table, Elihu now turns and addresses Job in person.

To Job (vv. 16–37)

The Accusation Is That Job Has Condemned the Righteous, Mighty God (vv. 16, 17)

> If you have understanding, hear this;
>> listen to what I say.
> Shall one who hates justice govern?
>> Will you condemn him who is righteous and mighty . . . (vv. 16, 17)

Turning from plural to singular verbs, Elihu speaks to Job. He denies Job's complaint that the one governing the universe "hates justice" and accuses Job of trying to condemn "him who is righteous and mighty" (v. 17). These two attributes of God, his justice and his power, are inseparable. This was the argument of verses 12–15; the one who is supremely mighty must be, by definition, the source and embodiment of justice.

This Is Wrong Because God Does Judge Justly (vv. 18–30)

Elihu continues by spelling out in some detail the way in which the mighty, righteous God exercises his judgment.

He Judges with No Favorites (vv. 18, 19)

> . . . who says to a king, "Worthless one,"
>> and to nobles, "Wicked man,"
> who shows no partiality to princes,
>> nor regards the rich more than the poor,
>> for they are all the work of his hands? (vv. 18, 19)

First, because God is supremely powerful, he is not cowed or influenced by power in others. Others can be pressured by powerful or rich people into showing favoritism toward them; not so the Almighty God. When kings, nobles, princes, and rich people behave wrongly, he has no hesitation in condemning them. Because of God's sovereign power, we may be sure his judgment is without favoritism; it is not in any way contingent upon human influence.

He Judges with No Uncertainty (v. 20)

> In a moment they die;
>> at midnight the people are shaken and pass away,
>> and the mighty are taken away by no human hand. (v. 20)

Second, God's judgment is not uncertain. When Elihu says that "in a moment they die," he is not saying that God's judgment is always immediate, but rather that its suddenness makes it very clear this is God at work. "At midnight," the time when people are asleep and feel secure, they die (as did the firstborn in Egypt, Exodus 12:29). Their judgment happens "by no human hand," no visible human agency, as proof that this is the judicial action of God.

He Judges with No Ignorance (vv. 21–25)

> For his eyes are on the ways of a man,
>   and he sees all his steps.
> There is no gloom or deep darkness
>   where evildoers may hide themselves.
> For God has no need to consider a man further,
>   that he should go before God in judgment.[8]
> He shatters the mighty without investigation
>   and sets others in their place.
> Thus, knowing their works,
>   he overturns them in the night, and they are crushed. (vv. 21–25)

Third, God judges with perfect knowledge. He has "eyes" that see "all" the "steps" of a person (v. 21). There is no possibility of hiding, not even in the "deep darkness" that speaks of cosmic "gloom" (v. 22). God doesn't need "to consider a man further," that is, to spend a long time investigating a man, before the case can come to trial (v. 23), as happens so often in human cases when the police take months, if not years, to accumulate all the evidence they need. God can execute "judgment" (v. 23), shattering even the most powerful people "without investigation" (v. 24) because he already knows all the facts. So the judgment of God is perfect not only because of his omnipotence but also by virtue of his omniscience.

He Judges with No Secrecy (vv. 26–28)

> He strikes them for their wickedness
>   in a place for all to see,
> because they turned aside from following him
>   and had no regard for any of his ways,
> so that they caused the cry of the poor to come to him,
>   and he heard the cry of the afflicted— (vv. 26–28)

Fourth, he will judge publicly, "in a place for all to see" (v. 26). There will be nothing secretive about his judgment. When men and women turn "aside from following him" (v. 27) and therefore become agents of social injustice (v. 28), he will give them the punishment they deserve, and he will do so publicly, so that the whole universe will see his justice.

He Will Judge Even If He Delays (vv. 29, 30)

> When he is quiet, who can condemn?
>> When he hides his face, who can behold him,
>> whether it be a nation or a man?—
> that a godless man should not reign,
>> that he should not ensnare the people. (vv. 29, 30)

But it is the fifth feature of God's judgment that is the climax of Elihu's case. What are we to say when God is "quiet," when he "hides his face" and doesn't seem to do anything about injustice (v. 29)? This, after all, is Job's problem. Elihu claims that when God is "quiet," it is still unacceptable and wrong to "condemn" him for injustice (as Job has done) (v. 29). For when "he hides his face" he is invisible ("who can behold him . . . ?"), and we cannot tell what he may be doing behind the scenes (v. 29). Neither on a national level nor on a personal level can we condemn God for his inaction.[9] Verse 30 seems to mean that we can still trust that God is working to ensure that godless people do not continue forever to reign and to trap and ensnare people.

The point here is that God's apparent inaction does not contradict his justice. "It indicates that during a period marked by God's 'silence and inactivity'—that is, between a cry for help and an intervention by way of answer—it is not permissible . . . to censure God, as Job has done."[10] "God's slowness to act does not deny his sovereignty,"[11] nor his justice.

For all these reasons—God's sovereign impartiality, God's definite judgments, God's omniscience, God's public judgments, and God's inscrutability when he delays—it is a wrong and terrible thing to accuse God of wrong. It is therefore natural that Elihu should close by calling upon Job to repent.

Job Must Repent of What He Has Said about God (vv. 31–33)

> For has anyone said to God,
>> "I have borne punishment;[12] I will not offend any more;
> teach me what I do not see;
>> if I have done iniquity, I will do it no more"?
> Will he then make repayment to suit you,
>> because you reject it?
> For you must choose, and not I;
>> therefore declare what you know. (vv. 31–33)

Verse 31 is not asking a theoretical question. Elihu is making a definite suggestion. The "anyone" here could be Job (v. 31)! Job is encouraged to put up his hands and admit that he has said things he ought not to have said and then to pray to God to teach him the things he has not understood (v. 32a) before pledging himself not to say these things again (v. 32b).

The meaning of verse 33 is not easy to unpack. To "make repayment" seems to refer to God admitting that Job is right. "[T]o suit you" would indicate God doing this on Job's terms. The words "because you reject it" may mean "despite your rejection of repentance" or "because you reject God's terms."[13] Perhaps we might paraphrase it, "You can't expect God to roll over and admit you're right. You must decide to repent of what you have said. You know that's the right thing to do." Elihu is appealing to Job's conscience. Before long his appeal will be heeded and Job will indeed repent of exactly the words of which Elihu says he needs to repent. Elihu's accusations are accurate and precise.

Job's Trial Must Continue Until He Repents (vv. 34–37)

Men of understanding will say to me,
    and the wise man who hears me will say:
"Job speaks without knowledge;
    his words are without insight."[14]
Would that Job were tried to the end,
    because he answers like wicked men.
For he adds rebellion to his sin;
    he claps his hands among us
    and multiplies his words against God. (vv. 34–37)

Finally Elihu spells out the seriousness of the issues. Hartley suggests that Elihu pauses after verse 33 to see how Job will respond. When Job's body language shows he is not persuaded, Elihu looks at the assembled company and gives this final warning. This is possible. But whatever the precise circumstances, these final words stress for us, as for Job, the great importance of what we say about God and his justice and goodness. Of what Job has said thus far, the verdict will be that Job speaks "without knowledge . . . without insight" (v. 35). This is the conclusion of Elihu's case.

But what are we to say about verse 36, where Elihu seems to call down a curse upon Job? Commentators are quick to condemn Elihu for being insensitive and cruel here. But they may have missed the point. When Elihu says that Job ought to be "tried to the end" he may refer—and in the context probably is referring—not to Job's sufferings but to the contest of arguments in which they are involved. The trial of arguments cannot end until Job admits that he is wrong in what he has said about God. This is confirmed by verse 36b: it is "because he *answers* like wicked men" that he must be "tried to the end." What Job is saying is very serious. Indeed he "adds rebellion to his sin," perhaps by undermining piety in others and encouraging them to rebel against God. He "claps his hands," which seems to indicate an impious and ungodly gesture (some rude, scornful gesture with his hands), and "multiplies his words against God." It is not that Job once let slip an unjustified remark about God, but that he goes on and on saying bad things about God's justice and goodness. It is this sustained attack on the good name of God that Elihu cannot endure. It is for this that he must challenge Job to repent.

Conclusion

I suspect our problem with Elihu—and the problem of many commentators— is with his intensity. It is easy to mistake his intensity for cruelty, insensitivity, or a self-obsessed arrogance.[15] But the plain meaning of the text is that Elihu is intense because the issues are serious. As Hartley puts it, "Elihu argues this point so intensely because he seems to fear that Job, in hardening his heart to God's disciplinary judgment, stands in danger of the final punishment, death. Therefore, he wants to convince Job to relinquish his complaint and submit himself to God."[16]

The central fact is that Elihu is right about the justice and goodness of God. To say anything else is to align ourselves with the snake in the garden. Although there are superficial similarities between Elihu and the comforters, the differences are significant. Jones puts it well:

> Elihu and the Friends deal with sin and suffering from diverse perspectives. While there can be no doubt that Elihu deals severely with Job in the light of the justice and power of God, he does so because Job had impugned God, explicitly as well as by necessary consequence. But that was done during and because of his affliction, and not prior to it (not that his words were any the less grievous on that account!). Whenever the Friends took Job to task for his sins, they were thinking of sins that Job had committed prior to his being afflicted by way of punishment. This was a supposition which they could not validate, whereas Elihu is highlighting sins that he can and does prove. What is more, they are sins that Job cannot and does not contest.[17]

30

Elihu's Third Speech:
What's the Point of
Being Good?

JOB 35

WHAT IS THE POINT OF BEING GOOD? From the parent telling the child, "If you're not good, Father Christmas won't come" to the sufferer asking, "What have I done to deserve this?" the connection between virtue and blessing and between wickedness and curse has been asked all through human history. It is in particular the question that the prosperity gospel and its cousin the therapeutic gospel characteristically ask and purport to answer: "If I am good, will God bless me?" "Yes, he will!"

Although at the start of the book Job firmly rejected this and showed that he worships God purely and simply because he is God and is worthy of his worship, it would seem that Job has faltered in this as his sufferings have continued. This short but dense speech by Elihu carries a sharp but necessary rebuke to Job and to any of us who fall into this trap, no matter how severe the suffering that prompts it.

Unlike the first two speeches, this one is entirely addressed in the singular to Job himself, with no separate address to the comforters or a wider audience (although Elihu expects them to be listening, v. 4b). But, as in the first two speeches, Elihu begins by summarizing something Job has said (vv. 2–4) before giving his answer or refutation. The refutation is in two parts (vv. 5–8 and then vv. 9–16).

The Question: What's the Point of Being Good? (vv. 1–4)

And Elihu answered and said:

> "Do you think this to be just?
>   Do you say, 'It is my right before God,'[1]
> that you ask, 'What advantage have I?
>   How am I better off than if I had sinned?'
> I will answer you
>   and your friends with you." (vv. 1–4)[2]

The key question is in verse 3. In his second speech Elihu has also quoted Job as saying this (34:9). Now he takes issue with it and makes it the main focus of the speech. "If I take trouble to live a penitent and godly life, what is the point if, despite my virtue, I experience such terrible suffering? Surely I might at least expect some measure of blessing instead of this dreadful pain." That is Job's question and objection. Elihu answers it with considerable robustness. There is no arm around Job's shoulder and no sympathetic cup of tea but rather a strong rebuke!

The First Answer: It's the Wrong Question to Ask (vv. 5–8)

> Look at the heavens, and see;
>   and behold the clouds, which are higher than you.
> If you have sinned, what do you accomplish against him?
>   And if your transgressions are multiplied, what do you do to him?
> If you are righteous, what do you give to him?
>   Or what does he receive from your hand?
> Your wickedness concerns a man like yourself,
>   and your righteousness a son of man. (vv. 5–8)

Elihu begins with an illustrative exhortation (v. 5). In essence he says, "Have a good look up at the vast high sky and the clouds so far above you! Think about the transcendence of God and how his dwelling-place is beyond your reach. He lives above and beyond this world of human mortals. Nothing you can do on earth will change what happens up there. You can murder and commit adultery or be generous and faithful, and the clouds will continue the same as before. You won't affect the sky because it is way up there."

In the same way, because God in his nature is transcendent (up there), two things follow. Negatively (v. 6) you can sin as much as you like, but you won't damage God; you cannot cause him to suffer or damage his essence. Positively (v. 7) you can be as good as you like, but you can never put God in your debt; he doesn't need your good deeds, and your good deeds do not give him anything. God in his very nature and eternal blessedness is impassible and immutable, unchangeably the same. Putting the two together (v. 8), both your wickedness and your righteousness (your bad behavior and good) can only affect human beings.[3]

Elihu is not suggesting that God does not care how Job or anyone else behaves. "After all, he is counseling Job in God's name to cease fighting with God and to submit to him";[4] so he clearly thinks our actions have moral and spiritual significance. He is saying that since we cannot affect the blessedness of God by our actions, there is no way we should expect to gain any kind of leverage with him. We cannot say to God, "If I stop sinning, I expect you'll feel happier and reward me" or "I'm sure my good behavior has made your day better, so it seems to me that you owe me one in return." So to ask what advantage I may expect to gain from my piety is the wrong question; it is a question that reveals I have not properly taken on board the transcendence of God and therefore his impassibility and immutability.

But if Elihu's first answer is blunt, his second is even more uncomfortable.

The Second Answer: Don't Expect an Answer (vv. 9–16)

> Because of the multitude of oppressions people cry out;
>   they call for help because of the arm of the mighty.
> But none says, "Where is God my Maker,
>   who gives songs in the night,
> who teaches us more than the beasts of the earth
>   and makes us wiser than the birds of the heavens?"
> There they cry out, but he does not answer,
>   because of the pride of evil men.
> Surely God does not hear an empty cry,
>   nor does the Almighty regard it.
> How much less when you say that you do not see him,
>   that the case is before him, and you are waiting for him!
> And now, because his anger does not punish,
>   and he does not take much note of transgression,
> Job opens his mouth in empty talk;
>   he multiplies words without knowledge. (vv. 9–16)

In verses 9–13 Elihu describes a nonspecific situation. The point will become clear in verses 14–16 where he applies it to Job. Here is the situation: all over the world there is oppression, and in this oppression the oppressed "cry out" and "call for help" (v. 9). So why doesn't God do something about it? The answer is a general answer without being a universal answer: because they are not exercising faith. This is the point of verse 10a. They don't ask, "Where is God my Maker?" This question "Where is . . . ?" is not asking for information but expresses the seeking of a heart that longs for God. Jeremiah uses the same idiom when he says of unbelieving Judah that "they did not say, 'Where is the LORD . . . ?'" (Jeremiah 2:6).

So the problem is that while these people cry, they do not pray; their cry is a cry of anguish, but it is not a cry directed with faith to God. The expression "who gives songs in the night" (v. 10) is unique in the Old Testament. It may refer to the songs of trust sung by believers in dark times or, perhaps more likely, to the objective "songs" given to us by God in the night—the morning stars, the proofs and indications that there is a morning coming. Whatever the meaning, the people Elihu is speaking about do not really pray, and this is why God does not answer.

Verse 11 may mean that God has given us more light than the beasts and the birds or that he has taught us by means of the beasts and the birds (i.e., he teaches us *by* the beasts, *by* the birds). Either way human beings ought to reach out in faith rather than just cry out in pain. So (v. 12) these people do "cry out" because proud evildoers oppress them,[5] but God "does not answer." Their cry is "empty" (v. 13), so Almighty God pays no attention to it. The word "empty" means deceitful and worthless; their cry comes from unbelieving hearts.

This is uncomfortable stuff! Elihu is not saying there are no people on earth who cry out in faith, pictured by the widow in Jesus' story in Luke 18. That would contradict many Biblical counterexamples. But he is saying that there are people—many people—whose cry is not a prayer. The point of this becomes evident when, in verses 14–16, he homes in on Job himself. Job has complained that he cannot "see" God, that his "case is before" God, and he is just waiting and waiting for God to hear his case (v. 14). He is perplexed that God does not punish evildoers and seems not to notice transgression (v. 15). But his problem is that his talk about God is "empty" (v. 16), just like the "empty cry" of the people described in verses 9–13. In a phrase echoed by the Lord in 38:2, Elihu describes Job as speaking "words without knowledge" (v. 16).

Conclusion

So what is Elihu saying to Job? He is telling Job that as long as he keeps saying these outrageous and impious things about God, he cannot expect God to answer him. God will not answer his cries any more than he can be expected to answer the cries of other sufferers who do not cry to him from faith. In our soft and liberal cultures we find this offensive. And yet it is true. Elihu is giving Job "the wounds of a . . . faithful . . . friend" (Proverbs 27:6); he is telling Job what he needs to hear. In his rough and uncompromising way he is doing

Job far more good than the soppy sympathy of one who dares compromise with the name of God. He is challenging head-on our natural and instinctive but sinful expectation that by our virtue we can put God in our debt and that in our painful cries we have a right to have God listen to us. Neither is true, for God is above and beyond us, unchangeable in his nature and consistent in his determination to listen only to the prayers of those who seek him because he is God, and not because of what they hope to gain from him.

31

Elihu's Fourth Speech: Cosmic Grandeur and Cosmic Justice

JOB 36, 37

PICTURE A LARGE MILITARY CAMPAIGN. In the course of this campaign an order comes down to a local commander. He can see that the order will result in heavy casualties for his troops; it seems to him to be a foolish instruction. But the fact is, the carrying out of this order is the only way in which the campaign can be won. The local commander neither understands the whole picture nor has the authority to command the whole army; both his understanding and his power are circumscribed. Only the commander-in-chief has the universal grasp of the military realities and the total command of all the troops; only he can know and do what is needed for victory.

This limited illustration may help us grasp the central point that Elihu is making in his climactic and final speech: only cosmic power can put into effect cosmic justice. Only the Commander-in-Chief of the universe has the universal understanding to know fully just how the victory of good over evil can be won; only he has the cosmic power to put this plan into effect. To a man in one locality, like Job, however great his regional power and however deep his local wisdom, it is not given to know what will finally result in cosmic justice.

Elihu's final speech would seem to be addressed entirely to Job, although one imagines that others were listening in. It has two main parts. After a brief introduction (36:1–4), in which Elihu says what he is seeking to do, the first main part concerns God's dealings with people (36:5–25). The second main part concerns God's government of the world (36:26—37:20), followed by a conclusion about God's glory (37:21–24). Each of the two main parts ends with an appeal to Job for response.

Introduction: A God-Given Defense of God's Justice (36:1–4)

And Elihu continued, and said:

> "Bear with me a little, and I will show you,
>> for I have yet something to say on God's behalf.
> I will get my knowledge from afar
>> and ascribe righteousness to my Maker.
> For truly my words are not false;
>> one who is perfect in knowledge is with you." (vv. 1–4)

Elihu begins briefly with an appeal, a motive, an authority, an aim, and a claim. The appeal (v. 2) is for Job to keep on listening: "Bear with me a little, and I will show you, for I have yet something to say . . ." Elihu knows that we do not naturally listen to God's truth; we need to be encouraged to keep on grappling with his truth.

The motive is that he is speaking "on God's behalf" (v. 2b). He is God's mouthpiece. Incidentally, the fact that God himself speaks in the succeeding chapters does not vitiate Elihu's claim to inspiration, any more than the perfect revelation of Jesus renders John the Baptist's prophecies less than God-given.

Elihu's authority comes because he has gained his "knowledge from afar" (v. 3a). The expression "from afar" may simply mean that he has traveled widely and trawled all the best libraries, scholars, and wise men of the world to inform what he says. But it seems more likely that he is claiming to have received his knowledge from the heavenly realm (the far-off realm where God dwells) and that this is an implicit claim to divine inspiration for his words. The expression "from afar" is often used to express the heavenly distance of God from people. We are told that "the haughty [God] knows from afar" (Psalm 138:6). The psalmist says to God, "You discern my thoughts from afar" (Psalm 139:2). In Jeremiah God calls himself "a God far away" (Jeremiah 23:23).[1] The expression "from afar" is repeated in Job 36:25, forming an inclusio around the first major part of the speech.

Elihu's aim is to "ascribe righteousness to my Maker" (v. 3b). This does not just mean to *say* that the Creator is just, but also to *prove* or *demonstrate* that he is just. This has been Elihu's aim in all his speeches; it was the motive that launched him on his intervention in the debates (32:1–5).

Finally Elihu claims that because his motive is right, his authority is God-given, his aim is God-honoring, and the content of what he says is reliable (v. 4). It is "not false" (that is, not twisted or perverted); he speaks with the voice of "one who is perfect [blameless, flawless] in knowledge." That is to say, he speaks as a prophet with the voice of "him who is perfect in knowledge" (37:16). Elihu is not being arrogant, but he is claiming to speak as a prophet.[2]

After this crisp introduction, Elihu expounds his two main points. Each of them focuses on the greatness of God; he defends God's justice by expounding his greatness. Jones has pointed out that the words "Behold, God . . ." are important and emphatic. Elihu begins this way three times in this speech; each one draws attention to the power of God. "Behold, God is mighty . . ." (36:5); "Behold, God is exalted in his power" (36:22); "Behold, God is great" (36:26). And right at the end of the speech Elihu says, "The Almighty . . . is great in power" (37:23). The logic of Elihu's argument is that only cosmic power can guarantee cosmic justice. The response Elihu calls for is entirely consistent with this. Job, and we, should bow in humble submission before the grandeur of God's cosmic power, trusting in his achievement of cosmic justice in the end.

God Acts Powerfully and Justly on People (36:5–25)

The Mighty Justice of God (vv. 5–7)

> Behold, God is mighty, and does not despise any;
>   he is mighty in strength of understanding.
> He does not keep the wicked alive,
>   but gives the afflicted their right.
> He does not withdraw his eyes from the righteous,
>   but with kings on the throne
>   he sets them forever, and they are exalted. (vv. 5–7)

In verses 5–7 Elihu begins (v. 5) by stating God's "mighty" nature. The phrase "strength of understanding" (v. 5b) is literally "strong of heart" and seems to refer to God's determination to work out his purposes of cosmic justice and not to be frustrated in this; he is set in his purpose. But in his mighty nature he "does not despise" human beings, who "are not his playthings."[3] This caring power is expanded in verses 6, 7 in deliberately unequal ways. Verse 6a affirms that God will not allow the wicked to stay alive indefinitely; he will punish them. But then, at greater length, verses 6b, 7 expound his gracious determination to vindicate the afflicted righteous, who trust in him (this is the meaning of "righteous" both here and in the Psalms). He will give them—and Job, if he proves to be one of them—"their right" (their vindication) and will exalt them to places of great dignity "with kings on the throne . . . forever" (v. 7).[4] Here is a God whose power is used emphatically in gracious justice for the believing oppressed.

The Just Discipline of God (vv. 8–10)

> And if they are bound in chains
>   and caught in the cords of affliction,
> then he declares to them their work
>   and their transgressions, that they are behaving arrogantly.
> He opens their ears to instruction
>   and commands that they return from iniquity. (vv. 8–10)

Verses 8–10 contradict the prosperity gospel of the comforters, for they recognize that those who are righteous by faith may be, and often are, "caught in the cords of affliction" (v. 8). The righteous do suffer. When this happens, God "declares to them their work"—that is, he shows them the true nature of their deeds and therefore their heart—and in particular "their transgressions, that they are behaving arrogantly" (v. 9). It is worth thinking carefully about this. Elihu does not deny that there is such a thing as suffering for those who are righteous; he does not therefore deny that this may be the case for Job, as indeed we know it is. But he is saying (and this is similar to his argument in 33:14–29) that suffering often brings out the pride and rebellion in our hearts, as it has done in Job. Even the Lord Jesus "learned obedience through what he suffered" (Hebrews 5:8), although he did so without sin.

So, says Elihu, God graciously "opens their ears to instruction" or discipline (v. 10). The expression "open the ears" indicates an obedient listening and submission (as shown by the servant of the Lord in Isaiah 50:4, 5—"the Lord God has opened my ear, and I was not rebellious"). In this way God summons them to repentance (v. 10b) from the pride and rebellion in their hearts. Elihu is saying something different from the comforters here. He can agree that Job is not being punished for unforgiven sin prior to his suffering. But he argues that Job's suffering has caused some sinful attitudes in Job's heart to come to the surface and to be expressed in his words, and he is right, for Job and for every believing sufferer except the Lord Jesus.

The Two Responses to God (vv. 11–15)

> If they listen and serve him,
>   they complete their days in prosperity,
>   and their years in pleasantness.

But if they do not listen, they perish by the sword
  and die without knowledge.

The godless in heart cherish anger;
  they do not cry for help when he binds them.
They die in youth,
  and their life ends among the cult prostitutes.
He delivers the afflicted by their affliction
  and opens their ear by adversity. (vv. 11–15)

In verses 11–15 Elihu spells out the two possible responses to the loving discipline of God. Positively, those who "listen and serve him"—that is, those who heed his discipline and bow down under it in humble penitence—are richly blessed (v. 11). On the other hand (v. 12), those who refuse to listen will "perish . . . and die without knowledge"—that is, for lack of a saving knowledge of God (as in Hosea 4:6).[5] What is happening for these people is that their suffering reveals the godlessness of their hearts, which is shown by their simply getting angry and resentful (v. 13a) and refusing to turn to God in prayer (v. 13b). "Suffering only intensifies their antagonism toward their God."[6] Their life is a downward spiral of vice and judgment (v. 14). But by contrast God delights to use affliction as his means to deliver "the afflicted" (v. 15), bringing them to the place of humble, open ears and soft hearts by means of adversity.[7] Paradoxically, there is an adversity gospel that goes far deeper than the so-called prosperity gospel.[8]

All that Elihu has described in verses 5–15 is God's mighty determination to save the righteous and to punish the wicked. That is to say, it takes the mighty power of God acting through suffering and discipline to keep the righteous humbled under his mighty hand and to bring the godless to judgment. Only cosmic power can bring to pass cosmic justice.

The Appeal to Job (vv. 16–25)
He also allured you out of distress
    into a broad place where there was no cramping,
    and what was set on your table was full of fatness.
  But you are full of the judgment on the wicked;
    judgment and justice seize you.
  Beware lest wrath entice you into scoffing,
    and let not the greatness of the ransom turn you aside.
  Will your cry for help avail to keep you from distress,
    or all the force of your strength?
  Do not long for the night,
    when peoples vanish in their place.

> Take care; do not turn to iniquity,
>   for this you have chosen rather than affliction. (vv. 16–21)

From verse 16 Elihu turns and addresses Job personally. These general truths of the sovereign grace of God bear on Job's case directly. "What has God been doing in your life?" he asks Job. Answer: "Surprisingly and wonderfully he has been alluring or luring you out of the very mouth or jaws of distress" (v. 16a). The words "out of distress" (v. 16) are literally "out of the mouth of distress," in the sense of beings rescued out of the very jaws of danger. These jaws would seem to be the greedy mouth of death and Hell, which are threatening to devour Job because of his attitude of proud defiance toward God. But by the sufferings Job is enduring God seeks to lure him back to "a broad place" (v. 16), an unconstricted place. Suffering confines and narrows our world and constrains our possibilities (as being housebound demonstrates most vividly). Job has been terribly constricted, but it is the purpose of God to free him and to give him plentiful blessing (v. 16c). (The old-fashioned expression "full of fatness" is not so attractive to our figure-conscious minds today [v. 16]. It means plenty of what is most desirable in life.)

The problem with Job is that instead of being "full" of God's blessings (v. 16c), he is "full" of the kind of false judgments about God that wicked people make (v. 17a), and therefore he is in a place of danger (v. 17b). It is not easy to understand verses 18–20.[9] The "ransom" of verse 18b may refer to the costly repentance that Job must undergo.[10] Job cannot save himself (v. 19). He must not long for death as a cheap way out (v. 20), as he has repeatedly done (7:21; 10:18–22; 17:13–16). He must not allow himself to go on speaking iniquitous things (v. 21a) as a way out of affliction. Instead he must submit humbly to the gracious discipline of God.

> Behold, God is exalted in his power;
>   who is a teacher like him?
> Who has prescribed for him his way,
>   or who can say, "You have done wrong"?
> Remember to extol his work,
>   of which men have sung.
> All mankind has looked on it;
>   man beholds it from afar. (vv. 22–25)

In verses 22–25 Elihu comes back to the greatness of God ("Behold, God is exalted in his power," v. 22a) but focuses in particular on how the power of God is used to instruct and teach people (v. 22b: "who is a teacher like him?").

God is the ultimate instructor who works powerfully and graciously in people to bring them by grace to glory.[11] In the words of the old hymn, we are "made by grace for glory meet."[12] Nobody has told God how to do it (v. 23a), and no one has the cosmic knowledge that would allow them to tell them he was doing it wrong (v. 23b). So Job must "remember to extol his work" (v. 24a), to respond to the workings of God with humble praise rather than arrogant protest. Faithful people have sung of this, and Job needs to be part of the choir of praisers (v. 24b). He needs to admit that he is one of those who look on the cosmic greatness, the cosmic grace, and the cosmic justice of God "from afar" (v. 25). He needs to listen to the God-given words of Elihu, whose wisdom has come "from afar" (v. 3).

In all this Elihu may seem harsh to Job, but he is actually bringing him great gospel truth. He is teaching him that only the cosmic power of the Sovereign God can bring cosmic justice to fruition. Job has suffered, and is suffering, terribly; but no matter how terribly he has suffered, to respond with arrogant protest toward God is wrong and dangerous, and he must repent.

Elihu knows that this kind of argument is accurate, but it lacks the persuasive force to change entrenched positions. What he now does in the remainder of the speech is to say what is doctrinally much the same, with imagery that engages Job (and us) with visceral force.

God Acts Powerfully on the World (36:26—37:20)

In the second section and conclusion of the speech two motifs are interwoven. On the one hand there is a sense of mystery, of the wonderful and awesome "beyondness" of God's government of the world. On the other hand there is explanation and teaching, or at least brief indications of purpose, clues as to why God governs the world as he does.[13]

God Acts in Power for Blessing and for Judgment (36:26—37:13)

> Behold, God is great, and we know him not;
> the number of his years is unsearchable. (vv. 26)

With his final "Behold, God . . ." Elihu gives us his headline, which is not only that "God is great" but also that he is beyond our understanding. The old-fashioned expression "we know him not" does not mean we cannot enter into relationship with him, but that he is "beyond our comprehension,"[14] "beyond our understanding."[15] He is inscrutable, not least because he exists above and beyond time (v. 26b).[16] So the great power of God carries with it the entailment that we cannot and must not expect fully to understand him.

> For he draws up the drops of water;
>> they distill his mist[17] in rain,
> which the skies pour down
>> and drop on mankind abundantly. (vv. 27, 28)

Elihu takes as his introductory example the wonderful process of evaporation, condensation, and precipitation. This process is both beyond normal human comprehension (or it was then) and yet is also clearly beneficial to human beings. These waters "drop on mankind abundantly" (v. 28). The process is at the same time mysterious and yet intelligible—mysterious in its means, but intelligible in its result.

> Can anyone understand the spreading of the clouds,
>> the thunderings of his pavilion?
> Behold, he scatters his lightning about him
>> and covers the roots of the sea.
> For by these he judges peoples;
>> he gives food in abundance.
> He covers his hands with the lightning
>> and commands it to strike the mark.
> Its crashing declares his presence;
>> the cattle also declare that he rises. (vv. 29–33)

Elihu then moves, very naturally, from the quiet processes of evaporation, condensation, and precipitation to the more dramatic and violent occurrence of a fierce thunderstorm. When the clouds gather, as it were with God riding them like a chariot (v. 29),[18] we are to picture God zapping the earth and the sea with fierce shafts of lightning so bright that they expose even the "roots" or depths of the sea (v. 30), symbolizing the most remote and dangerous corners of creation. It is an amazing picture, continued in verses 32, 33.

But again, as with the rain, it has a purpose: "For by these he judges peoples; he gives food in abundance" (v. 31). This is a double-edged purpose: a storm can cause terrible damage (as it had with Job in 1:16, 19), but the resulting rainfall can also lead to the fertilization and growth of crops. The same action of God, the same storm, brings judgment for some and blessing for others, just as the same affliction brings blessing to the righteous and judgment for the ungodly in heart (36:8–15). The fact that we cannot understand how God does it does not mean that we can accuse God of injustice or incompetence in his government of the world.

> At this also my heart trembles
>> and leaps out of its place.

Keep listening to the thunder of his voice
  and the rumbling that comes from his mouth.
Under the whole heaven he lets it go,
  and his lightning to the corners of the earth.
After it his voice roars;
  he thunders with his majestic voice,
  and he does not restrain the lightnings when his voice is heard.
God thunders wondrously with his voice;
  he does great things that we cannot comprehend.
For to the snow he says, "Fall on the earth,"
  likewise to the downpour, his mighty downpour.
He seals up the hand[19] of every man,
  that all men whom he made may know it.[20]
Then the beasts go into their lairs,
  and remain in their dens.
From its chamber comes the whirlwind,
  and cold from the scattering winds.
By the breath of God ice is given,
  and the broad waters are frozen fast.
He loads the thick cloud with moisture;
  the clouds scatter his lightning.
They turn around and around by his guidance,
  to accomplish all that he commands them
  on the face of the habitable world.
Whether for correction or for his land
  or for love, he causes it to happen. (vv. 1–13)

This next passage continues the vivid and dramatic description of the storm. But the theme here is that this is a way in which God speaks. It is "the thunder of his *voice* . . . the rumbling that comes from his *mouth*" (v. 2); it is the roar of "his *voice* . . . his majestic *voice* . . . when his *voice* is heard" (v. 4); it is the wondrous thunder of "his *voice*" (v. 5); it is how he "*says*" a command to the snow and the downpour (v. 6); it is "the *breath* of God" (v. 10); and by these phenomena the storms "accomplish all that he *commands* them" (v. 12).

Here again, and perhaps even more emphatically, is a phenomenon that evokes wonder ("my heart trembles and leaps out of its place," v. 1). He tells Job to "keep listening" (v. 2; literally, "Listen! Listen!") to this "voice" of God. It is an unconstrained public word from God, coming from "the whole heaven" and reaching "to the corners of the earth" (v. 3). It is an unrestrained voice (v. 4) and an incomprehensible voice (v. 5), a voice that brings "snow" and wild downpours (v. 6). When God acts like this, both human beings and animals have to cease their normal activities (vv. 7, 8). It is a strange voice that brings "ice" and "lightning" (vv. 10, 11).

But again it has a purpose, as verses 12, 13 make clear. All these wild and incomprehensible phenomena, these storm clouds, "turn around and around" (picture a hurricane or tornado) "by his guidance" and with a purpose—"to accomplish all that he commands them on the face of the habitable world" (v. 12). The wild things that happen in life are God's wild things, and all their wildness is under his control. With them he does "correction" (v. 13)—the works of discipline[21] (as in 36:8–15) or judgment—or brings blessing to the "land" or just out of "love" for people. Just as the storm of 36:31 might bring judgment for some and food for others, so this storm is a painful but necessary correction for some and the simple expression of God's love to others.

In all this Elihu wants to evoke in Job a sense of humble wonder and the realization that only God in his cosmic power can be trusted to work out his purposes of final and cosmic justice. So Elihu goes on to make his last appeal to Job.

The Appeal to Job (37:14–20)

> Hear this, O Job;
>   stop and consider the wondrous works of God.
> Do you know how God lays his command upon them
>   and causes the lightning of his cloud to shine?
> Do you know the balancings of the clouds,[22]
>   the wondrous works of him who is perfect in knowledge,
> you whose garments are hot
>   when the earth is still because of the south wind?
> Can you, like him, spread out the skies,
>   hard as a cast metal mirror?
> Teach us what we shall say to him;
>   we cannot draw up our case because of darkness.
> Shall it be told him that I would speak?
>   Did a man ever wish that he would be swallowed up? (vv. 14–20)

So far it has been an awe-filled but general description. Elihu speaks to anyone who is listening and asks questions like "Can *anyone* understand . . . ?" (36:29). But now suddenly it becomes very personal: "Hear this, O *Job* . . . Do *you* know . . . Do *you* know . . . *you* . . . Can *you* . . . ?" (vv. 14, 15, 16, 17, 18). These truths call for an individual response. Anticipating closely the Lord's speeches, Elihu asks Job questions to challenge the limitations of his knowledge ("Do you know . . . ?") and his power ("Can you . . . ?"). Elihu calls upon Job to "stop and consider," to pause in his complaints and laments and to think hard and long about "the wondrous works of God," which in this context means God's using his cosmic power to work his cosmic justice (v. 14). In verses 15,

16 Elihu asks Job if he can understand how God controls perhaps the most chaotic and unpredictable phenomena in the universe, the weather. God commands the clouds and the lightning, but how does he do it? Only God knows, for he is "perfect in knowledge" (v. 16), and he has given Elihu the words of "one who is perfect in knowledge" (36:4).

In verse 17 Elihu reminds Job of those stiflingly hot days when the wind comes from the dry southern desert, and whatever you wear you cannot help feeling that you can hardly breathe because of the heat. Jesus's contemporaries knew this phenomenon too: "When you see the south wind blowing, you say, 'There will be scorching heat'" (Luke 12:55). The point seems to be that Job knows what it is to experience the weather, but he cannot control the weather.

There are days when the sky is dry, hot, and oppressive, like a bronze mirror overhead (v. 18), with no possibility of rain and no hope for crops; these days are accursed according to Deuteronomy, when "the heavens over your head shall be bronze" (Deuteronomy 28:23). Job knows what it feels like to experience such misery, but he cannot control it.

In view of such mysterious and awesome greatness, in verses 19, 20 Elihu warns Job that it is presumptuous and dangerous to think he can "draw up [a] case" against God, for God dwells in the light of perfect knowledge, and Job is in "darkness" (v. 19). So to send God a message saying "I want to speak with you and to challenge you" is like wishing to be "swallowed up" (v. 20b). How much wiser it is to bow before God's sovereign wisdom.

Conclusion: God Is Overwhelmingly Glorious (37:21–24)

> And now no one looks on the light
>> when it is bright in the skies,
>> when the wind has passed and cleared them.
> Out of the north comes golden splendor;
>> God is clothed with awesome majesty.
> The Almighty—we cannot find him;
>> he is great in power;
>> justice and abundant righteousness he will not violate.
> Therefore men fear him;
>> he does not regard any who are wise in their own conceit. (vv. 21–24)

If Elihu has delivered this speech during an actual storm, perhaps now the storm is over. But whether it is an actual storm or a poetically imagined storm, the conclusion pictures that beautiful scene when the clouds are clearing ("when the wind has passed and cleared them") and the "bright" sun ("the light") shines low in the sky (v. 21).

Into this scene of dramatic and overwhelming brightness Elihu describes God coming "out of the north" in "golden splendor" in verse 22. Of course the sun never shines literally out of the north. But the north (Hebrew *zaphon*) in the ancient Near-Eastern religions was the place of the mountain of the gods (Mount Zaphon, analogous to Mount Olympus in Greek mythology). Thus the arrogance of the King of Babylon is described in terms of his saying in his heart, "I will ascend to heaven; above the stars of God I will set my throne on high; I will sit on the mount of assembly in the far reaches of the north" (Isaiah 14:13). In a more contemporary idiom, Isaiah would be saying to him, "You're so arrogant you think you're a god; while the rest of us have coffee with friends in Starbucks, you think you have a membership card for entry into the club of the gods!"

Elihu, like some of the psalmists, takes this polytheistic storybook language and appropriates it for the one true God. This is why Zion can be described as being "in the far north" (Psalm 48:2). This is not a geographical description, for Zion was in the southern part of the promised land; it is using storybook language to say that Zion is the true home of the one true God. In verse 22 Elihu pictures God coming in the most wonderful brightness and "awesome majesty," so much so that the only proper response is to bow in adoration of his beauty and his grandeur.

In verses 22, 23 Elihu says that because the Almighty God dwells in "the north," far away and above human reach, "we cannot find him." He is gloriously transcendent, "great in power," and—just as important—because he is great in power, we may be confident that he will "not violate . . . justice and abundant righteousness" (or he will not "oppress," which would contradict justice). That is to say, his cosmic power will guarantee not only that he knows how to achieve cosmic justice but that he will actually do so.

For that reason, in verse 24 Elihu concludes, the right response is to "fear him" with loving, reverent fear and to run a million miles away from being "wise in [one's] own conceit." To "fear" God was precisely what Job had done all his life (1:1, 8; 2:3); it defined his wisdom (28:28). And yet Elihu is concerned that some of the things Job has said in his pain have been conceited things. He is right to warn Job against these and to call Job back to the God-fearing wisdom that has characterized his life.

Retrospect on Elihu

Elihu has made four remarkable speeches. Neither Job nor the comforters have made any attempt to interrupt him. He has claimed to speak with the breath or voice of God, as God's prophet preparing the way (as it turns out) for God himself to speak directly. He has begun the answers to Job by focusing on the justice of God. Yes, he says in his first speech, God does speak. He speaks in prophecy, through conscience, and in suffering. He speaks to save. His speaking is a part of his working out justice for the righteous who trust in him. In his second, and perhaps most deeply theological, speech he has argued that God must be just simply by virtue of being God. To deny his justice is to challenge his deity. In the third speech Elihu challenges the prosperity gospel question, what profit is there in being pious? With his radical God-centeredness, Elihu says this is the wrong question and that God will not listen to us while we are so self-centered as to ask it. This is an uncomfortable and unpopular truth, but nonetheless true. Finally, in his last speech he helps Job not only to think with his mind but also to feel with his whole person the majestic cosmic power of God and to reflect that only such cosmic power can be trusted to put into effect cosmic justice. He calls upon Job and every believing sufferer to bow in humble adoration before this majestic God. In all this Elihu is a faithful prophet of God.

32

The Lord's First Speech, Part 1: What Wonderful Knowledge

JOB 38:1–38

HAD I BEEN PRESENT AT THE CREATION I would have given some useful hints for the better ordering of the universe." Those words are attributed to King Alphonso the Tenth, King of Spain in the thirteenth century, nicknamed "Alphonso the Learned."[1] Alphonso was not the first human being to think he could run the universe better than God. The learned and wise Job, nurtured in the wisdom tradition of the ancient east, trained from childhood to think deeply about life, has come to the conviction that he does not live in a well-run world. He has repeatedly questioned the wisdom with which the Almighty is governing his world. By implication he too considers he could have offered the Creator "some useful hints" for ordering the universe better—like not condemning a righteous man to misery, for instance. I know nothing about King Alphonso, but I do know that, however learned he may have been, there were no "useful hints" he could possibly have given to the Creator to enable the universe to be better governed. Nor could Job.

But how is he—and how are we, when we are tempted to feel the same—to be persuaded, deeply persuaded, of this? Elihu has begun the answers to Job. He has spoken, in my view prophetically, of the justice, loving mercy, and kindness of the God who speaks and governs and whose presence is as awesome as a massive thunderstorm. No one interrupts Elihu or questions his words. The three comforters are silent and Job is quiet as Elihu reaches the end of his fourth and final speech.

We may consider what happens next under the headings of the event, the issue, and the answers.

The Event: The Astonishing Voice of God (v. 1)

Then the LORD answered Job out of the whirlwind and said . . . (v. 1)

What happens next is astonishing. It is what Job has both desired most passionately and feared most deeply. God speaks, and speaks directly and personally, to Job himself. Back in chapter 9 Job has cried out, "If I summoned him and he answered me, I would not believe that he was listening to my voice. For he crushes me with a tempest . . . he will not let me get my breath . . ." (9:16–18). The prospect of an audience with God is terrifying. And yet it is this for which Job longs most urgently. "Oh, that I knew where I might find him," he has cried (23:3). "Oh, that I had one to hear me! (Here is my signature! Let the Almighty answer me!)," he has called out in his final speech (31:35). Eliphaz thinks this is unimaginable. "Call now," he has mocked, "is there anyone who will answer you?" (5:1). Even the prophet Elihu cannot imagine this: "The Almighty—we cannot find him" (37:23). And yet now it happens. Job does not find the Almighty, but the Almighty finds and speaks to him. We do not know by what physical or psychological mechanism Job heard the voice of God or whether this was an audible voice or a voice heard inwardly. The narrative simply records that God spoke to him.[2]

The story is recounted of Benjamin Jowett, when he was Master of Balliol College in Oxford. Apparently someone asked him at dinner, "Dr. Jowett, we would like to know what your opinion of God is," to which he is said to have replied, "I should think it a great impertinence were I to express my opinion about God. The only constant anxiety of my life is to know what is God's opinion of me."[3] In a similar way the tables are now turned on Job.

Four things at least mark this speech as significant. The first is that this is recorded as unmediated speech, like God's speech to Israel at Mount Sinai (Exodus 20:1, 19) in later years. If my understanding is correct, God has begun speaking to Job by the mouth of Elihu the prophet in chapters 32—37, but now he speaks directly. Just as the Ten Commandments, spoken immediately from God to Israel, are thereby designated as of great importance, so it is with these divine speeches spoken directly to Job. We need to listen to them with rapt attention.

The second marker of significance is the use of the covenant name "the LORD" (Yahweh) for the first time since chapters 1, 2.[4] Although this covenant name will not be revealed in its redemptive fullness to Israel until centuries later (Exodus 3 and 6), the narrator correctly tells us that the God who spoke to Job is the God who will later be revealed as the covenant God and the same God who has been sovereign in the heavenly scenes in chapters 1, 2. This signals to us both that the poetic body of the book (chapters 3—41) is integral with the prose introduction and conclusion (1:1—2:13; 42:7–17) and also that the book records the character and dealings of the God of Israel with a believer before and outside of Israel. In this way the drama of Job, although historically not set in Israel's story, is tied to the great story of the whole Bible with its fulfillment in Jesus Christ.

The third feature is that God speaks directly and personally to one man. In 28:28 we have read a general word of God to humankind, but this now is a word to Job himself.

Finally God speaks "out of the whirlwind," the awesome storm described by Elihu in chapters 36, 37, the storm that speaks of the scary and sovereign power of God, the storm that Job's own life has become. We meet this stormy God also at Mount Sinai (Exodus 19) and in Psalm 18. Elijah was translated into Heaven in such a whirlwind (2 Kings 2:11). Many centuries later Ezekiel in Babylon will see "a stormy wind . . . out of the north, and a great cloud, with brightness around it, and fire flashing forth continually . . ." (Ezekiel 1:4; cf. Ezekiel 13:11, 13) and meet with God. Zechariah prophesies that "the LORD GOD . . . will march forth in the whirlwinds of the south" (Zechariah 9:14).[5] This great God speaks when and to whom he chooses. He "neither hurried nor humbled himself to do what Job demanded."[6] Such a manner of speaking humbled Job, and humbles us.[7] In the midst of the storms of Job's life, God speaks to him.

So this is the event. But what is the issue? For what purpose does God speak to Job?

The Issue: Full Knowledge of the Universe (vv. 2, 3)

> Who is this that darkens counsel by words without knowledge?
> Dress for action like a man;
>   I will question you, and you make it known to me. (vv. 2, 3)

The Lord will speak twice, perhaps to parallel the two times he spoke in the parallel heavenly scenes at the start (1:6–12; 2:1–6).[8] Each speech begins with a challenge, which sets the agenda and signals the key point being addressed. These are different for the two speeches.

In this first address Job is accused by God of darkening "counsel by words without knowledge" (v. 2). In this context the word "counsel" is "a broad term for the mysterious and paradoxical way in which the world is ordered and operates."[9] Job is not convicted of the supposed secret sins of which the comforters have accused him. All along he has maintained his innocence of these, and he is right. But he has spoken "words," many words, and some of his words have lacked real wisdom and knowledge. Elihu has said that "Job speaks without knowledge; his words are without insight" (34:35); now God agrees with Elihu's verdict.

It is about Job's words that God challenges him. He has spoken words about the government of the world, not only as this government has impacted him, but also more generally about how it has affected others. For example, he has accused God of bringing "deep darkness to light" (12:22), which seems to mean introducing terrible evil into the world. He has accused God of shaking the earth and making its stable pillars tremble as he introduces disorder where there ought to be order (9:5, 6).

But Job has spoken these words out of ignorance, for he does not know as he has claimed to know. He has spoken as if he has cosmic knowledge, as if he really grasped how the universe is governed and could therefore be critical of the one who is governing it, but he does not have this cosmic knowledge.

Although at the very end God will affirm that Job has spoken rightly of him (42:7), Job has also said some very wrong things about God. We shall have to ask, when we get to chapter 42, in what sense Job's words have been right. For the moment we have to focus on where he went wrong.

God therefore challenges him to "Dress for action," literally to gird his loins, to tuck his robe into his belt and so be ready for vigorous action, probably something like a wrestling contest with God (v. 3).[10] He is to do this "like a man" (v. 3; the word "man" means something like "warrior" or "strong man"). In our idiom, Job is to "man up" for the task. While this may be sarcastic, it may also be affirmative. God is affirming Job the believer as one who can stand tall and engage in this vigorous thinking with God. He is challenged to a contest of words; it is a verbal engagement. Job will need all his faculties for the thinking that is to come. The Lord will question Job, and Job is invited to answer (cf. 13:22). Here is an answer to Job that consists mostly of questions! Job wishes to question God, but God will ask the questions of Job. The answer to each question is not simply for Job to admit, "No, not me"; it is to grant to God, "No, I didn't, but you did."[11]

It is of course a surprise that God does not choose directly to answer Job's questions, or ours. He does not tell Job what had transpired in Heaven in chapters 1, 2. But what he does tell him will answer him more deeply and mercifully than a straightforward unveiling of the heavenly scenes of chapters 1, 2 could ever have done.

The Structure of the Answer

The main body of the speech consists of about seventeen[12] fairly short sections. Probably the most natural major division is between those sections speaking about the inanimate creation (38:1–38) and those considering animals and birds (38:39—39:30).[13] At the end there is a final challenge (40:1, 2) followed by Job's brief response (40:3–5).

It is difficult to know whether or not we are intended to discern a precise structure in the speech, and there is no a priori reason why we should expect one. But to help us follow our way through I see the structure of the first part as follows.

Introductory challenge (38:1–3)
>   A. God's counsel is revealed in the inanimate created order (38:4–38)
>>   1. The place of evil in the good created order (38:4–21)
>>>   (a) The order of creation is joyful (38:4–7)
>>>   (b) Evil has a limited place in creation (38:8–11)
>>>   (c) The structure of creation shows that evil will one day be destroyed (38:12–15)
>>>   (d) The place of the dead is known to God (38:16–18)
>>>   (e) Light and darkness are controlled by God (38:19–21)
>>   2. The skies speak of creation order (38:22–38)
>>>   (a) Snow and hail are God's waters for trouble (38:22–24)
>>>   (b) Rain is God's water for life (38:25–27)
>>>   (c) Interlude: think about the different forms of water (38:28–30)
>>>   (d) The heavenly government of the world is under God's control (38:31–33)
>>>   (e) Life-giving water is under God's control (38:34–38)

In the next chapter we will consider the remainder of the speech, in which we will see God's counsel revealed in the animals and birds (38:39—39:30), God's final challenge (40:1, 2), and Job's response (40:3–5). Although the speech is one coherent whole, we are going to tackle it in these two main parts to make it more manageable for us and to ensure that we attend carefully to it all and that the overall effect of the speech does not blur into nothing more than a vague feeling of impressiveness in our hearts. We begin with the structure and order of the inanimate world.

The Answer (Part 1): God's Counsel Is Revealed in the Inanimate Created Order (38:4–38)

The Place of Evil in the Good Created Order (38:4–21)

The first five passages emphasize the place of evil in the created order, using the language of the sea, darkness, and death. In considering the way God runs the world (his "counsel" [v. 2]), Job needs—and we need—to think carefully about good and evil and where and how evil fits into the overall picture.

The Order of Creation Is Joyful (vv. 4–7)

> Where were you when I laid the foundation of the earth?
>> Tell me, if you have understanding.
> Who determined its measurements—surely you know!
>> Or who stretched the line upon it?
> On what were its bases sunk,
>> or who laid its cornerstone,
> when the morning stars sang together
>> and all the sons of God shouted for joy? (vv. 4–7)

First, the universe is pictured as a great building project. This building project has a "foundation" that has been laid (v. 4a). It has "measurements" drawn out by a surveyor's measuring "line" to ensure precision (v. 5). There are "bases" or secure footings, strong sockets for the pillars to rest in, and a "cornerstone" to ensure that the whole thing holds together firmly (v. 6). God is the architect who designed it, the surveyor who laid it all out in accordance with his design, and the builder who constructed it. Here is a building being built to last, a solid, secure, robust affair, replete with beauty and enduring majesty.

All this is Biblical imagery familiar from the Psalms and the Prophets.[14] It speaks of a creation that is properly and purposefully ordered, in which there are material, physical, chemical, and biochemical regularities that scientists call physical or natural laws, and there is moral, social, and relational order, a world with justice at its heart.[15]

In Proverbs 8 the metaphorical figure of "wisdom" speaks of being present at the creation alongside God, being, as it were, the agent of creation (Proverbs 8:22–31). Indeed, Wisdom is pictured as a fine lady who has built a grand house (Proverbs 9:1). Had Job been present at the creation, he would not only be wise, he would embody Wisdom in his person.[16] But of course he was not, and he does not. This is why he speaks "words without knowledge" (38:2).

The punch line is in verse 7. At the creation "the morning stars" sang with joy or, to put the same thing another way, "all the sons of God shouted" a great celebratory shout of "joy." The parallelism suggests that "the morning stars" here are using the stars that greet the morning in a metaphorical way to symbolize the heavenly angelic beings called "sons of God" whom we met in chapters 1, 2. These are not literal stars (such as were created on day four of the drama of Genesis 1), but stars used as metaphors for heavenly beings.[17] But the point is that they "sang . . . for joy." When the cosmos was brought into existence, the supernatural spiritual beings, who watched and saw its underlying order, rejoiced because they saw, as God himself saw, that this cosmos was and is very good.[18]

In *The Magician's Nephew* C. S. Lewis beautifully describes the creation of Narnia in the language of song.

> In the darkness . . . [a] voice had begun to sing. It was very far away and Digory found it hard to decide from what direction it was coming. Sometimes it seemed to come from all directions at once. Sometimes he almost thought it was coming out of the earth beneath them. Its lower notes were deep enough to be the voice of the earth herself. There were no words. There was hardly even a tune. But it was, beyond comparison, the most beautiful noise he had ever heard. It was so beautiful he could hardly bear it. . . .
>
> Then two wonders happened at the same moment. One was that the voice was suddenly joined by other voices; more voices than you could possibly count. They were in harmony with it, but far higher up the scale; cold, tingling, silvery voices. The second wonder was that the blackness overhead, all at once, was blazing with stars . . . you would have felt quite certain that it was the stars themselves which were singing, and that it was the First Voice, the deep one, which had made them appear and made them sing.[19]

This overwhelmingly beautiful song speaks of a superlatively good creation. It is this fundamental goodness in creation that Job has denied, especially in his dark anti-creation lament of chapter 3. To Job's jaundiced eyes, the evil and disorder in creation has wiped out its goodness, so that we are left with something essentially and fundamentally evil. No, says the Creator, when the cosmos was set in place, those who understood what was happening rejoiced, and they were right to rejoice. The question is whether or not Job will align himself with this song of joy and will praise the goodness of creation even in the midst of his loss and sorrow.[20]

It is important to be clear that evil did not intrude on this good creation from somewhere else. There was no outside from which evil could come, for the universe is, and was, the universe. So what God proclaimed to be good and the angels sang about with joy included in germ all that would transpire in its history, including what we call the fall and all its entailments of evil.

Campbell Morgan quotes lines from the poet Browning:

That what began best, can't end worst,
Nor what God blessed once, prove accurst.[21]

"Job," says the Lord in essence, "if you had perfect knowledge of creation, you would understand that it not only was but remains a source of cosmic joy." That is a strange and surprising thing to say to a man suffering as Job does, but it is true. The next section begins to answer the obvious question, but what about evil?

Evil Has a Limited Place in Creation (vv. 8–11)

> Or who shut in the sea with doors
>   when it burst out from the womb,
> when I made clouds its garment
>   and thick darkness its swaddling band,
> and prescribed limits for it
>   and set bars and doors,
> and said, "Thus far shall you come, and no farther,
>   and here shall your proud waves be stayed"? (vv. 8–11)

There is a place for evil in this world, but it is a place with strict limits. In verse 8 the imagery changes abruptly, and God invites Job to think about "the sea," that symbol in the Bible of disorder, chaos, danger, evil, and ultimately death. Job understands this imagery. Earlier he had asked God, "Am I the sea, or a sea monster, that you set a guard over me?" (7:12).

Picture a wild ocean coastline, with huge waves crashing against the cliffs under dark brooding skies, with wild winds and storm clouds. How are we—how is Job—to think of this symbol of all that has made his life a misery? With a strange dark humor, we are invited to think of this sea as being like a baby![22] Picture the breaking of a mother's waters at the end of pregnancy, and then her baby bursting out of the womb on its day of birth and causing havoc from that day on. (Some parents may identify with this imagery!) But here is a baby who is put in clothing and a "swaddling band" to restrain him (v. 9) and then put in some kind of playpen so that he cannot roam free and cause chaos everywhere (v. 10). Here is an unruly infant under discipline, with strict "limits" (v. 10; literally "statutes") constraining his movements and action. "Thus far . . . and no farther," say his firm parents (v. 11). In the same way the waves of the sea have a limit (cf. Psalm 104:9; Proverbs 8:29; Jeremiah 5:22). They meet cliffs and coasts. Even when they burst over these in the violence of a tsunami or a hurricane, they stop somewhere. Even though this is a continuing battle involving "the gnawing away of shores, cliffs, sands and headlands," even so "the ultimate restraining of the ocean is finely suggested."[23]

I remember one wild February day walking along the beautiful Welsh coastline with my wife. Our rocky path took us close to the sea, and we saw spray rising forty or fifty feet into the air. It was wonderful to watch. It would have been terrifying to be in such a strong and turbulent sea, but it was marvelous to watch how the cliffs forced the waves to halt. The spray was like a vain protest from the waves; the mere fact that the waves became "breakers" was a reminder that God said to them, "Thus far . . . and no farther," their power broken by the limits set them by God (v. 11).

Evil, if we dare say this with reverence and care, is God's baby. Not in the sense that God is the origin of evil, as if evil shows forth God's character, for that cannot be, but in the sense that evil is no more of a threat to God than a badly behaved infant is to his parents. When the power of evil is pitted against the power of God, we know who is stronger.

There are two important things to learn from this. First, and most obvious, evil has a limit. Always there is a point at which God says, "Thus far . . . and no farther," even to the sufferings of Job (v. 11). This has huge pastoral importance: a robust doctrine of the sovereignty of God is more comforting than the sickly alternatives suggested by process theism and its cousins. "[T]here are no belligerent cosmic forces beyond Yahweh's authority."[24]

But the other truth to learn—and this is so obvious that it is easy to miss— is that there is a place for evil in the created order.[25] The sea is both restrained and yet also protected by God,[26] as the language of an infant's clothing and swaddling bands suggests. In this foundational language the sea is "shut in," but it is not dried up (v. 8). Echoing Genesis 1, the deep has limits placed upon it, but it is not destroyed. In some strange and wonderful way, even disorder has a place in God's order.

If this is so, that raises a further question: will it always be so? If evil has a place—albeit a restricted one—in the created order, is this an enduring state of affairs? Must we reconcile ourselves to the presence of evil forever? It is this question that the third passage addresses.

The Structure of Creation Shows That Evil Will One Day Be Destroyed (vv. 12–15)
> Have you commanded the morning since your days began,[27]
>> and caused the dawn to know its place,
> that it might take hold of the skirts of the earth,
>> and the wicked be shaken out of it?
> It is changed like clay under the seal,
>> and its features stand out like a garment.
> From the wicked their light is withheld,
>> and their uplifted arm is broken. (vv. 12–15)

Again the imagery changes. Now, in place of the architect, surveyor, and builder, and in place of the disciplinary parent, God is portrayed as a commander or general. In verse 12 "dawn" or "the morning" is personified as a creature awaiting orders. The two halves of verse 12 are saying essentially the same thing: "Have you ever given orders to dawn/morning and told it to get up and get the world up?" In delightful imagery it is as if God shakes sleepy dawn in its bed, gets it up, and tells it that it is time to get the world up again, for the sun to rise and the light to return to a dark world.

In verse 13 "dawn" gets to work, and the picture changes again. Just as one might take a tablecloth by its edges and shake the crumbs off it, so dawn will take hold of the "skirts" or edges of the earth and shake "the wicked" out of it. Why "the wicked"? Because the wicked love darkness rather than light, because their deeds are evil (John 3:19), because the murderer and the adulterer prefer to do their evil deeds under cover of darkness (Job 24:13–17), because evil is by nature secretive.

So in verse 14 the Lord pictures that beautiful scene when you watch a dark landscape appear as first light dawns. From a gray two-dimensional nothingness, it takes shape, rather as flat clay becomes three-dimensional when impressed with a seal, and its features become visible, and it has color and texture like a piece of clothing. What is the point and purpose of all this? The paradoxical "light" (v. 15) of the wicked (which is darkness, for darkness is their preferred environment, and "deep darkness is morning to all of them; for they are friends with the terrors of deep darkness," 24:17) is "withheld," and the "arm" they lift up to threaten and harm "is broken." All of which is a vivid poetic way of saying that every time the sun rises, it is evidence that there is a judgment to come. Every time the light is switched on in creation, it reassures us that darkness will not last forever. Each new day is cosmic proof that evil has no enduring place in the created order. Sure, it must be part of this creation for now; it has a place in God's purposes, albeit a strictly limited one. But it will not be with us forever. There will come a day when the sea (in this symbolic sense) will be no more (Revelation 21:1). The wheat and the weeds may need to grow together for the present; but the day of judgment will come, when the weeds will be burned and the wheat gathered into God's barns (Matthew 13:24–30).

So God has set before Job a deep and penetrating portrait of the fundamental structure of the universe, a cosmos that is deeply and ultimately good, a cosmos in which there is a necessary place for evil and yet in whose structure the final destruction of evil is foreshadowed. This universe is deeper by far than the two-dimensional idea of the universe on which Job has been brought up and that still obsesses the comforters. Here is a universe in which the ugliness of evil is part of the creation of God and will ultimately serve the glory of God.

The natural question that now arises is, how can we be sure that evil is a part of God's creation and under the control of God? How can we be sure that lurking in the dark corners of the universe there is no independent and autonomous power of evil that might threaten the good purposes of God? It is this question that the next two passages address.

The Place of the Dead Is Known to God (vv. 16–18)
> Have you entered into the springs of the sea,
>   or walked in the recesses of the deep?
> Have the gates of death been revealed to you,
>   or have you seen the gates of deep darkness?
> Have you comprehended the expanse of the earth?
>   Declare, if you know all this. (vv. 16–18)

Extremes fascinate human beings. In our day we have extreme sports; in the past we had exploration of desperate, dangerous wildernesses. Still we watch in wonder as probes land on Mars or as we watch recordings of men walking on the moon. We read with fascination the accounts of the early adventurers to the North and South Poles. They were doing something we all long to do—although most of us prefer to do it from our armchairs—which is to press out to the extremities of the universe. Why do we have this instinct? Perhaps it is because we understand that only those who have explored the extremities of the world can be sure they understand the world and can therefore hope to control the world. The next passage takes Job to an extremity where no man had yet gone and returned—the place of the dead.

This place lies deep beneath normal existence. "The springs of the sea" or "the recesses of the deep" (v. 16) are the places deep down below the wild disordered sea, at the boundary between the deep dark sea and the place of the dead, Sheol, which lies below, in the poetic way in which the ancient writers described the universe. It is the place of Genesis 1:2: "darkness was over the face of the deep." "Have you been down there?" the Lord essentially asks Job. "If you have, you will have seen 'the gates of death . . . the gates of deep darkness' [v. 17]; you will have visited the entrances to Sheol itself."

In verse 18 "the expanse of the earth" is usually understood, from its context, to refer not primarily to the surface of the earth but to what lies beneath, to the vast expanse of the underworld,[28] and this is probably correct. Following on from verses 16, 17 the Lord asks Job if he has seen the underworld. It is all one big question: have you been to the extremity of existence that is death itself? Job may feel that he has, that in his sufferings he has been knocking on the doors of Sheol. And yet for all the darkness of his sufferings, he does not have the comprehensive and universal understanding of death that he needs in order to understand the universe. But by implication the Lord knows all about these nether regions, and their darkness is no threat to the goodness of his creation or the ultimate triumph of his purposes, for "darkness is as light" with him (Psalm 139:12).

The place of the dead is the deepest, the darkest, and the worst extremity in creation. It lies outside Job's area of knowledge and therefore beyond his region of control. But by implication it does not lie outside the Lord's area of perfect knowledge and entire control. If that is true for the place of the dead, then we may be sure that there is no shadowy nook or dark cranny of the universe—visible or invisible—that lies outside God's knowledge or control.

Unlike Job, we now know that one man has now been to, and right through, the gates of death. He has gone deep into the place of the dead, and he has returned victorious. That terrible place that has been known to God since it began is a place whose sting has been removed and whose terrors need terrify the Christian no more.

Light and Darkness Are Controlled by God (vv. 19–21)
> Where is the way to the dwelling of light,
>   and where is the place of darkness,
> that you may take it to its territory
>   and that you may discern the paths to its home?
> You know, for you were born then,
>   and the number of your days is great! (vv. 19–21)

In the next passage Job is taken to another extremity (or pair of extremities); these are over the horizon, or two horizons to be precise. In the poetic cosmology, somewhere over the eastern horizon there is a "dwelling" where "light" lives, from which it comes up in the morning to light the earth (v. 19). And over the western horizon there is a "place" where darkness lives (v. 19). Light and darkness are more than physical descriptors; they speak of goodness and evil, of order and disorder, of joy and gloom. The Lord asks Job if he has been where "light" dwells and where "darkness" lives (v. 19), so that he might conduct each to its home (v. 20), thereby showing that he is sovereign over light and darkness. If Job could answer yes, then he must be eternal, one who existed at the creation of the world (v. 21). But of course he cannot. Darkness is a great mystery to him; he cannot understand why this world has within its existence both light and darkness.

The Skies Speak of Creation Order (38:22–38)

The next five passages all call on Job—and us—to look upward to the skies and to reflect on what the skies teach us about the wonderful counsel of God in his government of the world. Four of the five are about water. Water is one of the most familiar parts of existence, and yet it is a puzzle.

Snow and Hail Are God's Waters for Trouble (vv. 22–24)

> Have you entered the storehouses of the snow,
>   or have you seen the storehouses of the hail,
> which I have reserved for the time of trouble,
>   for the day of battle and war?
> What is the way to the place where the light is distributed,
>   or where the east wind is scattered upon the earth? (vv. 22–24)

In the poetic cosmology, above the firmament or canopy of the sky there are "storehouses" containing the different precipitations that humans experience (v. 22). These storehouses have windows (the windows of Heaven) that may be, and sometimes are, opened by God to release their contents on the earth below.

The Lord highlights two of them here—water in the forms of "snow" and "hail" (v. 22). Why these two? Because each is associated with war and destruction, "the time of trouble . . . the day of battle and war" (v. 23). In the days of Joshua "the LORD threw down large stones from heaven" to terrify the Amorites (Joshua 10:11). Hail was one of the plagues of Egypt (Exodus 9:18–26) and is part of prophetic language about the wrath of God (e.g., Isaiah 30:30). Snow too is a weapon of war with God, as in Psalm 68:14, and as both Napoleon and Hitler discovered in the snowy depths of Russia when both of their armies suffered heavier losses because of the bitter cold than because of enemy action.

In this context "the light" of verse 24 seems to be the lightnings that come down from Heaven, and "the east wind" means a stormy wind that comes at the same time (v. 24). Together we are given a picture of destruction unleashed on the world from above. Job is asked if he has been to the places from which these things come; if he has, then he will understand why, how, and when they are unleashed, and he will be able to control them. But of course he has not and he cannot.

Rain Is God's Water for Life (vv. 25–27)

> Who has cleft a channel for the torrents of rain
>   and a way for the thunderbolt,

> to bring rain on a land where no man is,
>> on the desert in which there is no man,
> to satisfy the waste and desolate land,
>> and to make the ground sprout with grass? (vv. 25–27)

God now turns to another form of water. Water can fall as snow and hail to bring death and destruction, but it can also fall as life-giving "rain" (v. 25). In the poetry here the "channel" for the rain is the path the rain takes from the heavenly storehouses down to the ground (v. 25). This channel is "cleft," indicating deliberate action by God; it does not just happen by chance (v. 25).[29]

It is associated here with a "thunderbolt" (v. 25). We are to picture a massive rainstorm. But whereas the snow and hail brought trouble in battle and war, this water brings rain on "a land where no man is, on the desert in which there is no man," an uninhabited and uncultivated land, an utterly barren land, a land that would have no water if God did not send this rain (v. 26). Water in this form satisfies or saturates the wastelands and causes vegetation to sprout where there was nothing. This is life-giving water. What a contrast! The same element, sent by the same Creator, with such different consequences![30] (Of course it is also true that snow meltwaters bring spring life, and hail when melted brings growth. But the point of the contrast is that the same element in different forms and different contexts can have diametrically different results.)

Interlude: Think about the Different Forms of Water (vv. 28–30)
> Has the rain a father,
>> or who has begotten the drops of dew?
> From whose womb did the ice come forth,
>> and who has given birth to the frost of heaven?
> The waters become hard like stone,
>> and the face of the deep is frozen. (vv. 28–30)

God wants Job to pause and think deeply about what he can learn from water. So he inserts this beautiful interlude, "a poetic vignette of sheer lyrical delight."[31] In these three verses we think about "rain" (v. 28a), "dew" (v. 28b), "ice" (v. 29a), "frost" (v. 29b), and "frozen . . . waters" over "the deep" (v. 30). We think about their differences—rain and dew to make crops grow, ice and frost to threaten life, icy waters to cover the threatening "deep," perhaps even to hide the "chaotic terror lurking below."[32]

But as well as thinking about water in its different forms, we meditate on its Creator, in terms of its "father" (v. 28a), the one who has "begotten" it (v. 28b), from whose "womb" it came (v. 29a) and who "has given birth" to it (v. 29b). The imagery of origins is beautiful and intimate. It suggests an intimate relation between the Creator and water in all its forms, water that brings life and water that brings death. All these different experiences of water speak of a God who is intimately involved in his world, bringing both life and death. We are not at liberty to credit him with the times when we experience life-giving rain without also acknowledging that he is the one from whom death-dealing ice and frost come to us. He is the sovereign originator of them all.

The Heavenly Government of the World Is under God's Control (vv. 31–33)

> Can you bind the chains of the Pleiades
>   or loose the cords of Orion?
> Can you lead forth the Mazzaroth in their season,
>   or can you guide the Bear with its children?
> Do you know the ordinances of the heavens?
>   Can you establish their rule on the earth? (vv. 31–33)

In the fourth passage we are still looking up to the skies but are no longer thinking about water. Four names are given for heavenly bodies. "The Pleiades" and "Orion" (v. 31) are well-known and clearly identifiable constellations. But what does it mean to "bind" and "loose" their "chains" or "cords" (v. 31)? We cannot be sure. The poetic idea may be that these constellations are tied up before they rise and after they set and are set free to cross the sky in between, or that they are chained to their course across the sky while visible, but unchained when invisible (i.e., not on duty over the earth). We will see that the parallel with verse 32 may suggest the latter.

In verse 32 two other heavenly bodies (or groups of bodies) are spoken of. "The Mazzaroth" (a transliteration of the Hebrew) may be a reference to the planets,[33] to the constellations in general, or to some unknown constellation. "The Bear" is probably a constellation, although we do not know who "its children" are. In chapter 9 Job refers to God as the one "who made the Bear and Orion, the Pleiades and the chambers of the south" (9:9). Verse 32 speaks of leading them forth "in their season" or guiding them. This suggests that the "chains" and "cords" of verse 31 refer to these heavenly bodies being under constraint as they do metaphorical duty governing events on earth.

It was, of course, common in the ancient religions, as with modern horoscope users, to suppose that the stars influence and govern events on earth. While the Bible does not accept this, it unashamedly takes such well-known language and uses it to affirm the government of God through intermediate spiritual agencies. The stars are symbolic of the angelic spiritual beings by whose agency God governs the universe. We met them in the heavenly scenes in chapters 1, 2 ("the sons of God") and again—in parallel with the language of stars—in 38:7. So to speak of binding, leading, or guiding the heavenly bodies is to speak poetically of governing the world. This is why verse 33 concludes by asking whether Job has such controlling knowledge of "the ordinances of the heavens" (the decisions and edicts by which the heavenly bodies govern events on earth). Just as water from the skies has different effects but comes from one originator and controller, so the spiritual beings in the heavenly places do different things but under the supreme control of one binder, looser, leader, and guide. The words "their rule" (v. 33b) are strictly singular and may be translated either "its rule" (the rule of the heavenly bodies together) or—perhaps more likely—"his rule" (the rule of God).

We know from chapters 1, 2 what decrees were given when the sons of God met in Heaven; Job does not. But he may be confident that every decree has God as its sovereign originator and Lord.

Life-Giving Water Is under God's Control (vv. 34–38)

> Can you lift up your voice to the clouds,
>   that a flood of waters may cover you?
> Can you send forth lightnings, that they may go
>   and say to you, "Here we are"?
> Who has put wisdom in the inward parts
>   or given understanding to the mind?
> Who can number the clouds by wisdom?
>   Or who can tilt the waterskins of the heavens,
> when the dust runs into a mass
>   and the clods stick fast together? (vv. 34–38)

Finally, in verses 34–38 we come back to water. There is an old translation conundrum in verse 36. Since the very earliest translations of Job, no one has been sure of the meaning of the words translated here as "inward parts" and "the mind."[34] The context of verses 34, 35 and verses 37, 38 suggests that verse 36 has something to do with an understanding or control of rainfall, but what exactly we cannot be sure.

The main meaning of the passage is quite clear. In verse 34 Job is asked if he has the authority to call up to "clouds" so that they send a much-needed "flood" of life-giving rainwater. In verse 35 he is asked much the same thing, but in terms of having the authority to command bolts of lightning. This is a delightful picture—bolts of lightning reporting for duty before Job, standing at attention, and saying to him (as Isaiah says to the Lord in Isaiah 6), "Here we are; where will you send us today?" Verse 37 continues the same idea: is Job able to "number" (that is, not just count, but number in order to control) "the clouds" and, because this is about control, "tilt the waterskins of the heavens," a lovely image of the rain clouds being like full waterskins waiting for some supernatural being to tilt them so that the rain falls. Verse 38 either describes "the clods" of mud that result when the rain falls or the hard dry clods of earth that show the desperate need for rainfall. The parallel with the covenant curses of Deuteronomy 28, in which a hardened earth is a sign of drought (Deuteronomy 28:23), suggests the latter.

The main point is that no human being has the authority to command life-giving waters of blessing; no human being can command rain and prevent hail and snow; no human being can avoid suffering and ensure constant blessing. This is not within Job's power, and it is not within our power.

A Pause for Thought

How is Job—and how are we—to respond thus far? One striking observation is that although Job has to answer no to all the questions, it is to Job that the questions are asked. There is here an implicit dignity possessed by Job and by extension to redeemed humankind. Just as Adam was entrusted with the honor of governing the world on God's behalf, so even fallen human beings are given the dignity of being the ones to whom God asks these questions. He does not ask these questions of any other creature.[35]

A second thought concerns God's technique of using rhetorical questions rather than just making straight statements. After all, God could have rephrased the whole speech in terms like "Job, you don't know this, but I do." What does a rhetorical question do to Job and by extension to us? The answer is that it does what rhetorical questions always do: they draw in the listeners to the reasonings behind those questions, so that they begin to interiorize them, to make these truths their own as they think and then answer for themselves.

But the main response so far is to begin to think more deeply about how the doctrine of the sovereignty of God extends to his sovereignty over evil. We must banish from our thoughts any residual dualism in which evil is conceived as an independent or autonomous power. We are forced to consider the strange but wonderful possibility that evil is created to serve the purposes and glory of God and that in some mysterious way even darkness is necessary to show forth the light of God's goodness. There is a goodness in this mixed good and evil creation that lies below the surface and that will become fully evident only at the end, when the pure kindness and utter goodness of God will be vindicated for all to see. To grasp this goodness in the midst of suffering and evil needs a deeper faith in the absolute supremacy and universal sovereignty of God than Job can yet exercise. But by the grace of God he is on the way.

33

The Lord's First Speech, Part 2: Nature, Red in Tooth and Claw?

JOB 38:39—40:5

IN ONE OF HIS SONNETS the poet Robert Frost describes the hideous sight of a bloated spider and a dead moth, perched on what had been a beautiful flower. He meditates on that strange collocation of beauty and ugliness and asks what caused it all. "What" could have caused this, he concludes, "but design of darkness to appall?—If design govern in a thing so small."[1] By what design or plan is the world governed, if indeed it is governed? That is a good question. Is the "counsel" of God (38:2) a good counsel? Do we live in a well-run world? Or is the design of the world a "design of darkness to appall"?[2] This vital question lies behind the whole of God's first speech. So far as Job can perceive it, the purpose of the Almighty is a terrible, even an appalling purpose. In this first speech God begins his gracious work of bringing Job to repentance about the words he has spoken, which have shrouded the good purposes of God in darkness and made it impossible for he himself, or for others, to see in creation the goodness of God.

The Structure of God's First Speech
In the last chapter we studied the first half of the speech, with its focus on the inanimate created order. We move now to the second half. So let us now put together the first and second parts of the speech and overview the structure of the whole.

Introductory Challenge (38:1–3)
    A. God's counsel is revealed in the inanimate created order (38:4–38)
        1. The place of evil in the good created order (38:4–21)
            (a) The order of creation is joyful (38:4–7)
            (b) Evil has a limited place in creation (38:8–11)
            (c) The structure of creation shows that evil will one day be destroyed (38:12–15)
            (d) The place of the dead is known to God (38:16–18)
            (e) Light and darkness are controlled by God (38:19–21)
        2. The skies speak of creation order (38:22–38)
            (a) Snow and hail are God's waters for trouble (38:22–24)
            (b) Rain is God's water for life (38:25–27)
            (c) Interlude: think about the different forms of water (38:28–30)
            (d) The heavenly government of the world is under God's control (38:31–33)
            (e) Life-giving water is under God's control (38:34–38)
    B. God's counsel is revealed in the animals and birds (38:39—39:30)
        1. Predator and prey in the wild (38:39–41)
        2. God's time for life in the wild (39:1–4)
        3. Freedom and provision in the wild (39:5–8)
        4. Power and danger from the wild (39:9–12)
        5. Foolish wonder in the wild (39:13–18)
        6. Terror from the wild (39:19–25)
        7. Predator and prey in the wild (39:26–30)
Concluding challenge (40:1, 2)
Job's response (40:3–5)

Death, Life, and the Wild World

Before we immerse ourselves in this wonderful poetry and lose ourselves among this myriad of creatures, it is worth pausing to note two motifs. First, and perhaps most obvious, what God describes here is deeply wild. These creatures were not expected to be found on Job's farm. They represent animals and birds that are not tame, not domesticated, not under human control; they are "outside man's care and control."[3] Here is a tour of the part of the created order that lies outside the limits of the world that is domesticated and ordered by human beings. They will help answer the question, how do you and I respond when the wild world breaks into the farm, when the disorder and chaos of a dark world invades our ordered world and makes mincemeat of our plans and hopes? Come outside the farm, says the Lord to Job, and have a thoughtful tour of the wild world outside.

    The second motif is that of life and death. All the descriptions here live between the polarities of birth, sustenance, and life on the one hand and death and decay on the other. There is a particular emphasis on the vulnerable and defenseless young—whether it be the young lions (38:39), the young ravens (38:41), the young goats (39:4), the ostrich eggs and young (39:14–16), or the young eagles (39:30). And as we shall see, the two poles are inextricably tied in to one another; it is not possible to conceive of life as we know it with one of these but not the other.

God's Counsel Is Revealed in the Animals and Birds (38:39—39:30)

Predator and Prey in the Wild (38:39–41)

> Can you hunt the prey for the lion,
>   or satisfy the appetite of the young lions,
> when they crouch in their dens
>   or lie in wait in their thicket?
> Who provides for the raven its prey,
>   when its young ones cry to God for help,
>   and wander about for lack of food? (vv. 39–41)

The cameos of animals and birds begin and end with predators and "prey" (here and in 39:26–30).

Picture a cinematic sequence in a nature program. First, there is a shot of lion cubs. They look sweet, soft, beautiful, even cuddly. I remember cuddling a white lion cub in a game park outside Johannesburg; it was a magical experience, stroking these sweet and beautiful creatures (although we would not have dared do this when they were a couple of months older). But in this nature program, the (sweet?) lion cubs are hungry; if they are not fed soon, they will die. Next there is a shot of young ravens calling out for food; they too will die if they are not fed. Our hearts go out to these defenseless little creatures. Perhaps then there are some shots of a family of beautiful animals, perhaps oryx or springbok. Young and parents are grazing happily together; we admire their beauty and grace.

But then we see the lioness lying in wait, stalking her prey. At the critical moment the lioness chases with unbeatable speed, separates one of the animals from the family, and tears it apart with ruthless power. There is blood and flesh everywhere. The final shots show the lion cubs satisfied with plenty of meat, and then afterward vultures and ravens feed on the abundant leftovers (ravens, like vultures, do not kill their prey but feed on prey killed by others).

How do we feel about a sequence like that? It is hard to feel either unqualified pleasure or unalloyed distaste. There is here a tension that cannot be reconciled in a world of food chains, of predators and prey. If the beauty of the oryx is to be unspoiled, the beauty of the lions and the helplessness of the raven chicks will end in starvation and death. The survival of the one must be at the cost of the other. In our world if the lion were to lie down with the lamb, there would be a lot of starving lion cubs. We live in a world in which predation and starvation are the only alternatives.

We may be shocked, but God says (by implication) to Job that he himself is the one who "hunts the prey for the lion," who "satisfies the appetite" of the lion cubs (v. 39), and who "provides for the [young] ravens" the "prey" they need to live (v. 41). Psalm 147 says the same: "He gives to the beasts their food, and to the young ravens that cry" (Psalm 147:9). Indeed, when the oryx (or whatever) is torn limb from limb, this is an answer to prayer, for the young ravens "cry to God for help" (Job 38:41). Psalm 104 echoes this: "The young lions roar for their prey, seeking their food from God" (Psalm 104:21).

Is it possible that in the counsel of God this age is so ordered that suffering for some is necessary for the survival of others? Is this process of predation also a pointer to a deeper truth, perhaps even the truth of redemptive suffering, that the day will come when the suffering of one innocent man will be God's means to bring life to a whole redeemed humanity?

God's Time for Life in the Wild (39:1–4)

> Do you know when the mountain goats give birth?
>   Do you observe the calving of the does?
> Can you number the months that they fulfill,
>   and do you know the time when they give birth,
> when they crouch, bring forth their offspring,
>   and are delivered of their young?
> Their young ones become strong; they grow up in the open;
>   they go out and do not return to them. (vv. 1–4)

The second cameo directs Job to the questions of times and of existence. God invites him to think about a particular "time," a significant time, a time when life begins. He is asked "when" (v. 1a) the shy, elusive mother ibex gives birth, to "number the months" (v. 2a) of her pregnancy, to "know the time" (v. 2b) when she gives birth, "when" (v. 3) she crouches in labor and is delivered of her calves. Here is a time that is beyond Job's knowledge, a time that is months of waiting, then a crisis of pain, and finally the fulfillment of joy and new life. What is more, this new life will grow to strength, independence "in the open," and will soon leave the mother's care to be cared for in the wild by God's generous hand alone (v. 4).

The God who brings "the time of trouble" (38:23) also brings the time of birth and life. As "the Preacher" or "Qoheleth" (Ecclesiastes 1:1, ESV margin) will say, "For everything there is a season, and a time for every matter under heaven: a time to be born, and a time to die . . ." (Ecclesiastes 3:1–8). One of the concerns Job has voiced has been God's mishandling of times. Human beings are given "days like the days of a hired hand . . . months of emptiness, and nights of misery" (7:1–3). Indeed "every morning . . . every moment" God watches and visits misery on Job (7:18). The "set time" for vindication that Job longs for never seems to come (14:13). If only God were the righteous Lord of time!

In reply God says he is. He is the one who knows, not only with cerebral head knowledge but with personal caring oversight, "when the mountain goats give birth" (v. 1); he observes the calving, not watching with the dispassionate eye of a mere observer or student, but watching and caring in love as she calves. He has "numbered the months" of pregnancy, not merely counting, but loving and watching (v. 2).[4] These "shy elusive creatures of the mountains"[5] are the objects of his tender care; their times are in his hands.

The problem with time is the waiting. As every human mother who has been granted a safe birth knows, there is a waiting for conception, there is waiting and hoping during gestation, there are all manner of pains of pregnancy and labor, but in the end there is life and joy. If this is true for mountain goats, how much more is it true for human beings in pain struggling to remain believers. "Yahweh's veiled answer" to Job "is that the rhythm of times which governs the perilous birth cycles of shy creatures also operates for human beings. If Job does not know the function of regular times in the natural cycle of things, he can scarcely appreciate the implications of proposing a time out of time when a mortal would return from the dead for personal vindication."[6] And yet the time would come when days, months, and years of hatred and evil, indeed the apparent ultimate victory of that evil, will be reversed in one glorious morning of new life. Job needs to learn—and we need to learn—to entrust ourselves to the righteous Lord of time.

Freedom and Provision in the Wild (39:5–8)

> Who has let the wild donkey go free?
>> Who has loosed the bonds of the swift donkey,
> to whom I have given the arid plain for his home
>> and the salt land for his dwelling place?
> He scorns the tumult of the city;
>> he hears not the shouts of the driver.
> He ranges the mountains as his pasture,
>> and he searches after every green thing. (vv. 5–8)

The third cameo shifts the focus onto wild freedom. Here is a "wild don-key" who has been set "free," whose "bonds" have been "loosed" and who can run "free" and "swift" (v. 5), who chooses, paradoxically, to live in "the arid plain . . . the salt land" (v. 6), perhaps that dead region south of the Dead Sea running south to the Gulf of Aqaba. Job is to picture him mocking at his poor domesticated relations as they are whipped and driven by cruel drivers in the hubbub of the city (v. 7); by contrast, he roams free and "ranges the mountains" looking for food—"every green thing" (v. 8).

He has this strange, wild, fast, arid freedom. And yet—and this is the point—this freedom is the precise gift of God. It is God who has "let the wild donkey go free" and "loosed" his "bonds" (v. 5); it is God who has "given" him the dry salty land as his "dwelling place" (v. 6). He is "free" and "wild" (v. 5); he lives in a deeply inhospitable place, a place of death rather than life. And yet his choice, his freedom, and his survival do not in any way compromise the absolute providential control of God over all of life; rather they express the wild wonder of God's providence right to the margins of life. There is not one inch of strange wildness that lies outside the counsel of God.

Power and Danger from the Wild (39:9–12)

Is the wild ox willing to serve you?
  Will he spend the night at your manger?
Can you bind him in the furrow with ropes,
  or will he harrow the valleys after you?
Will you depend on him because his strength is great,
  and will you leave to him your labor?
Do you have faith in him that he will return your grain
  and gather it to your threshing floor? (vv. 9–12)

This fourth cameo speaks of dangerous power. The "wild ox" (v. 9) was a two-horned creature, some bulls more than six feet across at the shoulders,[7] and a legendary terror. In Psalm 22 David puts being rescued "from the horns of the wild oxen" alongside being saved "from the mouth of the lion" (Psalm 22:21). When Balaam needs to speak forcefully about how God fights with overwhelming power for Israel, he says that God "is for them like the horns of the wild ox" (Numbers 23:22; 24:8).

There is therefore a wild irony in this description. "Why not try this?" God asks the farmer Job. "Go out into the wild and find a wild ox. Walk up to it, pat its head, let it eat some food out of your hand, talk to it, be an 'ox-whisperer,' lead it quietly back to the farm to feed overnight at your feeding trough. Then watch as it bows its meek head to let you put a harness on it and willingly plods with its docile strength 'after you' (that is, he is subservient to you) through the fields. In fact it is so docile you can entrust it to pull safely after the youngest farmhand. And you know you can trust it to do the job." The whole scenario is absurd! Job knows perfectly well that even to try it would be suicidal. The most stupid farmer in the world knows better than to seek to domesticate this fierce creature. "This challenge to domesticate and humanize the wild ox anticipates Yahweh's challenge for Job to control Behemoth and Leviathan."[8]

God is saying to Job, "You know there is some wild stuff out there, beyond your control, outside the farm, and some of it is deeply dangerous." The cameo does not spell out the implication of this, but it is not difficult to begin. It would be wonderful to be able to harness the strength of the wild ox in the service of agriculture; here is a power to be envied and desired. But—and this is the point—it will take a wisdom and counsel wider and deeper than Job's to achieve this. And by implication such counsel lies with God alone. Job is to bow before the wisdom that can take the wild dangerous power of the wild ox and subdue it to his own purposes. Here is the wisdom that in centuries to come will use a death to defeat the one who has the power of death (Hebrews 2:14).

Foolish Wonder in the Wild (39:13–18)

> The wings of the ostrich wave proudly,
>   but are they the pinions and plumage of love?[9]
> For she leaves her eggs to the earth
>   and lets them be warmed on the ground,
> forgetting that a foot may crush them
>   and that the wild beast may trample them.
> She deals cruelly with her young, as if they were not hers;
>   though her labor be in vain, yet she has no fear,
> because God has made her forget wisdom
>   and given her no share in understanding.
> When she rouses herself to flee,
>   she laughs at the horse and his rider. (vv. 13–18)

In some ways the fifth little portrait is the odd one out. There are no rhetorical questions (the translation of verse 13b is very uncertain), God refers to himself in the third person (v. 17a), and the ostrich is the only creature portrayed in a mainly negative light. Perhaps for these reasons the LXX omits it, and many scholars consider it to be an interpolation. But there is no Hebrew manuscript evidence for its omission, and if it is not original, it is hard to see how and why such a strange passage would have been interpolated later.

Besides, the proverbial strangeness of the ostrich is not so out of place in a catalog of wild and strange creatures; rather it takes their strangeness to a new level, and no doubt with some humor as well!

Here is a creature with "wings," but it cannot fly (v. 13a), a creature with the reputation of leaving her new-laid eggs vulnerable and defenseless on the warm ground (v. 14),[10] not caring about the danger of their being trampled upon (v. 15)—perhaps by a "wild beast" (v. 15) like the lion, the mountain goat, the wild donkey, or the wild ox in the previous cameos. Although she has gone through pregnancy, labor, and the laying of the "eggs" (v. 14), she doesn't seem to care if "her labor be in vain" (v. 16). Indeed, she is a very stupid creature (v. 17)! And the reason she is so stupid is that God, in his sovereign counsel, "has made her forget wisdom" (that is, he has not endowed her with wisdom) and has chosen not to give her the expected share of common sense! Here is a creature whom God has created stupid! And yet—and here is the surprising punch line—although she flaps her wings without being able to fly, she can run so fast that even a horse spurred on by a rider cannot catch her (v. 18)! In this respect she is more powerful than the nuclear weapons of her age (see the next cameo); to "laugh" at the horse and rider is to claim superiority (v. 18).[11] God has made a creature with an amazing burst of speed and a comical lack of common sense.

I am not sure there is meant to be a precise point for Job to learn except that there is in the universe much unintelligible strangeness and paradox. If there is a strange paradox with the ostrich, how much more ought Job to admit that there may be stranger and more paradoxical matters in the government of the world. And who knows, God may make it clear in the end. One day a man will walk this earth with extraordinary and surprising abilities to heal, to walk on water, to raise the dead—abilities no one would have guessed when they looked at his very ordinary appearance (Isaiah 53:2b)—and yet who will end his life being treated as if he were an utter fool. And yet in this mysterious paradox will lie the key to the universe.

Terror from the Wild (39:19–25)

> Do you give the horse his might?
>> Do you clothe his neck with a mane?
> Do you make him leap like the locust?
>> His majestic snorting is terrifying.
> He paws in the valley and exults in his strength;
>> he goes out to meet the weapons.
> He laughs at fear and is not dismayed;
>> he does not turn back from the sword.

Upon him rattle the quiver,
the flashing spear, and the javelin.
With fierceness and rage he swallows the ground;
he cannot stand still at the sound of the trumpet.
When the trumpet sounds, he says "Aha!"
He smells the battle from afar,
the thunder of the captains, and the shouting. (vv. 19–25)

It is important for us to feel the grim, dark terror of this portrait of the warhorse. It is "an eerie and haunting picture."[12] We begin with "his might" (v. 19a); he is a massively powerful creature. For many centuries a warhorse, whether carrying a warrior rider or pulling a chariot, was the epitome of ultimate power; it was the nuclear weapon of most past centuries. We must expel from our minds all pictures of domesticity or tameness. His neck is clothed "with a mane" (v. 19b). The word "mane" is normally derived from the root "to thunder"; his mane speaks of almost divine power. He can "leap" and jump with astonishing power; picture a "locust" scaled up many times (v. 20a)! When he snorts in anger, there is a dark majesty that "is terrifying" (v. 20), giving to those watching a foretaste of the terror that comes from being in the presence of death and the God who can send body and soul into Hell. The word "majestic" is associated with God (v. 20). "O Lord my God, you are very great! You are clothed with splendor and majesty" (Psalm 104:1). The word "terrifying" is associated with God in his anger, not least by Job himself (Job 39:20; e.g., 9:34, "let not dread of him terrify me"; 13:21, "let not dread of you terrify me"). Here is a dark, dangerous, Godlike creature. Those familiar with J.R.R. Tolkien's The Lord of the Rings might think of the Dark Riders.

Then in verse 21 we see him on the verge of battle, ready to charge, pawing the ground eagerly with his front feet, hyper-confident in his strength, itching to be let loose against the weapons of the enemy. He has no fear and experiences no terror or dismay (v. 22a); you will not see him fleeing from "the sword" of the enemy (v. 22b). Picture him as he charges, with "the quiver" rattling against his flanks, "the flashing spear" and "javelin" against his side (v. 23). Feel the power of his "fierceness and rage" as he metaphorically eats up the ground in his charge (v. 24a). When "the trumpet sounds" for war, you cannot hold him back (v. 24b), for he cries "Aha!" with joy that now, at last, he can do what he was created for, which is to bring death and destruction (v. 25).

Here is a quasi-divine, supernatural, eerie, terrifying creature whose business is killing, who loves nothing more than the blood and shrieks of battle. And yet—and we ought to be getting used to this by now—there is one who has given him his might (v. 19a), clothed him with his warlike "mane" (v. 19b), and has given him the nature and strength to "leap like the locust" (v. 20).

Here, as with the wild ox, is a creature who is a threat to Job, who symbolizes the dangers and the destruction experienced by Job. Perhaps the Sabeans and the Chaldeans had ridden upon just such warhorses when they devastated Job's life (1:15, 17). And yet this warhorse has a Master; there is one to whom it owes its strength, its nature, and its victories. And therefore there is one to whom it must one day give an account and who is sovereign over all its warlike acts. Job cannot hope to overcome this ultimate weapon of war; he must bow and entrust himself to the only one who can.

Predator and Prey in the Wild (39:26–30)

> Is it by your understanding that the hawk soars
>   and spreads his wings toward the south?
> Is it at your command that the eagle mounts up
>   and makes his nest on high?
> On the rock he dwells and makes his home,
>   on the rocky crag and stronghold.
> From there he spies out the prey;
>   his eyes behold it from far away.
> His young ones suck up blood,
>   and where the slain are, there is he. (vv. 26–30)

In our final cameo we return to the food chain, to predators and to prey, with a truly awful (in the proper sense) description of birds of prey. We see "the hawk" (perhaps sparrow hawk, falcon, or kestrel) soaring into the sky and migrating to "the south" in the autumn (v. 26) and then "the eagle" mounting up (literally, on eagles' wings) to his eyrie high on an inaccessible cliff face (v. 27). We see him there, making his home "on the rocky crag and stronghold" (v. 28), a place utterly impregnable and invincible. As we read this description from the world of nature, we can't help but think about how often the eagle has been used as a symbol for human empires.

But instead of admiring his beauty or the grace of his flight, our attention is fixed on what he does. From the great height he attains "he spies out the prey . . . from far away" (v. 29) with the legendary sharpness of eye that birds of prey have, perhaps seeing a field mouse hidden in the long grass of a field from many hundreds of feet above. Between verse 29 and verse 30 he has dived, pounced, carried his prey back to his eyrie, and torn it piece from piece for his young. The poetry spares us no detail. There is no disneyfication of the scene. We are not told blandly that the young eagles eat their dinner; they "suck up blood," and the nest is a place "where the slain are" (v. 30).

In case we were in any danger of forgetting, it is by the "understanding" (which includes plan and purpose) of God that all this happens and by his "command," not by Job's (vv. 26, 27). God does not permit predators to kill their prey; he commands them to do it! Verse 30 is a shocking end to the seven animal and bird cameos as we watch the young eagles around a dead body with blood dripping from their lips—and all at God's "command" (v. 27).

The Lord's defense of his "counsel" (38:2) is not like so many Christian celebrations of the wonders of creation, in which our calendar photos are carefully chosen to be beautiful, full of grace and majesty, showing no violence or death. Rather, the Lord gives Job a brutal, in-your-face portrait of death and danger, as well as of birth and life. There is in the universe a great deal of death, violence, predation (both among animals and, metaphorically, humans), danger, and terror, he says. "You know that, Job. You know that all this is inextricably entwined in the world you know; you cannot take out the death and leave just life alone, for there would be no life without death." Any plan, any government of this world in which good is ultimately to triumph, must necessarily have within it a plan to overcome evil with good. Job could not expect, we cannot expect, a shallow, trite, banal, simple solution to the problem of evil. We must not be surprised if the counsel of God is inscrutable; we must not challenge his counsel with the arrogance of human claims to superhuman knowledge. This leads to the concluding challenge.

Concluding Challenge (40:1, 2)

And the Lord said to Job:

> "Shall a faultfinder contend with the Almighty?
> He who argues with God, let him answer it." (vv. 1, 2)

With a fresh introduction for emphasis and calling for a response ("And the Lord said to Job . . ." [v. 1]), the concluding challenge is given. Job is "a faultfinder" (that is, one who finds fault with the way God runs the world); he is one who "argues with God," a man who has spoken and thought above himself and has seriously suggested that he could have given some useful hints to help God run the world better (v. 2). Job has no secret sins of which he has not repented; the comforters were wrong about that. But he has spoken sins, sins of arrogance, of which he does need to repent. Elihu was right about that.

Amazingly and soberingly, to the man whose wealth God has confiscated, whose family God has taken away, whose greatness God has removed, and whose health God has ruined, God says in summary, "I have made no mistake. I know exactly what I am doing in your life and in every detail of the government of the world. My counsel is perfect; I have got nothing wrong."

How will Job respond?

Job's Response (40:3–5)

Then Job answered the LORD and said:

> "Behold, I am of small account; what shall I answer you?
>   I lay my hand on my mouth.
> I have spoken once, and I will not answer;
>   twice, but I will proceed no further." (vv. 3–5)

At the start the Lord challenged Job to give an answer (38:3); now he does. Or does he? He makes one admission and one declaration. The admission is that he is "of small account" (v. 4). This has the sense of being small or light and hence metaphorically unworthy relative to God. Implicitly he is beginning to bow before the greatness of God, although he still focuses on himself. It will not be until after the second speech that he explicitly makes a confession about God. Still, it is a start.

After this admission he makes his declaration—namely, that he will make no further declarations. He puts his hand over his mouth as if to discipline his unruly tongue and lips and prevent them from saying anything else that they ought not to say. He admits he has already spoken "once . . . twice" (v. 5), which has the sense of "time and time again." Now he will stop.

Shortly before Clement Attlee won a landslide victory in the British General Election of 1945, he had a lot of trouble from the Chairman of the Labour Party, one Professor Harold Laski. Apparently Laski kept writing to Attlee telling him how to do his job or that he ought to resign. Attlee ended his reply to one of these tiresome letters with the pointed words, "a period of silence from you would now be most welcome." God sometimes wants to say that to us, as he did here to Job: "My dear Job, thank you for all your twenty chapters worth of letters telling me how to run the world and suggesting I could do it better than I am. A period of silence from you would now be most welcome." And Job gets the message. He is utterly awed. "Oh, yes, I'll shut up. In the presence of the Creator of the world, I'll shut my big mouth" (40:3–5). As Derek Kidner has written, God's speech "cuts us down to size, treating us not as philosophers but as children—limited in mind, puny in body—whose first and fundamental grasp of truth must be to know the difference between our place and God's, and to accept it."[13]

But we are still left with at least two loose ends. First, does God's speech answer Job's question? The question is, "Why do I, Job, who do not deserve it, suffer as I do?" The answer so far seems to be, "Look around and you will understand that I the Lord am the creator and sustainer of life. I am in control of all the world, and therefore you may trust me with your life and your unanswered questions." Is this an answer? Yes and no.

Of course, we know Job has always been a true worshipper. He has never denied that the Lord is God, really God, in control, supreme, sovereign, all-powerful. And yet somehow this first speech forces him to look around and admit that the Lord really is God, who made and who sustains *all* the created order. And as the Lord speaks this word to him, Job bows down deeper than ever, and somehow his questions may be left safely at the feet of this Almighty God.

And yet there is still a problem. And this is something Christians always face when we say, in the words of that classic Louis Armstrong song, "What a wonderful world." The problem is this: yes, it is a wonderful world, and yet it is also a world touched by terrible evil. It is a world where a cultured man may listen to Mozart while being commandant of an extermination camp at Belsen or Ravensbruck, a world where the beauty of sex may be twisted into infidelity and abuse, a world where the wonder of man's technological wizardry is used in the service of mass destruction. And it is a world in which blameless Job suffers.

So the puzzle is this: what about the evil in the world? It is all very well for the Lord to be the good Creator of a good world. But what about the world we actually have to live in, a good world touched by darkness and death? And this *is* the world we have to live in. It is the world Job lives in. It is the world any honest believer lives in. A world with pain, injustice, perplexity, and sorrow. What about that world, the real world? As we have seen, there have been hints of an answer in the first speech. There will be more in the second.

The other loose end concerns Job himself. Although Job has admitted something about himself, that he is "of small account," he has not yet said anything—or at least nothing explicit—about God. "He has acknowledged his own insignificance, but has not exalted the Lord's knowledge and wisdom." He is therefore "only sobered but not humbled."[14]

And so, with these two loose ends on our hearts, we move to the Lord's second and climactic speech.

34

The Lord's Second Speech: Terrifying Evil

JOB 40:6—42:6

EVIL FRIGHTENS ME. This book has been the hardest I have ever had to write. As I have written it I have struggled with painful and perplexing evil in some relationships. I have been frightened by the evil thoughts and desires bubbling up within my own heart. I have found myself scared at the supernatural power of evil in myself and in others, in addictions, in dysfunctional relationships, in sickness and death, in stubborn self-centeredness, in destructive rivalries, and in depressive illnesses. I am scared of evil. And one of the most evocative ways of conveying the sort of terror I sometimes feel is in the language of monstrous beasts.

> My mind [was] paralysed by the dreadful shape which had sprung out upon us from the shadows of the fog. A hound it was, an enormous coal-black hound, but not such a hound as mortal eyes have ever seen. Fire burst from its open mouth, its eyes glowed with a smouldering glare, its muzzle and hackles and dewlap were outlined in flickering flame. Never in the delirious dream of a disordered brain could anything more savage, more appalling, more hellish be conceived than that dark form and savage face which broke upon us out of the wall of fog.

Thus Arthur Conan Doyle describes the hound of the Baskervilles in perhaps the most famous of the Sherlock Holmes stories. He conjures up a vision of a dog with supernatural overtones that inspires terror in its victim and in his readers. As this hound breaks out of the fog upon them, for a moment all the powers of Hell seem to be unleashed. To hear this description, to imagine oneself there, is to elicit a visceral fear.

But it is not only fictional creatures that can inspire terror. In 2007 the crew of a New Zealand fishing boat hooked a Patagonian toothfish in the deep waters off Antarctica when they realized something bigger was also trying to swallow it. Two hours later they hauled up one of the most mysterious and frightening predators of the deep—a colossal squid about thirty-nine feet long, weighing nearly a thousand pounds, with eyes as big as plates and twenty-five razor-sharp hooks on the end of its tentacles. If calamari rings were made from its tentacles, they would have been the size of tractor tires.[1] Imagine coming face-to-face with that in the sea; the prospect is terrifying beyond belief!

It is these kinds of visions that confront us as we hear God's final speech. How are we to respond when mind-numbing, terrifying, supernatural evil breaks into the ordered, domesticated life of the farm, the world in which we exercise some reassuring measure of control, where life seems to dominate rather than death, and where there is a predictability that makes normal life possible and sustainable? What do we do when we hear an unexpected diagnosis of a terminal disease for ourselves or for one we love? How are we to think when violent crime robs us of our physical health or a trauma leaves us paralyzed with post-traumatic stress disorder? Where do we turn when the stability of our mind is overturned by the onset of some crippling psychiatric disorder, or when a secure relationship with a spouse, parent, or child is broken—or threatened with fracture—by the unpredictable and unexpected behavior of another, perhaps the terrible revelation of an infidelity or the frightening illogicality and instability of another's response to some word or event? These things are full of dread; they are the realities in our lives of which storybook monsters can only begin to convey the fear and numbing terror.

Orientation for God's Second Speech

But we are getting ahead of ourselves. Let us first orient ourselves to listen to this second speech. We will consider briefly the structure, the point at issue, Job's response, and what all this suggests about the significance of the speech.

The Structure of God's Second Speech and Job's Response

The structure is simple and as follows.

> Introduction (I): The Accusation (40:6–8)
> Introduction (II): The Challenge (40:9–14)
>   Two Portraits
>   The Behemoth (40:15–24)
>   The Leviathan (41:1–34)
>   Job's Response (42:1–6)

Differences between the Second Speech and the First

We must note that the second speech addresses a different issue from the first and elicits a different response from Job. Whereas the first speech focused on God's government of the world, his "counsel" (38:2), the second is concerned with his justice (40:8). And while the first speech ended with a sobered and silenced Job (40:3–5), the second ends with Job affirming very strongly a truth about God (that he can do anything, 42:2) and a qualitatively deeper experience of God (42:5, "see[ing]" rather than just "hearing"), before humbling himself in explicit repentance (42:6). It is a radically deeper and stronger response.

Putting these together—the different point at issue and the deeper response—we are led to expect that in some way the second speech will do more than just supplement the first with a bit more of the same kind of argument. Rather we will not be surprised to discover in the second speech a qualitatively stronger truth that addresses the radically deeper issue and elicits a wonderfully richer response. In particular we will see that whereas the first speech spoke of the natural created order in ways that hinted at supernatural forces and agencies, the second speech portrays these supernatural agencies in vivid forms.

But first we must attend to the issues.

Introduction (I): The Accusation: You Must Not Call God Unjust (40:6–8)

Then the LORD answered Job out of the whirlwind and said:

> "Dress for action like a man;
>   I will question you, and you make it known to me.
> Will you even put me in the wrong?
>   Will you condemn me that you may be in the right?" (vv. 6–8)

Verses 6, 7 are a repetition of 38:1, 3. But whereas at the very start of the Lord's first speech he accused Job of darkening his "counsel" (38:2), here he makes a different and sharper accusation. In verse 8 he accuses Job not just of failing to understand God's wise ways of governing the universe but of seeking to put God on trial, to condemn God in order to justify himself. Bildad has denied that God ever perverts justice (8:3). But Job has impugned God's justice, and it is this accusation that God addresses now. But he does it in what is, to us, a most surprising manner.

Introduction (II): The Challenge: Can You Judge the World? (40:9–14)

> Have you an arm like God,
>   and can you thunder with a voice like his?

Adorn yourself with majesty and dignity;
    clothe yourself with glory and splendor.
Pour out the overflowings of your anger,
    and look on everyone who is proud and abase him.
Look on everyone who is proud and bring him low
    and tread down the wicked where they stand.
Hide them all in the dust together;
    bind their faces in the world below.
Then will I also acknowledge to you
    that your own right hand can save you. (vv. 9–14)

Instead of going over aspects of God's governance of the world, defending himself point by point, explaining his judgments and actions, as we might expect in a human trial, in verses 9–14 God challenges Job to have a go himself at being the judge of all the earth. We will have to think about why he does this. But for the moment let us enter into the irony and drama of the scene. God begins with reference to his "arm" and his "thunder" (v. 9a, b). In this context God's upraised "arm" speaks of his powerful actions in judgment, rescuing the righteous and punishing the wicked.[2] Elihu earlier eloquently introduced to us his thunderous voice (37:1–5). God speaks with a voice of "thunder" and reaches out his outstretched strong "arm" when he comes to rescue his own and punish his enemies.

Now he asks Job if he is able to take God's place and do that. He expands on this challenge with a beautiful rich irony in verses 10–14. God in effect says, "Here are my royal robes, my judge's wig and gown of majesty and dignity [v. 10a]. Why don't you put them on? Go on. You will look glorious and splendid with them on [v. 10b]. Oh, you do look fine and dandy! Okay. Now let your anger at injustice overflow [v. 11a]; look at all the arrogant, wicked people and bring them down [v. 11b]; bring them low, tread them down [v. 12],[3] bury them in the dust [v. 13a], tie them up in the place of the dead, which is your dungeon [v. 13b; cf. Jude 6, "kept in eternal chains under gloomy darkness"[4]]. For, as you know, I have a day against 'all that is proud and lofty' [Isaiah 2:12ff.]. How are you getting on? Is it going well, your efforts to put the world to rights? What's that? Your angry speeches don't seem to have made much difference? How frustrating that must be! Keep trying a bit longer, a touch harder; I'm sure you'll manage it. It's not difficult, surely, to run the world better than I have been doing. After all, I seem to have been making rather a mess of it. I'm so glad you're here to help." And so on. We can picture this darkly comic scene and hear the tones of voice.

And then, at the end, "Look," says God, "when you finally succeed, I will roll over and admit that you have it within your power and wisdom to 'save' yourself [v. 14]. Then I will gladly abdicate and hand over the government of the universe to you." It is a little like that light movie *Bruce Almighty* in which Jim Carrey plays a TV reporter, Bruce Nolan, who complains about God one time too often, and God responds, giving him some divine powers and the opportunity to try running things for himself. Although at one level the movie is blasphemous (having "God" appear in a rather silly human form), actually the main burden of the plot is the comic stupidity of Nolan and his patent failure to do anything beyond making a complete mess of things. The comedy of this light movie is not dissimilar to the irony of this challenge from God to Job.

It would be easy to misunderstand this challenge, as if God were throwing up his hands and saying, "Look, mate, you have a go. It's not as easy as you think, this governing the world. I'm doing my best. Don't get so cross when I don't get it right all of the time; you couldn't do any better." But as we shall see, he is not saying this. Yes, he is saying that the government of the world is harder than Job thinks (and harder than the comforters think), much harder. But he is not saying that he is doing his best and Job mustn't complain if he doesn't get it right all the time. Not at all.

James and John did not "know" what they were asking when they asked to share in Jesus' victory over evil, for there is first a cup to be drunk and a baptism of death with which to be baptized (Mark 10:38). In the same way Job does not know what it will mean to conquer and subdue evil. As we will later discover, that will necessitate the cross of Christ, for only by death can death be destroyed.[5]

We will now consider the two word portraits that follow without explanation. Whereas there was a concluding challenge at the end of the first speech (40:1, 2), the second just stops at the end of the Leviathan portrait. Clearly these portraits are of great importance. We will need first to listen to them and then to think carefully about them before we too learn to respond like Job and say, "I know that you can do all things, and that no purpose of yours can be thwarted" (42:2).

The Behemoth (40:15–24)

Behold, Behemoth,
    which I made as I made you;
    he eats grass like an ox.
Behold, his strength in his loins,
    and his power in the muscles of his belly.
He makes his tail stiff like a cedar;

> the sinews of his thighs are knit together.
> His bones are tubes of bronze,
>> his limbs like bars of iron.
> He is the first of the works of God;
>> let him who made him bring near his sword!
> For the mountains yield food for him
>> where all the wild beasts play.
> Under the lotus plants he lies,
>> in the shelter of the reeds and in the marsh.
> For his shade the lotus trees cover him;
>> the willows of the brook surround him.
> Behold, if the river is turbulent he is not frightened;
>> he is confident though Jordan rushes against his mouth.
> Can one take him by his eyes,
>> or pierce his nose with a snare? (vv. 15–24)

The first portrait is of the Behemoth. This is a plural name for a creature that is singular in more senses than one; it is singular in that it is one creature and not many, and it is singular in that it is unique. The word "Behemoth" is the plural of the word for something like a farm animal (v. 15). Here the plural seems to be a plural of majesty, conveying something like "The Superbeast." We are told first of his origins, his diet, and his strength. His origins are with God, for he is a creature ("which I made as I made you," v. 15b). His diet is "grass"; he is a creature who feeds on the grass in the wild, "like an ox" (v. 15c). To eat "like an ox" is to have a hearty and insatiable appetite (as we would say, "he wolfed down his lunch"). His strength is energetically described in verses 16–18. His "loins" and "belly" muscles are immensely powerful (v. 16). Verse 17 either describes a massively powerful tail and thighs or, possibly, a huge erect penis between gigantic testicles (if "tail" is a euphemism for penis and "thighs" are a euphemism for testicles).[6] Either way the verse speaks of tremendous strength and virility. Verse 18 describes "bones" and "limbs" as strong as "bronze" and "iron." Here is a hard, strong, impressive creature. And Job is invited, in his mind's eye, to "behold" him (vv. 15, 16), to look at him, to fill his mind with the sheer strength of this creature.

Then in verse 19, after Job's mind is filled with the outline of this powerful creature, he is told of its primacy and yet its vulnerability. This creature is "the first"—that is, the preeminent one—"of the works of God" (v. 19a).[7] He is not to be messed with. And yet he is vulnerable. The words "let him who made him bring near his sword" (v. 19b) mean that the one who made him—and no one else—is able to approach him with a sword. However powerful he is, and whatever primacy he has in creation, his Maker does have the power and authority to come near it with his sword, to express his dominion over it, to subdue it, to keep it in its place, and even finally to kill it. In Revelation "a sharp sword" will come from the mouth of the rider on the white horse to destroy the beast and the false prophet (Revelation 19:15ff.).

Verses 20–22 paint a picture of a creature that is always present and always hungry. "The mountains" (that is, those who dwell on the mountains) supply him endlessly with food (v. 20). The words "yield food" suggest the bringing of food as tribute from defeated foes; his food is the price he exacts for his victory (v. 20). Sometimes he may be concealed "under the lotus plants" and "in the shelter of the reeds and in the marsh" and in "the willows" at the water's edge (vv. 21, 22). But always he is there, and always he is being fed (v. 20a). This picture suggests a land creature, but one who is at home in rivers. The surging waters of a frightening "river," the turbulence of the "Jordan," in the old days when it was a great river, do not frighten him (v. 23). He is a very strong creature, unfazed and "not frightened" by water in all its dangerous forms (v. 23). And he is untamable; no human being can capture him and take him to a zoo (v. 24).

So here is a powerful, hungry superbeast, untamable by human beings, who is yet made by God and can be tamed by God. We shall ask later who or what he may be. But first let us fill our minds and hearts with the second portrait.

The Leviathan (41:1–34)

The Leviathan is given a long and climactic description. Thirty-four unbroken verses paint a picture of this terrifying creature, with no explanation at the end. Clearly we are meant first to see, hear, imagine, and feel this creature in all his majesty.

> Can you draw out Leviathan with a fishhook
>   or press down his tongue with a cord?
> Can you put a rope in his nose
>   or pierce his jaw with a hook?
> Will he make many pleas to you?
>   Will he speak to you soft words?
> Will he make a covenant with you
>   to take him for your servant forever?
> Will you play with him as with a bird,
>   or will you put him on a leash for your girls?
> Will traders bargain over him?
>   Will they divide him up among the merchants?

Can you fill his skin with harpoons
  or his head with fishing spears? (vv. 1–7)

We begin in verses 1–7 with a devastating sequence of questions. God is speaking, we must assume, to a man who knew what the Leviathan was. Certainly in his lament in chapter 3 Job has spoken of those who are ready to rouse Leviathan, a creature with power to erase his conception night and birth day from the calendar (3:8). "So, Job, how about sitting by the ocean's edge with your fishing line and see how you get on if the Leviathan takes your bait [v. 1a]?" It would be like one of those disaster movies where we see a little old fisherman sitting at the end of a wooden pier with his line, trying to reel in what seems like a big fish but turns out to be a monster who devours him and makes firewood of the pier before devastating the whole town behind him. "And how about putting a cord around his tongue and jaw to make him harmless? Have a go at that! Or a rope through his nose or a hook through his jaw? [vv. 1b, 2]." The very idea that you could succeed with this is absurd, like the idea of taming the Behemoth (40:24).

"Or here's an idea, Job: do you think that when you have tied him up, he will plead with you, 'Ow, Job, that hurts! Please loosen the cord. I promise I'll be good. I will. I will. I tell you what—I'll make a binding agreement (covenant) with you[8] and promise to be your servant always [vv. 3, 4].'" Again the idea is absurd and was prefigured in the unlikely scenario of the farmer Job domesticating the wild ox (39:9–12). "Or just imagine having him as a pet [v. 5], as you would a parrot, or put him on a leash as you would with the family dog. Imagine coming home one evening, ringing the doorbell, and your little daughter answers and gives you a kiss. 'Hello, darling,' you say, 'I've brought you a pet.' 'Oh, thank you, Dad.' 'It's called a Leviathan.' And then this monster roars in and devours the whole family."[9] This is dark humor. "Can you imagine seeing his dead body laid out on the fish market floor ready to be auctioned [v. 6], as merchants do with tuna in the Tsukiji fish market in Tokyo early each morning? No, you can't! Because nobody is able to kill and catch him; no one can successfully harpoon him or kill him with fishing spears [v. 7]. The idea is stupid and unthinkable."

Lay your hands on him;
  remember the battle—you will not do it again!
Behold, the hope of a man is false;
  he is laid low even at the sight of him.
No one is so fierce that he dares to stir him up.
  Who then is he who can stand before me?

Who has first given to me, that I should repay him?
Whatever is under the whole heaven is mine. (vv. 8–11)

Verses 8–11 follow the questions with some statements. "Just you try laying hands on him," says God (v. 8). "You won't forget the battle that follows; you won't try that again, if you have any sense. He is far too dangerous and strong for you." Indeed any hope human beings have of defeating him is make-believe (v. 9a); we only have to see him to collapse in terror (v. 9b). There is no human being so strong and "fierce" that he dares to "stir . . . up" Leviathan from the depths where he lives (v. 10a). Lovers of The Lord of the Rings are reminded of the foolish hobbit who accidentally stirs up the Balrog from the depths under Mount Moria (as we considered when expounding 3:8). A kid might wake up the family dog to have some fun with him, but no human being with sense will dare to wake up Leviathan when he sleeps.

But—and here is the surprise in verse 10b—here's a different kind of question: "Who then is he who can stand before *me*?" "If you think it would be scary to stand in Leviathan's presence, just ask yourself what it must be like to stand in *my* presence. No one—not even Leviathan—has any purchase on, any call on, any rights over me (v. 11). I owe no creature anything. I am the Creator of Heaven and earth, and 'whatever'—really whatever, including Leviathan (and Behemoth)—'is under the whole heaven is mine' (v. 11). Think about Leviathan and tremble; then think about what it means for me to be the Sovereign Almighty Creator. And think what this must mean for Leviathan too."

I will not keep silence concerning his limbs,
    or his mighty strength, or his goodly frame.
Who can strip off his outer garment?
    Who would come near him with a bridle?
Who can open the doors of his face?
    Around his teeth is terror.
His back is made of rows of shields,
    shut up closely as with a seal.
One is so near to another
    that no air can come between them.
They are joined one to another;
    they clasp each other and cannot be separated.
His sneezings flash forth light,
    and his eyes are like the eyelids of the dawn.
Out of his mouth go flaming torches;
    sparks of fire leap forth.
Out of his nostrils comes forth smoke,
    as from a boiling pot and burning rushes.
His breath kindles coals,

and a flame comes forth from his mouth.
In his neck abides strength,
    and terror dances before him.
The folds of his flesh stick together,
    firmly cast on him and immovable.
His heart is hard as a stone,
    hard as the lower millstone. (vv. 12–24)

There follows in verses 12–24 a description of the Leviathan. Just as the Behemoth's primary characteristic was strength, so it is with Leviathan (v. 12); he is a beefy, muscular creature. And you can't get under his skin to attach "a bridle" to him (v. 13). He is wild and untamable. He has a very frightening "face" (v. 14), with "doors" consisting of rows and rows of teeth. To look into his face is to know the terror of facing a hungry great white shark at sea or a voracious crocodile. Verses 15–17 describe a back covered with impregnable shields of hard armor, with no vulnerable spaces between them where you might hope to land a harpoon or a sword. Verses 18–21 describe a fire-breathing dragon of a creature, with "eyes" so bright they outshine "the dawn" (v. 18) and "breath" that will solve your problems in lighting your barbecue (vv. 19–21). The fire that emanates from his nostrils and mouth reveal the heat and anger of the hatred and malice in his heart. They remind us of God's "lightnings" in Elihu's final speech (36:30).

His neck muscles are terrifying and hard (v. 22a). He is an utterly scary creature who smells of death (v. 22b). There are no soft places in his skin (v. 23). And his chest or "heart" (v. 24) is hard like "the lower millstone."[10] The word translated "heart" may speak of him as a hard-hearted creature (cold inside) or may just mean that his chest is rock-hard.

When he raises himself up the mighty are afraid;
    at the crashing they are beside themselves.
Though the sword reaches him, it does not avail,
    nor the spear, the dart, or the javelin.
He counts iron as straw,
    and bronze as rotten wood.
The arrow cannot make him flee;
    for him sling stones are turned to stubble.
Clubs are counted as stubble;
    he laughs at the rattle of javelins. (vv. 25–29)

Verses 25–29 show what happens when human beings attack him. The Leviathan is "crashing" around (v. 25) in a terrifying way. You can attack him with swords (close combat) or with spears, darts, and javelins (weapons from a distance), but they will have no effect. You can detonate a hydrogen bomb under him, and he will scarcely notice. He is a storybook monster, tearing these weapons to pieces as if they were mere "straw" or "rotten wood" (v. 27). Arrows, sling stones, clubs, javelins—he laughs at them all (vv. 28, 29). He is invincible to human attack.

> His underparts are like sharp potsherds;
>   he spreads himself like a threshing sledge on the mire.
> He makes the deep boil like a pot;
>   he makes the sea like a pot of ointment.
> Behind him he leaves a shining wake;
>   one would think the deep to be white-haired. (vv. 30–32)

In verses 30–32 we see him thrashing around in the mud and the water. His underside, where we might have hoped to find a point of weakness, is "sharp" and hard (v. 30). He lives in "the deep" (the place of chaos, disorder, and death), thrashing around and making it white with the foam of his movements (vv. 31, 32). In these verses "the deep" (vv. 31, 32) is mentioned twice, as well as "the sea" (v. 31) and "the mire" (v. 30). Here is a sea monster, a fire-breathing sea dragon, whose dwelling place is associated with evil, danger, hostility to God, and death.

> On earth there is not his like,
>   a creature without fear.
> He sees everything that is high;
>   he is king over all the sons of pride. (vv. 33, 34)

The description ends with his uniqueness (v. 33a: "On earth there is not his like"); he is unlike all other creatures. He fears nothing and no one in the created world (v. 33). "He is king" (v. 34). The world is full of proud and arrogant people, but he is the proudest, the strongest, the ruler of them all. He is the one who can really say, "I am the greatest."

So who is he? And who is the Behemoth? Before we consider this vital question, we must listen to Job's response.

Job's Response (42:1–6)

Then Job answered the LORD and said:

> "I know that you can do all things,
>   and that no purpose of yours can be thwarted.
> 'Who is this that hides counsel without knowledge?'
> Therefore I have uttered what I did not understand,

> things too wonderful for me, which I did not know.
> 'Hear, and I will speak;
>   I will question you, and you make it known to me.'
> I had heard of you by the hearing of the ear,
>   but now my eye sees you;
> therefore I despise myself,
>   and repent in dust and ashes." (vv. 1–6)

Job's response is in three parts. He speaks of something he now knows, of things he did not know, and supremely of one he has now seen. First, he now knows that God "can do all things" and that "no purpose" of his "can be thwarted" (v. 2). This is a very strong statement. At one level Job has never doubted this. He has repeatedly called God "the Almighty" and has echoed the confidence of the comforters that the Almighty really is omnipotent. But it seems that he now knows this truth in a deeper and fuller way. We will have to ask why and what this means.

Second, in verse 3 he speaks of something he "did not know." He echoes God's rebuke to him at the start of the first speech: "Who is this that hides counsel without knowledge" (cf. 38:2). (Incidentally, this echo from the start of God's first speech suggests that Job's response here is his considered response to the cumulative effect of both of God's speeches together.) He now admits clearly and explicitly that he has done exactly that of which the Lord accused him. He has indeed spoken of "what I did not understand, things too wonderful for me, which I did not know." The word translated "wonderful" speaks of matters that only God can do (referring to his power) and that only God can understand (referring to his wisdom). These are things "too great and too marvelous for me," as David will put it in Psalm 131:1. At the end of the first speech, Job admits he himself is "of small account" (Job 40:4); but his statement here is stronger. He admits clearly that he has said things he ought not to have said, he has made accusations he ought not to have made, he has spoken as if he understood things he does not understand. It is only after God's second speech that he admits this clearly; in some way the first speech softened him without moving him to a clear surrender.

Finally, in verses 4–6 Job echoes God's introductory challenge to both speeches: "I will question you, and you make it known to me" (see 38:3; 40:7), prefixing the echo with the words, "Hear, and I will speak" (v. 4). His focus now is on what he "heard" when God spoke. In one of the most famous verses in the book, Job contrasts a previous hearing with a new seeing (v. 5). Before the terrible events of this book, Job's knowledge of God was "by the hearing of the ear" (v. 5). In the context of the book, this must refer to the framework of understanding that he shared with the comforters and with so many morally serious philosophers and theologians throughout history. He has heard the traditions of these people; the assured results of their traditional understanding had come into his ears from childhood. He had heard that there was one Almighty God, that this God was righteous and all-powerful, and that therefore certain things might be expected, morally, in the world by way of crime and punishment, virtue and reward. All this he had heard "by the hearing of the ear." "But now my eye sees you" (v. 5). On the face of it this is a strange thing to say after God has given him word-portraits of two terrible creatures, the Behemoth and the Leviathan. He has had no mystical vision of God; a beatific vision has not been granted to him. Rather he has seen in his imagination two terrible beasts or monsters. He has not had Isaiah's later vision of the Lord lifted up in the temple (Isaiah 6) or Ezekiel's strange vision of the Lord on his chariot throne (e.g., Ezekiel 1). He has not literally seen anyone or anything. He is still on his rubbish heap licking his wounds, surrounded by unhelpful comforters and the challenging presence of the prophet Elihu. And yet, as he has heard the Lord's words (by whatever psychological or physical mechanism they might have come), he has seen the Lord with a clarity he has not approached before. And in response to this aural vision (for it is a vision that enters him through his ears) he repents (v. 6), for the first and only time in the book. He not only admits he has spoken what he ought not to have spoken—he turns from these words and repents in deep contrition for his sin. It is an extraordinary and surprising response from the man who has steadfastly refused to repent of the supposed sins of which the comforters have repeatedly accused him. Clearly it signals a climax in the book.

So we must come back to the question, who is the Behemoth, and who is the Leviathan, that their portraits could elicit such a response?

Who Are the Behemoth and the Leviathan?

In the history of the interpretation of Job, there have been two main approaches to the Behemoth and the Leviathan. On the one hand, some have understood them to be actual creatures, of the kind one might nowadays find in a zoo.[11] So typically the Behemoth has been understood to be the hippopotamus and the Leviathan to be the crocodile. The other main approach has been to understand these two creatures to be storybook creatures from the stories of the gods and goddesses well known in the ancient Near East.

It is not difficult to see how the descriptions have called to mind features of actual creatures. The Behemoth is a powerful river and land animal, like the hippopotamus. The Leviathan has terrifying rows of teeth, like the crocodile. The techniques to be used for hunting them "correspond to the hunting techniques for the hippopotamus and the crocodile."[12] Moreover, there is evidence to suggest that in Egyptian mythology both the hippopotamus and the crocodile were "symbols of chaos" and needed to be subjugated.[13]

But there are serious difficulties with understanding them to be merely natural creatures; these difficulties cumulatively make it clear that they are storybook creatures.

The first difficulty is that neither portrait fits perfectly with any known creature on earth.[14] For example, the Leviathan is described as a fire-breathing monster and an ocean-dwelling creature, neither of which is true of the crocodile. On its own this is not an insurmountable objection, for we must allow room for poetic hyperbole in these descriptions. But it is a problem, for there are no such hyperbolic features in the descriptions of natural creatures in the first speech.

A second difficulty is that it is hard to see how Job's inability to catch and tame a hippo and a crocodile really addresses the question of his inability to administer cosmic justice; the issues and stakes are much higher than this. Tied in with this difficulty is, as we have seen, the extraordinary depth and clarity of Job's response to this second speech. A speech that was no more than a couple of afterthoughts to the first ("Oh, and by the way, I forgot to mention that you haven't managed to tame a hippo or a crocodile") would hardly elicit such a response. It would be anticlimactic, when in fact it is a tremendous climax.[15]

Allied to these evidences from within the book of Job is clear evidence from elsewhere in Scripture that the Leviathan is a well-known storybook creature. Job has implied his own understanding of this in 3:8 ("Let those curse it who curse the day, who are ready to rouse up Leviathan"). Isaiah describes Leviathan as a "fleeing serpent . . . the twisting serpent . . . the dragon that is in the sea" in the context of God's sovereign victory over it (Isaiah 27:1). In Psalm 74 Asaph speaks of the exodus in terms of God breaking "the heads of the sea monsters" and having "crushed the heads of Leviathan" (Psalm 74:12–14), suggesting that Leviathan is a many-headed sea monster whose power and enmity to God are such that only the redemptive power of the exodus can subdue him. In a wonderfully ironic passage, Psalm 104 describes Leviathan as a sea creature for whom God has made the sea as his playpen (Psalm 104:25, 26).

The book of Revelation takes the imagery of beasts, dragons, serpents, and sea monsters and applies it explicitly to Satan. "And the great dragon was thrown down, that ancient serpent, who is called the devil and Satan, the deceiver of the whole world" (Revelation 12:9). "And he seized the dragon, that ancient serpent, who is the devil and Satan, and bound him" (Revelation 20:2). So we have clear Scriptural evidence that Leviathan is a strange and terrifying sea monster, a many-headed, fire-breathing dragon who conveys to us the terror and evil of Satan himself. He is "the embodiment of cosmic evil itself."[16]

Luther expresses it well in his best-known hymn, *"Ein Feste Burg"*:

> The ancient prince of hell,
> Has risen with purpose fell;
> Strong mail of craft and power
> He weareth in this hour,
> On earth is not his fellow.

This means that our identification of the Leviathan with Satan is not dependent upon extra-Biblical sources. However, there are plenty of extra-Biblical sources suggesting that sea monsters or dragons were symbolic of hostile spiritual forces—for example, in the polytheistic stories of the religions of the ancient Near East. In the ancient world, as today, when you wanted to speak about the world you often did so in terms of stories or myths. And one of the stories that made the rounds was of some kind of dragon god or serpent god or sea monster god who was the archenemy of the chief god in the pantheon. And in the old stories all sorts of battles were fought between this monster god and other gods. I agree with Habel: "It is difficult to imagine that an Israelite audience would have heard the name Leviathan without making these associations."

The background to these myths was always polytheistic: behind the visible world are many gods and goddesses. This raises a problem for some people. Can we really imagine the firmly monotheistic Old Testament authors referring to creatures from polytheistic stories? Are they suggesting that the Lord has to subdue the Leviathan in a cosmic battle whose outcome is in doubt, as Baal had to confront the god of the sea and the sea monster in the Canaanite myths? Not at all. Sometimes the Old Testament writers use the language of these myths to teach what is actually true about the one living God. The creatures are often referred to as mythological. But this word is unhelpfully ambiguous. It is often understood to mean something like fictional or untrue. But from the pens of the firmly monotheistic Old Testament authors these creatures are neither part of a polytheistic pantheon nor untrue. They are a way of taking well-known storybook imagery, of a kind that would immediately convey chaotic supernatural terror, and bringing it firmly into a monotheistic worldview. They are saying that the Leviathan in all his supernatural wild hostility has no existence independent from the Creator and exercises no agency in autonomy from the Creator; he is stronger than us, but he is a creature of God. Behemoth and Leviathan are storybook creatures, but they are also utterly real and true; it is just that their truth is conveyed to us in storybook descriptions that arouse in us a response of visceral fear. In this way they convey to us the truth of Satan much more powerfully than a calm and measured theological description would do. To a generation more familiar with the Harry Potter stories, we might want to compare Satan to Voldemort.[17]

We are therefore on strong Biblical ground when we identify the Leviathan at the end of the book of Job with the Satan at the start. This also answers a popular objection to the integrity of the book, namely, that the Satan plays a critical role at the start and then disappears from view. He does not disappear from view; he appears in all his evil terror at the end.

The fact that this kind of symbolism is used for human powers that defy God does not mean they have no real spiritual referent. For example, in Ezekiel the power of Egypt is described as "the great dragon that lies in the midst of his streams" (Ezekiel 29:3).[18] This means more than that Egypt is like a dragon. It suggests that in its power used against God, Egypt takes on something of a satanic character. The same would be true of the power of Rome to which similar symbolism is applied in the book of Revelation.

But what of the Behemoth? Here we cannot be so sure and must make a more tentative suggestion based more on hints and nuances in the text. Jones sees an echo of Behemoth and Leviathan in the two beasts (one a land beast, one from the sea) in Revelation 12, 13, and this is possible. Robert Fyall has argued carefully that the Behemoth portrays death himself (with echoes of the Canaanite god Mot).[19] This ever-hungry superbeast is always devouring, like the grim reaper in modern cartoons, the hooded figure of death with his sickle picking off one and then another to keep feeding his insatiable appetite. This suggestion is attractive in terms of Biblical theology as well as expository evidence, for Scripture associates death with Satan in many places. And it will enable us to see a persuasive Christological climax to the book of Job.

Fyall ties the two readings together helpfully: "It is not that they *are* the hippopotamus and the crocodile, but that these beasts in their size, ferocity and untameable nature are evidence of that dark power rooted in the universe itself which shadows all life."[20]

How Should We Respond to Behemoth and Leviathan?

G. K. Chesterton suggests that as Job listens to God's speeches, "he feels the terrible and tingling atmosphere of something which is too good to be told. The refusal of God to explain His design is itself a burning hint of His design."[21] What is conveyed to Job and to us in the Behemoth and Leviathan descriptions is indeed almost too good to be told. And yet it is true.

It seems that the Behemoth may be the storybook embodiment of the figure of death. And the Leviathan in Biblical imagery is the archenemy of God, the prince of the power of evil, Satan, the god of this world (as Jesus calls him), the one who holds the power of death. And in the Leviathan we see the embodiment of beastliness, of terror, of undiluted evil. When, at the climax of his description, we read that "he is king over all the sons of pride" (41:34), we are reading of the one who elsewhere is called "Beelzebul, the prince of demons" (Matthew 12:24).

This second divine speech to Job is precisely addressing the problem of supernatural evil in the created order. This is clear in Job 40:8–14. Job has questioned God's justice (40:8). So God challenges him to do the job of the judge of all the earth (40:11)—that is, to bring low the proud and to tread down the wicked (40:12). "If you can do that," says the Lord in essence, "then I will admit that you can save yourself. But you can't" (40:14).[22]

So the figures of the Behemoth and the Leviathan come not as an anticlimax but rather use the language of well-known stories to make the point that only the Lord can keep evil on a leash. The Leviathan is "the ruler of this world" (John 12:31), "the prince of the power of the air"—that supernatural region that lies above us but below God's Heaven (Ephesians 2:2). So here is a creature that is the ruler of all the proud. "If you can tame *him*, Job, then we may be sure you can tame all the proud. But you can't, Job, can you?" Indeed we saw in Job 19 that it is precisely this monster who has been savaging Job and making his life such utter misery all this time. Job cannot take him on. The point of Job 41 is to make us tremble at the awesome and fell power of the prince of evil. If we thought evil was bad, when we come face-to-face with the Leviathan we realize it is infinitely more frightening than we had thought. "You cannot begin to take on the problem of evil, Job. And you know that."

"But *I* can!" says the Lord. That is the point. This awesome monster is "a *creature*" (41:33), a created thing. "I made him too, and I can tame him. And he is on *my* leash, even if he cannot be on yours" (41:5). We see similar deprecating comedy in Psalm 104:26 with its calm description of Leviathan as placed in the sea to frolic, as a parent might put an unruly child in a secure playpen to play.

Now this is the point. A walker enters a farmyard and is terrified by wild dogs, yapping, snarling, and snapping around his ankles. He is scared. And the question he is bound to ask is, "Are these dogs restrained in any way?

Are they on a leash? Is there an owner around who can call them off?" As Job suffers, his greatest and deepest fear is that the monster who attacks him is unrestrained, that the attacks will go on forever, with unrelieved ferocity, and that the monster has been given a free hand, unlimited access to Job and his life. He is afraid that there is no sovereign God who has evil on a leash.

But there is. And when Job grasps that, he is filled with awe (42:2). We, the readers, have already seen this in chapters 1, 2, in which it is clear that Satan is restrained (1:12; 2:6). On both occasions Satan obeys to the letter. Satan, the Leviathan, is a horrible monster. But he cannot go one millimeter beyond the leash on which the Lord keeps him.

Now this does not answer our questions. It does not give us a philo-sophically tidy schema that can explain the problem of suffering and evil. But it does something deeper: it opens our eyes to who God is. He is the only God, without rival. Even the mystery of evil is his mystery. Even Satan, the Leviathan, is God's Satan, God's pet, if we dare put it like this. This means that as we suffer, and as we sit with others who suffer, we may with absolute confidence bow down to this sovereign God, knowing that while evil may be terrible, it cannot and will not ever go one tiny fraction beyond the leash on which God has put it. And it will not go on forever, for the One to whom we belong is God.

It is not until the New Testament that we learn what it cost God to win this victory over the Leviathan. Neither the Behemoth nor the Leviathan can finally be defeated by the imposition of a greater force of the same kind; evil cannot be defeated by evil, but only by the redemptive suffering of pure good-ness. This was no Olympian victory won from a great height by a tyrannical and remote god. On the contrary, this victory was won, paradoxically, on the cross of Christ. As the writer of the letter to the Hebrews explains, the reason the Son of God became a fully human being was so "that through death he might destroy the one who has the power of death, that is, the devil" (Hebrews 2:14). The reason the Leviathan monster has a hold over human beings is that we have surrendered to his cruel sovereignty by rebelling against God. "The sting of death is sin" (1 Corinthians 15:56). We owe this evil monster our dark allegiance and cannot escape his clutches until our debt is paid. That debt was paid at the cross.

> And you, who were dead in your trespasses and the uncircumcision of your
> flesh, God made alive together with him, having forgiven us all our tres-
> passes, by canceling the record of debt that stood against us with its legal
> demands. This he set aside, nailing it to the cross. He disarmed the rulers

and authorities and put them to open shame, by triumphing over them in him. (Colossians 2:13–15)

The One who is Lord even over Leviathan suffered on the cross. He is the Lord who deals in scars, for he bears them in person as God's only Son. When the darkness of the Leviathan's presence overwhelms us, we may turn with confidence to this Savior alone. Shortly after World War I, at a time when Europe reeled under the burden of unutterable darkness, the poet Edward Shillito wrote a poem that captures something of this truth:

If we have never sought Thee, we seek Thee now;
Thine eyes burn through the dark, our only stars;
We must have sight of thorn-pricks on Thy brow,
We must have Thee, O Jesus of the Scars.

The heavens frighten us; they are too calm;
In all the universe we have no place;
Our wounds are hurting us; where is the balm?
Lord Jesus, by Thy Scars, we claim Thy grace.

The other gods were strong; but Thou wast weak;
They rode, but Thou didst stumble to a throne;
But to our wounds only God's wounds can speak,
And not a god has wounds, but Thou alone.

Centuries after Job, horrified people watched evil unmasked as the destructive forces within a demonized man they called "Legion" catapulted 2,000 pigs over a cliff into the sea. As they watched, they grasped in their horror the true power and disorder of evil, and at the same time they watched the man who was and is Lord over that evil exercise the authority he was to win at the cross (Mark 5:1–20).

Evil frightens me. It is meant to. I am meant to be humbled by supernatural evil so that I know—deeply know—that it is too strong for me, that I cannot resist it on my own. Death and the one who hold the power of death—that is, the devil—are too strong for me. But my response is not meant to end in terror. For at the climax of the book of Job is this assurance that both death (the Behemoth) and the one who holds the power of death (the Leviathan) are creatures entirely under the control of the Sovereign God who is my Savior.

I am not skilled to understand
What God has willed, what God has planned;

I only know at His right hand
Stands one who is my Saviour.

I take Him at His word indeed;
"Christ died for sinners"—this I read;
For in my heart I find a need
Of Him to be my Saviour.[23]

The assurance that he can do all things and that no purpose of his can be thwarted is the comfort I need in suffering and the encouragement I crave when terrified by evil. He does not merely permit evil but commands it, controls it, and uses it for his good purposes. The most evil deed in the history of the human race, the moment when the Leviathan and the Behemoth seemed ultimately victorious, was the moment that was brought about by "the definite plan and foreknowledge of God" (Acts 2:23), and that was the moment of the Behemoth's and the Leviathan's definitive defeat. This God who knows how to use supernatural evil to serve his purposes of ultimate good can and will use the darkest invasions into my own life for his definite and invincible plans for my good in Christ. Hallelujah! What a Savior!

Epilogue

The End Comes at the End

JOB 42:7–17

NOW WE COME TO the marvelous conclusion of the book of Job.

> After the Lord had spoken these words to Job, the Lord said to Eliphaz the Temanite: "My anger burns against you and against your two friends, for you have not spoken of me what is right, as my servant Job has. Now therefore take seven bulls and seven rams and go to my servant Job and offer up a burnt offering for yourselves. And my servant Job shall pray for you, for I will accept his prayer not to deal with you according to your folly. For you have not spoken of me what is right, as my servant Job has." So Eliphaz the Temanite and Bildad the Shuhite and Zophar the Naamathite went and did what the Lord had told them, and the Lord accepted Job's prayer.
>
> And the Lord restored the fortunes of Job, when he had prayed for his friends. And the Lord gave Job twice as much as he had before. Then came to him all his brothers and sisters and all who had known him before, and ate bread with him in his house. And they showed him sympathy and comforted him for all the evil that the Lord had brought upon him. And each of them gave him a piece of money and a ring of gold.
>
> And the Lord blessed the latter days of Job more than his beginning. And he had 14,000 sheep, 6,000 camels, 1,000 yoke of oxen, and 1,000 female donkeys. He had also seven sons and three daughters. And he called the name of the first daughter Jemimah, and the name of the second Keziah, and the name of the third Keren-happuch. And in all the land there were no women so beautiful as Job's daughters. And their father gave them an inheritance among their brothers. And after this Job lived 140 years, and saw his sons, and his sons' sons, four generations. And Job died, an old man, and full of days. (vv. 7–17)

The End Comes at the End

The end comes at the end. And this is important because although we have reached the end of the book of Job, in our lives we are not yet at the end. When we wake up in the morning, what do we expect our day to be like? We may, of course, have expectations for a particular day, the prospect of a good party or apprehension about a visit to the dentist. But in general what do we expect of a normal day? For a Christian, what ought to be our idea of the normal Christian life? This is important because our idea of normality will govern whether we end up delighted or disappointed at the end of the day.

The book of Job ought to shape our expectation of the normal Christian life. We may think that a perverse suggestion since Job is such an extreme book, and yet it is true. Although the book of Job paints in primary colors how God treats his friends and placards before us supremely how he treats a peculiarly blameless believer, nonetheless we have no reason to expect that he will treat us in any radically different way if we belong to Christ.

We ended our last study at a moment of high drama where the Lord himself spoke to Job and Job responded. To break off there was a bit like those ice cream vans that play part of a tune and then suddenly stop partway through, and we wait for the end, the resolution, some sense of closure, some rounding off of the tune so that we can relax and go home knowing it is finished. We want to know what happens next.

In 42:7–17 we have the closure to the story, the resolution, the conclusion, the end. But what are we to make of it? On the face of it, it is a bit of an anticlimax. It goes back from poetry to prose, and frankly it feels a bit prosaic. After the dramatic imagery and the soaring heights of the poetry, it feels like a bit of a comedown: the Lord has a quiet word of rebuke for the friends, Job prays for them, and they are forgiven (vv. 7–9). Then it all ends happily: Job is restored to greater prosperity, is given a new family, and generally rides off into the sunset (vv. 10–17). Is that not a bit flat, a bit sugary even? And yet there are depths in this conclusion that are neither shallow nor sugary.

Alongside this final prose section of Job, let us take for our text a verse in the letter of James. James is speaking to believers under pressure; he wants them to persevere, and he writes: "Behold, we consider those blessed who remained steadfast. You have heard of the steadfastness of Job, and you have seen the purpose of the Lord, how the Lord is compassionate and merciful" (James 5:11).

James focuses on two people: Job with his perseverance and the Lord with his compassion and mercy. Let us begin with Job.

The Perseverance of Job

Job's perseverance or "steadfastness" or patience is an active quality, a pressing on, not a passive sitting back and letting it all wash over him (James 5:11).

I want us to consider two aspects of Job's perseverance—perseverance in warfare and perseverance while waiting.

Perseverance in Warfare

The book of Job is so refreshingly honest about this. Although Christians sometimes groan at the prospect of studying Job, again and again they are surprised and refreshed by the sheer honesty of this book. We have seen that Job the believer is fighting a battle. There is a battle going on; the Lord has been challenged by Satan, the Leviathan, a monster masquerading as god. And as they war, it is not so much that Job is on the battlefield; he *is* the battlefield. The battle for the soul of Job is fought out in his struggles as the monster tears at his life. It is a dark warfare. Satan fills Job's mind with images of despair, darkness, death, and futility. Job is taken through the valley of the shadow of death.

He is taken there as a believer suffering for his faith; he is suffering because he is a believer. We saw this in Job 1, 2. God singles out Job and says in essence, "Look, there's a believer." Satan attacks Job for precisely that reason. Job is not about human suffering in general; it is about the suffering endured by a believer because he or she is a believer. Job is being persecuted not by human enemies but by Satan. He endures disaster, tragedy, and sickness because he fears God.

Supremely this dark warfare is fulfilled in Jesus Christ. Jesus is the blameless believer. And as we see in the Gospels, Satan focuses his attack on Jesus with an even greater ferocity than upon Job. From Herod's attempt to have him slaughtered as a toddler through the temptations in the wilderness to the agony of the cross, Satan tears at Jesus' soul—by temptation, discouragement, loneliness, betrayal, misunderstanding, and agony. Day by day the Lord Jesus awoke to dark warfare.

Indeed Job is fulfilled in Jesus, and every follower of Jesus is called to follow in the footsteps of Job. Job foreshadows Jesus, and the disciple cannot avoid the shadow. As Jesus said to Simon Peter, "Simon, Simon, behold, Satan demanded to have you [plural], that he might sift you like wheat, but I have prayed for you [singular] that your faith may not fail" (Luke 22:31, 32).

Jesus did not pray that his disciples would be spared the sifting and that Satan would be forbidden his demand. Rather he expected the demand would be granted, as it had been for Job. And he prays that in this painful sifting Simon's faith may not fail. We ought to expect this. Every morning we ought to wake up and say to ourselves, "There is a vicious, dark spiritual battle being waged over me today." Satan is very busy; wherever on earth there is a believer walking with God in loving fear, God says, "Look, there's a believer," and Satan says, "May I attack him/her? I want to prove whether this is a real believer." And sometimes the Lord grants that terrible permission. When he does, we ought not to be surprised, "as though something strange were happening" to us (1 Peter 4:12).

Patricia St. John wrote a poem called "The Alchemist" in which she said:

> God seeks no second site on which to build,
> But on the old foundation, stone by stone,
> Cementing sad experience with grace,
> Fashions a stronger temple of his own.

So here is one inescapable element of the normal Christian life: warfare. That expectation relates to our circumstances. The second relates to our attitude of heart.

Perseverance in Waiting

Job perseveres by waiting, an active prayer-filled waiting. In 42:7 God says to Eliphaz, "You have not spoken of me what is right, as my servant Job has." Now on the face of it this is a surprising thing for God to say. It is not surprising to us that God says the friends were wrong, but it ought to surprise us that the Lord says that in some way Job is right, for again and again Job says terrible things about God. And yet in spite of the fact that Job charges God with being a wrongdoer (which is both serious and untrue, and God has rebuked him for it), God can say at the end that Job has spoken rightly of him. How is this?

It is possible that God's affirmation refers only to Job's humble response to God's speeches (40:3–5; 42:1–6), and it is true that this is "the simplest and clearest explanation" of what God says here.[1] And yet I think there is a deeper truth here. It seems to me that God's affirmation applies somehow not only to what Job has said but to who Job is. The answer would seem to be this: the friends have a theological scheme, a tidy system, well-swept, well-defined, and entirely satisfying to them. But they have no relationship with the God behind their formulas. There is no wonder, no awe, no longing, no yearning, and no prayer to meet and speak with and hear and see the God of their formulas. They are content with the rules of The System they have invented.

Now some of their statements considered on their own are correct. For example, in 5:13 Eliphaz says that God "catches the wise in their own craftiness"; the clever person will be called to account by God. That is true, and we have seen that Paul quotes Eliphaz with approval in 1 Corinthians 3:19. But although the friends make some statements that are true, they do not as a whole speak rightly of God because they have no relationship with God, no seeking of God, and no longing for God. For them he is a dead doctrine and an abstract theory.

But Job does speak rightly. We have seen that one of the great motifs of Job's laments is that he longs to bring his perplexity to God himself. Job cannot be satisfied with any system: he must know God and speak to the living God. He must, for nothing else will satisfy him. This heart longing of Job is the core reason why the Lord says Job has spoken rightly of him. And of course it leads to Job's speaking rightly of the Lord in his humble responses to the Lord's speeches. The rightness of Job's heart throughout leads to the repentance of Job's lips at the end. The unambiguously "right" thing he says is at the end, but all his words have sprung from the heart of a believer. While the friends want a system, Job wants God. The friends would not have been at church prayer meetings—they had no need. But Job would if he could: "Oh, that I knew where I might find him" (23:3).

The Lord's response to Job is instructive. In his affirmation of Job, in spite of the terrible things Job says about God, "we are forcibly reminded that God, for all his rough handling of his servant's rude demands, reads between the lines and listens to the heart."[2]

We ought to expect that the normal Christian life will be full of unresolved waiting and yearning for God. This is the mark of a believer, of real and personal religion. So we should never be fatalists. A fatalist looks at circumstances and says, "What will be, will be—there is some impersonal power up there sorting it all out." Sometimes we Christians say that, but we ought not to. We ought to say, "What is God doing, the God who is my maker and my friend? Where is this personal God in all this? If only I could speak to him; if only I might find him." Such directed, prayer-filled, intentional waiting is the integrating arrow of hope that holds together the authentic Christian life.

So we learn from the perseverance of Job that we ought to expect warfare and waiting, struggle and prayer. Now let us move on from the perseverance of Job to the mercy of God.

The Compassion and Mercy of the Lord

James says, "You have . . . seen the purpose of the Lord, how the Lord is compassionate and merciful" (James 5:11).

Few of us would have described God's behavior in Job as "compassionate and merciful." After all, was it not under God's sovereignty that the Satan was sent to destroy Job's possessions, to kill Job's children, and to ruin Job's health? Yes, it was. The book is quite clear about that. Is that compassion and mercy? Not obviously. It would be more common to say of God that he never really cared about Job, that he is some kind of bitter and distant deity.[3]

Earlier we considered the analogy of the Satan as a fierce dog biting someone and yet held on a leash by its master. However, in normal life we hold the owner responsible for the violence inflicted by the dog, and the book of Job makes no attempt to dodge this objection. We saw at the start that there is no hesitation both at start and finish in insisting that the Lord alone is the Sovereign God. The Satan is not an equal and opposite power, so that God says, "I'm doing my best to protect you, but I can't win them all." There is no dualism here. God is in control, and he is responsible for what happens.

So what does James mean when he says, "The Lord is compassionate and merciful" (5:11)? He says this because of "the purpose of the Lord," referring to the end or goal for which God has been working. We see this end in Job 42. Here are three elements from Job 42 of the compassion and mercy of the Lord.

Humbling (42:1–6)

Let us go back to verses 1–6 for a moment and see how God loves Job enough to humble him. When God speaks, Job responds with few words and silent awe. We see this in 40:4, 5 and again in 42:1–6. Job says:

> [T]herefore I despise myself,
>   and repent in dust and ashes. (42:6)

When Job says he repents, he does not mean the friends have been right all along, that Job has secret sins and finally has to admit them and repent. He maintains his integrity at the end as he has all along. But he realizes he has been presumptuous: he has spoken of things he does not understand and has overreached himself (42:3). Now in the presence of the living God he bows down in silent worship.

And that is a good thing! For Job to be brought low so that he despises himself and exalts God is not a bad thing. We understand that for us to go around thinking we are worms in relation to our fellow human beings is a destructive thing. That kind of inferiority complex, pathological low self-esteem, is not to be encouraged. In a sense it's better to say, "I'm OK; you're OK," as the pop psychology book had it. But in the presence of the living God, to bow down low and to grasp how great he is and how small I am is a healthy thing—because it is true. It is a mark of the love of God that he brings Job low, for this is where a creature ought to be.[4]

That is true for us as well. We often pray for success, both for us and for others; we pray for good exam results, for good job offers, etc. And yet so often success leads to pride, and pride to self-confidence, and self-confidence to independence from God, and independence from God leads to Hell. The most deeply compassionate and merciful thing God can do is to humble us and bring us low so that we bow before him and lean on him and trust him. That is the first mark of the compassion of God: he loves enough to humble us, as he humbled Job, under his mighty hand.

Perhaps for some of us there has been, or there will be, a time in life when everything goes wrong. A time perhaps of pain and failure, even of disaster and misery. And it may be that God in his compassion is bringing us low so that we will lean on him alone. This was for Job a hard truth, but it was nonetheless a mark of the mercy of God that he would bring Job very low.

Acceptance (42:7–9)

The technical term is *justification*. God vindicates Job; he declares him to be in the right. God acknowledges Job as one of his people. We saw earlier how desperately Job longs for this. God does this in three ways.

First, in verse 7 he says that Job has spoken rightly of him, whereas the friends have not.

Second, in verse 7 (once) and verse 8 (twice) God calls Job "my servant" exactly as he had done in Job 1, 2. This is a title of dignity; it is how God characteristically described Moses and the prophets. It is a word that speaks of covenant relationship.

Third, in an ironic reversal the friends are told that Job will pray for them. If we had been Job's friends, we would have been stunned, for we would have expected God to take us to one side and say, "I want you three, because you are righteous and the prayer of a righteous man has great power in its effects [James 5:16], to pray for that sinner Job." But in fact God does the reverse. Job, the intercessor and bearer of sacrifices at the start (1:5), now intercedes for those who offer sacrifices at the end (42:8). And this means it is Job who is righteous, justified, vindicated, in right relation with the Lord. Only people in right relationship with God can pray and expect their prayers to be answered. The one who longed for a mediator (9:33; 16:19; 19:25) becomes the mediator and foreshadows the only mediator between God and people, the man Christ Jesus (1 Timothy 2:5). Indeed, Job "has always been a man of prayer.

Even his fiercest denunciations have been a determination not to let God go until he blesses him."[5]

So in these three ways God makes it clear that he accepts Job. "This man is mine; he belongs to me, and I will make sure he is mine forever.'" And this justification, this right relationship with God, is what Job has so deeply longed for throughout the drama. It is a mark of the mercy of God that he vindicates Job. And if we are in Christ, God will vindicate us. At the end he will look on each of us and say, "This one is mine; they belong to me; he or she is my honored servant." It is hard to think of a greater mark of God's compassion and mercy than this, however hard the path we tread to get there.

Blessing in the End (42:10–17)

And then, lastly, God blesses Job. The end comes at the end. He gives him greater prosperity in a restoration of his fortunes (v. 10) that foreshadows the return of Judah from exile[6] and ultimately foreshadows the resurrection, ascension, and heavenly rule of the Lord Jesus Christ. Job receives sympathy and comfort that echoes the intention of his three friends (compare v. 11 with 2:11) but achieves that which they failed to achieve. God gives him renewed celebration (v. 11); this meal is the first celebration since 1:4. His isolation is replaced by a joyful return to life among others. Joy comes back into his life. God gives him a new and bigger family, with daughters of legendary beauty (v. 15). He gives him a long life, double the normal three score years and ten (v. 16). What are we to make of this?

Let us note that God *first* restored Job to relationship and then blessed him. Job cried out, "now my eye sees you" (42:5) before he was blessed. This is important. Job proves he is a real believer because he bows down to God in a time of pain. It is not that God first blesses him and then Job says, "You seem to be a good God after all; I will worship you." He worships because God is God, and then in the end he is blessed. And when he worships he has no proof or certainty that he will be blessed. He lives by faith, not by sight.

Also let us note that the blessing is not a reward for worship. It is not that God says, "Well done, old chap. You've persevered jolly well; now you can have the sweets I promised you." Not at all. In fact the doubling of his wealth points to grace; God is pouring out undeserved blessing. We must never see the sufferings of Job as undermining the grace of God. God is no man's debtor.

But the most important thing about the blessing is that it happens *at the end*. James understands this perfectly: "Be patient, therefore, brothers, *until the coming of the Lord*. . . . You have heard of the steadfastness of Job, and you have seen the purpose of the Lord, how the Lord is compassionate and merciful" (James 5:7, 11).

The purpose of the Lord to show mercy and compassion will be seen finally only when the Lord Jesus returns in glory. Job 42 anticipates the return of the Lord Jesus Christ. Like all the Old Testament types of Christ, Job dies at the end of his story (v. 17); and his death proves he is not the one to come, but merely one in whose sufferings are foreshadowed that one whose sandals neither Job nor any Old Testament prophet nor even John the Baptist will be worthy to untie.

The end comes at the end. The normal Christian life is warfare and waiting and being loved and humbled by God and being justified by God, all in the here and now. But it is the expectation of blessing *at the end*. Often we do get blessed now. God graciously pours out all manner of blessings here and now. But the blessings we get now are just a tiny foretaste of the blessings to be poured out at the end.

And the blessings God will pour out on the believer at the end will be every bit as *real* as the blessings of Job. Job knew real prosperity, real joy and celebration, real fruitfulness and real beauty (his dazzling daughters). The blessings of the new heavens and new earth will be rock-solid real. We look forward to beauty that makes the most beautiful woman in the world seem dull. We look forward to fruitfulness that will make the most abundant family in the world seem barren. We look forward to prosperity that will make the Forbes list of the world's billionaires seem poor. And we look forward to celebration that will make the best party in the world seem like a quiet glass of apple juice. So as we end this study, let us remember what we ought to expect of the normal Christian life. Let us see what Job foreshadowed, now fulfilled in the sufferings, faith, life, death, resurrection, ascension, and heavenly reign of Jesus Christ. Let us expect to suffer with him if we will ultimately reign with him, for by grace we will.

Conclusion

So What Is the Book of Job All About?

TOO OFTEN WE COME TO the book of Job (as to other parts of the Bible) expecting answers to our questions, and especially to questions about suffering. The main human character certainly suffers, but the book of Job is not fundamentally about suffering. Job suffers *because he is a believer*, and he suffers *as a believer*. And because he is a suffering *believer* the central character and subject of the book of Job is not Job who suffers but about the God with whom he has to deal. The book of Job is about God. This ought not to surprise us, but it is easy to forget. If we take our eye off the central focus and major instead on suffering, we will be disappointed, for we do not find in Job the answers to the questions we have chosen to pose.

Instead we find what Job found when he ultimately had to listen to God: God asks him questions more than Job poses puzzlers to God. And this turns the tables, as they must be turned. The book of Job is not about Job but about God—his character, sovereignty, justice, goodness and, yes, even his love. Above all it is about God the Creator of everything, the One who is God, who made everything, even the wildest corners of the created order. He is the God who made and who entirely controls the Leviathan, the Satan, the beast and monster who seeks to destroy Job. Even this hideous monster is God's monster, God's creature.

And therefore Job is about true worship, about our bowing down in reality and in the darkness to the One who is God, leaving even our most agonized unanswered questions at his feet, for we are creatures, and he alone is the Creator.

Because Job is about God and the worship of God, it is also about humility—the humility to admit (as Job 28 shows) that there is so much about this world that we do not understand. Wisdom with a capital W is God's preserve. It is presumptuous of us to act as if we had made the world, which is what we do the moment we suggest that we could run this world better than God. Humility means to do precisely what Job was doing at the beginning and what 28:28 affirms: to bow before God in loving fear and to "turn away from evil." In New Testament terms it is to repent and believe, to hear and to heed the gospel. Here is the gospel in Job—repentance and faith practiced at the start and repentance and faith affirmed at the end.

But of course Job is also about Job. He is the central human character in the drama, introduced at the start and blessed at the end. He is addressed personally by the Lord, whereas the other human characters are either ignored or rebuked. So Job points us to the mystery at the heart of the universe: a blameless believer who walks in fellowship with his Creator may suffer terrible and undeserved pain, may go through deep darkness and then at the end be vindicated. There is such a thing in the universe as suffering that is not a punishment for the sin of the sufferer.

And therefore Job is passionately and profoundly about Jesus, whom Job foreshadows both in his blamelessness and in his perseverance through undeserved suffering. As the blameless believer par excellence, Jesus fulfills Job. As a priestly figure who offers sacrifices for his children at the start and his friends at the end, Job foreshadows Jesus the great High Priest. The monstrous ferocity of the beast Leviathan reaches its vicious depths in the life and death of Jesus, who in his passion endures deeper depths and a more solemn and awesome darkness even than Job. The drama, the pain, and the perplexity of Job reach their climax at the cross of Jesus Christ. In the darkness and God-forsakenness of those terrible hours of lonely agony, the sufferings of Job are transcended and fulfilled. And as the blameless believer accused and despised by men but finally vindicated by God in the resurrection, Jesus fulfills the drama and longings of Job for justification.

And because Job is about Jesus, it is also, derivatively, about every man and woman in Christ. Every disciple, called to take up the cross and walk in the footsteps of Christ, must expect in some measure to walk also in the footsteps of Job. So in the end we may conclude that Job is in some measure about us. Not primarily about us, for it is above all about God. Not centrally about us, for its central human character foreshadows Jesus Christ. But for each of us as a believer walking through this world in union with Christ, Job is an unavoidable part of the pathway of faith. Our final justification will come through present suffering. Those who today are not recognized as children of God will one day publicly be acknowledged as his (see Romans 8:19). So as we return again and again to this book of Job and meditate on its depths, let us pray to be given grace to bow down, especially in the darkness, to the God who is God. It is this God, who is God even of the wild, evil, and seemingly random fringes of life, whom we are called to love and to trust. In the footsteps of the Lord Jesus we too may entrust ourselves "to him who judges justly" (1 Peter 2:23).

Soli Deo gloria!

Bibliography

Commentaries on Job

Ash, Christopher, *Out of the Storm: Grappling with God in the Book of Job* (Leicester, UK: IVP, 2004).

Atkinson, David, *The Message of Job*, The Bible Speaks Today (Leicester, UK: IVP, 1991).

Benfold, Gary, *Why Lord? The Book of Job for Today* (Epsom, Surrey, UK: Day One, 1998).

Clines, David J. A., *Job 1—20* (Dallas: Word Books, 1989).

————, *Job 21—37* (Dallas: Word Books, 2006).

————, *Job 38—42* (Dallas: Word Books, 2011).

Gordis, Robert, *The Book of Job* (New York: The Jewish Theological Seminary of America, 1978).

Habel, Norman C., *The Book of Job* (Philadelphia: Westminster Press, 1985).

Hartley, John E., *The Book of Job*, New International Commentary on the Old Testament (Grand Rapids, MI: Eerdmans, 1988).

Janzen, J. Gerald, *Job*, Press Interpretation series (Atlanta: John Knox, 1985).

Jones, Hywel R., *Job* (Darlington, UK: Evangelical Press, 2007).

Pope, Marvin H., *Job*, The Anchor Vale Bible (New Haven, CT and London: Yale University Press, 1965).

Rowley, H. H., *The Book of Job*, The New Century Bible Commentary (Grand Rapids, MI: Eerdmans, 1980).

Other Books Relating to Job

Fyall, Robert S., *Now My Eyes Have Seen You: Images of Creation and Evil in the Book of Job* (Leicester, UK: IVP, 2002).

————, *How Does God Treat His Friends?* (Fearn, Ross-Shire, UK: Christian Focus, 1995).

Glatzer, Nahum N. (ed.), *The Dimensions of Job: A Study and Selected Readings* (New York: Schocken Books, 1969).

Gordis, Robert, *The Book of God and Man: A Study of Job* (Chicago and London: University of Chicago Press, 1965).

Kidner, Derek, *Wisdom to Live by: An Introduction to the Old Testament's Wisdom Books of Proverbs, Job and Ecclesiastes* (Leicester, UK: IVP, 1985), especially chapters 4 and 5 (on Job).

Morgan, G. Campbell, *The Answers of Jesus to Job* (London: Oliphants, 1964).

Acknowledgments

I am grateful to IVP (UK) for permission to make use of material first published in *Out of the Storm: Grappling with God in the Book of Job,* my first attempt at opening up the book of Job. That short volume had its origin in a sermon series preached in All Saints, Little Shelford near Cambridge, England and is dedicated to "all the saints at All Saints, Little Shelford." I remain grateful to them for their love and encouragement in those early days. I am also grateful to many other congregations and conferences who have allowed me to preach from Job, including the Klang Valley Bible Conference in Malaysia, the Timothy Project in Singapore, the City Partnership Summer School from St. Helen's Bishopsgate in London, and the students of Moore Theological College in Sydney. But most of all I am thankful to God for ten cohorts of students at the Proclamation Trust's Cornhill Training Course, who have sharpened up my thinking year after year.

I thank God for the patience and prayers of my wife Carolyn and of our daughter Lizzie, who was living at home during the writing of the book. I am grateful also to Beckie Hollands, my PA, for her help in all sorts of practical ways and for reading through the manuscript.

My own interest in Job was first stirred by Bob Fyall's excellent and provocatively entitled book *How Does God Treat His Friends?* I have also been helped by commentaries, especially those of Hywel R. Jones, Norman C. Habel, and John E. Hartley, and by Bob Fyall's scholarly work *Now My Eyes Have seen You.*

To Bob Fyall in particular my debt is considerable, both in exegesis and in illustrative material.

Notes

Where no page number is given in a commentary citation, the reference is to where the commentator is expounding the verse under consideration. For full source information on quoted works, see Bibliography.

Preface
1. Quoted in Gordis, p. xii.
2. G. Campbell Morgan, *The Answers of Jesus to Job*, p. 9.

Introduction: What Is Job All About?
1. All Saints, Little Shelford near Cambridge, England. These studies were first expanded and written up in a shorter book, *Out of the Storm: Grappling with God in the Book of Job* (Leicester, England: IVP, 2004).
2. Paraphrase of Job 21 from *The Message*.
3. *Romeo and Juliet*, Act II, Scene II.
4. Gerard Manley Hopkins, "Sonnet 41."
5. Gordis, p. xi.
6. *The Week*, September 20, 2008, p. 13.
7. In an interview Rico Tice once said, ". . . the gospel is not, 'Oh Lord, my life is empty, fill me.' The gospel is 'Oh Lord, I'm an offence to you, rescue me.'" *Christianity* magazine, July 2011, pp. 21–23.
8. Susie Orbach, *Bodies* (London : Profile Books, 2009), p. 55ff.
9. Quoted from Gaius Davies, *Genius, Grief and Grace* (Fearn, Ross-shire, UK: Christian Focus, 2001), p. 8.
10. Gordis, p. xxv.

The Structure of the Book of Job
1. I have generally followed the persuasive structural analysis of Norman C. Habel here. See Habel, *The Book of Job*, pp. 26, 27.
2. See the exposition of chapter 28 for discussion of the "voice" we hear in this chapter.

Chapter One: Welcome to a Well-Run World
1. Gordis suggests that since Nathan uses this formula, "there was a man" to introduce his parable in 2 Samuel 12:1, the words indicate to us that the book of Job is a fictional narrative. But as both Hartley and Clines say, this is a non sequitur. There is good reason to believe that Job was a historical figure, and the references to him in Ezekiel 14:14, 20 support this. But see Daniel J. Estes, "Fiction and Truth in the Old Testament Wisdom Literature," *Themelios* 35-3 for the view that "The book of Job . . . may well be explained . . . as a divinely-inspired work of imaginative literature, in which the author explores the lofty theme of the problem of evil by setting forth an ideal case study and then by constructing a series of speeches that represent the best efforts by humans to resolve the issue" (p. 18).

2. So Gordis and Clines. In addition to this, the clearest clue, there are two others. In Genesis 36:28 and 1 Chronicles 1:42, Uz is the son of an Edomite tribal chieftain. And in Genesis 22:21 a man named Uz is the brother of Buz, which appears as a place name in Jeremiah 25:23 in association with Dedan and Tema, towns in northwest Arabia, not far south of Edom.

3. Clines.

4. So Clines, Hartley. Gordis, admitting that it was a common name in the second millennium B.C., thinks it had a folk etymology from the verb "to hate" and meant something like "the hated, persecuted one." But the evidence for this is not conclusive. More likely, as Clines says, "in the Old Testament context the name has no particular significance, and nothing in the man's name, any more than in his character, presages his history."

5. Clines.

6. Gordis.

7. Hartley.

8. Here he uses an adjectival form from the same root.

9. C. Bridges.

10. "And . . ." Contemporary English translations do not translate the *waw* consecutive here. While it is not necessary to translate it, here it does seem to reinforce the implicit message that Job's prosperity was in some way the result of his piety. Clines says it "delicately suggests" this connection.

11. See Hartley.

12. In 31:38–40 Job speaks of his land and what grew on it.

13. Critics who suggest that the Job of the prose prologue is a city dweller, whereas the Job of the poetic dialogues is a seminomad, are thinking too woodenly. As Gottwald observes, "agriculture and pastoral nomadism are by no means mutually exclusive" (quoted in Hartley, p. 68, note 18).

14. Gordis says there is no suggestion that Job's sons were "inveterate revelers devoting themselves exclusively to extended feasting and riotous living."

15. So Gordis, who points out that this makes sense of Eliphaz pulling rank on him in 15:10 and of the vehemence of Job's grief. This is not an old man facing death; it is a man in the prime of life.

16. This is the likely meaning of "when the days of the feast had run their course." It may mean a once-a-year event, when all seven birthday parties had finished (as Gordis suggests), but more likely Job did this at the end of each party (so Clines).

Chapter Two: The Testing of Your Faith

1. *The Valley of Vision: A Collection of Puritan Prayers and Devotions* (Edinburgh: Banner of Truth, 1975), p. 13.

2. I have rendered the Hebrew literally, "the Satan" (ESV, "Satan"). It has the article here and in Zechariah 3:1, 2. In 1 Chronicles 21:1 "Satan" appears as a proper name without the article.

3. So Clines.

4. This is a famously puzzling passage. It is not clear whether these are heavenly creatures or powerful human princes.

5. Gordis rightly rejects the suggestion that this expression means here "to stand *against* God."

6. So Clines.

7. As, for example, in this word's use in Genesis 23:10 (where Ephron sits "among" his fellow-Hittites), in Genesis 40:20 (where the baker and cupbearer are "among" Pharaoh's servants), or 2 Kings 4:13 ("I dwell among my own people").

8. Janzen.

9. Archibald MacLeish, in his play *JB*, has one of his characters repeat this refrain (Boston: Houghton Mifflin Company, Sentry Edition, 1956), p. 11.

10. The same word is used in Numbers 11:8 of the people going about looking for manna and in Jeremiah 5:1 of the prophet running to and fro through the streets of Jerusalem searching for a righteous man.

11. Bob Fyall's excellent introduction to Job is entitled *How Does God Treat His Friends?*

12. John Chrysostom, *St. Chrysostom's Homilies on the Gospel of St. John and the Epistle to the Hebrews*, Nicene and Post-Nicene Fathers of the Christian Church, Part 14.

13. So Gordis.

14. Kidner, p. 56.

15. Clines.

16. As Clines vividly paraphrases the colloquial and impudent speech of the Satan here.

17. Clines makes the interesting suggestion that the Satan's role is analogous to the role of the "devil's advocate," the *advocatus diaboli*, in the Roman Catholic process for testing a claim to canonization. Those who support canonization ask the "devil's advocate" to test the claim ruthlessly to make quite sure that it is genuine before going ahead. Although the "devil's advocate" speaks against the candidate, his role is necessary in order to make sure that the successful candidacy will be seen to be beyond criticism.

18. Clines says that the Satan is "a manifestation of the divine doubt, an embodiment of the demonic wrath of God, an expression of the 'dark' and sinister side of the divine personality." Clines admits that his reading "is not—we may suppose—the storyteller's intention." Indeed it is not.

19. G. Campbell Morgan, *The Answers of Jesus to Job*, p. 19.

20. The technical term for this sub-Christian theology is Open Theism. There are good discussions and critiques of it, including Bruce A. Ware, *God's Lesser Glory* (Wheaton: Crossway, 2000) and John M. Frame, *No Other God: A Response to Open Theism* (Phillipsburg, NJ: P&R, 2001).

21. The Sabeans may be from Sheba (i.e., Shabeans), "a distant land" in southwest Arabia (1 Kings 10:1; Isaiah 60:6; Jeremiah 6:20). Or they may be from northern Arabia. See Gordis.

22. In 2 Kings 1:10 lightning is called "fire . . . from heaven" and in Numbers 11:1 "the fire of the LORD."

23. "The young people" is the same word as used earlier for the farm servants, but clearly here it includes Job's children (as is clear from Bildad's barbed statement in 8:4).

24. So Fohrer (in Clines).

25. The words, "Blessed be the name of the LORD" are the same as in Psalm 113:2.

26. This may mean something like "the skin of others—the outer skin of my possessions and family—will be sacrificed if I can keep my own skin, my own life and health."

27. Both are quoted in Clines.

28. As Rashi suggested. See Clines, p. 55.

29. As Clines puts it, "it is of the essence of the Book of Job that from this critical moment onward heaven is sealed off and silent."

30. "His body is already speaking for him; the damaged and broken skin represents the onset of Job's breakdown" (Kahn, quoted in Clines).

Chapter Three: The Loneliness of Job

1. "For the news to reach the Friends in their several countries and for them to arrange for a meeting suggest that Job's suffering has extended over a considerable period of time" (Gordis). Clines suggests an interval of some weeks, or possibly months.

2. Clines unkindly suggests that they came together because Job was now a dangerous person publicly to associate with, and they needed to protect one another from becoming contaminated by contact with him. But if this was in their minds, why come at all?

3. ". . . to show . . . sympathy" means to shake the head to and fro as an act of identification with the sufferer (Clines).

4. Jones.

5. Ibid. This positive reading of their motives is in accord with the text so far. Clines is unjustifiably skeptical of their motives.

6. See Janzen, p. 57.

7. The genealogy also appears in 1 Chronicles 1:32.

8. Gordis.

9. Janzen, p. 58.

10. Clines suggests we should take "recognize" in the sense of "acknowledge," rather as one government might "recognize" another. He cites Genesis 37:32, 33, where Jacob recognizes (acknowledges) that the bloodstained robe is Joseph's, and Genesis 38:25, 26, where Judah is asked by Tamar to recognize (that is, to acknowledge) that the staff she holds belongs to him. The friends will not acknowledge Job as a living being with whom they can have relationship.

11. Janzen notes this sad contrast.

12. Clines.

13. The expression "sprinkled dust on their heads *toward heaven*" has suggested some strange interpretations. Gordis thinks it was "an apotropaic rite, in order to ward off the evil from themselves," but this seems speculative, and he gives no evidence for this reading. Habel compares it to Moses's throwing soot into the air to bring boils on Egypt (Exodus 9:10) and suggests the friends are symbolically calling forth "the same sickness on themselves" as has fallen on Job "as an act of total empathy. They are one with the dust of death and one with Job in his distress." This also seems unlikely.

14. Gordis.

15. Atkinson, p. 29.

16. Habel, p. 98.

17. Ewald, Peake, Andersen, all quoted in Clines, p. 64.

18. Clines.

19. Ben Sirach (Ecclesiasticus) 22:12 says, "Mourning for the dead lasts seven days."

20. Rowley.

21. Quoted in *The Dimensions of Job: A Study and Selected Readings*, ed. Nahum N. Glatzer (New York: Schocken Books, 1969), p. ix.

22. Charles H. Gabriel, "I Stand Amazed in the Presence," 1905.

23. Jean Danielou, quoted in *The Dimensions of Job: A Study and Selected Readings*, p. 109.

Chapter Four: Weep with Those Who Weep

1. Fyall, p. 102.

2. Janzen: "In words addressed to no one but himself, and thereby in words which deepen his solitariness, Job speaks" (p. 61).

3. See Chapter 3 in Gaius Davies, *Genius, Grief and Grace* (Fearn, Ross-shire, UK: Christian Focus, 2001).

4. The similarities between this lament and Job 3 are unlikely to indicate any literary dependence. Clines is right to say they probably reflect a common tradition of lament.

5. Fyall, p. 33.

6. John Gibson, "Jesus, We Celebrate Your Victory," 1987.

7. Dave Bilbrough, "I Am a New Creation," 1983.

8. Chris Williams, Paul Richards, Ingrid Whitton, *I'm Not Supposed to Feel Like This* (London: Hodder, 2002).

9. Clines observes that here we move "from the external description of suffering to Job's inner experience."

10. Habel rightly says Job did not curse God but came to "the brink of cursing God." Had he done so, his protestations of innocence later would be empty.

11. Compare Pharaoh's day (his "birthday") in Genesis 40:20. Clines suggests that "his day" in Job 3 is a way of speaking of his whole life, as in 30:25: "him whose day was hard." But in view of how the curse goes on in verse 3, it seems better to translate this "the day of his birth."

12. The word *geber*, used here, "connotes a powerful man . . . a full-blooded, stalwart person . . . a distinguished person" (Hartley, p. 92).

13. Arthur Koestler's evocative title.

14. The compound word *tsalmaweth*, translated "deep darkness," is sometimes translated, from its separate parts, "shadow of death."

15. Clines.

16. Janzen calls it "this cry of sexual ecstasy." Clines says, "The 'cry of joy' . . . he wishes had never been uttered is the sound of his parents' lovemaking that resulted in his conception."

17. But not to "control" him (TEV—*Good News Bible*) or "tame" him (NEB). The verb is the same as in 41:10.

18. Clines, p. 79.

19. Closing the doors may possibly refer to preventing the fetus from emerging from the womb alive. But the opening of the womb in Bible imagery refers elsewhere to conception, as, for example, when the Lord "opened [the] womb" of Leah (Genesis 29:31) or "closed [the] womb" of Hannah (1 Samuel 1:5).

20. Clines (p. 97) correctly identifies verse 26 as the "nodal verse" and comments that the presence of turmoil and the absence of rest is "the dominant image of the poem."

21. Janzen (p. 61) describes this as Job's "existential contraction and expansion."

22. So, for example, Gordis and Pope.

23. The ESV takes it this way.

24. Hartley. The word "house" is used for Sheol in 17:13 ("If I hope for Sheol as my house . . ."). It is called "the house appointed for all living" in 30:23. Ecclesiastes speaks of man "going to his eternal home" (Ecclesiastes 12:5). Ezekiel 26:20 speaks of the pit (Sheol) as a place of "ruins."

25. Clines is right to reject this suggestion of Davidson.

26. I owe the central insight of my analysis here to Clines, who seems to me to be persuasive.

27. Ecclesiastes 6:4, 5 echoes this sentiment.

28. Primo Levi, *If This Is a Man and The Truce* (London: Penguin, 1979) p. 379ff.

29. Clines comments that Job's anxiety arises "from the intellectual-existential significance of what has happened to him. The suffering and the loss is one thing, but it is not on the same level as the mind-blowing and foundation-shaking threat that the exceptional suffering of the exceptionally pious poses for OT notions of cosmic order, divine justice and human values" (p. 91).

30. The repetition of the words "why is light given" from verse 20 are not in the Hebrew but are implied and have to be supplied in English translations to make it readable English.

31. Quoted by Clines regarding verse 22.

32. Quoted in Fyall, p. 39.

33. The word is different but synonymous.

34. We see this same imagery in Lamentations 3:7 ("He has walled me about so that I cannot escape") and in Hosea 2:6 ("Therefore I will hedge up her way with thorns").

35. Hartley.

36. C. S. Lewis, *A Grief Observed* (London: Faber, 1966), p. 7.

Chapter 5: Introducing Job's Comforters

1. Helmut Thielicke, *The Prayer That Spans the World: Sermons on the Lord's Prayer* (Cambridge, UK: James Clarke, 1960), p. 65ff.

Chapter 6: Eliphaz's First Speech

1. Clines refers to "the general consolatory tendency of this speech" and says that Eliphaz is "the kindliest representative of the orthodox dogmatic position" (p. 123).

2. Habel, p. 118ff. argues persuasively that there is no reason to take Eliphaz's mood here as belligerent or paternalistic.

3. Eliphaz "responds to Job diffidently and tentatively, seeking to offer him the encouraging advice he formerly had offered others in times of their misfortune" (Janzen). He "shares a common heritage with Job" (Habel).

4. See Ezekiel 7:17 ("All hands are feeble, and all knees turn to water") or Ezekiel 21:7, where the expression is associated with a melting heart. Hebrews 12:12 refers to "drooping hands . . . weak knees."

5. Job himself portrays this beautifully in chapter 29.

6. Cf. Matthew 27:42: "He saved others; he cannot save himself."

7. NIV "strikes" is better than ESV "touches," which is too weak a word.

8. The word "pious" expresses well what is literally "your fear," that is, the fear of God.

9. As in Psalm 18:15, "at the blast of the breath of your nostrils."

10. See also Proverbs 28:15 where a wicked ruler is compared to "a roaring lion or a charging bear."

11. Habel translates this "in the traumas of night visions."

12. Habel calls it a "bizarre collage" of experiences that "has no identified origin and is delivered by no known messenger. Eliphaz' message is a faint sound uttered by a fleeting spectre."

13. Andersen, in Clines, says it is "very spooky."

14. So Clines, Habel.

15. See Jantzen, p. 73ff.

16. See also 10:9; 33:6.

17. Or possibly we are so fragile that a moth can squash us. Habel thinks this is the meaning and that it represents "rich ironic style."

18. Similarly violent imagery is used in Isaiah 30:14: "its breaking is like that of a potter's vessel that is smashed so ruthlessly that among its fragments not a shard is found with which to take fire from the hearth, or to dip up water out of the cistern."

19. Paul uses this same "tent" imagery for human fragility in 2 Corinthians 5:1ff. Peter does the same in 2 Peter 1:13 ("body" in that verse is literally "tent").

20. Hartley.

21. ". . . and I declared his estate to be suddenly cursed" (Hartley). "And at once I declared his dwelling would be cursed" (Habel); so also Gordis.

22. So NIV "suddenly his house was cursed," following the LXX by translating with a passive (so also Pope, Rowley).

23. So Habel, Pope. The imagery of devouring is used of death in 18:13: "It consumes the parts of his skin; the firstborn of death consumes his limbs."

24. See Fyall, p. 118ff. Reshef (or Resheph) was a god of plague and pestilence.

25. Habel, Pope.

26. Habel's word.

27. The phrase "But if it were me" (v. 8a) gets the sense well.

28. Very much as in Hannah's song (1 Samuel 2:1–10) or Mary's song (Luke 1:46–55).

29. Proverbs 3:11, 12; Psalm 94:12; 118:18; Hebrews 12:5–11.

30. So Hartley, p. 128: "Eliphaz sides with the Satan against God . . . for he seeks to motivate Job to serve God for the benefits that piety brings."

31. "Understandably Eliphaz does not yet realize that Job has lost confidence in the God of his past religion" (Habel).

Chapter Seven: Job's First Reply to Eliphaz

1. *As You Like It*, Act 2, Scene 1.
2. The NIV translates the word consistently as "terrors" in both verses.
3. Habel, p. 141.
4. Habel uses this striking expression. For Job, above is the spy and tormentor of mankind, below is the place of peace. "Thus the hierarchy of good is reversed; the underworld, the earth, and the heavens become the sufferer's ranking of desirable realms in the cosmos."
5. The word "crush" appears also in 4:19; 5:4; 22:9; 34:25.
6. See also 27:8: ". . . when God cuts him off" and Isaiah 38:12: ". . . he cuts me off from the loom."
7. Jones.
8. So Clines, persuasively. The alternative interpretations of Habel, Pope, and Hartley are less persuasive.
9. In 5:12 Eliphaz says God "frustrates the devices of the crafty, so that their hands achieve no success." It is the same word (translated "success" in both places in the NIV).
10. Some translate verse 14 to mean that friends ought to continue to show kindness even when someone forsakes the fear of the Almighty. This seems unlikely, not least since Job maintains that this is not true of him.
11. Psalm 37:20 uses the similar image of smoke vanishing to speak of God's judgment on the wicked.
12. From Dante's *Inferno*.

Chapter Eight: Bildad's First Speech

1. Jones: "There is nothing theoretical about it."
2. See Gordis, "Special Note 10," p. 521; also Hartley, Habel, Janzen.
3. Hartley.

Chapter Nine: Job's First Reply to Bildad

1. Habel suggests this should be translated "He [i.e., God] would not answer one charge in a thousand," the problem being that we cannot summon God into court. While this is true, Hartley is probably right (with the ESV) to see that the problem is human inability to answer God. As Hartley points out, this is what happens at the end of the book: Job does not and cannot answer God.
2. See Christopher Ash, *Marriage: Sex in the Service of God* (Nottingham, UK: IVP, 2003), chapter 4.
3. There is uncertainty about the precise identification of these constellations, and in particular whether the fourth one is an individual star or a constellation of stars. But nothing hinges on this.
4. Cf. 26:12; Psalm 89:10; Isaiah 51:9.
5. See G. Campbell Morgan, *The Answers of Jesus to Job*, chapter II.
6. Fyall, p. 41.

7. Habel: "The genuineness of his yearning for God shines through this line."

8. Cf. Psalm 139.

Chapter Ten: Zophar's First Speech

1. Hartley: "Zophar unwittingly aligns himself with the Satan's position found in the prologue by encouraging Job to seek God for personal gain." Jones: "If Job does this in order to recover his prosperity, he demonstrates insincerity; if he refuses to do so, he demonstrates his perversity. Integrity is forfeited either way, and if it is, then Satan wins."

2. H. H. Rowley, "The Book of Job and Its Meaning," in *From Moses to Qumran* (Cambridge, UK: Lutterworth, 1963), p. 178 (quoted in Kidner, p. 58).

Chapter Eleven: Job's First Reply to Zophar

1. Some take the first section to end at 3:17.

2. Hartley explains that in pre-exilic times the *'am* had this connotation; "the gentry" (citing Pope).

3. Shakespeare, *Romeo and Juliet*, Act II, Scene 2.

4. The meaning of verse 6c is unclear. It may mean (a) they are idolaters, having "gods'" they can hold in their hands; (b) their "hands" (their abilities and autonomy) are their gods—they believe themselves to be like gods; or (c) the sense may be reversed to mean "those God has in his hand" (NIV), though this seems less likely.

5. So Gordis and Clines among others.

6. Clines.

7. The idiom does not appear elsewhere in the Old Testament, and its meaning is uncertain. But the parallelism suggests it must mean something similar to taking our life in our hands (v. 14b).

8. The exact meaning of this famous verse is not certain. The KJV reads, "Though he slay me, yet will I trust in him." But the exact tone is not certain. It may express a confident trust, or it may express resignation: "I have to speak to him, because The System doesn't work and I have no choice; but I don't know how it is going to end." However, the confidence of verse 16 suggests that the traditional reading is a correct understanding. Although Job is terrified, ultimately he does believe he will be vindicated.

9. Helmut Thielicke, *The Prayer That Spans the World: Sermons on the Lord's Prayer* (Cambridge, UK: James Clarke, 1960), p. 21.

Chapter Twelve: Eliphaz's Second Speech

1. Jones.

2. Pope.

3. Pope makes this perceptive observation.

4. This last phrase comes from Habel.

5. Habel, p. 251 helpfully lists these verbal echoes.

6. The expression "*from* their fathers" more likely should be translated "*by* their fathers." The sense is not that wise men hid these things from their ancestors (a strange idea), but that the ancestors did not hide it from them, and they did not hide it from us. This is open tradition. Hence the NIV (following the sense of most com-

mentators, including Clines, Gordis, Habel, and Hartley) renders this: "what the wise have declared, hiding nothing received from their ancestors."

7. Habel.

8. This sense is supported by Clines, Habel, Hartley, and Pope and fits much better with the context.

9. Verse 30c ("and by the breath of his mouth he will depart") is not easy to understand. The word "his" may refer to God or possibly to death (as Habel suggests).

Chapter Thirteen: Job's Second Reply to Eliphaz

1. Jones.

2. It is possible to translate the idiom of "shaking the head" in a positive light, as a sympathetic shaking of the head (so Hartley, Habel). If so, it would lead smoothly into verse 5.

3. Habel.

4. Ibid.

5. Ibid.

6. Fyall.

7. Driver and Gray, followed by Habel and Fyall, suggest that "resting place" here has the connotation of Sheol.

8. Clines's suggestion that the witness is Job's own cry is not persuasive. Job needs an intercessor outside of himself, one who is on the level with God himself.

9. Jones.

10. The word translated "scorn" (v. 20) in the ESV may mean "intercessor" (as in 33:23; Isaiah 43:27, in both of which the ESV translates the word as "mediator[s]" or Genesis 42:23 where the ESV translates the word as "interpreter"). In this case Job may be saying, "My intercessor is my friend" (NIV), continuing the thought of verse 19.

11. Fyall, p. 44.

12. From Dante's *Divine Comedy*.

13. E.g., Habel, Clines.

14. John Calvin, *Commentary on Psalms*.

15. The ESV rendering "before whom men spit" misses the meaning. The phrase "before whom" in this context means "in the face" (Habel, "upon whose face").

16. Verse 12 is puzzling. Is it a quote from his friends, telling him in a shallow and banal way that there will be light at the end of his tunnel (if he repents)? Or is Job expressing his own hope for light to come (as in the NIV: "Yet the desires of my heart turn night into day; in the face of darkness light is near," vv. 11, 12)? We cannot be sure.

Chapter Fourteen: Bildad's Second Speech

1. For more on the concept of creation order see O. O'Donovan, *Resurrection and Moral Order*; also Christopher Ash, *Marriage: Sex in the Service of God* (Leicester, UK: IVP, 2003), chapter 4.

2. Habel.

3. William Shakespeare, *Hamlet*, Act 3, Scene 4.

4. Habel takes verse 11 with verses 7–10 as the conclusion of the trap section. It is equally possible to take it with verses 12–14. It serves as a link between the two sections.

5. See also 24:17; 27:20; 30:15.

6. Habel.

7. See Christopher Ash, *Remaking a Broken World* (Crownhill, Milton Keynes, UK: Authentic Media, 2009), chapters 2 and 5.

8. Not knowing God is not about intellectual ignorance but about moral perversity and disobedience, as the parallel with "the unrighteous" demonstrates.

Chapter Fifteen: Job's Second Reply to Bildad

1. The phrase "ten times" means repeatedly or often, as when Jacob says it of Laban's behavior in Genesis 31:7, 41.

2. While the word "erred" is sometimes used of minor, inadvertent sin (e.g., Numbers 15:29, 30), we cannot be sure it has this limited scope here. It is often used more widely, as Clines points out. The meaning of verse 4b is disputed. It is unlikely to mean, "It's none of your business" (cf. NIV), for why then would Job continue the dialogues?

3. Habel: "the supreme irony of this vivid portrayal lies in the closing line. The mighty fortress against which God has marshalled his entire siege works and militia is, in fact, a mere 'tent.'" Habel calls this "a bitter example of divine overkill."

4. In verse 17 "breath" (*ruach*) may be translated "soul" or "life." It may be that Job's physical breath is repulsive or that his whole being is repulsive; perhaps both.

5. Fyall comments, "It is the interplay of the hand of God and the hand of Satan that is presented with such subtlety in the prologue" (p. 45).

6. The cry "Oh, that . . ." punctuates the book and expresses the longings of Job's heart (e.g., 14:13; 23:3, 4; 31:35).

7. Fyall, p. 45.

8. The word "For" (ESV, "For I know") is not *ki* but simply *waw*. The NIV omits it. Fyall translates this "Yet" to make the point that this is not so much a logical deduction from his longing as a wonderful contrast between dead stone and a living vindicator.

9. Numbers 35:16–28; Deuteronomy 19:6–13; 2 Samuel 14:7, 11.

10. E.g., Leviticus 25:25–28; Jeremiah 32:6–11.

11. Hartley. See the helpful and persuasive discussion in Fyall, pp. 48–50.

12. ". . . a juridical term meaning to rise (stand) as a witness in a trial" (Pope).

13. This is a famous exegetical crux. See the discussion in Fyall, p. 51.

14. Fyall, p. 47 calls this "a striking parallel" with Job's context. See also Psalm 24:6; 27:4.

15. "This thought was so intense that it almost recognized itself. Job's assurance of seeing God was so vivid that it virtually became a vision of God and he faints in the ecstasy of his faith" (A. B. Davidson, quoted in Fyall, p. 51ff.).

Chapter Sixteen: Zophar's Second Speech

1. C. F. Alexander, "There Is a Green Hill Far Away," 1847.

2. Bildad has said much the same (8:11–13), as has Eliphaz (15:29–33).

3. Isaac Watts, "O God Our Help in Ages Past," 1719.

4. Pope.

5. Habel.

6. As the Assyrian emperor did to besieged Jerusalem in Hezekiah's day (2 Kings 18:31, 32).

7. This anecdote is told of various very rich men!

8. The NIV follows most commentators in translating verse 28, "A flood will carry off his house, rushing waters on the day of God's wrath." This makes the imagery even more vivid.

Chapter Seventeen: Job's Second Reply to Zophar

1. Pope.

2. Clines, p. 521.

3. Derek Kidner, *The Message of Jeremiah*, The Bible Speaks Today (Leicester, UK: IVP, 1987), p. 60.

4. Clines, p. 521.

5. In Genesis 31:27 Laban says to Jacob that he would have sent him away "with mirth and songs, with tambourine and lyre." Isaiah 24:8 links these same instruments with "mirth" and "the noise of the jubilant."

6. Habel.

7. Ibid.

8. Pope says their prosperity is not in their control (Hartley similarly).

9. The word translated "pails" (v. 24a) occurs only once in the Old Testament. It has been translated "intestines" (Habel), "haunches" (Pope), or "testes" (Hartley). The parallel with healthy and moist bones (the opposite of brittle bones) in verse 24b suggests it is a picture of old age without decrepitude.

10. Cf. Moses' burial in a valley (Deuteronomy 34:6).

Chapter Eighteen: Eliphaz's Third Speech

1. Neither the strong man nor the wise man can "do anything that puts God under obligation" (Hartley).

2. Habel.

3. Hartley.

4. Habel.

Chapter Nineteen: Job's Third Reply to Eliphaz

1. Jones.

2. Hartley.

3. Habel says that the way this wish breaks the usual pattern of the speeches "heightens its significance."

4. Jones.

5. Job will reiterate this in 31:6, 7.

6. Jones, Hartley.

7. Hartley. Habel is similar.

8. Habel, p. 356ff. Habel, however, does not think this speech comes from Job's mouth but from one of his friends, perhaps Zophar.

9. Habel.

Chapter Twenty: Bildad's Third Speech

1. Hartley. Habel says, "Clearly Bildad's speech is too short . . . if the pattern of the previous speeches proves any guide." But why should it prove a guide?

2. Ironically, Habel supplements Bildad's speech with 26:5–14 and keeps all of chapter 27 in Job's speech, whereas Hartley supplements Bildad's speech with 27:13–23 and keeps 26:5–14 in Job's speech!

3. Pope.

4. Pope is incorrect in suggesting that Job has admitted the truth of verse 4.

Chapter Twenty-One: Job's Third Reply to Bildad

1. Hartley comments, "Often in his speeches Job recites hymnic lines in praise of God. They encourage his faith in God." This is true. But Jones perceptively notes, "Job here silences Bildad (and by implication his friends as well) by answering him in his own coin and by speaking about God in terms that exceed those that Bildad has used. He beats Bildad in theology as well as anthropology," first by insisting that the scope of God's activity includes all of creation, and second (in v. 14) by suggesting that there is more to God's self-revelation than can be discerned in creation and providence.

2. Jones.

3. Habel.

4. Habel says this formula "probably refers to the formal oath and imprecation character of the speech that follows."

5. The NIV heads chapter 27 "Job's Final Word to His Friends."

Chapter Twenty-Two: Job Begins to Sum Up

1. The same or similar expressions are used in 1 Samuel 14:39, 45; 2 Samuel 2:27.

2. Jones.

3. Habel argues from the singulars here that the enemy is God himself. But it makes much more sense to take this as a generic singular, as Habel himself admits it is when we get to verse 13. "Job is describing *all* enmity, rather than *an* enemy." In particular he is thinking of the friends and ultimately of the Satan, whose spokesmen they have unwittingly become (Jones).

4. There is a similar prayer in Jeremiah 18:21.

5. Habel.

6. Habel writes of "the wind whistling its sinister mocking sounds through the deserted ruins where the wicked once lived in splendor."

Chapter Twenty-Three: Why God Won't Answer My Question

1. "The speeches surrounding it are frenetic, unlike the calm, measured tone of this passage" (Fyall, p. 65).

2. This is Fyall's suggestion.

3. Derek Kidner writes, "It appears to be the author's parenthesis rather than Job's" (Kidner, p. 80).

4. Fyall says, "In essence the picture of mining becomes a metaphor for Job's search for the divine wisdom that lies behind creation" (p. 69).

5. See discussion on 27:1.

6. Fyall, p. 66ff. quoting Andersen.

Chapter Twenty-Four: The Longing

1. Mircea Eliade, quoted by Martin Wärnelid, in *Evangelicals Now* (December 2004), pp. 16, 17.

2. Quoted by Martin Wärnelid from a 1942 radio talk (see ibid.).

3. The word "prime" means literally "autumn" in the sense of ripe maturity in contrast with imminent decline (see Hartley, following Pope).

4. Hartley thinks it unlikely that there is a reference here to the servant boys, on the grounds that having servants was not a special blessing to a great nobleman; but surely the point is that they were an indication of being a nobleman, an indication no longer present for Job.

5. Jones.

6. In the original there is no "and" between v. 8a and v. 8b; the withdrawal of the youths and the respectful standing of the elders are simultaneous. It is a striking scene.

7. The expression "him whom I did not know" means the stranger, the one who has no local power networks, no influential friends locally to look out for his interests. To "search out the cause" means to research their case carefully.

8. See Habel.

9. In Isaiah 62:3 the word is translated "crown." In Zechariah 3:5 it is on the head of the high (ruling) priest.

10. Habel is wrong to say that Job's speech is "tantamount to a speech of self-praise"; in saying this, Habel lines himself up with Job's comforters.

11. The LXX translates "sand" as *phoinix*, and it has been suggested there may be an allusion here to the myth of the phoenix dying and then rising from the ashes of its funeral pyre. While this is possible, it seems more natural to understand Job as expecting a very long life.

12. Cf. Genesis 49:24; 1 Samuel 2:4; Jeremiah 49:35.

13. There is no need to suggest that because verses 21–25 echo and to some extent repeat an earlier theme they must necessarily have been misplaced. Such is the woodenness of some liberal criticism.

14. "I smiled on them when they had no confidence" (ESV) may also be translated "When I smiled at them, they scarcely believed it" (NIV, following most commentators, including Habel and Hartley).

15. To "sit" as chief was to take the position of authority, as Jesus "sat" before teaching (e.g. Matthew 5:1; Luke 4:20).

16. Bringing comfort in grief is perhaps an ironic allusion to the comfort Job's friends have failed to bring him.

17. We see these hopes vividly expressed in Psalm 89:1–37.

Chapter Twenty-Five: The Lament

1. This is a gloating mockery, like that of Judah's enemies described in Lamentations 1:7.

2. Habel.

3. 1 Samuel 17:43. Abner does the same in 2 Samuel 3:8.

4. The description of verses 2–8 would seem to be of the young mockers rather than of their fathers (although Clines thinks it is the fathers). But it doesn't much matter; one suspects the description of fathers or sons would be much the same.

5. Pope.

6. Clines suggests that "bray" alludes to their having sex in the open air but adduces no evidence for this.

7. Habel.

8. Ibid.

9. As in Lamentations 3:14.

10. ~~As in Habel.~~

11. Hartley, p. 402, n11.

12. This idiom of "standing" to petition is used in Jeremiah 15:1: "Though Moses and Samuel stood before me . . ."

13. See Psalm 18:10.

14. Cf. "I will make lamentation like the jackals, and mourning like the ostriches" (Micah 1:8).

Chapter Twenty-Six: Job's Last Word

1. See Christopher Ash, *Pure Joy* (Nottingham, UK: IVP, 2012; Phillipsburg, NJ: P&R, 2013).

2. "This statement was not drawn up in a solicitor's office!" (Jones, p. 220).

3. I am grateful to Habel for his insights into the structure of the chapter and have largely followed his reading.

4. Cf. Matthew 5:28, "looks at a woman with lustful intent"; 2 Peter 2:14, "eyes full of adultery."

5. See Christopher Ash, *Marriage: Sex in the Service of God* (Leicester, UK: IVP, 2003), chapter 8.

6. So the chiastic structure is not very tidy. English translations usually put verse 6 either as a parenthesis or between dashes.

7. It is hard not to be reminded of Lady Macbeth's exclamation, "Out, damned spot!" William Shakespeare, *Macbeth*, Act V, Scene 1.

8. To "arise" or "stand up" refers to legal proceedings, as in 30:28b, where Job stands up "in the assembly," Micah 6:1, where God challenges Israel to "Arise, plead your case," or Psalm 76:9 ("When God arose to establish judgment").

9. Verse 14 has a neat chiastic structure: (a) "what then shall I do" (Job's guilt), (b) "when God rises up" (God's judgment), (b') "When he makes inquiry" (God's judgment), (a') "what shall I answer him?" (Job's guilt).

10. Cf. 14:13; 19:23.

11. In Ezekiel 9:4, 6 the "mark" of innocence put on the foreheads of God's people is literally a *taw*.

12. Cf. Isaiah 9:6 and Isaiah 22:22, where "the government" or "the key of the house of David" is put on Messiah's "shoulder."

13. The esv follows the rsv with "breathe their last"; but to lose one's "spirit/breath" (*ruach*) may also mean to lose heart (hence niv, "broken the spirit"); the parallel in Jeremiah 15:9 supports the niv here.

14. Job "is in tune with nature and thus his case deserves an answer" (Fyall, p. 68).

Chapter Twenty-Seven: Elihu and the Justice of God

1. I do not agree with those who call him "an angry young man" in a disparaging way. It seems to me that his anger is essentially godly and parallel to the anger that drove the Lord Jesus to overturn the tables of the money-changers.

2. Jones, p. 229.

3. There is no good reason for Clines to reposition Elihu's speeches, along with chapter 28 (which he also assigns to Elihu), after chapter 27. They make perfect sense after Job has had the final word in chapters 29—31.

4. I have changed my mind on this. When I wrote *Out of the Storm: Grappling with God in the Book of Job*, I suggested that Elihu gave us a mixture of truth and error and that part of our learning wisdom was to learn discernment between the two. Although most of the critical commentaries were very negative about Elihu, I was persuaded—partly by John Hartley—that we ought to view him more positively. Since then, and the more I have taught these chapters, I have come to the conclusion that Elihu quite simply gives us truth from God and speaks as a prophet.

5. W. Whedbee (see Hartley, p. 427, n1).

6. Clines, vol. 2, pp. 708–711 gives plenty of examples. Jones, pp. 223–227 is very helpful on these issues. Habel's otherwise helpful commentary is skewed in these chapters by his conviction that the author of the book of Job is subtly undermining Elihu, even as Elihu speaks. This is a very subtle reading, and we ought not to accept it unless a more straightforward reading is utterly impossible (which it is not). Janzen says that the Elihu chapters contain an implied critique of the prophetic tradition and are there to force us to choose between false prophecy (exemplified by Elihu) and the true word of the Lord, which follows. This again is a convoluted reading.

7. For example, Hartley refers to Elihu's "verbose, overly apologetic style" that "offers comic relief to break the tight, fearful atmosphere created by Job's oath" (p. 427).

8. This is all the more so if the Buz here is the descendant of Abraham's brother named in Genesis 22:21.

9. Jones, p. 226.

10. I agree with Jones that Elihu "has suffered from bad press and needs to be rehabilitated" (p. 228).

Chapter Twenty-Eight: Elihu's First Speech

1. For example, the "you" in 32:6 is plural.

2. "I said" is literally "I said to myself." Likewise in verse 10.

3. Although he does not think Elihu's claim is true, Janzen is right to see that Elihu is indeed claiming divine inspiration in 32:8, 18; 33:4; 36:3, 4; 37:16.

4. Habel argues that the emphatic "Yes, I will!" implied here and twice in verse 17 has a wordplay with Elihu as a man of anger. He reads this negatively. But equally it can be read as a wholesome, emphatic confidence.

5. Jeremiah 20:9.

6. Habel says Elihu is portrayed as unwittingly describing himself as a "windbag" and therefore a fool (cf. 15:2). But the metaphor can speak equally of a man who has an overflow of truth bursting to get out of him.

7. Cf. Deuteronomy 32:1, 2; Isaiah 1:2; Micah 6:1.

8. Elihu does not accuse Job of claiming sinless perfection but of being "clean" and "pure" in the sight of God, with no unforgiven "iniquity in" him (Habel).

9. The word translated "occasions" in verse 10 is used in Judges 14:4 where God seeks a pretext to start trouble with the Philistines.

10. Cf. Psalm 62:11.

11. The words "from perishing by the sword" may mean "from crossing the river" (NIV footnote), in the sense of crossing the river that divides the living from the dead (e.g., the river Styx in Greek mythology). See Fyall, p. 111.

12. NIV: "and keep them from pride."

13. ". . . those who bring death" may refer to the angels or messengers of death, whose task is to bring human beings down to the place of the dead.

14. C. S. Lewis, *The Problem of Pain* (London & Glasgow: Fontana Books, 1957), pp. 80, 81.

15. That is, "he"—the sufferer—sees "his"—that is God's—"face."

16. Habel.

Chapter Twenty-Nine: Elihu's Second Speech

1. See also verses 5, 6, 10, 12, 17, 18.

2. Hartley: "*Right* stands for that which is legally correct and *good* for that which is morally sound." Habel translates "good" as "defensible." But it seems to have a stronger and more rounded meaning, including moral goodness, the kind of government that gives us pleasure because it is attractive and—to use Elihu's metaphor—tastes good.

3. The ESV follows the RSV in making an unnecessary emendation here. The original refers to "arrows," such as in 6:4, "the arrows of the Almighty." Hence NIV, "his arrow inflicts an incurable wound."

4. Hartley. Habel suggests that Elihu is particularly engaging with what Job says in 12:13–25. He gives some parallels between the two passages. While this may be true, Elihu's engagement is more broadly with what Job has repeatedly said and implied.

5. Habel says this accusation is groundless and betrays Elihu's prejudice against Job. But this misses the point; the accusation is based not on some supposed prior secret sin of Job but on his actual words.

6. Cf. Psalm 104:29.

7. "Since his right to rule is inherent in his being, any challenge of his rule is a disparagement of his person" (Hartley).

8. There is a translation issue in verse 23, which may possibly mean that it is not appropriate for human beings to set times for God to come and give judgment in court. But the translation of the ESV makes perfect sense.

9. This is one possible meaning of "whether it be a nation or a man." Another possible reading is represented by the NIV, which takes verse 29c as the start of a new sentence: "Yet he is over individual and nation alike, to keep the godless from ruling, from laying snares for the people" (vv. 29, 30).

10. Jones.

11. Hartley.

12. The meaning of "I have borne punishment" is "I am guilty" or "I have made a mistake." It is not so much about his punishment (as the ESV suggests) as about his admission of guilt.

13. Hartley.

14. Habel puts all of verses 35–37 in quotation marks, as what wise people will say about Job. Since Elihu clearly agrees with all this, it doesn't much matter whether this is what wise people will say or what Elihu says.

15. For example, Habel accuses Elihu of presumption because he is concerned to defend God without going into the specifics of Job's case.

16. Hartley, pp. 449, 450.

17. Jones, p. 244. Hartley agrees that Elihu "locates Job's plight in his inflamed rhetoric rather than in any continuance of past sins. Therein Elihu departs from the judgment of the comforters that Job is suffering because of some hidden sin that he had committed" (p. 462).

Chapter Thirty: Elihu's Third Speech

1. The ESV "It is my right before God" is not easy to understand. It means either "I am in the right before God" or possibly "I am more righteous than God."

2. Hartley calls Elihu's style "verbose, overconfident"; but we might equally say that he speaks with authority because he has a God-given authority.

3. The expressions "a man like yourself" and "a son of man" both simply mean "your fellow human beings." The NIV expresses this clearly: "Your wickedness only affects humans like yourself, and your righteousness only other people."

4. Jones, p. 250.

5. ". . . because of the pride of evil men" probably means that this aggressive pride is the cause of the oppressed crying out. It might possibly mean that the "evil men" are the oppressed who cry out but whose real nature is proud. But this seems less likely.

Chapter Thirty-One: Elihu's Fourth Speech

1. Hartley says, "Here, as in ch. 32, Elihu claims that his words are inspired."

2. Habel, with characteristic skepticism, accuses Elihu of falling into the trap of playing God. This would only be true if Elihu were a false prophet, which Habel fails to demonstrate. Far from claiming to be God, Elihu is claiming to speak for God, as all true prophets do.

3. Jones.

4. Cf. Hannah's song in 1 Samuel 2:1–10 or Mary's song in Luke 1:46–55.

5. The same two responses and results are given in Isaiah 1:19, 20.

6. Habel.

7. Cf. Psalm 119:67, 71, 75.

8. Christopher Ash, *Bible Delight* (Fearn, Ross-Shire, UK: Christian Focus, 2008), chapter 9, "The Adversity Gospel."

9. Hartley says of verses 19, 20, "The text of these two verses is so obscure that it is next to impossible to establish any meaning for them."

10. Jones makes this attractive suggestion.

11. Regarding God as teacher, cf. Psalm 25:8–12: ". . . therefore he instructs sinners in the way. He . . . teaches the humble his way. . . . Him will he instruct in the way that he should choose."

12. Francis H. Rowley, "I Will Sing the Wondrous Story," 1886.

13. Habel speaks of a "a balanced interplay between mystery and meaning."

14. Habel.

15. Hartley.

16. Cf. Psalm 102:27: ". . . your years have no end."

17. The same word "mist" is used in Genesis 2:6 of God's waters over the earth.

18. This storm-god imagery has its parallels in other ancient Near-Eastern religious traditions. It also appears elsewhere in the Old Testament, for example in Isaiah 19:1 ("Behold, the LORD is riding on a swift cloud") or in Psalm 18.

19. The expression "seals up the hand" means to stop people from working (the hand symbolizing action).

20. To "know it" means to acknowledge that this is the action of God himself.

21. The word "correction" can mean "rod" or "scourge."

22. For "the balancings of the clouds" the NIV has "how the clouds hang poised."

Chapter Thirty-Two: The Lord's First Speech, Part 1

1. Quoted by the American Secretary of State Dean Acheson, at the start of his autobiography *Present at the Creation: My Years in the State Department*. See Robert L. Beisner, *Dean Acheson: A Life in the Cold War* (Oxford: Oxford University Press, 2006), p. 636.

2. Against most commentators, I am assuming this speech, like the others, to be historical and not merely a creation or composition of the author of the book of Job.

3. This story is told by Morgan, p. 54.

4. There is another possible use of "the LORD" in 12:9, but there are uncertainties about this.

5. Cf. Isaiah 29:5, 6; Jeremiah 23:19; 25:32; 30:23; Nahum 1:3.

6. Jones, p. 263.

7. "Each worshipper, drawn out of his self-centred existence as by a powerful magnet, bows reverently before his God." Hartley, p. 490.

8. Jones makes the suggestion that this signals to us that we are to read the end in the light of the beginning.

9. Habel.

10. Perhaps like Jacob in Genesis 32. Possibly a "belt wrestling" match (Hartley). In 1 Kings 18:46 Elijah girds up his loins before running. In the prophetic description of an army in Isaiah 5:27 "not a waistband is loose."

11. Habel says the answers to the rhetorical questions are neither "Who knows?" nor "I did not" but "You alone did."

12. It is not always clear exactly what constitutes a section. For example, should the raven's prey (38:41) be considered separately from the lion's prey (38:39, 40)? Should the section about the different forms of water (38:28–30) be considered as distinct from the preceding verses about rain (38:25–27)? These decisions are not of any great significance.

13. Hartley takes his major division between 38:24 and 38:25. He calls 38:1–24 "The Structure of the World" and 38:25—39:30 "The Maintenance of the World" (Hartley, p. 389, n1). One problem with this is the section about the heavenly bodies (38:31–33), which would seem to fall most naturally into the structure of the world and is not clearly about its maintenance.

14. E.g., Psalm 24:2; 89:11; 102:25; 104:5; Proverbs 3:19; Isaiah 48:13; 51:13; Zechariah 12:1.

15. See also the exposition of Job 28.

16. Eliphaz has already taunted him, saying, "Are you the first man who was born? Or were you brought forth before the hills? Have you listened in the council of God?" (15:7, 8).

17. Hartley, p. 495, n21; Fyall, p. 73: "these natural phenomena are visible symbols of the heavenly court."

18. This speech shows God's creative purpose "as one which is meaningful, worthwhile, and evocative of exuberant celebration" (Janzen, p. 243).

19. C. S. Lewis, *The Magician's Nephew* (Harmondsworth, UK: Penguin Books [Puffin], 1963), pp. 93, 94 (cf. pp. 97–99).

20. Janzen.

21. Morgan, p. 20.

22. Cf. the dark humor in Psalm 104:26, where Leviathan is simply a pet in a fishpond.

23. Fyall, p. 74.

24. Hartley.

25. "The sea, even as primal chaos, is limited to, yet given, a place in the scheme of things" (Janzen, p. 235).

26. Janzen notes this ambivalence.

27. The phrase "since your days began" simply means "ever" or "in your lifetime."

28. Hartley: "the underworld's vast expanse." Habel: this apparently refers "to the vast netherworld domain of which the ground is but the visible surface."

29. The same divine purpose is indicated in 28:26 ("when he made a *decree* for the rain . . ."). "Both passages therefore emphasize the principle of divine cosmic order" (Habel).

30. The connection is also shown by the repetition of "way" in verse 24a (for destructive lightning) and "way" in verse 25b (for the thunderbolt accompanying the life-giving rain). This is noted by Habel.

31. Ibid.

32. Ibid.

33. This is Hartley's suggestion.

34. The interpretation of these two Hebrew words "has been in dispute since the ancient versions first attempted a translation" (Habel).

35. Janzen, p. 229: "humankind is that part of creation whom God addresses with questions concerning the rest of creation."

Chapter Thirty-Three: The Lord's First Speech, Part 2

1. Robert Frost, *Design*, in *Robert Frost: Selected Poems* (Harmondsworth, UK: Penguin, 1973), p. 179.

2. Janzen alludes to this sonnet.

3. Jones, p. 269.

4. Hartley rightly observes that the idiom to "number the months" implies compassionate care "for a mother during the days of her pregnancy."

5. Habel.

6. Ibid.

7. Hartley.

8. Habel.

9. Translators have very different opinions about how to translate verse 13. In verse 13a the verb translated "wave proudly" may well mean "rejoice" (hence Hartley, "beat joyously"). It is hard to be sure what verse 13b means.

10. "According to ancient folklore she was considered the epitome of stupidity" (Pope).

11. Fyall, p. 76.

12. Ibid., p. 78.

13. Kidner, p. 72.

14. Jones.

Chapter Thirty-Four: The Lord's Second Speech

1. Reported in *The Week*, March 10, 2007.

2. Cf. Exodus 15:16; Psalm 89:13, 14.

3. There is a clear chiasm in verses 11, 12. To "pour out" and to "tread down" (vv. 11a, 12b) are parallel; to "look on" is almost identical in verses 11b, 12a.

4. Cf. Job 17:16, "the bars of Sheol."

5. I am grateful to Janzen for this insight.

6. The Syriac and Vulgate translate "thighs" as "testicles," which suggests that "tail" may be a euphemism for the penis.

7. I am following Gordis here in seeing "first" as indicating preeminence rather than primordial existence. The suggestion of Habel that it means "primordial" (analogous with Wisdom in Proverbs 8:22) does not fit well with the idea that the Behemoth is symbolic of death.

8. Here the "covenant" (v. 4) is made in response to a defeated foe suing for peace. Job is ironically portrayed as the one who can dictate the terms of this covenant.

9. "The poet creates a sense of the absurd with his picture of a violent sea-monster being fondled as a pet like the tiny birds of young girls." Habel.

10. The lower millstone has to be of harder stone than the rotating upper millstone, as it must bear the weight of the upper one.

11. For a vigorous exposition of this viewpoint, see Gordis, pp. 569–572.

12. Habel.

13. So Kubina (1979), quoted in Habel, says, "Links with the hippopotamus and crocodile suggested by the language of this passage arise from the use of these figures as symbols of chaos in Egypt."

14. The identification with natural creatures has been far from unambiguous. For example, Aquinas identified Behemoth with the elephant. The New English Bible, following G. R. Driver, translated Behemoth as "crocodile" and Leviathan as "whale."

15. Fyall quotes George Bernard Shaw's quip that God really needs to do better, when challenged about his justice and providence, than retort, "You can't make a hippopotamus, can you?"

16. Fyall, p. 157.

17. I am grateful to Grant Retief for this suggestion.

18. Similarly, in Jeremiah 51:34–44 Babylon is described as a monster.

19. Fyall, chapter 6. Fyall concludes, "I would submit, then, that these contextual, linguistic and structural considerations make the identification of Behemoth with Mot, the god of death, a very strong probability" (p. 137).

20. Fyall, p. 127.

21. Quoted in Glatzer, p. 234.

22. The fact that Job is challenged to "save" himself (40:14) counts against the strange view of Habel (in my opinion) that Job is meant to see himself as a potential

threat to God, just as Behemoth and Leviathan might be. "Perhaps Job should see himself as a similar threat." But Job needs saving, not subduing.

23. Dorothy Greenwell, "I Am Not Skilled to Understand," 1873.

Epilogue: The End Comes at the End

1. Jones.

2. Kidner, p. 73.

3. In Archibald MacLeish's Pulitzer Prize-winning play *JB*, this is the gist of a powerful telling of Job's story that fails to do justice to its Biblical fullness and ends up being more of a rant against suffering and injustice in the world.

4. Cf. Glynn Harrison, *The Big Ego Trip: Finding True Significance in a Culture of Self-esteem* (Nottingham, UK: IVP, 2012).

5. Fyall, p. 181.

6. Jones makes this point helpfully: "Job's sufferings were a kind of bondage and his restoration was a kind of deliverance or redemption."

Scripture Index

General Index

Index of Sermon Illustrations

a message of first importance to the sufferer," 158

Theories
James Dobson, "I used to have four theories on child-rearing and no kids. Now I have four kids and no theories," 94

Therapeutic Gospel
Customer feedback survey beginning with, "We want to know how we left you feeling," 20

Trouble
Helmut Thielicke quote, "Goethe . . . once said in his old age that he could hardly think that he had been really happy for more than a month in his whole life," 169

Vindication
Older brother on playground protects younger brother, 271

Waiting
Example of an earthquake blocking main roads so best route is disrupted, 96

Weakness
Quote, "It is as if I go for a night's camping on my own . . . . I wake . . . and all around me are tanks and gun emplacements," 211

Wisdom
The poet knows that if we can grasp the architecture or structure of the Universe, then we will know the answer to the question, "Why?" 280
The architecture of a piece of hardware or software, 280

Worldview
Heroine from *The Sound of Music* sings, "Perhaps I had a wicked childhood . . . ," 92
Elderly Christian woman saying to author, "What have I done to deserve this?" 92

Worshippers
It is loss that reveals the true worshipper and separates the fair weather Christian from the true worshipper, 118